Cities of Power

Cities of Power

The Urban, the National, the Popular, the Global

Göran Therborn

VERSO
London • New York

First published by Verso 2017
This paperback edition published by Verso 2021
© Göran Therborn 2017, 2021

To the best of the publisher's knowledge, the images reproduced here
are in the public domain. Should that be incorrect in any instance, Verso
will seek to rectify the mistake in future editions of this work.

1 3 5 7 9 10 8 6 4 2

Verso
UK: 6 Meard Street, London W1F 0EG
US: 20 Jay Street, Suite 1010, Brooklyn, NY 11201
versobooks.com

Verso is the imprint of New Left Books

ISBN-13: 978-1-78478-545-1
ISBN-13: 978-1-78478-547-5 (US EBK)
ISBN-13: 978-1-78478-546-8 (UK EBK)

British Library Cataloguing in Publication Data
A catalogue record for this book is available from the British Library

Library of Congress Cataloging-in-Publication Data
A catalog record for this book is available from the Library of Congress

Typeset in Minion Pro by Hewer Text UK Ltd, Edinburgh
Printed and bound by CPI Group (UK) Ltd, Croydon CR0 4YY

The city . . . is the point of maximum concentration for the power and culture of a community.

—Lewis Mumford, *The Culture of Cities* (1938)

Architecture is a kind of eloquence of power in forms – now persuading, even flattering, now only commanding.

—Friedrich Nietzsche, 'Skirmishes of an Untimely Man' (1888)

Contents

Introduction:

The Urban, the National, the Popular and the Global

This is a book about meetings and relationships between four social forces: the urban, the national, the popular and the global. We shall be watching how they meet and how they change the urban habitat during the lifetime of the national, up until now. The urban is old: cities have existed for thousands of years, but they have been transformed by the arrival of the national in the form of nation-states, just over two centuries ago. The national transformation of cities has focused on the urban centre of the nation-state, its capital, which is the object of this study. Mostly pre-national cities of different kinds were changed into national cities, but sometimes nation-states built new cities for themselves. Nation-states arrived at their chosen capitals along different historical pathways and after long or short, rough or smooth journeys. These historical experiences left enduring marks on each capital city.

Nationalism and nation-states were part of a much larger epochal change, the rise of modernity as a new historical era, rejecting authorities and institutions of the past (inner-worldly ones above all) and trying to create new societies, new cultures, a new world. The national and the global first met in this context, as global nationalism. Major meeting-places of this encounter were the national capitals, which now had to adapt to global models of a capital 'worthy of the nation', taking in the avenues of Second Empire Paris, the infrastructure of London, in some places the Mall and the Capitol Building of Washington.

Nations developed and changed and the constitutive elites of nation-states were faced with popular challenges from the ascendancy of originally subaltern classes, ethnicities/races and gender groups. Occasionally these challenges were strong and successful enough to create distinctive popular moments of power, manifested in urban history. National struggles for power could take extreme and violent forms, not only destructive and ephemeral, like wars and riots, but also, for a time, forms cemented in the capital city, which we shall also look at.

In recent times the global has taken centre stage, first of all in the form of global, transnational capitalism. To not a few contemporary authors, the national is on the verge of becoming an extinct species, particularly in big cities. We shall look into those claims, sceptically but seriously, trying to disentangle the intertwined dynamics of the global, the national and the local in the new style of globalist urbanism, of verticality, novelty and exclusivity. At the very end we shall venture a glance into the future of our four forces.

Underlying my interest in the choreography of the urban, the national, the popular and the global are old analytical interests in forms and relations of power and in meanings, ideology and symbolic forms. Cities affect us by their spatial structuring of social relations and by their provision of meanings of social life. This might be seen as urban power, but cities in the nation-state era are not actors of power of the same weight as the national, popular and global forces. Cities of our time had better be approached as manifestations and representations of power. Our main research question here is: What kind of power does the urbanity of the capital cities under investigation manifest and represent?

The study is global and historical, from the first national capitals, revolutionary Paris and Washington, D.C., up to today and the flamboyant new capital of Kazakhstan, Astana. But it is, of course, neither an encyclopaedia of the capitals of the world nor a world history of power. It deals with a set of significant examples of the four major kinds of nation-state and national capital formation in the world, with some historical moments of power change and with how capitals of the different national types have had to confront the challenges of popular and global moments.

This has been a project long in coming, arising out of free time in Budapest in 1996, as the incumbent of a temporary European Chair of Social Policy at the ELTE University and many times interrupted by seemingly more urgent obligations. It was initially inspired by a history of the drama of the city's Heroes' Square.* A first study analyzed the processes and symbolic transformations which turned major dynastic residence cities of Europe into national capitals. Due to a couple of editorial mishaps it was published only in 2002.[1] Then I managed to get some funding (from two now-defunct Swedish public research funds, FRN and HSFR, and from the INTAS of the EU, also passed away) and to link up with urbanist colleagues of various disciplines from all over the world, resulting in a series of joint regional publications.[†] As always, my research is the product of an individual craftsman, not an industrial output by a factory of research assistants.

---

* Andras Gerö, *Modern Hungarian Society in the Making* (Budapest, 1995), chapter 11. The square and its Millennium Monument, at the end of the city's main boulevard, were a frequent destination of my walks.

† Regional projects launched as part of this work include one on Eastern European capitals organized as a Helsinki conference, with the generous support of Markku Kivinen and Anne Haila and published as *Eastern Drama: Capitals of Eastern Europe 1830s–2006* in a special monographic section of the *International Review of Sociology* 16:2 (2006); a second Eastern European project with EU funding, together with Larisa Titarenko of the University of Minsk, Anelie Vosiliute of Vilnius and Afgan Abdullayev of Baku, focusing on Baku, Minsk and Vilnius and reported in a Russian book edited by Titarenko, *Postsovietskie Stolitsy, Minsk, Vilnius, Baku* (2009); a collaboration with Fernando Pérez Oyarzún at the Catholic University in Santiago, Chile, on a Latin American–US conference in 2007, which did not issue into a publication but was fruitful in itself; a workshop on Southeast Asian capitals in Bangkok in 2008, co-organized with K.C. Ho of the National University of Singapore and published as a section of *City* 13:1(2009). Thanks to Laurent Fourchard of the University of Bordeaux and Simon Bekker of Stellenbosch University, South Africa, I got access to French Africanist workshops, out of which Bekker and I could organize a conference on capital cities in Dakar in 2010. It was published as a book, in association with the African research network CODESRIA: Bekker and Therborn (eds), *Power and Powerlessness: Capital Cities in Africa* (Cape Town: HSRC Press, 2012). Finally, there was a global collective effort. Professor In Kwon Park and the *International Journal of Urban Sciences* asked me to guest edit a special issue on cities and power, which materialized in March 2015 (vol. 19, no. 1). Routledge published the issue as a book in 2016: G. Therborn (ed.), *Cities and Power*.

Alongside the collective joint projects, my work on cities of power has also included some individual essays: 'Transcaucasian Triptych' (*New Left Review* 73, 2007), on Tbilisi, Yerevan and Baku; 'Identity and Capital Cities: European Nations and the European Union', in F. Cerutti and S. Lucarelli (eds), *The Search for a European Identity* (2008), on Brussels and the competition for the capital of the EU; and 'Modern Monumentality: European Experiences', in J. Osborne (ed.), *Approaching Monumentality in Archaeology* (2014).

Without original intention, this book has become part of a tetralogy of global studies, which started with *Between Sex and Power: Family in the World, 1900–2000* (2004). It was followed in 2011 by *The World: A Beginner's Guide* and in 2013 by *The Killing Fields of Inequality*.

For me this book has been an immensely stimulating and enriching learning experience, one which included, of course, the opportunity to visit the cities treated here. Critical analyses of power more often make one angry than happy. But I do hope that I will be able to convey also something of the excitement at learning about cities and their diversity in time and space.

During this long process, I have piled up an enormous debt of gratitude. My wife, Sonia Therborn, has accompanied me on most of my often strenuous urban explorations since she retired from clinical psychology (and often before) and has transferred her sharp psychological eye onto urban anthropology, enlightening a myopic macro-sociologist.

Perry Anderson's characteristically kind and generous encouragement of my first venture into urban studies gave me both courage and motivation to continue. Anne Haila brought me into a most inspiring network of urban scholars working on 'urban science' for the European Science Foundation. Markku Kivinen, director of the Helsinki Alexander Institute, was crucially supportive, both of my first regional workshop and in providing me with an interpreter and companion to Astana. At the end of my stint as co-director of the Swedish Collegium for Advanced Study in the Social Sciences, my colleague Björn Wittrock granted me the opportunity to bring together a set of eminent urban scholars as fellows for a year or a semester. This was an enormously stimulating time together with Simon Bekker, Swati Chattopadhyay, Kumiko Fujita, K.C. Ho, Laura Kolbe, Abidin Kusno, Fernando Pérez Oyarzún and Karl Schlögel and the start of lasting personal friendships as well as of the cooperation mentioned above.

The various joint regional projects involved working together with effective, generous and interesting co-organizers: Simon Bekker, K. C. Ho, Fernando Pérez Oyarzún, Larisa Titarenko and an impressive array of scholars.

A long list of informants have helped me by sharing their knowledge of their city. After all these years, I have to apologize that any list would have been incomplete. Several informants are footnoted below and are here publicly thanked for their kindness. Several people even organized guides or brief research assistance for me: Judith Bodnar in Budapest informed me of many things and connected me with Judit Veres, Chang Kyung-Sup, who also personally accompanied me several times in Seoul, Anand Kumar in Delhi, Alan Mabin in Pretoria, Enzo Mingione put me into contact with Alberto Violante in Rome, Jo Santoso in Jakarta, Alicia Zicardi in Mexico. Swedish embassies in Cairo, Harare, Ljubljana and Singapore have been very helpful, as have the Norwegian legations of Lilongwe and Maputo. Special Russian-language help in Astana as well as collegial companionship was provided by Tapani Kaakkuriniemi and, on a second trip, by Larisa Titarenko. In Paris, Edmond Prétceille has been both a helpful colleague and has taken me around the *banlieue*. Patrick Le Galès, with whom I once wrote an article on European cities,[2] has been a very inspiring paragon of rigorous urban scholarship.

Ljungbyholm, Sweden
Midsummer's Eve 2016
Göran Therborn

1
Cities, Power and Modernity

Cities and Power

Cities emerged as concentrations of power, and of wealth, some five thousand years ago. Lewis Mumford once defined a city as a 'point of maximum concentration for the power and culture of a community',[1] and later began his list of 'chief functions of the city' with 'to convert power into form'.[2] Cities now contain more than half of humankind; power and wealth are reaching unprecedented degrees of planetary concentration. At the dawn of planetary urbanization, understanding the inscriptions of power in our built urban environment is not only a scholarly, but, even more, a civic imperative.

Despite Mumford's declarations, power has slipped out of the grasp of mainstream urban history and social science more often than not, or it has been relegated to the past. After the Baroque, Mumford's own interests veered to technological and economic change. A recent (and good) collective work with the seductive title *Embodiments of Power* both starts and stops with the Baroque.[3] Leonardo Benevolo's monumental *History of the City* makes the European revolutions of 1848 a divide between the 'liberal' and the 'post-liberal' city, but Benevolo loses most of his interest in power after 1848.[4] The late Sir Peter Hall presents a cultural axis in *Cities in Civilization*, but his Book Four on the 'urban order' is not very concerned with the political order.[5]

The great historian-cum-sociologist Charles Tilly was a sharp critical analyst of power, but a resolutely materialist network structuralist with little interest in meaningful forms, whether of cities – which he mainly saw as sites of capital concentration – or of states. He never grasped, or thought important, the difference between Baroque, absolutist, dynastic states and states of nations, with their national capitals.[6] In his view, after Charles V's imperial abdication in 1557, 'nation-states began to get priority', particularly after 1700.[7]

Synergetic encounters of political theory/history and urbanism have been few and fragile enough to allow the great urbanist, Peter Hall, to get away – twice or thrice, first in 1993, then in 2006, with a paperback repetition in 2010[8] – with the following typology of capital cities:

1. Multi-function capitals
2. Global capitals
3. Political capitals
4. Former capitals
5. Ex-imperial capitals
6. Provincial capitals
7. Super capitals

With all due respect, this list reminds me of a list of animals which Michel Foucault, without citation, claimed Jorge Luis Borges had excavated from an ancient Chinese encyclopaedia, according to which the animal kingdom comprised the following types:

a. belonging to the Emperor
b. embalmed
c. tamed . . .
e. sirens
f. fabulous . . .
j. innumerable . . .
n. which from afar resemble flies[9]

In the currently prevailing urban discourse, power is submerged in conceptions of economic nodality, certainly a legitimate and important research topic in itself – but with city power measured by the zip codes of major corporations and/or business services firms.[10] For all its other merits, which are many and have been deservedly applauded, this approach has two limitations in a context of cities and power. Its economism leaves out the power manifestations of the urban built environment itself. Even the most capitalist city imaginable is not only business offices and their connections to business offices elsewhere. Second, the political economy conception of world/global cities seriously underestimates the power of states in the current world.* After all, this is a world where the latest US president (Barack Obama) has been at war for the whole of his two terms of office, longer than any president in US history, making war in seven different countries of the world.†

The analytical framework deployed here – forms of state formation and their consequences, combining structural and symbolic perspectives on the city, identifying and exploring moments of major historical urban change worldwide – does not seem to have been used before. But no claim to originality is made with regard to studying power dimensions of contemporary cities. Apart from the vast monographic literature, which will be referred to repeatedly below, there are a number of distinguished comparative contributions. As this is not an academic thesis requiring a literature review, I shall confine my collegial respect to a short list only.

The portal work in the modern field is Lawrence Vale's *Architecture, Power and National Identity*, a masterly study of architecture and capital city design in a wide range of national contexts, focusing on 'capitol complexes' of governmental buildings, with a critical political sense and the professional eyes of a city planner.[11] Also contemporary and intercontinental in scope are Wolfgang Sonne's deep-digging Swiss dissertation (Habilitation) *Representing the State*[12] on the early-twentieth-century design of some capital cities, from Washington to New Delhi, and the

---

* A critique of some, in my view extreme and untenable, claims of the political economy approach to urban studies is given in my 'End of a paradigm: The current crisis and the idea of stateless cities', *Environment and Planning A* 43: 272–85. But I would like to add that I consider Saskia Sassen and Peterl Taylor great urban scholars, from whom I have learnt much.

† The Obama regime has 'intervened' militarily in Afghanistan, Iraq, Libya, Pakistan, Somalia, Syria and Yemen. See the *New York Times*, 16 May 2016, 1, 4. True, making war has not been Obama's only preoccupation, but it has been surprisingly important for a Nobel Peace Prize laureate.

collective overview edited by David Gordon, *Planning Twentieth-Century Capital Cities*. An impressive global study on the relocation of capitals is Vadim Rossmann's *Capital Cities: Their Development and Relocation*, similar to this book.[13]

Incisive, non-parochial analyses of power in contemporary cities have also come significantly from outside the academia of urban history and social science, from architecture and architectural criticism. Two works have blazed the trail: Deyan Sudic's *The Edifice Complex*[14] and Rowan Moore's *Why We Build*,[15] both focusing on architects and their patrons. From a similar milieu also comes Owen Hatherley's remarkable *Landscapes of Communism*.[16]

All built environments in human settlements are manifestations of the power relations among the inhabitants. Two sources and several kinds of power are highlighted in this book, which is not meant to be a general treatise on power. With its focus on the capital cities of nation-states, political power is naturally central. But political power in itself means no more than power by coercion and/or persuasion through institutions and processes of government. We are here explicitly interested in the character and the operation of political power in capital cities of the world.

Modern processes of urban power form a quadrangle of competing actors and types of influence. In one corner is political authority – national and/or urban – identifying the character of which is a major aim of this study, with variable powers and resources of design and regulation; in a second corner is capital, global as well as national, with economic power and resources of design and 'development'; third, there are the classes of privilege, with their desires, fears and resources; and finally, there are the popular classes, with their grievances and their capacities of resistance and of change.

We begin with the national elites' political power, emerging from the welter of nation-state formation. In this macroscopic global analysis, the national elites will be approached through the specific contexts of nation-state construction and the latter's relationship to prevailing capitalism.

Then we shall look into two types and two eras of challenges to the historical national elites. One is a popular challenge, coming out of the rise of social and political forces once excluded from the nation-making process. The other is a global challenge of non-national forces and issues. The former is clearly a different kind of political power; the latter may posit a supremacy of economic power.

Political power can, of course, take many different forms, from the same or similar social roots. Here we shall look into the apotheosis of national elite power under perceived popular threat, i.e., at fascism and kindred military dictatorships. Furthermore, we shall analyse urbanistic Communism as an enduring radical popular challenge to historical elite rule, and into post-Communism as a new kind of political power.

After World War II there was concern with democratic versus non-democratic architecture and urban design, especially in West Germany.[17] This is here taken into account, but it would not work as a master distinction, given the fact that most of the nation-states of the world for most of the 225 years covered in this book were non-democracies.

Popular political power has asserted itself in different ways: in access to institutional power, as in 'municipal socialism', welfare-state cities or, recently outside Europe, in city governments by middle-class coalitions with the urban poor, but also in successful protest moments: stopping the ravages of the 'Car City' in the North Atlantic of the late 1950s to 1970s and, even more recently, in a spate of urban revolutions – or better called, given their basically ambiguous (but always non-working-class) social character, extra-constitutional regime changes. It may also make up bargaining power in cities where public participation in urban planning and development is recognized.

Capital cities are by definition sites of political power. But popular challenges mean that they are often also sites of resistance, of political counter-power, of protest rallies and headquarters of opposition movements, parties and trade unions.

Most of the constitutive national elites were capitalist or pro-capitalist, and their imprint on their nation and its capital is duly taken into account. But there is also the raw economic power of capital and wealth outside political channels. This – economic – is the second source of power we have to pay attention to. It operates in two major ways in our story. One is its imprint on the spatial layout and on the patterning of buildings, and most specifically through skyscrapers. The other refers to the urban exclusivity of wealth and economic prosperity, as manifested in gating and private cities of the privileged.

At some level, all systems of political power need representation, in the sense of public display. Power needs public representation to be recognized, respected, awed or admired, in order to be obeyed and followed. A new reign of power is publicly and ceremoniously inaugurated. Secondly, modern nation-state power (in particular) needs representation in order to give direction to the self-identity, thoughts, beliefs, memories, hopes and aspirations of its citizens. This is the second function of monumentality, as well as of flags, cocardes, symbolic pins, public banner slogans and rhetorical addresses to the nation.

Economic power as such needs no representation; money is force enough in itself. Many times it is wiser to let it operate in the dark rather than in broad daylight.* Corporations and capitalists often want to display their wealth, though, and to bask in admiration of their buildings.

'Representation' has a connotation of intent, which would be much too narrow a perspective for what we are trying to do here. Basically, our interest is in manifestations of power. Representations make up an important part of the latter, but there are also power manifestations through ignorance, neglect or rejection of certain areas or parts of the population, and there are power manifestations of order and disorder, of competence and incompetence.

Reading the Urban Text

Cities are shaped by power in two different ways. First, urban social relations are structured through the constitution of city space, in terms of division/connection, of centre/periphery, of hierarchy/equality and of comfort/discomfort/misery. Second, power constructs the meaning of life in the city: the opportunities and the limitations, the sense and the priorities of urban living, identities in the city, the meanings of the city's and the nation's past, present and aspired future. The urban text of

---

* A comic example of monetary discretion is the instructions apparently given to the guards, civilian as well as uniformed, protecting the head office of Goldman Sachs at 200 West Street in Battery Park City in New York, an imposing but by no means spectacular skyscraping slab. If you walk up to one of them asking what building it is, you get the answer 'An office building.' What office building? 'Oh, just an office building.' 'I thought Goldman Sachs should be here somewhere, do you know where it is?' 'No.' (Conversation recorded on 13 April 2016.) The comic aspect is that the building is indicated on official city maps, and the address is easily Googled.

power can be read along these two lines. The key variables we are then going to look at are often simultaneously socially structuring and meaning-conveying.

The spatial layout

The urban layout is a production of social space, in Henri Lefebvre's felicitous phrase.[18] In the ancient grand civilizations, such as the Indic and the Sinic, it was designed as a cosmological representation of the city's connection to the cosmic order. Later, for instance in European and modern history generally, the space produced is usually that of terrestrial power relations. The basic elements of the spatial design are its paths or system of streets; its allocation of the size of building lots; its 'edges' or boundaries within the city as well as its boundaries to the non-/other city (currently often blurred); its open places; its nodes of circulation; its delimited areas, districts or neighbourhoods; and what we may call their mode of orientation, i.e., their conception of centre–periphery and their use of the given topography, for example, a landscape of alternating altitudes.*

We are not dealing with metric variables of power or with clear-cut universal categories, and our analysis has to be tentative and contextualized. Some rules of thumb about where to start looking might be worth mentioning.

What constitutes the centre of the city or, in big cities, often the centres (plural)? Historically, the polar cases were, at one end, an open public space, an agora or forum (as in republican Athens and Rome), and, at the other, a castle or palace (as in Beijing and Edo/Tokyo and in monarchical Europe) or a temple (like in Tenochtitlán). What are the functions of the centre(s)? How is/are the centre(s) connected to the rest of the city? Here the main inherited alternatives are structurally linear-axial or concentric. That is, either through linear thoroughfares, as in both ancient Chang'an and in modern Brasília, Islamabad and Abuja, or through rays of streets radiating out through a concentric urban space

---

* I am here largely if not exclusively leaning on Kevin Lynch's *The Image of the City* (Boston: MIT Press, 1960), chapter III, and Spiro Kostof's *The City Shaped* (New York: Bulfinch Press, 1991), especially chapters 3 and 4, although their concerns were not primarily with power.

like an Indic mandala, in Yoruba Ife, or in European Baroque Versailles, Karlsruhe and Saint Petersburg. Blurring these alternatives of stark centrality indicates more complex configurations of power.

Seclusion of the centre from the periphery is a manifestation of a power of social exclusivity. A dramatic example is, of course, former apartheid cities, where the working and servant classes were kept in 'townships' far away from the centre, separated, as in Pretoria, by unbuilt wasteland. Paris has maintained a clear boundary between the city proper and its suburbs or *banlieues*, separated by a motorway running on the demolished city walls.

The regularity of the street system, for instance a grid, and the uniformity or harmony of its buildings demonstrate a power concerned with urban structure – which Islamic rulers, for instance, historically were not – and capable of implementing its design. The width, and sometimes also the length, of streets are often deliberate manifestations of power. Pierre L'Enfant, the designer of what became Washington, D.C., called for avenues 'proportioned to the greatness which . . . the Capital of a powerful Empire ought to manifest'.[19] The Paris of the mid-nineteenth-century Second Empire would make wide avenues a standard of national capitals and of all ambitious cities.

Archaeologists have long paid attention to the size patterns of building lots as indicators of hierarchy and inequality. An extreme example of spatial density differentials is offered by contemporary Nairobi. In 1999 there were between 360 inhabitants per square kilometre in Karen and 80,000 in Kibera, pointing clearly to the power of the few over the many.[20] A similar indicator of inegalitarian power is the existence and extension of built-up, non-produced space – in plain English, of slum areas on raw land, without prepared streets, a water supply or sewers.

A topography of hills and plains is often used as a power gradient. The (high) plateau of Abidjan and Dakar, for instance, is the site of first the colonial and then the national elite. The High City of Brussels or Kyiv is historically the city of political and religious power, the Low City of the secondary economic power of merchants and traders. But it may also be used as an instrument of hierarchical integration. In pre-modern Edo and Addis Ababa, the lords lived on the hills with their retinue around them, below. In Addis this is still visible, albeit rapidly disappearing, in poor neighbourhoods adjacent to modern buildings of wealth and power.

Still another important variable of a city's spatial layout is accessibility of space. We may here distinguish between official, private and public space: the first accessible only to the proper authorities, the second only to the owners and the public to everybody. The relative size and importance of the three can be read as manifesting the relative power of an exclusive state, of private property and of the citizenry, respectively. Recently, post-Communism has meant a reduction of official space but, like in most other capitalist cities, an expansion of private-only space, through private shopping malls replacing public markets (or department stores) and private gating slicing up the urban space.

It should not be forgotten that the 'public' can be, has been and in some cities still is gendered* and/or racialized. Racial exclusion from public areas has become prohibited, but a female public presence is still contested in Arabic and West Asian Islamic and in North Indian Hindu cities.

Functionality

The functioning of a city has two main dimensions, their supply of opportunities – of money and employment, above all – and their supply of services. In this study, the former is partly covered by our focus on political capitals, although we shall have reason to take notice of variations in their socioeconomic structure. The extent and the distribution of urban services, on the other hand, are direct manifestations of city power.

Urban life is significantly structured by the availability and accessibility of a number of necessary urban services. First of all, water supply, sanitation, electricity, garbage collection and waste management: are they provided, adequately, for everybody? Street lighting, pavement, safety and policing, mail delivery? Housing, food and employment are often left to markets: to what extent are they kept functioning and

---

* Until recent times, the 'public' and the 'public sphere' have been either overwhelmingly or exclusively male, apart from some strong-headed mistresses and European salon hostesses. But women played a crucial role in at least two decisive events in European history on the threshold of modernity: in October 1789, when a procession of angry Parisian women brought the King back to Paris from Versailles, and in Petrograd in 1917, when women's demonstrations for bread ignited the February Revolution.

properly regulated? To what extent is there adequate public transport? Are urban roads properly maintained? Are there schools, health clinics and basic stores in all areas and accessible to everybody?

In today's North Atlantic region, the functioning and accessibility of these services are basically taken for granted, but their history is rather short, even here. Their full importance was brought home to me during a collective study of African capitals, most of which have a huge service deficit.[21] Only a third of households in Addis Ababa and Kinshasa had (as of around 2005) piped water on the premises, in Abuja 40 per cent. Only half of the population of Kinshasa had access to sewage or latrines, in Addis less than one in ten.

Poverty and underdevelopment are one reason for this, the power-lessness of the African powerful. But there is also a question of priority, between what Mussolini once called tasks of 'necessity' and tasks of 'grandezza'. Historically, while the Paris of Napoleon III and his prefect Haussmann became a world model of grandeur, Victorian London was both a European pace-setter and the leading world exporter of water and sanitation services.

The functioning of urban services is currently a major political issue in a number of cities: the Washington Metro, public transport in Bogotá and the supply of water and electricity in Delhi, for example. The exclusivity or inclusivity of city power can be gauged by the city's functionality.

Patterning of buildings

The pattern of buildings might be seen as a special aspect of the spatial layout. It refers to the relative location and size of buildings, above all in the city centre. What kinds of buildings occupy the most central location? How do the central buildings relate to each other?

For example, all over Latin America, except in Montevideo, Bogotá, and Brasília, the Presidential Palace is the overpowering or dominant central building, with Congress clearly offside. In Mexico, until recently, it was almost anonymous, and in Chile it was relegated to a refurbished hospital in Valparaíso. In Ottawa, Washington, Montevideo and Brasília, on the other hand, the congress or parliament building has centre stage. In the new Malaysian capital of Putrajaya, the dominant building is the prime minister's office. City halls have no prominence in any American capital, while they are major buildings in Tokyo, Seoul and Copenhagen and clearly, if not quite successfully, compete with the state buildings in Vienna. When the Belgians created their national capital in the mid-nineteenth century, the Royal Palace was larger than the Parliament opposite it, but the largest building of all was the Palace of Justice. The main government building, whatever it is, is usually protected against construction competition by various rules of permissible height (as in Washington, D.C., for instance) and distance. But in Tokyo the official office of the prime minister is overshadowed by the non-descript corporate tower of an undistinguished insurance company. Some cities, Paris for instance, have no central representative governmental building at all: what does that imply?

The patterning of buildings takes other significant expressions, too, such as the uniformity and harmony or unrelated heterogeneity of buildings along main streets, or the extent of contrast between main-street buildings and back-street or peripheral buildings. Moreover, there is a noteworthy temporal dimension. When a regime embarks upon a building programme, what representative buildings are given priority and how are the priorities of time and money set between representation and utilitarian construction, service infrastructure or housing? Are there meaningful clusters of representative buildings?

These are just a few examples, and before jumping to conclusions of interpretation we had better see them, and others of their kind, as first of all raising questions and providing incitements to historical and contextual queries.

Architecture

Architecture is often what first catches the eye looking at a city. It has two dimensions. One is aesthetic, expressed in historical styles or in contemporary iconicity. The style chosen is loaded with meaning, which any urban scholar has to pay attention to. However, the meaning is historically path-dependent, depending upon the historical experience of the power-holder. The European Gothic of the Westminster Parliament is the style of the 'free-born Englishman', the Gothic of the Strasbourg Münster or the Kölner Dom is *echt deutsch*, that of the

Vienna City Hall is the style of autonomous cities, in the Flemish tradition. Neoclassicism is republican in Washington and imperial in Paris and Saint Petersburg.

The second dimension is political, viewing built forms as expressing a 'grammar of power', as the Norwegian architectural theorist Thomas Thiis-Evensen has called it.[22] I have found his sketch very useful. Six building variables and their power implications are listed in this 'grammar':

- Closure: the more closed, the more inaccessible
- Weight: the heavier
- Size: the larger
- Distance: the more distant from its immediate environment
- Symmetry: the more symmetrical
- Verticality: the taller the building, the more concentrated and the more authoritarian the power of the builder is likely to be.*

Five of the six may be interpreted as indicators of imposing awe, pomp, haughtiness, even arrogance. Symmetry is an expression of order, of a central mastering of the whole.

By size, modern power tends to be overshadowed by ancient, showing a certain popular approximation of power. The *château de Versailles* was 16 acres, the Moscow Kremlin 68 acres and the Vatican compound about 110 acres, which may be compared to the 175 acres of the Beijing Forbidden City, the 255 acres of the Delhi Red Fort and the 1,200 acres of the 200 BC *er fang* complex of Chang'an. But Saint Peter's in Rome is much larger than the main temples of Tenochtitlán and, even more, of Cuzco. In terms of verticality, the Great Giza Pyramid of 2500 BC, at 146 metres, commanded the skies until the skyscrapers of the twentieth century.[23]

The 'grammar' will not be used for any declension exercises of a Latin-school type, nor for any taxonomy. It is a list of variables to bear in mind when looking at buildings and thinking about their meaning.

---

* A similar, perceptive analysis of interior civic space, such as parliaments and city halls, is made by Charles Goodsell, *The Social Meaning of Civic Space,* Lawrence: University Press of Kansas, 1988.

Monumentality

Monumentality is directly geared to the production of meaning. The Latin *monere* means to remind. Through its built ensembles, statues, plaques and museums, a city's monuments try to remind us of events and persons and to convey a particular historical narrative, urban and/ or national. A built landmark may also constitute a monument, without an intrinsic narrative but reminding us of the identity of a place. Beijing's Tiananmen is such a monumental landmark, figuring in China's national emblem. Though not in the national heraldry, the Brandenburg Gate and the Eiffel Tower play similar roles for the identity of Berlin(ers) and Paris(ians).

Monumentality is often neglected in hard-nosed urban social science and was dismissed by the modernist architectural and urbanist vanguard of the years between the two world wars. However, in 1943, three leading figures of CIAM (Congrès International d'Architecture Moderne, the architectural vanguard movement) – its soon-to-be president Josep Lluís Sert, the long-term secretary Sigfried Giedion and the painter Fernand Léger – published 'Nine Points on Monumentality', pleading for a modernist reconsideration.

> Monuments are human landmarks which men have created as symbols for their ideals, for their aims and for their actions . . . Monuments are the expression of man's highest cultural needs . . . They have to satisfy the eternal demand of the people for translation of their collective force into symbols . . . Monuments are therefore only possible in periods in which a unifying consciousness and unifying culture exist.

From their sixth point the authors then move on to argue for a new, modernist monumentality without being very concrete, other than arguing for 'modern materials and new techniques', for 'mobile elements' and projections of colour.* They evade answering their own implied

---

* J. L. Sert, F. Léger, and Sigfried Giedion, 'Nine Points on Monumentality', reprinted in Joan Ockman (ed.), *Architecture Culture 1943–1968*, New York: Rizzoli, 1993 pp. 29–30. The *Architectural Revuew* (104), 117–28, 1948, organized a high-level modernist symposium on monumentality, with Lucio Costa, Sigfried Giedion,

question, whether a 'unifying consciousness unifying culture' still exists. We do not need to answer that question here, because monumentality can also thrive among divided consciousnesses and cultures.

Madrid at the end of 2014 is a good illustration. On 15 October the Spanish king inaugurated in Madrid a big monumental statue to the eighteenth-century admiral Blas de Lezo. It had started as a private initiative, which soon got the enthusiastic support of the then right-wing mayor of Madrid. This happened in the build-up to the Catalan crisis, and knowledgeable Catalan nationalists soon pointed out that de Lezo had taken part in the bombardment (and final Spanish capture) of Barcelona in 1714. The Barcelona municipal council formally demanded the withdrawal of the statue, something the Madrid mayor declared she would never do under any circumstances.[24]

In Budapest in the same autumn of 2014, liberal opinion was very upset by a new sculptural ensemble with a monstrous bird descending on an angelic Hungary, commemorating the 'German occupation' (from March 1944 to the end of World War II). It is interpreted, correctly, as whitewashing the reactionary, anti-Semitic regime that ruled Hungary after 1920 and aligned itself with Nazi Germany at the outbreak of World War II.[25]

Monumentality may actually be a good indicator of the division of the country. By the outbreak of the protest rallies in Kyiv in the autumn of 2013, Lenin had been taken down in the country west of Kyiv, surviving in the capital with a battered nose, but stood tall east of the Dnipro River in the main square of every important city. After the successful regime change, Lenin is now confined to the Donbass region.[*]

Modern monumentality in the narrow sense of statues, triumphal arches, allegorical and other sculptural ensembles, pantheons and columns is of Greco-Roman European origin, and processional portraits are of Christian European origin. Monumentality has had its golden ages – imperial Rome and nineteenth-century Paris – but it is very much still with us, capable of arousing civic passion. This symbolic repertoire

---

Henry-Russel Hitchcock and others, where the Swedish functionalist design organizer and art historian Gregor Paulsson was the only anti-monumentalist: 'Intimacy, not monumentality should be the emotional goal'.

[*] In the winter of 2016 there was a foiled nighttime attempt on the life of the monumental Lenin in Donetsk.

has been imported into other civilizations in modern times and its relative scarcity in, for example, East Asia, should be interpreted in the context of its alienness. Mausoleums and symbolically charged tombs, on the other hand, are part of the heritage of all Asian cultures.

Toponymy

Urban meanings are also constructed through naming streets, places, buildings, institutions – by *toponomy*. The official naming of streets was a European post-medieval practice. The original, vernacular naming referred to a street's artisans and shops, some feature of its natural location or some colourful inhabitant of the neighbourhood. Concentrated national and city governments had more representative concerns.

The first such street of any note was probably the Via Giulia in Rome, named after the great early-sixteenth-century Roman planner Pope Giulio II. In London, beginning with Henry VIII, several King Streets were laid out, none very grand. In 1765 a law was passed that all streets and squares should have a name and a name tablet.[26] In Paris official names started to appear in the seventeenth century, first drawn from royalty, but soon also from statesmen and high servants of the king: Colbert, Mazarin, Richelieu. By the eighteenth century, before the revolution, there were also streets named after guild heads and city leaders, and after 1728 there was a police ordinance that all Parisian streets should have a name plaque.[27] In the 1630s, the idea of official street naming reached the new (short-lived) big-power capital of Stockholm, whose Regency government began by commemorating itself, in *Regeringsgatan* (Government Street).

The practice later radiated across the European imperial area and into Republican Beijing,[28] but it never stuck in Japan, which has kept a block-based address system. In contrast to Communist Europe, street (re)naming was not important in Communist China, although it did happen occasionally. In the 1990s, the World Bank put out a manual of street naming, mainly aimed at Africa.

Washington, D.C., has its major avenues named after the states of the Union, with Pennsylvania Avenue outshining all others, followed by New York, in connecting Capitol Hill to the White House. The current American affection for toponymy of airports, hospitals, university buildings, etc., seems to be rather recent. US cities pioneered the utterly pragmatic manner of numbering streets, or, as in Washington, using the letters of the alphabet.

Some methodological problems

The meaning of the city text cannot be fully grasped from the existing cityscape, however sharp the urbanistic vision. Most cities are old, which means they consist of different time layers of spatial layout and of manifestations of meaning. At most given points in time, cities have to be read diachronically. You have to dive into city history and into the city's plans, unrealized as well as realized. In general, contemporary cities have to be approached through a perspective of cultural geology. City texts have to be deciphered in archival contexts, making use of the historian's privilege over the archaeologist.

Oslo furnishes a nice illustration of the necessity of keeping historical layering in mind when interpreting a contemporary cityscape. The central, commanding building of modern Oslo is the Royal Castle, built in the nineteenth century for the lieutenant-governor of the Swedish king, but the current centre of power is the parliamentary *Storting* building on the main street below the Castle. The configuration of the two buildings tells us something interesting about the transition from royal Swedish to parliamentary Norwegian rule, but it would be misleading as a guide to power in contemporary Norway.

We have already taken note of the polyvalence of architectural styles. But even politically analyzed built forms are not always understandable from general principles of construction. Transparency, for instance, is currently interpreted as a feature of democratic government and therefore of democratic architecture, underlined in the self-presentation of the EU parliamentary complex. However, a famous example of Italian Fascist modernism, the *Casa del Fascio* in Como by Giuseppe Terragni, is a light four-storey structure with large glass doors to the piazza and big windows, intended to convey the transparency of Fascism as a 'glass house' with 'no obstacle between the political leaders and the people'.[29]

National Power and the Pathways to Modern Nation-States

In a politico-cultural perspective on world history, the rise of national power and nation-states appears as a major historical divide, the key political dimension of modernity. By 1700, no single state in the world was claiming to be a state of the sovereign power of a nation. Britain, for which a bold sixteenth-century national claim has been made,[30] was after a short republican interlude again ruled as a dynastic monarchy, and its revolutionary settlement of 1688 was a compromise between two pre-national monarchical principles. The Tory one held that 'the King is the source of all justice & authority' and the Whig one, which became preponderant, 'that King James the 2nd . . . by breaking the original compact between King & people . . . has thereby abdicated the government & left the throne vacant'.[31] The Netherlands was a confederation of towns and local communities created from seven United Provinces.

Today, all states – except Saudi Arabia and the Gulf emirates – present themselves as nation-states. What this planetary transformation of political power, which did not stop with the proclamation of nation-states, has meant for cities and urban representations of power is a central theme of this book.

National power, nation-states and national capitals are distinctive phenomena, differing from the much more researched and hotly controversial topics of national identity and nationalism. National identities are part of a vast field of 'Othering' – distinguishing 'us' from 'the others' – and have, as such, ancient roots. Nationalism belongs to the secular ideological field of 'isms' emerging in Europe after the French Revolution.*

National power is a conception of legitimate power, breaking with previous conceptions of the 'grace of God', 'Mandate of Heaven', of descent – whether of princely dynasty or oligarchic *regimentsfähigen Familien* ('families fit for rule', as it was called in the Swiss city cantons) – or of age-cum-descent, as of tribal elders. National independence from empires started in the Americas about two centuries ago and became a

---

* The vast literature on these topics may be seen as summarized by the key contributions of, in alphabetical order, Benedict Anderson, Ernest Gellner, Eric Hobsbawm and Anthony Smith.

major feature of twentieth-century history. It is in this sense that national power is the political core of the vast cultural transformation we call modernity. Basically, the nation was the population of a territory; national power, national sovereignty, was its claim to rule. For a long time this population was, at most, no more than its adult, non-servile males, setting the stage for subsequent struggles about who the nation is. A nation-state is the practical institutionalization of national power. In urban terms, the struggle for national power was focused on transforming the princely *Residenz* city, the oligarchic mercantile city, the religious centre (e.g., Rome), or centres of imperial/colonial power into national capitals. In the 'White Dominions' of the British empire, national capitals were built as political replacements of the colonial.

Modernity, nation-states and their four main historical pathways

'Modernity' may be used as a shorthand for a current or recent culture. In the arts it has come to designate the reign of a style or a stance, 'modernism'. Into sociology it has been imported to label a (largely pre-defined) social process, 'modernization'. Post-classical Latin *modernus* means no more than 'current, of today'. In my opinion, concepts should do better than just providing a label. They should trigger curiosity, stimulate new research questions. Concepts should be leveraged.

Leveraging concepts of modern and modernity would then mean asking: what does it mean to be modern? How and when can a social period be interpreted as modernity? Should such periods be specified by socio-cultural domains and/or by territorial areas?

In my opinion, the best and the least idiosyncratic definition of being modern is to be unbound by tradition, by the wisdom of our fathers, by the skills of our masters, by any ancient authority. To be modern is a *cultural time orientation* to the present and towards the future, no more and no less.

A modern culture, then, would be a culture where this time orientation is predominant, modernity an epoch of such predominance. Instead of fixing a label on what we are observing and writing about, we would then be confronted with a number of questions, without any self-evident answers: when did modernity happen? Variously in different cultural spheres, in science, the different arts, in conceptions of history, politics, economics, family life? Did it take place in different ways and at different times in the world? If so, do the variable pathways to modernity affect today's social and cultural life?

Hopefully, the advantages of seeing modernity not as 'modes of social life which emerged in Europe from about the seventeenth century onwards',[32] but as something which has to be discovered and specified, come out of the sample of questions above. Here we have to concentrate on three issues: first, accepting that modernity breaks through in different socio-cultural domains at different times, in a comparative global perspective, is there any sectoral breakthrough which can be taken as more important than the others and is thereby useable as a benchmark? I am arguing that the modernity of political power, of the polity, is the decisive variable because of its intrinsic capacity to affect all other socio-cultural realms. However, the impact of modern political power on the traditionalism/modernity of society may be big or small, fast or slow. There is also a pragmatic reason: political change tends to be eventful and therefore much easier to pin down and date than economic change.

Second, what is, then, a modern polity? The answer, for analytical instead of ideological purposes, had better not be weighed down by particular institutional features, usually derived from the scholar's native or otherwise ideal country. A simple, straightforward and non-aprioristic answer is, a *nation-state*. True, nations often refer to their past, but when they emerge, the politics of the nation assert the power of the present against the past. The nation-state is a self-constituted body claiming to rule itself into an open, non-prescribed future, unbound by past precedence, abolishing or marginalizing the rights of princes, under whatever title, denying colonial powers and transcending the traditional rights and powers of tribal elders or hereditary urban oligarchies.

Third, can the arrival of political modernity be globally typologized in a way that is analytically manageable as well as empirically warranted? Yes, it dawned upon me, as I was making a global study of the development of the right to vote,[33] that there were four major routes to modern national citizenship, four major pathways into modernity, defined by the conflict lines for and against the new, between modernity and tradition, between modernity and anti-modernity. They can be distinguished in general analytical terms and can therefore be used not only to sort groups of countries but also as ideal types, two or more of which may have been taken in a particular country.

How was the new political culture generated? Internally, in the given society, or imposed or imported from outside? Who were the forces of the new? A new stratum within the given society, an external force or a part of the old internal elite? Where were the main forces of anti-modernity, of traditional authority and submission – inside or outside?

In this vein we may distinguish four main conflictual configurations in the world. They emerged as empirical generalizations, but they can also be used as ideal types, especially as they can be located in a logical property space.* This possibility has operated above all in two great hybrid cases: Russia and China. But the four main actual roads to modernity were opened up in the following ways.

Table 1. Roads to/through modernity by the location of forces and cultures: for and against.

Pre/Anti-Modernity Forces	Pro-Modernity Forces		
	Internal	External	
		Imposed	Imported & Learnt
Internal	Europe	Colonial Zone	Reactive Modernization
External	'New Worlds' (Settler States)		

Note: Countries of reactive, or externally induced, modernization include Japan, Qing China, Ottoman Empire/Turkey, Iran and Siam/Thailand.

The new future orientation of the last centuries first emerged in Europe not as a natural emanation of European civilization but out of conflicts internal to Europe, primarily north-western Europe, including wars about European overseas empires. In other words, the European route was one of civil war, which pitted the forces of reason, enlightenment, nation/people, innovation and change against those of the eternal truths of the Church, of the sublime wisdom and beauty of ancient philosophy and art, of the divine rights of kings, of the ancient privileges of

* Not all logical combinations have been empirically significant.

aristocracy and of the customs of fathers and grandfathers. It was related to the rise of commerce, capital and industry, built upon colonial accumulation overseas.

In a global perspective, two aspects of the European nation stand out. One is its anchorage in a popular and territorial history, distinguished from the landed property of princely power. The other is its heavy, distinctive cultural load, with spoken language at its core. Standardizing and homogenizing a national language was a central part of national political programmes, of 'making Italians' and turning 'peasants into Frenchmen', as Eugene Weber's beautiful book names it.[34] The creation of a national language through dialect selection and grammatical and orthographic codification became a major task of European small-nation intellectuals in the nineteenth century, from the Balkans to Norway. Where possible, minority languages were driven out of national culture.

The settler states of the Americas had to create new nations, which mythologically and emblematically, of course, drew upon historical examples as symbolic resources – ancient European republicanism in the case of the United States, historical Catholic experiences and pre-Columbian (e.g. Inca and Aztec) high culture in Hispanic America – but which claimed no ethno-cultural territorial history and shared their language with the colonial metropolis.

Most distinctive of the New World was its conception of the *nation as a club* to which desirable members could and should be recruited. Targeted immigration from Europe was a major dimension of nation-formation. 'To govern is to populate', a prominent mid-nineteenth-century Argentine politician and politician, Juan Bautista Alberdi, said.[35] Particularly in Latin American discourse – in Brazil as well as, for instance, in Argentina – this club-member recruitment was explicitly referred to as 'whitening' or 'civilizing' the nation.[36] For a long time, only people of external, European descent were regarded as a full citizens of the new nations of the Americas and Australia.

Nations of the Colonial Zone constitute a third variety, *nations identified as ex-colonies*. There were no historical territories, no singular historical peoples, only colonial boundaries. In a rare wise decision, African nationalist leaders decided to accept all such boundaries, however arbitrary and culturally divisive. Ali Jinnah did not, and British India, which was larger than any pre-colonial state of India, broke up into India – which Nehru refused to call 'Hindustan' – Pakistan and Bangladesh, through terrible pogroms and wars of divorce.

The maintenance of the colonial language is arguably the most ostentatious legacy of the colonial pathway to modernity, with its ensuing complicated and hierarchical relations of nation and culture, though also pragmatically practical in multilingual nations – such as Nigeria, with 400 to 500 languages according to different estimates,[37] or India, which has at least 122, according to a recent linguistic census analysis.*

The European notion that a nation is defined by its language could not be applied in the ex-colonies. When it was, as in Pakistan, it had disastrous results, from 1952 bitterly dividing the Bengali east to the Urdu-promoting leaders of West Pakistan, where the Mughal hybrid of Urdu was not the majority mother tongue either.[38]

A general legacy of anti-colonialism is a strong nationalism as the decisive modern mass politics. Post-colonial culture also tends to be starkly divided between elite and mass culture. Elite culture is usually conducted in the language of the former colonial power, a language which the majority of the population does not understand. In the capital city, the colonial divide is usually reproduced, the post-colonial elite taking over the official buildings and the private mansions and villas of the colonizers. Colonial administrative practices tend to be kept, although often subverted by corruption and/or lack of state resources.

Traditional authorities and rituals tend to persist, drawing upon both their colonial institutionalization and their national credentials. In spite of their use in colonial indirect rule, traditional leaders were often incorporated into modern anti-colonial nationalism. The founding programme (from 1948) of the radical Convention People's Party in Ghana, for instance, demanded as its first objective 'independence for the people of Ghana and

---

* Lincoln Mitchell, *The Color Revolution*, Philadelphia: University of Pennsylvania Press, 2012, chapter 7. The only exceptions developed in areas of developed pre-colonial inter-lingual trade, in the Indonesian archipelago, where a Malay *lingua franca* developed, in the mid-twentieth century renamed Bahasa Indonesia by the nationalists (see Benedict Anderson, *Language and Power*, Ithaca Cornell University Press, 1990, part II), and in East Africa, in Tanzania and Kenya, where less successfully Swahili, a Bantu language, developed out of the Arabian trade and was adopted as the national language, along with English and local vernaculars (Ch.Githiora, 'Kenya: Language and the Search for a Coherent National Identity', and F. Topan, 'Tanzania: The Development of Swahili as a National and Official Language', both in Andrew Simpson (ed), *Language and National Identity in Africa*, Oxford: OUP, 2008).

their Odikros [traditional rulers]'.[39] Modern Malay nationalism, as the national Tunku Abdul Rahman Memorial museum in Kuala Lumpur narrates, started after World War II as a protest against British plans to reduce the powers of the traditional rulers and to institute an equal colonial citizenship for Malays, Chinese and Tamils alike. Independent India, on the other hand, did away with the princely states of India.

The nation of reactive modernization is the *pre-modern realm*, defined by the writ of the prince, the emperor, the king or the sultan. This was how the successful modernizers of Meiji Japan saw it, as did the less successful rulers of Siam and Abyssinia and the soon-defeated modernizers of Joseon Korea, Qing China and the Ottoman empire. It was a historical legacy of rule, synonymous with its ruling dynasty, who often (though not in Japan) gave the realm its everyday name. The modern task here was not national emancipation but building the realm into a nation. In Japan this was greatly facilitated by the high ethnic homogeneity of the country and the low salience of intertwined religions. The most important measure of national unification was the abolition of the feudal *daimyo* domains, returning their lands 'to the emperor'. The Meiji modernizers built a modern Japanese nation around the symbol and mystique of the Emperor, whose status, but not his power, was more and more exalted as the modernization process progressed, culminating in the 1930s and during the Pacific War.

In Japan and Thailand in the twenty-first century, the monarch is a sublime national icon, in comparison with which even British monarchical deference and protocol pale into civic celebrity – but an icon of the nation, not the owner of the land. The great modernizer of Siam, King Chulalongkorn (Rama V), has even become a figure of religious devotion, as I noticed at his equestrian statue in Bangkok in 2007.

National language and culture were not primary issues. They were given by the realm, although the status of Sinic civilization and culture came to suffer from the recurrent defeats of China. They became primary when the Turkish nation succeeded the failed Ottoman empire.

The national capitals coming out of emancipation from colonialism and from reactive modernization both have a tendential duality, abruptly juxtaposing urbanistic elements from different civilizations. The hegemonic combination is different, though. The centre of the colonial city was built by the conquerors and then taken over by the ex-colonized, de facto reproducing the characteristic duality of the colonial city. The centre of reactive modernization – usually the princely palace and its surroundings – remained in native hands, though 'modernized' by foreign imports of style and amenities. Paraphrasing the doctrine of socialist realism, we may say that it was foreign in form and native in content.

The two great hybrids

The meandering of actual history is rarely captured by the straight lines of scholarly ideal types. In the history of modernity there are two great hybrids weighing heavily on the twentieth- and twenty-first-century worlds: Russia and China. Russia was a part of Europe from the time when the latter was still subsumed under the worldview of Christianity. In the fifteenth century, a Muscovite prince married a Byzantine princess and invited Italian architects to the Kremlin to bolster a claim to being a Third Rome. Peter I had learnt about the modern world in the Netherlands, and in the later eighteenth century the court of Catherine II was part of the Francophone Enlightenment, harbouring Denis Diderot as the court *philosophe*. In the nineteenth century, Tsarist Russia became a European precursor of the global Cold War United States, the *gendarme* of last resort against any rebellions against the status quo. Inside Russia there also developed powerful currents of the European labour movement, Marxist social democracy.

However, Russia was also an underdeveloped part of Europe, and among its ruling elite self-consciously so, from Peter I to Lenin. Reactive modernization—catching up with resourceful enemies—was a second crucial part of the Russian path to modernity, from Peter's use of his absolutist power to build the city of Saint Petersburg rather than a Peterhof replica of Versailles, to Lenin's and Stalin's conceptions of socialism as electrification and breakneck industrialization, respectively.

Late imperial Qing China did attempt some reactive modernization, without much success as the devastating imperialist invasion of Beijing in 1900 brought home. Nevertheless, China was never properly colonized; no alien governor-general ever ruled it. But it was partially colonized: its main ports were largely foreign imperialist 'concessions' and a major revenue source, the Customs, was controlled by an inter-imperialist consortium.

The hybridity of China included a third, non-negligible component, an offshoot from European class structuration and mobilization. The Communist Party of China has undergone multiple mutations, but its ultimately successful character of a Marxist class organization derives from Europe and the European labour movement, transmitted through the Comintern (the Communist International) in the 1920s.

While post-Ottoman Turkey may be seen as a late case of reactive modernization, after the failed half-hearted Sultanate attempts, Egypt, an autonomous important area of the empire, had to experience the mutation of extravagant khedival modernization into semi-colonial bondage.

Summing up

Nation-states constituted tipping-points of modernity, creating a political space of open horizons of action regardless of whether the nation saw itself as rooted in ancestral territory and culture or not. At their very core of nation conception and constitution, nation-states arose out of very different kinds of power constellations, following from their history of development. Their capital cities have varied accordingly, in ways never before explored systematically, if at all.

There were four main routes to national statehood:

1. The European road: externally overdetermined internal reform or revolution
2. The 'New Worlds' of European settlers seceding from the motherland: outgrowing European traditions
3. The colonial road to independence: turning colonial modernity against the colonizers
4. Reactive modernization from above: defending the realm in a new way against novel challenges

These pathways may also be seen as ideal-type trajectories, which may be combined in a given country. The two main centres of twentieth-century Communism – Russia and China – were the two great hybrids of modern state formation. My hypothesis is that this nation/modernity hybridity was crucial to the victories of Communism in Russia and in China, but that is another story.

Furthermore, the new national capital cities bear witness not only to the context of nation-state formation, but also to its political process, whether ruptural or gradual. Did the nation-state arise out of a ruptural violent conflict, a revolution, a civil war, a war of independence, or did it grow into being through an accumulation of gradual shifts of power, or, alternatively, through negotiated transfer?

In the next chapter we shall investigate the constitution and construction of the major capitals along the four major routes of nation-state formation. Later we shall look into how moments of popular and global challenge to the national elites have appeared in national capitals of different constitutive origins. The hybrids of Moscow and Beijing will be dealt with in a special chapter on the coming and going of Communism.

2

National Foundations:
Europe – Transforming Princely Cities

Europe was a world pioneer of modernist breaks with past authorities, wisdom and aesthetic canon. However, in a global context, the most striking aspect of European nation-states and their capitals is historical continuity as well as continuity of territory, language, religion, art, architecture and urban layout. This paradox of pioneer modernism combined with de facto conservationism is mainly explained by European imperialism. Europe was the only part of the world which did not have its pre-modernity conquered, shattered or fatally threatened and humiliated. Therefore, its pre-national, pre-modern background and legacy matter more than to capitals coming out of other national pathways. With respect to cities, this background had two main features: a particular urban system and form of urbanism, and a historically evolved repertoire of architectural language and symbolic forms.

The core of European civilization was uniquely urban in a specific sense; it developed in sovereign cities, in city-states which were part of regional systems of exchange, rivalry, competition, warfare and alliances. City-states developed on other continents, too, but nowhere else did they constitute political and cultural systems of comparable significance. This was ancient Greece, succeeded by ancient Rome, a city building an empire; by Byzantium, another city holding an empire; and, after the collapse of the Mediterranean urban powers of antiquity, ancient civilization revived in Florence and the other city-states of the Renaissance.

European cities were distinctive legal-political entities, characterized by the civic, in Germanic languages *Bürger*, rights of its free men.[*] Even when not sovereign states, European cities and towns usually had institutions of collective self-governance, in the big and wealthy cities represented by magnificent city halls. They had their own legal system which spread around the urban networks from certain nodes, such as Magdeburg law eastwards to Kyiv, among others, and Lübeck law northwards into Baltic towns. A key element of European urban form was a central public space: the Greek *agora*, the Roman *forum*, the Italian piazza, the Romance *place/ plaza*, the German *Platz*, the Russian *ploshchad*.

Architectural Greek and Roman antiquity defined classicism in European building. It was a form of language which, in spite of its ups and downs in the cycles of taste, never left European – and overseas- migrated – architecture until the mid-twentieth-century victory of the modernist movement. It could even blend with modernism, as in some of the best architecture of Italian fascism – for instance, EUR, the exhibition complex built in Rome for the World Exhibition that never was. Indeed, modern nationalism, first of all French Revolutionary and Napoleonic symbolism, drew more heavily on the classical heritage than the *ancien régime* preceding it, in pageantry, painting, nomenclature – the Temple of Reason, the Field of Mars, the Pantheon and, in monumental architecture, the Vendôme Column and the Triumphal Arch. The new United States was very much part of the early-nineteenth-century so-called Greek Revival, as the public buildings of Washington, D.C., testify. Pre-modern European architecture developed a whole repertoire of styles, which in the nineteenth century were often blended into something known as Historicism or Eclecticism. Classicism apart, the most important element of the repertoire was the medieval Gothic, from the French 'era of the cathedrals'. It made a powerful comeback in the nationalist age.

Before the Nations

The paradigmatic European nation-state grew out of an existing pre- national state, and its capital evolved out of a long pre-national history.

***

[*] The classical study of the distinctive, autonomous European city is Max Weber's long section on it in his *Economy and Society*.

Although our proper story begins with nation-states and national capitals, because of the strong pre-national legacy in most of Europe, some prologue history might be helpful.

The Church, the land, the city and the king sum up the prehistory of nation-states and of national capitals. The Church was the decisive conduit of the classical heritage in the Dark Ages. The Classical Pantheon, built under Agrippa just before the Christian era and reconstructed by Hadrian around 130 CE, was consecrated as a church dedicated to the Virgin Mary and All the Martyrs in 609. When the popes started to rebuild Rome after their return from Avignon (in the late fourteenth century), one of their contributions was to add a Christian statue and/or an inscription of themselves to the imperial columns. Two famous examples are the columns of Trajan and of Marcus Aurelius Antonius (at what is now Piazza Colonna), then provided with statues of Saints Peter and Paul, respectively, on top, and an inscription commemorating the contribution by Pope Sixtus V.

The Church was the monumental builder of the Middle Ages and also later, from Renaissance and Baroque Rome to seventeenth-century London after the Great Fire. The Cathedral of Notre Dame, Westminster Abbey and the later Saint Paul's Cathedral, the Cathedral of Saint Stephen and the Basilica of Saint Peter were the unrivalled pre-modern constructions of Paris, London, Vienna and Rome. So was the Matthias Corvinus Church in Budapest. El Escorial outside Madrid was both a monastery and the most awe-inspiring of the royal palaces. Only the Kremlin of the Muscovy Tsars and the city hall of the rich merchants and manufacturers of provincial Brussels indicated overwhelming secular power or wealth.* Berlin was not a medieval city of significance and became architecturally ambitious only in the second half of the eighteenth city. In other words, Berlin had no important pre-modern centre of monumentality, but there was the castle of the Hohenzollern, electors of Brandenburg-Prussia.†

The Church organized the rituals of the collectivity, from Mass to royal coronations and funerals, and church buildings provided the

---

* The enormous Kremlin contained churches inside it.
† In Sweden, Uppsala, about 80 kilometres north of Stockholm, was the ecclesiastical capital, with the coronation cathedral, so the royal castle dominated the political centre.

most important space for homage and remembrance of worldly figures: royal, aristocratic and occasionally even poetical tombs, statues and busts.* London's Westminster Abbey, since Tudor times, and Saint Paul's Cathedral seem to have harboured a larger number and, more certainly, a wider range of commemorative monuments than most major churches of Europe.† On the whole, tombs had a very important place in dynastic monumentality, most famously, perhaps, in the abbeys of Saint-Denis and of Westminster and the Viennese *Kapuzinergruft* of the Habsburgs.

Occasionally – and in papal Rome frequently – the townscape was also adorned with saintly statues and votive monuments, such as the early-eighteenth-century Plague Columns in Vienna and in Buda (now part of Budapest), or the Charles Church in Vienna, also built in gratitude for relief from the plague.‡ In the seventeenth century, Christopher Wren built not only a new Saint Paul's Cathedral but fifty other churches in the City of London.[1]

Papal Rome, from its height to the end of its full splendour, contributed two further features to urban monumentality, the Cathedral of Saint Peter apart. One was the straight axial road with its long urban vista, the Via Pia, from the Quirinale to Porta Pia, constructed from 1561 to 1562, long antedating the wider Nevsky Prospekt, the Champs-Élysées and all the others.[2] The second was the grandiose piazza in front of Saint Peter's, capable of receiving in a grand manner the hundreds of thousands of pilgrims coming to Rome. It got its final shape with Bernini's colonnades from the years around 1660, becoming arguably the most elegant monumental public space in the world.

---

* The Poets' Corner of Westminster Abbey was de facto named and institutionalized in the eighteenth century, although Geoffrey Chaucer, for instance, had a grave monument there in 1556 (Nikolaus Pevsner, *London I: The City of London*, Pevsner Architectural Guides, New Haven, CT: Yale University Press, 1957, 383ff).

† This is my tentative conclusion from comparing my own superficial impressions with the thorough survey by Nikolaus Pevsner (ibid., 122ff, 360ff).

‡ The London Monument in memory of the Great Fire of 1666 was similar in character, though officially secular. In 1681 it got a hateful anti-Catholic inscription, accusing 'Popish frenzy' of having caused the fire. The inscription was removed in 1831 (Weinreb and Hibbert [eds], *London Encyclopedia*, 541).

The Rise of Territorial Capitals

Before any central urban monumentality could emerge, there had to be a capital city. The European Middle Ages started out as a massive reruralization of social and political life. The idea of a capital city passed away.[3] Even the greatest of early medieval rulers, Charlemagne, did not need one, although Aachen (Aix-la-Chapelle) was his preferred residence in the latter part of his reign. Paris became *caput regni* only in the first half of the fourteenth century.[4] And that was not irreversible. In the last decades of the long and powerful reign of Louis XIV, Paris became a huge suburb of Versailles. In his last twenty-two years, Louis visited Paris only four times. Until the revolution, the relationship of Paris to Versailles was never quite clear.[5]

London assumed permanent capital functions by the twelfth century. Before that, Winchester was the modest political capital of England, where the regalia and the royal treasure were kept and where the survey results for the Domesday Book were returned.[6] However, the capital functions centred around Westminster, that is, around the royal palace and the Abbey, which was the coronation church. The City of London was still for some time rather a twin city to Westminster, some kilometres down the river to the east.

Vienna became the permanent capital of the Habsburgs in the course of the seventeenth century – Prague was the major alternative – and definitely only when the Ottomans began to be rolled back, after their failed siege of Vienna in 1683.[7] Russia grew out of Muscovy, but Peter I moved the capital from Moscow to Saint Petersburg after his decisive victory in the Northern War at Poltava in 1709. After the October Revolution, Moscow became again the main capital: 'main' because in Tsarist Russia, the USSR and post-Communist Russia, the two cities both have both a special standing as *stolitsy*, capital cities (originally meaning 'throne cities').

Berlin had housed the main residence of the Brandenburg Hohenzollerns since the 1440s, but that meant more a feudal manor than a national centre. In the eighteenth century, when Brandenburg-Prussia was becoming a great power, Potsdam was alongside Berlin the official 'residence city', the one much preferred by Frederick II (the Great). To the Hohenzollerns, Potsdam was a possible capital even of the German Reich; Bismarck had to push the new German emperor into accepting Berlin.[8]

The Spanish royal court moved to Madrid in 1560 and the city soon became very dominated by the court and its needs, but the former kept an ambulatory life for another good half-century, with El Escorial as the grandest and most important alternative in the surrounding region. Even when a permanent royal palace was built in the 1630s, the Buen Retiro Palace, it was actually (just) outside the city. This led to the symbolic and highly ceremonial entry into Madrid of a new king or queen through one of the city gates, the Puerta de Alcalá.[9]

Ofen, or Buda, had gathered most of the capital functions in Hungary after the abortive revolution in 1848, at the onset of which the Hungarian Diet met in Pozsony, currently Bratislava. It became Budapest only in 1873, uniting the three cities of traditionally German Buda (Ofen), the rapidly growing economic centre Pest across the Danube and ancient and aging Obuda, a bit to the north, where the Roman Aquincum had once been. Brussels, finally, had been the site of the Dukes of Brabant and of Habsburg plenipotentiaries, but became a state capital only in 1830.

Pre-Nation Cities

It has already been hinted at that there was no straight road from the rise of capital cities to national capitals. The city was in a sense also part of the prehistory of the nation. The City Belt, from the Italian peninsula up through the Swiss Alpine passes into the Rhineland and to the North Sea, was the European *pièce de résistance* to the formation of territorial states.[10] The cities on the southern shores of the Baltic succumbed earlier, but as long as they could, the Hanseatic cities fought the rise of sovereign territories. In the period of transition from the Middle Ages and the New Age, cities, rather than territorial states, were often the main sites of power and wealth: Florence, Venice, Genoa, Lübeck, Augsburg, Nuremberg, Antwerp and Amsterdam are, perhaps, the most famous examples.

Among European capitals today, London is unique in being both an ancient, indeed Roman, trading hub and the old medieval capital of a dynastic territorial state. No wonder that it took some time for its two parts, the City (of London) and Westminster, to coalesce.

The wealthy and powerful trading cities coming out of Europe's Dark Ages had their own pre-national monumentality. Their grand town halls and guild halls, the most splendid of which were built by Flemish cloth-makers, their magnificent town gates and sometimes a prominent weigh-house and/or exchange represented a specific urbanity: autonomous, proud, capitalist and rich. The main buildings of the city and its commerce were generally laid out at or around the main square – typically called in Germanic Europe the 'big market' (*grosse/grote markt*), which often but not always also had the main church.

Amsterdam was special in the Calvinist austerity which wrapped its enormous wealth, but its huge mid-seventeenth-century city hall in the main square (the Dam) highlights well its pre-national monumentality. Amsterdam was then the capital of the United Provinces and of its major part, the province of Holland. The city is still officially the capital of the Netherlands, although the Hague is the site of the monarchy and the government. But it is the *city* hall – now formally a royal palace – that is Amsterdam's most monumental piece of architecture.

Brussels, another part of the City Belt, still testifies eloquently to a rich pre-national urban iconography. In spite of the national trimmings after 1830, to which we shall return below, the symbolic centre of Brussels is still its *grande place/grote markt*, dominated by its mid-fifteenth century Gothic town hall and surrounded by various guild halls, mostly in Flemish baroque save for one in reconstructed Gothic, all with nicknames out of the city argot. The topological city centre, Place de Brouckère, is named after a mayor.

The Peace of Utrecht in 1713, ratifying the eclipse of the United Provinces by Great Britain, signalled the beginning of the end for the city republics. The French Revolution, the Napoleonic Wars and the Congress of Vienna did the rest. The United Provinces were reconstituted as the Realm of the Netherlands under the Orange dynasty, and Venice was handed over to the Habsburgs as part of a package. Only the now rather marginal Swiss city cantons kept most of their autonomy, for another thirty-five to sixty years, and Lübeck still lingered on in a shadowy existence until the unification of Germany.

Royal Absolutism

The European power configuration preceding the national state was usually the dynastic territorial state, governed with royal absolutism. This general rule had one major exception, though, apart from the decaying city-states, which were ruled by closed commercial oligarchies. There was the ascending, post-absolutist Kingdom of Great Britain, governed in the name of the king by a land-owning aristocracy while dominating world trade and starting an Industrial Revolution. Nevertheless, the major style was that of absolutism, set since the time of Louis XIV at Versailles, from which it radiated to the Habsburg Schönbrunn and to the peripheries of absolutist Europe.

The centrepiece of royal architecture and monumentality in general was the royal palace – in eastern Europe initially built as a fortified castle – or palaces plural, then regularly at least a winter and a summer palace. Versailles (and, in imitation, Karlsruhe) was laid out as a radial city, beaming out from the royal palace. A huge, well-sculptured park became an important feature of a truly royal seat in the course of the seventeenth century, a *sine qua non* for palaces outside city centres. In addition, there might be some other palaces of royal power and largesse, of organization for war, a mint perhaps, or a veterans' hospital or nursing home, like the Hôtel des Invalides in Paris or the Royal Hospital for Seamen at Greenwich. The European absolutist monarch was not a god on earth nor some other power floating above the earth. He or she stood at the apex of an aristocratic pyramid.[11] Aristocratic palaces, then, also contributed significantly to the royal townscape, as in Saint Petersburg.

There was a royal ritual rhythm that played an important part in the life of dynastic capitals, of royal births, birthdays, marriages, coronations and funerals, with public ceremonies and popular festivities as well as court protocol and temporary monuments of arches and tribunes at coronations and royal marriages. There could also be military parades, and some cities, such as Berlin, Potsdam and Saint Petersburg, had very centrally located parade grounds.

Extra-palatial monumentality was less thought about and developed, but it did exist. The equestrian statue was an ancient Roman monument, although perhaps secondary. Charlemagne was enthralled when he saw one of Theoderic in Ravenna and brought it to Aachen, but it seems to have passed into medieval obscurity. The custom was revived with the Italian Renaissance and developed by French seventeenth-century absolutism. In Paris, Henry IV got a statue by the Pont Neuf in 1614; Louis XIV got a number in France and several in Paris.[12] In London, Charles II was put up in King's (now Soho) Square and outside Chelsea Hospital. Before his deposition, James II was elevated in Whitehall.[13] In Vienna, the oldest equestrian statue – or at least the oldest still standing – dates only from late eighteenth century. It portrays Emperor Franz Stephan (1708–65) and was founded in 1781 and first put up in 1797; it is now to be found in the Burggarten, né Kaisergarten.[14]

There was also the royal square, with a name referring to some royalty or royal exploit and, usually, with a statue. The Paris of Henry IV provided the model, the Place Dauphine (Crown Prince Square) on the Île de la Cité, beside the statue of the king, and Place Royale (now the Place des Vosges), successfully built to become the centre of elegant life in town, with a statue of Louis XIII. In spite of his personal move to Versailles, Louis XIV did invest in the royal grandeur of Paris as well. The more ephemeral Place des Victoires, with an extremely triumphalist statue of Louis XIV, was a private initiative by a rich admirer, whereas the almost simultaneous Place Louis le Grand (today's Place Vendôme, after the old palace of the Duke of Vendôme), was somewhat more restrained in the symbolism of its equestrian statue of the Sun King. The Throne Square got its name from the city entry of Louis XIV and the temporary throne then installed there. What is now known as the Place de la Concorde started out in the last third of the eighteenth century as Place Louis XV, with a royal statue.[15]

Saint Petersburg was the absolutist city par excellence, a magnificent manifestation of pre-national monarchical and of royally derived *court aristocratic* wealth and will, built by imported Italian architects, to Russian taste. War, religion, monarchy and aristocracy set their first imprints upon the city. The Palace Square was shaped by the Tsar's Winter Palace and the General Staff opposite it. Nearby, somewhat back, was the hulk of the Senate and Synod, the heads of the civilian and the ecclesiastical administration. The grandiose long boulevard Nevsky Prospekt ran from the Admiralty to the Nevsky monastery.

Moscow became less imperial and less aristocratic and, with late-nineteenth/early-twentieth-century textile industrialization, embourgeoised.

But it retained a central role of pre-modern Russia. Tsars were crowned in the Kremlin Dormition Cathedral and after the Napoleonic invasion of 1812, the city became a proto-national symbol due to its sacrificial burning, forcing the Grande Armée to its disastrous retreat.

The Nation versus the Prince(s)

The European nation-states built their capitals upon these pre-national traditions of Greco-Roman antiquity, medieval churches, town and guild halls and monarchical and aristocratic palaces, all still visible historical layers of the modern national cities. No new capital was built, except for Reykjavik in Iceland, which harboured no pre-modern city at all. Athens had to be rebuilt as a city, and some other Balkan capitals were tiny and rustic. The European tradition did include a separate city government, but by the end of royal state power, most capital cities had lost most of their civic autonomy. Modern London had no unified city government at all, and both London and Paris got fully elected city governments only in the 1970s.

The nation entered Europe's capital cities in two big and two smaller waves. One centred on the French Revolution, its vicissitudes and its (largely Napoleonic) repercussions, spanning the continent from the British Isles – where important changes had started earlier – to Russia, from Norway to Spain and the Balkans. The carapace of medieval traditions, urban oligarchies and royal power cracked, either wide open with a bang or stealthily ajar. The second wave rolled in from the mid-nineteenth century, including but not peaking in the European Spring of 1848 until Albanian independence just before World War I, bringing national Belgrade, Brussels, Bucharest, Budapest, Copenhagen, Rome, Sofia, Tirana and national-cum-imperial Berlin. Here the people-prince conflict was embedded in a range of large-scale processes of social change and transformation of rural-urban relations population growth, railway connections and industrialization, in a complex geopolitical power game among the big powers of the continent.

After that, there was a third brief wave in 1919 and 1920 along the East-Central strip between Russia and Germany, upon the final break-up of all the remaining pre-national regimes in Europe,

Romanov Russia, Hohenzollern Germany and Habsburg Austria-Hungary. The Ottoman Balkans had been nationalized just before the Great War. Finally, a fourth wave surged in the 1990s, with the end of the multinational Communist states of the USSR and Yugoslavia, a wave which also included a ripple in the United Kingdom, with Scottish and Welsh devolution and corresponding new national Scottish and Welsh institutions and buildings. National issues have been revived in the 2010s, with the Scottish referendum and the Eastern Ukrainian semi-secession in 2014, the continuous restiveness of Flanders and the rise of Catalan sovereignty claims. What will come of this is unclear.

The first three waves all centred on conflicts between peoples, constituting themselves as nations, and monarchical power – in the Netherlands and Switzerland against hereditary *Regenten* or *regimentsfähigen Familien*. The fourth was a rejection of multi-national nation-states.

This is not the place to theorize or explain the rise of nation-states. The task here is to locate them in time and to grasp their impact on the capital city. However, we do need some clear criteria. First of all, we are not dealing with questions of nationalism and national identity here, but with the constitution of state power.

A state is a nation-state when its sovereignty and power are claimed to derive from a nation (or people). Although claims to being a nation are often, particularly in Europe, derived from an interpretation of the past, the power of a sovereign nation is open to the future, unbound by descent and custom. The sovereign power of the nation is modern. Because of its radiation of power into the whole society of its rule, the establishment of a nation-state may be seen as a country's tipping point into modernity.[16] Its polar opposites are states which belong to a prince by 'divine right' or the 'mandate of heaven', by legitimate succession or by conquest. These two poles do not exhaust the historical roster of human polities, but their opposition largely defines the field in which nation-states had to establish themselves. In Europe, though, there did develop very early a conception of a territorial realm, belonging to one prince or another but separable as a geographical concept from its ruling family. In Asia, this was often not the case; the Ottoman (Osmanli) and Mughal Empires were dynastic names, and so was Choson (today's Korea). China, Zhongguo, did have a territorial meaning, while also, for instance in Korea, being referred to as a dynasty.[17]

When does a state become a nation-state? The continuities of European state history complicate the task, often necessitating indicating a timespan of variable length. A very important aspect of this continuity was the unique European process whereby princely rule could gradually evolve into a purely symbolic monarchy. Even the French case is not without possible options. Clearly, the revolution from 1789 onwards made France into a nation-state, but the crucial date, or even year, has been debated. For instance, in 1880 when the National Assembly was to decide the Day of the Nation, it had at least eleven alternatives in front of it.[18] The alternatives considered included the one most proper in my eyes, 20 June 1789, when the Third Estate of the Estates-General turned itself into a Constituent National Assembly. The date finally chosen, 14 July 1789 (the storming of the Bastille), was arguably a wise compromise, a moderate way of commemorating the revolutionary people of Paris.

In Parisian iconography, an embryonic national streak was visible already under the monarchical hegemony of the *ancien régime*. When major streets started to get official names in the seventeenth century, some were given to non-royal statesmen, like Richelieu, Colbert and Mazarin; later they were given to the provost of the merchants and to city aldermen and, finally, in the 1780s, to famous writers such as Racine and Molière.[19]

One of the first urbanistic conquests of the revolutionary nation was ending the duality between Paris and the royal court city of Versailles. The Estates had been convoked to Versailles, and it was there that the French nation constituted itself as such. It was in buildings around the royal castle of Versailles that the Third Estate turned itself into the National Assembly, in the Hall of Minor Pleasures (Salle des Menus-Plaisirs), and swore the Oath of the Tennis Court (Jeu de Paume) not to part before providing the nation with a constitution. This spatial duality ended abruptly in October 1789, when a very angry procession of Parisian market women and an only slightly less angry march of Parisian National Guards forced the king and the court to return to Paris, to the Tuileries. The National Assembly followed, and installed itself in the Riding House (Salle du Manège) of the same royal palace.

The revolution unleashed a huge iconoclasm, not quite unprecedented,* similar to that of later Communist revolutions and anti-Communist counter-revolutions. As the revolution did end the *ancien régime* – after a short counter-revolutionary Restoration of 1815 to 1830 – the pre-revolutionary toponymy and monumentality did not return, unlike in parts of post-Communist Europe, but nor did the revolutionary thrust endure. Place Louis XV became Place de la Révolution, the site of the guillotine and the execution of Louis XVI. In 1795 the Directory gave it its present name, Concorde, briefly interrupted by the Restoration. The Place du Trône became the Place du Trône Renversé (the Square of the Toppled Throne) and then finally settled down as the Place de la Nation. The Place Royale lost the statue of Louis XIII and, after a brief stint dedicated to the 'Fédérés' (the army and the National Guard) became the sedate Place des Vosges in honour of the first province to contribute to the military campaign of 1799. The Restoration, of course, restored its monarchist original, but then lost out. Place Louis le Grand became definitively Place Vendôme, and Louis XIV was replaced by the Column of Austerlitz, modelled after Trajan's column of ancient Rome. The victorious commander of the battle (Napoleon) was taken down from the top during the Restoration, but was restored there afterwards. The Bastille prison was demolished. Instead came the Place de la Bastille, with its July Column topped by the Spirit of Liberty, erected in the 1830s, commemorating the martyrs of the July Revolution.

Already the national Orléans monarchy coming out of the 1830 revolution tried to bask in Napoleonic glory, completing the Arc de Triomphe with its recording of tri-continental imperial French victories. The battle-fields of Napoleonic victories are all over the streets of central Paris: Aboukir, Austerlitz, Eylau, Friedland, Iéna, Pyramides, Ulm, Wagram and so on, commemorated by three republics as well as by the Second Empire. The early victories of the Second Empire and the two world wars then added to the extraordinary war-path character of the streets of central Paris.

During the mid-nineteenth-century Second Empire and the power and design of the imperial Prefect of the Seine, Georges-Eugène

---

* The Roman process known as *damnatio memoriae* involved the destruction of portraits and statues of (dead or toppled) 'bad emperors' and their obliteration from historical records (see Eric Varner, *From Caligula to Constantine: Tyranny and Transformation in Roman Portraiture*, Atlanta: Michael C. Carlos Museum, 2000).

Haussmann, Paris got a largely new spatial layout of long, wide boulevards lined with homogenous architecture and long horizontal lines of
wrought-iron balconies, all testifying to a wealthy authoritarian power
unrestrained by any parliament or by individualist property rights. This
Paris became what Walter Benjamin called the 'capital of the nineteenth
century', and David Harvey the 'capital of modernity' and a transconti-
nental model was seen particularly in Latin America.[20]

However, the main enduring capital-city effect of the revolutionary
French route to political modernity and a nation-state is this: national
Paris has never had the time and/or money to construct monumental
buildings of national institutions, although from the very beginning of
the Revolutions there were grandiose plans.[21] The Palais de l'Élysée, the
Presidential Palace, is an ordinary aristocratic town palace in a side
street of the Rive Droite, once belonging to Madame de Pompadour, the
most notorious of royal mistresses. The National Assembly has a nice
location by the river, but is no more than a former palace of a minor
Bourbon royalty. During the Paris Commune of 1871 it had to move to
Versailles, and in 1875 it decided on this principal site of the *ancien
régime* as its permanent location (a permanence reversed after four
years). France did not have an official prime minister (then called
Président du Conseil) until 1946, but this position existed de facto from
1934, lodged in Palais Matignon, another former aristocratic townhouse, on the Rive Gauche. The last royal palace, the Tuileries, was burnt
down during the Paris Commune.[22]

Instead of institutional landmark buildings, Paris has a set of *places
de ruptures*, heavily invested with meaning to this day. The eastern
Places de la Bastille, de la République and de la Nation all refer to domestic French history, and they all have a left-of-centre connotation and a
similar function of gathering or demonstrating arrival.

Correspondingly, the French right have their places of assembly and
destination to the west, mainly commemorating external wars, from the
Jeanne d'Arc statue and Place de la Concorde along the Champs-Élysées
to the Arc de Triomphe, or, at the Rive Gauche, les Invalides. To this day,
French politics is much better at mass demonstrations and short strikes
than at building institutions and organizations.

When did Britain become a nation-state, a multinational one of (at
least) the English, the Scots and the Welsh, and London a national capital? These are questions rarely raised in British historiography, in

contrast to questions of national identity and nationalism.[23] *Terminus ab quo* is the 'Revolution' of 1688, which, whatever its unintended modern consequences, was basically a revolution in the pre-modern sense, literally a 'rolling back'* to the Tudor times of 'free-born Englishmen' and Protestant monarchs. No section of a nation-state, and no party wanting to create a nation-state, can possibly invite a foreign prince to conquer the country and rule the state, like the seven 'gentlemen and aristocrats'† who invited the Dutch *stadhouder* Prince William of Orange on 7 June 1688, did. The official motivation of 'the Great Restorer', as John Locke aptly called William, 'to appear in Arms' was 'Preserving of the Protestant Religion, and for restoring the laws and liberties of the ancient kingdom of England, Scotland, and Ireland'.[24] Through his marriage to the daughter of King James II, William also had a claim to the succession. The year 1688 was part of a two-centuries-long armed and religiously impassioned dynastic rivalry and inter-state princely power game over the British crown – also involving the French and the Spanish monarchs – that went on until 1746, when the army of a new Hanoverian Protestant dynasty finally defeated that of the Catholic Stuarts.

Terminus ad quem would be the 1830s. Iconographically, 1830 was a crucial year, when the new central square in London was in the end not called King William Square as expected. With the king's consent, it became instead Trafalgar Square,[25] on which the National Gallery was soon built and Nelson's Column erected. Parliamentary reform – now meaning looking forward and not back to some pure past – in 1832 made at least the House of Commons less a medieval privilege and more of a modern representation of the nation. Its new monumental landmark building, the Westminster Parliament, was decided upon in the late 1830s and began to open in 1847 (starting with the House of Lords).

The eighteenth century saw a gradual nationalization in Britain, of state power as well as of public monumentality. Wars were no longer financed by grants and loans to the king but by a 'national debt', a

---

* It was only in the course of the French Revolution that the word *revolution* acquired its modern meaning, of 'a way to open a new future', and lost the meaning of its prefix *re* – meaning 'back'.

† In an acclaimed and interesting book, the Yale historian Steve Pincus, without bothering much with the concepts of 'modern' and 'revolution', calls 1688 the 'first modern revolution' (*1688: The First Modern Revolution*, New Haven, CT: Yale University Press, 2009).

neologism of the 1730s, guaranteed by Parliament. In 1760 the king traded his property and income from it for a parliamentary Civil List grant.* By the time of the Hanoverian invitation to the throne in 1714, the power of Parliament to install a proper Protestant succession to the throne was established.[26] The power of the former grew steadily and that of the monarch faded gradually into ritual respect; 1834 was the last time a British monarch could appoint a prime minister against the opposition of the House of Commons.[27]

Somewhat bewilderingly, British patriotic celebrations during the Napoleonic Wars 'subsumed national achievements in glorification of the monarch'.[28] Characteristically, the new elegant main street of London's West End was named Regent Street, though it ended in Waterloo Place, where the prince regent then resided. (Below, we shall encounter some similar national monarchism in Japan.) Enthusiastic and very profitable Scottish investment in the empire furthered national Britishness.

Around Chaucer's tomb monument, there developed in the eighteenth century a Poets' Corner of national memorials in Westminster Abbey, including Shakespeare, Milton and others. In the 1790s, the main church of the City of London, Saint Paul's Cathedral, put up statues of four national benefactors: the lexicographer Samuel Johnson, the Orientalist William Jones, the painter Joshua Reynolds and the prison reformer John Howard. Linda Colley ends her great work *Britons* with a conclusion around a prominent 1822 Royal Academy painting, *Chelsea Pensioners Reading the Gazette of the Battle of Waterloo*, displaying diverse representatives of a victorious British nation.

Final British victory in the Napoleonic Wars shaped the new national iconography of London, generating Waterloo Place, Waterloo Bridge, Trafalgar Square, the Wellington Arch and Nelson's Column. The latter, including its reliefs of Nelson's four major victories and his guard of lions, took three decades to complete (in 1867), even though the column and the statue upon it were visible from November 1843. The government was reluctant to put any money into celebrating the nation's hero.† No domestic event or hero has ever been

---

* Leo Hollis, *The Stones of London*, London: Orion, 2011, 200. In 1857, Parliament separated the courtiers of the List from a Parliament-governed 'civil service' (Norman Davies, *The Isles: A History*, Oxford: Oxford University Press, 2000, 632).

† See Rodney Mace, *Trafalgar Square: Emblem of Empire*, London: Lawrence and Wishart, 1976, chapter 4, and Hood, *Trafalgar Square*, 46ff. The Column was originally

commemorated with such grandeur. No national building of worship was added to, not to mention ever replaced Westminster Abbey and Saint Paul's Cathedral, but the latter expanded its function as a national pantheon with an extraordinarily pompous tomb monument to the Duke of Wellington.

London grew as an imperial city, the world's largest by 1800. Apart from national-imperial iconography – including its majestic new Parliament – nation-state London was little nationalized. The old duality of the commercial and financial City of London, with its own Lord Mayor and guild institutions, and, on the other side, the royal and aristocratic Westminster and West End continued, although the two were increasingly connected by new land transport rather than by river boats. Before the nineteenth century, the City (with a capital C), had been a kind of sober, Protestant, liberal area of mercantile residence as well as offices, a sort of 'Amsterdam' in contrast to the more luxurious and exorbitant 'Venice' of the aristocratic West End. In the nineteenth century it was largely emptied at night, while opening in the morning, filled up with offices of world trade and finance.[29]

National London was in the grip of parliamentary power, which did pay attention to the functionality of the capital, establishing (in 1855) the Metropolitan Board of Works, which, overdue, produced the most extensive sewer system in the world and a metropolitan police force, while the City of London maintained its own. It also funded extensions and embellishments of a rather second-rate aristocratic palace (Buckingham), which in the eighteenth century became the townhouse of the Hanoverian kings, without ever allowing a royal presence in London on par with that in Paris of the Louvre or Tuileries, in Vienna of the Hofburg, in Berlin of the Stadtschloss, or of smaller capitals like Stockholm and Oslo. Street layout remained largely traditional, on the whole without parade axes similar to those of Paris, Vienna and Berlin. London was a city of imperial wealth and power, but not of royal or national splendour.

an initiative of a private, but of course high-level, Nelson Memorial Committee, which turned out to be incapable of financing its completion. The Treasury then agreed to step in, but first with cost-saving demands. The ruling elite of Dublin, 'second city of the Empire', was much more alert and efficient, putting up Nelson in its main street already in 1809. In 1966, on the eve of the fiftieth anniversary of the Irish Easter Rising against the British, the Irish Republican Army dynamited the column.

In some sense the London equivalent of the royal and national-imperial landmark planning of Paris – and the alternative to the *grands boulevards* – are the West End squares, laid out in the seventeenth and eighteenth centuries by wealthy aristocrats who were also big urban property owners, with homogenous architecture for aristocratic or gentlemanly townhouses, usually with an enclosed garden in the middle. The squares usually carry the names of their creator-owners, Grosvenor (the family name of the wealthiest of them all, the Dukes of Westminster), Bedford, Russell, Sloane and so on, still bearing witness to the unique British blend of landed aristocracy and urban capitalism. The similar Parisian Place Royale was a royal precedent, discontinued.

Even if they did not finish the *anciens régimes*, the French Revolution and Napoleon's armies rattled or challenged their *iconostases*, from London to Saint Petersburg, from Madrid to Berlin. In the fissures, new national imagery began to emerge. The Napoleonic invasions spawned ferocious nationalisms, from the guerrillas of Spain to the 'Patriot' (or 'Fatherland') War in Russia, via the Prussian Wars of Liberation. On the literary front, what the latter-day German historian Hagen Schulze has called *Hass-und Totschlagspoesie* (poetry of hatred and killing) was unleashed. Saint Petersburg got its first national monuments after the war: statues of the two major Russian commanders Barclay de Tolly and Kutuzov were erected outside the Kazan Cathedral, and Russian folklore motifs were added to the triumphal Narva Gate. The only major capital of Europe where nothing national was allowed – for the time being – was Vienna, the base of the oldest and proudest of the royal dynasties.[30]

By the 1830s, the nation-state situation in Europe may be summed up as follows. The two leading states, Britain and France, had become consolidated nation-states by steady evolution and by the failure of the counter-revolutionary Restoration, respectively. The oligarchic confederation of the Low Countries had become a national monarchy and so had, by an 1830 revolution, Belgium. End of the list of nation-states.

Sweden, in its rustic and modest way, had an evolution rather similar to that of the British, an eighteenth-century post-absolutist, quasi-parliamentary, Estates-governed Age of Liberty, and in the early nineteenth century the Estates deposed a king and asserted their right to make a new constitution before electing a new king. But the Swedish polity was still of four historical estates, not one nation, and coupled to Norway by a personal monarchical union. Denmark was still under absolutist rule, with a king who was also ruling German dukedoms, and as such a prince of the German Confederation. In Spain and Portugal the national banner had been planted, but the battles with royal absolutism had not yet been finally won. Switzerland was an oligarchic confederation of local urban and rural provincial polities, coming together as a nation-state only in 1847. The whole of central and eastern Europe was under princely domination, including the curious case of Greece: a state carved out of the Ottoman Empire by foreign powers on religious, ethnic and geopolitical grounds and put under the absolutist rule of a German prince.

The nationalization of Europe took more than a century. Only by 1920 were pre-modern patrimonial states gone from the sub-continent. The final blow was the defeat and ousting of the Habsburg, Hohenzollern, Ottoman and Romanov dynasties. Out of this protracted, complex, by no means linear history, we shall here only pick up a few themes bearing upon the capital cities.

The European national capitals were previous centres of their part of Old Europe, with – except for the Balkans – strong cultural and archi-tectural legacies of Greco-Roman classicism and of the Baroque, the Renaissance and the medieval Gothic. The exceptions were relatively marginal. Before the nineteenth century, Iceland did not have a single city, but the few ecclesiastic and administrative central functions there were had gathered in the area where Reykjavik emerged from the begin-ning of the twentieth century. The Hague, before the nation, and Berne, for the nation, were chosen by deliberation: the Hague because of its insignificance as a neutral meeting place of the Estates-General of the United Provinces,* Berne as the most central of the major cantonal cities, ethnically – straddling the border between French and German speak-ers – as well as geographically.

As its full Dutch name – 's-Gravenhage (the Count's Wood) – indi-cates, the Hague has an aristocratic origin as the seat of the medieval counts of Holland and during the federal republic also of the *stadhouder* (commander-in-chief), when there was one. The Estates gathered in its

---

* In the national monarchy of the Netherlands, the main city, Amsterdam, is defined as the capital city of the realm, but the usual defining criteria for a capital – the site of the head of state, the government and the legislature – apply only to the Hague. The cities-dominated republic of the United Provinces never recognized the Hague as a city.

Ridderzaal (Knights' Hall), where Parliament now assembles. Berne had been a small oligarchic city republic before becoming, in 1831, the capital of the strong canton of Berne and, in 1848, the permanent seat of the Federal Assembly of the Swiss nation-state. A modest assembly house was built in the 1850s in a square dominated by a casino.* In the 1890s the latter was replaced by a new parliament building, gradually accompanied around the quiet Bundesplatz by the National Bank, the Kantonalbank and the Crédit Suisse.

Balkan Ruptures

The ancient cities of Athens and Sofia (originally Roman Serdica) had shrunk radically and were no longer even regionally dominant, but were soon chosen by the new states: Athens for historical reasons – although the new Bavarian authorities originally planned to demolish the Parthenon and install a new royal palace there[†] – and Sofia in a complex geopolitical game with several somewhat larger Bulgarian cities.[31] To Greek nationalists, Athens was for many decades a provisional capital, a kind of Bonn to the prosperous diaspora while Constantinople was still Ottoman.

Athens and Sofia also exemplify the limitations of the sovereignty of the new Balkan states. Greece and Bulgaria both owed their statehood to foreign armies and navies: the former to an alliance of Britain, France and Russia, the latter to Russia. Greece not only got an absolutist Bavarian king – as neutral between the three big powers – but also a Bavarian administration, and Athens got German architects.[32] All this generated two revolutions in Athens, in 1843 and in 1862, leading to a national constitution and a new dynasty. The square in front of the Bavarian Royal Palace became Syntagma (Constitution) Square. From 1909 until its demise, the monarchy had to keep up with a more laid-back mansion, first intended for the crown prince of the new dynasty; the palace was, after lengthy renovation, taken over by Parliament in

---

* Like in Europe, casinos were not houses of gambling but housed (mainly) restaurants and entertainment.

† Eleni Bastéa, *The Creation of Modern Athens*, Cambridge: Cambridge University Press, 2000, p.89ff. The great German architect Schinkel had drawn up a plan for it, but it was soon abandoned, mainly, it seems, due to objections within the Bavarian royal family.

1934. As far as I know, this is only the second example in the world of a single building representing the change from royal absolutism to parliamentarism.*

Sofia too got a German king, Alexander von Battenberg – of the family later known in Britain as Mountbatten – and a heavy input of Viennese architecture. It is one of the two European capitals whose main street is named after a foreign prince – the other is Oslo, still paying homage to the ex-Napoleonic marshal who was elected king of Sweden and who, under the name of Karl Johan, conquered Norway in 1814. Sofia dedicates its principal avenue to the Tsar Osvoboditel (the Tsar Liberator), meaning Alexander II of Russia, who conquered Bulgaria for the Bulgarians. The Tsar himself stands in a semi-circle in front of the national parliament at one end of the avenue. He is still there, and also remained during Communist times. The first monument erected in ex-Ottoman Sofia was to a national independence hero, though, Vasil Levski.[33]

In the Balkans, the national was first of all anti-Ottoman and anti-Muslim. The national was largely centred around Orthodox churches, for which grand new cathedrals were built – in Belgrade, in Habsburgian Baroque, already in the 1830s after Ottoman recognition of Serbian autonomy;† in Athens, Bucharest and Sofia in neo-Byzantine splendour. Another priority building was a royal palace, at a time when royalty was still more anti-Ottoman than national. More genuinely national was the Bucharest Academy, where Romanian was first taught and which soon turned into a university.‡ Serbian Belgrade built its

---

* It should also a ring a bell of caution against facile socio-political interpretations from architecture, given the frequent rule of strongmen and dictators, rather than of parliament, in Greece from 1934 to 1974. The Copenhagen example is more appropriate, although also contingent. When a constitutional monarchy succeeded an absolutist, in 1849, the two chambers of the Diet moved in with the king into Christiansborg Palace, but in 1884 the palace was severely damaged by fire. The king moved to a smaller but exquisite late-eighteenth-century palace, somewhat off centre, in Amalienborg, while the Diet was lodged in former military barracks. In 1918 the Diet moved back to Christiansborg, whereas the royal family stayed at its new palace.

† The sovereign Kingdom of Serbia, like Bulgarian and Romanian independence, resulted from the inter-imperial Berlin Conference of 1878.

‡ The collective work *Capital Cities in the Aftermath of Empires*, edited by Emily Gunzberger Makkas and Tanja Damiljanovic Conley, London: Routledge, 2010, is a good introducory overview of the early history of national capitals in the Balkans and in East-Central Europe.

parliament on the former site of the main mosque,[34] and in Sofia the main mosque was turned first into a Russian military hospital, then a national library and finally a national museum.[35] The Muslim population fled en masse after the defeat of the Ottoman troops. Another thrust was de-Orientalization and Europeanization, for which architects and city planners were invited from Germany, Austria and sometimes France (especially to Bucharest) and other parts of Western Europe, from Italy in the case of Tirana.

For these reasons, the Balkan national capitals do not share the urbanistic continuity of the rest of Europe. Indeed, their rupture with the previous layout of space and architecture is unique in modern times, without any equivalent among the capitals of the ex-colonial zone, among the capital changes of those of reactive modernization, nor among any of the later Communist capitals (except for American-bombed-out Pyongyang). The avidly imported European ideas of public space – wide streets and open places, grid planning and exterior-oriented (instead of inward-turned) residential and public buildings – clashed totally with the Ottoman tradition. Even the architecture of the buildings of Ottoman power was seen as unattractive. Only as a temporary stopgap could the Bulgarian king think of living in the *konak* of the Ottoman governor, and Romanian Bucharest had no use for the fortified *caravanserais* which had been the landmarks among the vineyards and gardens of the semi-rural city.

Though facilitated by the massive flight of the 'Turks', the whole cities were, of course, not transformed over a decade or two. But certain central areas were, in a dramatic way. In Athens three new avenues were laid out in the centre, with the 'academic trilogy' of impressive neoclassical buildings along one of them: University Street, for the university, the Academy and the National Library, designed by the Danish architect Hans Christian Hansen and his brother Theophil. Bucharest gave priority to building and widening a set of boulevards, which after the 1877 war (which won Romania total independence) were all named after events or heroes of the war, fronted by Calea Victoriei with a triumphal arch.[36] I have already mentioned Sofia's Tsar Liberator Avenue. Poor Belgrade changed more slowly, but the street joining it with the road to Istanbul became the main boulevard. Zagreb and Ljubljana were never under Ottoman rule and could therefore follow the European mainstream of continuist change. Tirana became the permanent capital of

Albania only in 1925, fifteen years after a proclamation of independence during the first Balkan War, as a small town of 10,000. It was not purged of mosques and Muslims like the other Balkan capitals of the time, but came under strong influence from Italy and Fascism in the 1930s.

Ethnic Change in the East-Central Strip

The ethnic national character of the East-Central European capitals had luckily been decided before the nation-state came onto the top of the agenda. By and large it was decided by immigration from the country-side, driven by rural proletarianization, urban industrialization and rail transport. In the nineteenth and early twentieth centuries, ethnic city government and impact was a hot issue in almost all the future national capitals of East-Central Europe. Only three or four among twenty future capitals had by the mid-nineteenth century an ethnic majority from their coming nation: Warsaw, Ljubljana, Zagreb and perhaps tiny Tirana. Helsinki was mainly Swedish-speaking, Tallinn (known as Reval) and Riga were German-dominated, Vilnius was Jewish (and Polish), Minsk was Jewish and Yiddish-speaking, Prague was primarily German and Bratislava was called Pozsony and was until the 1840s the coronation city of the Hungarian crown and the most frequent seat of the Magyar Estates. Budapest consisted of Buda, Obuda and Pest, all three predominantly German in the early nineteenth century. Belgrade was Muslim; Bucharest was Greek-dominated; Skopje more Muslim than Macedonian; and Sofia a multi-ethnic, largely Muslim city. In Sarajevo the Muslims, today's 'Bosniaks', remained a (large) minority until sometime between 1948 and 1991, while in 1926 Ukrainians were less than half of Kyiv's population and Romanians less than half of Chişinău's.[37]

Inter-ethnic friction and conflicts festered in East-Central Europe throughout the twentieth century and even after, but the character of the nation-state capitals was never in doubt, except for Vilnius, which was not the capital of the inter-war Lithuanian Republic because it was ruled by Poland and got a Lithuanian ethnic majority only late in Soviet times.

The bitter inter-ethnic conflicts which accompanied Eastern European nationalism have been best chronicled with respect to Prague, which does not necessarily mean that they were sharper there than elsewhere. But with that qualification, the fate of Mozart in Prague in 1913 is a good illustration of rival symbolic nationalism. The Prague Society for the Promotion of German Sciences, Arts and Literature wanted to put up a statue of Mozart in front of the (German) Estates Theatre, where *Don Giovanni* was first performed in 1787. However, this required the use of a small piece of municipal land outside the theatre. The city council, Czech-dominated since 1861, rejected the petition, officially for traffic reasons.[38]

However, the modern history of East-Central Europe should not be reduced to national conflicts. It too was part of the European route of *continuisme* and class. The new Balkan states of Bulgaria, Greece and Romania, with their powerful German kings, exemplified an eventful but nevertheless gradual transition from princely absolutism to the nation-state, although not to democratic monarchies. The modern history of East-Central Europe is much more dramatic than that of north-western Europe, with the gradual national evolution of its capitals inter-foliated by moments of revolution.

For all its national/ethnic complexity and conflicts, the Strip also experienced the typical European modern primacy of class. Its major intra-state violent conflicts were structured not by ethnicity or religion but class. The Finnish Civil War of 1918 pitted Red industrial workers and crofters against the White yeomanry and professional-managerial strata. The Baltic post–World War I wars had a triangular shape, pitting Balto-German landowners (with German troops); Estonian-Latvian farmers (with a tiny professional stratum), helped by British military; and Estonian-Latvian-Lithuanian workers and worker-soldiers against each other. The Budapest Commune of 1919 rallied urban workers (and a large part of the Jewish intelligentsia) against the upper and middle classes. The Greek post-post–World War II civil war had perhaps a more ideological character, dividing the popular classes, but its poles were the Communist-led popular resistance against the Nazi occupation, on one side, and on the other the collaborationist turned Anglophile upper and middle classes.

The Pre-National Central Powers

During World War I, Austria-Hungary and Germany were, in neutral speech, often referred to as the Central Powers for their location in the middle of Europe. The Habsburg monarchy never became a nation-state, but from its stiff neo-absolutism, after 1860 it gradually came to accommodate national elements. With Russian help and under some able military commanders it finally survived and crushed the revolution of 1848. What started its decline and increasingly accommodationist stance was the loss of its Italian lands in 1859 to French and Piedmontese armies, and the decisive blow came in 1866 with its defeat to Prussia at Königgrätz (also known as Sadowa).

In Vienna, what became the grandiose Ringstrasse around the Baroque inner city out of the open military grounds around the city wall, the glacis, was announced by the Emperor in 1857: 'It is My will that . . .'[39] The original plan was for new military barracks as well as cultural institutions and a dynastic votive church.[40] The plan included a city hall – elective municipal government was being adopted in Austria – but no parliament.*

With the defeat at Königgrätz, Habsburg absolutism was doomed and the Ringstrasse changed its character in a bourgeois national direction. The liberal city of Vienna built itself a majestic Gothic city hall, which was interpreted as referring to the proud and autonomous Flemish cities, once part of Habsburg lands. Nearby, Theophil Hansen designed a new version of his Athens Academy as an impressive Reichsrath (Council of the Realm, in fact Parliament), but without any national symbolism. Already, in the early 1860s, a society for the promotion of the arts had petitioned for a monumental programme in honour of non-royals, but mostly of aristocrats connected to the city; it was effectuated in 1867. The liberal city leadership then expanded the programme, primarily with respect to great artists.[41]

1867 was also the year of the Austro-Hungarian Compromise and the establishment of Austria-Hungary under a double monarch: emperor of Austria and king of Hungary. Financed by rich land rents and soaring wheat exports, the ruling Hungarian aristocrats embarked on a very ambitious national course, peaking in the millennium celebration in 1896 of the Magyar conquest of Hungary, including a World Exhibition and the world's second underground line (after London's). The emperor

---

* This appears from a contemporary leaflet of the 1859 plan reproduced in facsimile in Schorske, *Fin-de-siècle Vienna*, 32–3. It is not mentioned in Schorske's otherwise very illuminating chapter devoted to the Ringstrasse.

and his Vienna government had to acquiesce. In 1882 a statue of the poet and 1848 revolutionary initiator Sándor Petőfi was erected in Budapest. In 1894 the remains of the exiled national revolutionary leader Lajos Kossuth were brought back to the city and given a grand official burial. In 1904 the world's largest parliamentary building, the Országház (House of the Nation), was opened on the Pest side of the Danube, a duel in stone with the Habsburg Castle on the Buda Hills across the river. In location and in layout it refers to the Palace of Westminster, but it is built in a hotchpotch of historical styles, crowned by a gilded dome.

Prague was part of the Austrian half of the double monarchy and since the 1860s under Czech city government, with the support of which the Czech community built its own national institutions, from the neo-Renaissance National Museum towering over central Wenceslas Square to the Art Nouveau Obecní Dům (Municipal House), an entertainment centre meant to overshadow the German casino. The last national challenge the Catholic emperor had to swallow before the war was the city's decision to put up a huge monument in Old Town Square to the heretic Czech preacher Jan Hus for the quincentenary of his burning at the stake in 1415.

Berlin is another capital where, beneath a dramatic history, there is a strong streak of continuity between the pre-modern and the modern, between the pre-national and the national. The latter does not constitute a fateful German *Sonderweg* (special path) in contrast to an enlightened 'Western' mainstream. It is a variant of the pathway of London, for example. In contrast to Habsburg Vienna, Hohenzollern Berlin did take on a few national features out of the Napoleonic Wars, which unleashed a Prussian/German nationalism similar only to the Spanish. Post-Napoleonic Berlin got a national monument, an off-stage temple-like structure on a hill topped by an iron cross, the new rank-independent medal for military valour. When the quadriga on top of the Brandenburg Gate was brought back to Berlin (having been looted by Napoleon and taken to Paris), the peace goddess Eirene was replaced by Prussian Victoria with an iron cross on her spear. Non-dynastic military commanders Bülow and Scharnhorst flanked the exquisite Neue Wache (New Guardhouse) in the city centre. Urban hubs were renamed after Prussian victories against Napoleon: Leipziger Platz (after the battle in 1813) and Pariser Platz (after the city it conquered and occupied in 1814).[42]

Nevertheless, Prussia remained a dynastic state. Nor did German unification in 1871 create an unambiguous nation-state. In fact, its act of creation was almost provocatively dynastic and non-national. The German Reich was proclaimed in the Hall of Mirrors at Versailles (after the crushing defeat of the Second French Empire) by assembled German princes. No elected representatives of the nation or of Berlin were invited.

The Wilhelmine capital of the Reich rapidly developed into the national centre of Germany, with fast population growth and economic as well as cultural concentration. Although it never reached the national dominance of London or Paris, it was the main node of Germany's railway system, its main industrial city, its culturally leading city. But the realm was a federated monarchy with a substantial set of princes, from kings to dukes, under the emperor. Symbolically, the dynastic maintained the upper hand in Berlin. The main city centre (east of the big Tiergarten park) was dominated by the Imperial Palace, outside of which there was a monumental ensemble with an equestrian statue of the first emperor, appropriately carrying the double name of Emperor Wilhelm–National Monument. Off centre stage in the east was the monumental Reichstag, whose dedication the Emperor had finally agreed to after about a decade of wrangling: 'To the German People'. The square in front of it was still Königsplatz (Kings' Square, referring to the kings of Prussia). The imperial family pushed the construction of sixty-six Protestant churches in Berlin, including a new neo-Baroque cathedral in the front of the Imperial Palace and the Kaiser Wilhelm Memorial Church. In the Tiergarten the Emperor had in 1902 'donated' to the city a dynastic Victory Avenue (Siegesallee), with twelve Hohenzollern rulers arranged like medieval pilgrimage stations.*

---

* This pompous dynastic monument survived the November 1918 revolution, thanks to the Social Democrats, the Weimar Republic, and the Third Reich. It was damaged during World War II, and after the war the French occupants were particularly adamant in demanding its destruction. In 1947 the occupying Allies decided not to dynamite it but to remove it, which was effectuated in 1950 (Uta Lehnert, *Der Kaiser und die Siegesallee: Reclame royale*, Berlin: Reimer, 1998, 321ff.

Scandinavia

The exact dating of the Swedish nation-state may be argued over. It may be seen as a protracted, almost bicentennial process. The starting point was the end of absolutism with the death in battle of Charles XII (in 1718), issuing into a quasi-parliamentary, but Estates-based, 'Age of Liberty'. Royal *auto-golpes* in 1772 and in 1789 put an end to the former, without quite restoring absolutism. After the catastrophic war of 1808 and 1809, when Finland was conquered by Russia, the army deposed the king, and the Estates ensured that a new constitution was adopted before a new prince was elected. But the Estates remained the base of the polity until 1866, and the country was part of a personal monarchical union with Norway until 1905. Royal power was gradually waning in the course of the nineteenth century, but a new national polity freed from the entrapments of the medieval Estates and of a deferential royal administration was slow in developing.

By 1905 and the Norwegian union crisis, at least it was there, and government by national politicians rather than by court-connected civil servants began. In the 1890s, provoked by Norwegian nationalism, the Swedish flag had become a popular symbol, not just a royal and official ensign. The national character of Stockholm developed with this calendar. The city got its first significant national institution in 1866, a National Museum (of art), housing the former royal art collection.[*] In 1905, the Diet at last got its own building, in heavy North German granite, close to and clearly subservient in size to the royal castle. In 1923, Stockholm had its new city hall, this time clearly challenging the royal castle across the water, as an alternative icon of urban glory – it is currently the site of the Nobel Prize banquets.

Denmark was another old monarchy, absolutist until 1848. Constitutional Denmark did not immediately become a nation-state, though. The king of Denmark was also duke of Schleswig, Holstein and Lauenburg, with their distinctive political arrangements, including, in the case of the two latter, membership in the German Confederation. Only after the disastrous war against Prussia in 1864 did Denmark become a nation-state, shed of the king's German possessions.

---

[*] Already after the death of Gustavus III in 1792 the new Regency government asserted that the art collection was not the personal propoerty of the king but was property of the realm. It was to be gathered in a Royal Museum, provisionally located in the royal castle.

Copenhagen was the one royal residence city which celebrated its new status as a national capital, after a belated end to royal absolutism, by recentring itself around a new city hall which overshadowed everything else in the city. It was inspired by the city of hall of medieval Italian Siena and Verona: in front of it a vast City Hall Square was laid out, becoming the new public centre of the city. The burghers of Copenhagen had been a potent force even under (and in support of) royal absolutism, and its representatives played a central role in ending it in 1848. Ironically, the new centring of the city was brought about by a city council exclusively composed of the royalist right, in the wake of the 1864 discredit of the National Liberals.

Norway became a nation-state in 1905, peacefully seceding from the union with the Swedish monarchy. For two decades its capital kept its Danish name, Kristiania (after a Danish king), and its main street is still named after the country's first Swedish king, Karl Johan.* Finland seceded from Soviet Russia in December 1917. Its national self-determination was recognized by Lenin's government, but the country plunged into an internal class war, won by the bourgeois Whites, with significant but hardly decisive support of German troops. The fifth Nordic nation-state, Iceland, under British protection, left Denmark, then occupied by Nazi Germany, in 1944.

Latin Europe: Nation-States and Organized Religion

All the main religions of the world are ancient. Their clash with modernity is therefore not very surprising. Astonishing, however, is the rarity of their confrontation with nationalism and the nation-state. Important conflicts between nation-state and organized religion are basically confined to Latin Europe. In the internal struggles of emergent modern national Europe, the high clergy, of all the Christian denominations, tended to side with the forces of conservatism and anti-modernity, laying the ground for the unique twentieth-century secularization of Europe. But nations in their emergence were culturally ambiguous, and the European clergy also sometimes played a significant part in national

---

* In spite of this unusual toponymical magnanimity, conventional Swedish opinion holds Norwegians to be almost comically nationalist.

movements, above all in multi-religious states where the ruling prince adhered to a different religion – be it Islam in the Ottoman Balkans, Orthodoxy in Tsarist Poland and the Baltics, Catholicism in Habsburg Bohemia or Protestantism in British Ireland. Above, I have paid attention to the de-Islamization of the Balkans, and it may be added that after World War I the new Polish state blew up the Orthodox Alexander Nevsky Cathedral in central Warsaw.

Its (then) militant conservatism apart, the Catholic Church had two major liabilities in the eyes of the builders of new nation-states. First, it was a supra-state power and hierarchy demanding obedience to a supra-state leader, the pope. Second, it was extremely wealthy, the largest feudal landowner and owner of built real estate. Along with theological disputes, opposition to this had gone a long way in accounting for the Reformation in countries from Sweden to England, thereby laying the basis for resourceful Renaissance monarchies enriched by expropriated Church wealth. The French Revolution came ideologically out of the Enlightenment, with its strong rationalist and deist currents. The rupture of the revolution with the Church started with the former's demand that the French clergy pledge allegiance to the national constitution, which the pope refused to allow.

The historical conflict of nation-state and Church are visible today in two landmark buildings in Paris, the Pantheon and the Sacré-Cœur basilica. The Pantheon, 'To Great Men: A Grateful Fatherland', was originally built at the end of the dynastic regime as a votive church to Saint Geneviève and was turned into a national mausoleum in 1791. Voltaire, Mirabeau and Rousseau were the first entrants. The building was reconsecrated by Napoleon I, who ended the revolution's war with the Church, then became a national necropolis again under the July Monarchy; reconsecrated by Napoleon's nephew Napoleon III; and finally de-sacralized by the Third Republic on the occasion of the state burial of Victor Hugo. The blazing white Sacré-Cœur on the top of Montmartre was built by the Church (originally with state approval) as a penitence for and sign of revival from the moral decline of France since the revolution, punished by its defeat against the Prussians and expressed in the sins of the Paris Commune, a radical insurrection in 1871, starting on Montmartre.

The clash between nation-state and Catholic Church was most frontal in Italy, part of which was directly ruled by the pope, including the city of Rome. The French army had saved papal rule from the 1849 revolution and from the unification of Italy in 1860. But in the face of defeat by the Prussians, the French troops withdrew in 1870, and Italian ones entered Rome after a short bombardment of the Pious Gate. The nation-state took over the palaces of the papal court and administration as well as a large number of the many convents and monasteries. The pope's main palace, the Quirinale, became the Royal Palace and, after World War II, the presidential one. The national Senate and the Chamber of Deputies were (and are still) lodged in Renaissance palaces used by the papal government. New national offices were built along a new street, Via XX Settembre (20 September), the date of the armed Italian entry into papal Rome.

The pope retreated to the Vatican by the Basilica of Saint Peter, the smaller part of a now deeply divided city. 'To their [the national] congresses and society, [we put forward] other societies and congresses', declared the pope.[43] Guelph (pro-papal) forces remained important in Rome, but the anti-clericals had the backing of the national government. In 1889, the latter scored a major symbolic triumph: a monument to Giordano Bruno was unveiled in Campo de' Fiori, where in 1600 the Inquisition had burnt him as a heretic.[44]

The fact that the national parliaments of Portugal and Spain are housed in former convents and monasteries has a historical context of its own. Both monarchical states were devastated by French invasions and British interventions in the Napoleonic period, leaving the legacy of a half-century (Spain) to a full century (Portugal) of dynastic rivalries, civil wars between royal absolutists and liberal constitutionalists, military coups and counter-coups. In the mid-1830s the liberals and anti-clericals were in power in both countries. For fiscal as well as for political reasons, the national governments abolished the religious orders, freed their vast lands to the market and expropriated a large number of convents and monasteries in Lisbon and Madrid. Through all the political vicissitudes, these measures stuck. They had the most impact on Lisbon, where the dissolved religious orders provided housing not only for the Senate and Chamber of Deputies but also for army offices, law courts, the prefecture, the national conservatory, the national library, the academy of sciences and the site of the main railway station, the Santa Apolónia.[45]

City Politics and City Space

National capitals were much more national than municipal, but some kind of municipal self-government was part of the post-absolutist programme of the nineteenth century, and even papal Rome, since the mid-century, had a partly elected municipal government.[46] As the capital of national revolutions from 1789 to 1871, the city of Paris had an eminent role, and in the beginning of revolutions its Hôtel de Ville (City Hall) was an important meeting and brokering place. But the city never became a major institutional player. Brussels belonged to the pre-national City Belt of Europe, running from Italy to the Low Countries, where territorial state centralization never coalesced.[47] In its Grande Place, the Gothic city hall towers over the building of the Habsburg imperial representative at the opposite side of the square. Belgian Brussels maintained what was probably the most powerful capital-city mayoralty of nineteenth-century Europe.* The two most significant mayors, Jules Anspach and Charles Buls, have their names inscribed in the boulevards of the city's north-south axis. The Rathaus of Vienna is one of the most impressive city halls of the era, built by a wealthy bourgeois elite. Vienna also got Europe's first rabble-rousing or 'populist' mayor, for two years vetoed by the emperor: the Christian-Social Party's Karl Lueger, still remembered in part of the Ringstrasse as Karl-Lueger-Ring.†

The spatial layout of the old European capitals changed substantially. In some cities, Vienna and Copenhagen in the late 1850s particularly, restructuring was a compound of national politics and changes of situated military technology and considerations, making city walls and the glacis, the open field of shooting range in front of them, obsolete. In Paris a similar de-fortification took place at the same time, but further out from the centre, bringing suburban villages like Belleville, Bercy, Montmartre and La Villette into the city and little directly affecting the layout of the latter.[48] In Paris, the process of turning 'bulwarks' into

---

* Cf. Thomas Hall, *Planung europäischer Hauptstädte*, Stockholm: Almquist & Wiksell, 1986, 212ff. Anspach in particular shaped the layout of central Brussels. The later Buls had to contend with the king.

† Lueger was also a notorious anti-Semite and apparently a figure of inspiration to Hitler.

'boulevards' had started already in the late seventeenth century.[49] However, in the 1840s, a new defence ring around Paris was built, which stayed until 1919 and was only in the 1960s turned into the Périphérique ring road. In London, the walls had been torn down by the mid-eighteenth century. In Berlin, dismantling started at about that time too, but an 'excise wall' began to be built for fiscal reasons.[50] The wall around Rome was not regarded as a barrier to the expansion of the national capital, although it had prevented the emergence of a suburban periphery around the papal city.[51]

The rise of national politics of variable kinds transformed the urban space more consistently with its demands for representational spaces, the need to control unruly crowds and the need for open arteries for the circulation of commodities and people. The homo- or heterogeneity of the resulting built environment depended on the planning powers and the control of the land rent. In Europe, there have been, in modern history at least, four pertinent planning regimes. The strictest one was that of Haussmannian Paris, manifested in its boulevards of buildings of the same height and style, with long horizontal rows of wrought-iron balconies. Another one is the Berlin *Bauordnung* prescribing rules of height, proportions of building size and street width, but not style. The London one is a third example, of insular planning by individual (mainly aristocratic) investors of clusters of homogenous buildings around a square and for the rest a free-for-all, with some restrictions of height (until recently). Fourth, there is the thoroughly liberal Athenian pattern, largely followed in Ringstrasse Vienna, mainly depending on big individual investors, their taste and their choice of architect. National governments dominated the planning of most national capitals, with some exceptions: Brussels, Copenhagen, Rome, Stockholm. The active interest of the Berlin and Vienna national governments was limited.[52]

Ensanche (widening) was the keyword of the changes of central urban space.* Haussmann used the dramatic verb *éventrer* (literally meaning 'opening up the stomach').[53] Improving the circulation of people, commodities and air was a major drive. The result was a new pattern of long, wide, tree-lined avenues, with ample sidewalks and

---

* A Spanish word used in the 1860 plan for Madrid (Santos Juliá, *Madrid: historia de una capital*, Madrid: Fundación Caja de Madrid, 1995, chapter 3) and since then also used to designate urban parts built according to a widening plan.

showy buildings, and of large squares or roundabouts, usually displaying some national monument. These were not yet the motorized escape
routes of twentieth-century American cities, for a while attractive also
to European planners. The Balkans apart, the changes were most
dramatic in Paris and in Brussels. The Vienna Ringstrasse was a landmark ring, but it left the inner city, imperial and ecclesiastical, intact.
The widening of Madrid took a long time, due to political instability,
but Lisbon and Budapest were soon recentred along Avenida da
Liberdade and Andrássy út, respectively. Central Berlin was transformed in Prussian rather than German times by the master architect
Karl Friedrich Schinkel around the Schlossplatz, with the Schlossbrücke
connecting to the Unter den Linden, the Lustgarten and its museum.
The Brandenburger Tor was then at the western end of the city. West of
Tiergarten was another city, Charlottenburg, incorporated into Great
Berlin in 1920. Already, under Bismarck, construction had started of
the later main axis of West Berlin, Kurfürstendamm. Central London
got its major facelift in the immediate post-Napoleonic era, with Regent
Street and Trafalgar Square.

The nation-states required new, and more, public buildings, particularly in the Balkans, where few of the Ottoman edifices were deemed
acceptable: parliaments, ministries, law courts, a roster of buildings for
national cultural institutions, museums, theatre, opera, concert hall,
library, university and, for communications, post, telegraph and telephone offices – the latter most splendidly housed in Madrid's Palacio de
Comunicaciones, recently recycled into seat of the city government –
railway stations, with Paris's Gare du Nord and London's Saint Pancras
arguably the most remarkable.

Surprisingly few new parliament buildings were constructed in the
nineteenth and early twentieth centuries, reflecting the deep historical
roots of European modernity – London, Budapest and, on a small-state
scale, Berne were the only capitals with landmark parliaments. In the
Balkans, Berlin, Brussels, Kristiania/Oslo, Stockholm and Vienna they
remained subordinated, or at least secondary, to the palaces of the
monarchs. In the Hague, Lisbon, Madrid, Paris and Rome, existing
buildings were recycled for parliamentary use, and in Athens and
Copenhagen the new parliamentarians first moved in as lodgers into the
king's palace. After constructing the first round of buildings for its new
national kingdom, with the royal palace larger than the parliament

opposite it, Brussels then built a huge Palace of Justice as a national monument.

Urban services – power, water, transport and so on – expanded greatly but unevenly. Particularly great efforts were made on sewage systems, which were heavily challenged by rapid population growth, as dramatized by the Great Stink of the Thames in 1858. Between 1860 and 1878, Paris built almost 400 kilometres of underground sewage networks, on top of 228 pre-existing ones.[54] The Parisian achievement is dwarfed, though, by that of Joseph Bazalgette, the chief engineer of the London Metropolitan Board of Works, who built a total of 1,300 miles of sewers.[55]

The European national capitals were – with few exceptions, Rome being the largest – centres of their nations' capitalism and of its increasingly prosperous bourgeoisie. This meant whole new residential areas, whole new *beaux quartiers* in western and north-western Paris or London, along new *grands boulevards* like Kurfürstendamm in Berlin or Andrássy út in Budapest, of luxurious apartment buildings with separate servants' entrances, or townhouses in London or Amsterdam. The rise of European nation-states was intimately 'correlated with' – bracketing tricky questions of causality – the rise of large-scale industrial and banking capitalism. This meant new kinds of imposing private buildings – besides factories, which were sometimes also built for impression as well as for function, a stock exchange (Budapest built the largest), banking, industrial headquarters and department stores. Industrial capitalism also raised a new issue of urban policy: workers' housing.

Capitalist economic development moved the de facto urban boundaries and transformed the totality of the urban space, if much less so the historical centres. Real estate speculation became a major economic activity in the nineteenth century. The City of London came to display its character as the hub of world finance and its Docklands gained the buzz of the world's greatest port. Berlin got its *Bankenviertel*, in Behrenstrasse near Unter den Linden. The Stock Exchange, or Bourse, became the central buildings of Paris and Brussels. Huge working-class areas were sprouting in the peripheries, often slum-like in character, lacking most amenities and consisting of mainly self-built shacks, much like those of the Third World in the twentieth century.

The architecture of the national capitals remained, by and large, within the inherited European-style repertoire, with varying accents and combinations. Neoclassicism and neo-Gothic dominated the most central public buildings, but there was historicism of the nineteenth century itself, as well as neo-Renaissance and neo-Baroque. Under nationalist auspices, the old styles were given national interpretations, as we have already noticed.

However, European bourgeois nationalism did bring forth or promote some new styles. The most significant was, ironically, an antidote to the emerging standardized, industrial machine age, with curvaceous lines, floral decorations and bright colours. It was rather a family of kindred styles under several different names in different parts of Europe: Art Nouveau in Belgium and France (where it is also known as modern style) *modernisme* in Catalonia, Secession in the Habsburg area, *Jugendstil* (Youth Style) in Germany and Scandinavia and Arts and Crafts, Free Style or Art Nouveau in Britain.

Around the turn of the nineteenth and twentieth centuries, this style became distinctively popular among nouveau-riche national bourgeois on the European periphery, most boldly in Barcelona and well represented in Brussels, Prague and Riga, and more limitedly in Glasgow. Mostly it was used for private residences, but it could also be employed for fashionable stores and occasionally for public buildings, such as the Maison du Peuple in Brussels and the Municipal House in Prague. In Finland there developed a National Romanticism in heavy, crude grey granite, mainly for public cultural buildings such as churches and museums. The swelling Hungarian nationalism was sometimes expressed in a Magyar Orientalism.*

The European national capitals, spearheaded by Paris of the early Third Republic, succumbed to a 'statue mania'. Between 1870 and 1914 Paris erected 150 statues, not counting other kinds of commemorative monuments.[56] This was a tradition from ancient Rome, largely forgotten during the medieval era and revived during the Renaissance as a monarchical self-celebration. Now it was devoted to the leaders, heroes and stars of the nation: politicians, generals, scientists and artists working in all genres.

---

* However, the aristocratic elite governing Hungary rejected Budapest's foremost Secessionist architect, Ödön Lechner and in 1902 banned him from further public commissions. (Robert Nemes, 'Budapest', in *Capital Cities in the Aftermath of Empires*, 147.)

The imperialist nations of Europe flaunted their empires as national exploits. The national museums displayed colonial loot and conquests, most famously the British Museum's marble statues from the Athenian Parthenon. Many capitals had official colonial museums, among them Amsterdam, Brussels and Paris. The World Exhibitions had special colonial pavilions, and in 1931 Paris staged a large-scale 'International Colonial Exhibition'.[57] Trafalgar Square included two generals commanding British conquests in India (Charles Napier and Henry Havelock). Madrid installed a Plaza de Colón with a statue of Columbus in 1893 along the new south-north axis, Paseo de la Castellana. Murals in the Copenhagen City Hall boast of Danish colonies, from the West Indies to Greenland. In the twentieth century, between the two world wars, the authoritarian government of Portugal commemorated its maritime fifteenth- and sixteenth-century 'discoveries' and conquests in a major ensemble by the Tagus (Tejo) River; Mussolini's Rome celebrated the fascist conquest of Ethiopia and laid out a grand Via dell'Impero. Street names remind us of colonial exploits: in Berlin's Dahlem, of the German participation in crushing the Chinese Boxer Uprising, for instance. Colonial street naming, mainly geographical but also including some colonial governors and commanders, was particularly widespread, it seems, in the Netherlands. It started in the Hague, a favourite homeland retreat of Dutch colonialists in the 1870s, and later culminated in Amsterdam, which contains sixty-three colonial streets.[58]

3

National Foundations: Settler Secessions

Only settlers from Europe built nation-states and national capitals over-seas, and their notions of statecraft and urbanism were naturally imported from their motherlands and/or other parts of Europe.* However, the socio-cultural and political parameters of their state and city building were fundamentally different, and so were the outcomes behind the surface similarities. The major conflict line in the Americas was not national versus princely sovereignty, but between local settler sovereignty against overseas imperial rule. In the thirteen colonies of British America, opposition against the latter focused on taxation; in Hispanic America, on trade monopolies and high-office discrimination. In British as well as Hispanic America, settler rebellions started as pro-monarchical,† and Brazil entered the world stage of nation-states as a monarchy.

Settler secession was not like the artistic rebellion against the Vienna *Kunstverein,* which started the artistic and architectural rebellion known in Austria-Hungary as Secession. It was not the launch of a new culture, although it did contain rejections of Old Europe's aristocratic manners.

---

* While global in intention, this is not a study with encyclopaedic ambitions. Many minor states are not dealt with here, including Israel, also a settler state, in a time zone of its own and with a specific history.

† The Thirteen American Colonies saw their conflict as one with the British Parliament and claimed that the king had legitimate prerogatives to override it, in favour of the settlers (Eric Nelson, *The Royalist Revolution: Monarchy and the American Founding,* Cambridge, MA: Belknap, 2015). Southern Americans rebelled upon finding out that the legitimate Spanish king had been deposed by Napoleon.

It was more like the divorce of a middle-aged couple who had spent quite some time together but who had grown apart, with offspring cared for by the American part.

Metaphors aside, secession meant a different conception of the nation than the European one: no longer based on language, religion, culture, history, but on a territorial *club* of conquerors and settlers. The nation was a club of members, open to anyone entering the territory with the proper ethnic credentials. Like any club, the club-nation engaged in recruiting new members, advertising and subsidizing European immigrants, preferably from Northern Europe. This was a practice of underdeveloped, pre-national dynastic states, for example Frederick of Prussia inviting French Huguenots or Catherine of Russia inviting Germans, and was discontinued by the European nation-states.

In Europe, a central question of domestic politics was how many rights should be granted to the different classes, or orders, of the nation. In the settler nations, the rights of the people were less controversial. Instead, the key issue was: who are the people? Slaves were universally held as non-people, often ex-slaves and their descendants too. Natives and Mestizos were non-eligible for the club nations of the British secession, with the exception of New Zealand and its Maoris, too many and too powerful to be kept out. In Iberian settlement nations, Natives and Mestizos were usually accepted as members of the people and of the nation, even if they were de facto most frequently marginalized.* The settlers on one side against Natives, slaves and slaves' descendants on the other is the constitutive fault line of all settler nations.

These nations faced two other specific issues, which also have borne the iconography of their capital cities. One has been their relationships to their extra-nation motherland, from which the settlers' racial pride as well as their language and their culture came, but from which they also seceded. Another derives from the recruitment drives and their production of a multi-ethnic settler club-nation.

Among the nation-states of seceding settlers there is a noteworthy internal division very much pertaining to the construction of their

---

* See Hilda Sábato (ed.), *Ciudanía política y formación de las naciones*, Mexico: Fondo de Cultura Económica, 1999; Marie-Danielle Demélias, *La Invención Política: Bolivia, Ecuador, Perú en el siglo XIX*, Lima: 2003. The nationalist liberator of Peru, San Martín, who came with an army from Argentina, officially abolished the category 'Indian' in favour of 'Peruvian'.

capitals, deriving from settlement history, between secessions from the British Empire and from the Iberian ones of Spain and Portugal.

Centring Former British Settlements

Settler secession from the British Empire always resulted in new capitals being built: Washington, Ottawa, Wellington, Pretoria, Canberra. The reason is the kind of imperial settlement, made possible by imperial power and protection but not exclusively established by imperial conquest. It was also a refuge for religious dissenters, a dump for convicts, or a meeting ground for adventurers from different empires. From very early on, the different settler colonies within the imperial territory mattered, and secession polities had to respect and balance them. This, it came to be viewed, could be achieved only by creating new capital centres.

Within this category, we have to distinguish three groups. First, there is pioneering Washington, capital of a state of ruptural secession by a war of independence, capital of a slavery state and with a very weak and vulnerable indigenous population. Second, there are the capitals of the three White Dominions, with a very gradual emancipation from the motherland, all without slavery and two with marginal Native populations: Ottawa, Wellington and Canberra. Third, there is the capital of the finally failed settler state, Pretoria, South Africa.

The thirteen American rebel colonies seceding from the British Empire were divided into two economic and cultural blocs, North and South, centred on the significance of slavery, which was the basis of the Southern plantation economy. At first the United States had an itinerant Congress; in 1783 it opted to have two capitals: one in southern Virginia, the other in northern Delaware. A statue of the victorious commander-in-chief General George Washington, was proposed that would be transported between the cities.[1]

The following year's Congress selected New York City as its permanent site, but Southerners, including George Washington, started to intrigue against it. Finally, in 1787, a deal about the handling of the national debt secured Northern support for a Southern solution. President Washington was authorized to select an area on the Potomac River (near his home) and commissioners to build a new 'Federal

District' to be opened by 1800. In September 1791 the commissioners decided that the district should be called Columbia – an oblique way of referring to the European background of the settlers, although Columbus never reached any part of what became the United States. The city itself was to be called Washington.* The President engaged a recent French immigrant, the painter and engineer Pierre-Charles l'Enfant, who had grown up at Versailles, to make a plan for the city.

L'Enfant made a grandiose Baroque plan: a grid with diagonal grand avenues 160 feet wide and roundabouts meant to include monumental landmarks. It had two central nodes, the President's House and Congress House, the latter soon being given precedence, up on a hill. The two were to be connected by a Grand Traverse Avenue while forming a great triangle, of which the Avenue was to make up the hypotenuse; the Capitol, the President's House and a Washington Monument would be the three corners, connected by parks as the two smaller sides of the triangle. The central diagonal avenue was named Pennsylvania Avenue, a kind of consolation prize to the main state of the North, which lost the location battle. The federal character of the capital is further emphasized in all the other original main avenues being named after states.

L'Enfant was explicitly planning a 'Capital of [a] vast Empire'. It took about a century for it to be realized, revived by a Senate Planning Commission of 1902. Congress was always stingy with city finances, and most of the capital's construction had to be financed by land sales.[2]

The Supreme Court had no place in the original plan; it did not emerge as a major power until the 1830s, and in spite of its significance ever since and its late, stately building, it has never been properly fitted into the city plan. A major building L'Enfant did plan, on the other hand, was never realized: halfway between President and Congress he had envisaged a non-denominational church and a kind of pantheon for the heroes of the nation.[3] Persistent American religiosity has spawned a large number of houses of worship in central Washington, but religious

---

* This seems not to have been a public political decision. I once asked the eminent early US historian Gordon Wood when and how the naming was decided. With frank honesty he replied that he did not know, but thought it had been implied in the federal district project from the beginning. According to the monumental history of the city by Joseph Passonneau (ibid., 18), the decision was taken by the president-appointed commissioners.

pluralism has not favoured religious monumentality. Only since 1990 has there been one such claim, the Episcopalian Washington National Cathedral, the building of which Congress authorized a century earlier.

When L'Enfant couldn't (or wouldn't) produce the engravings of advertising for the land auctions of city plots – the United States already being a country of capitalist commerce – Washington fired him. Thomas Jefferson, Washington's secretary of state and the third president, became the major architectural influence, which meant, *inter alia*, 'antiquity' for Congress and 'modern' for the President's House.

Jefferson did not at all share L'Enfant's and Washington's grand ambitions for the city, which he always referred to as the 'federal town'. Jefferson oversaw the Capitol building and the President's House, but for the rest he was very restrictive with respect to the capital. For principled moral reasons, Jefferson was basically anti-urban. In his view, big cities were 'pestilential to the morals, the health and the liberty of man',[4] and he did not want Washington to resemble the 'overgrown' cities of the North, like Philadelphia and New York.[5] The vast Federal District and its city remained, in fact, a rustic area of separate villages for more than half a century, until the Civil War, largely due to frugal policy but also because the big geo-economic plans of George Washington and other Virginia gentlemen dried up. The Potomac silted up and was out-competed by Northern connections to the west, and Baltimore outdid Washington as a port.[6] Charles Dickens, who visited Washington in 1842, found the Capitol a 'fine building' but was full of contempt for the rest: 'Spacious avenues, that begin in nothing, and lead nowhere; streets, mile-long, that only want houses, roads and inhabitants; public buildings that need but a public to be complete'. But he was wrong in his conclusion: 'Such as it is, it is likely to remain'.[7]

Jefferson's idea of a government town was actually part of a virtually unique US configuration of seats of political power. Most US state capitals are not the largest cities of their states, and many are not even big cities. For instance, the capital of New York State is Albany; of Michigan it is Lansing, not Detroit; of Illinois, Springfield, not Chicago. California's capital is Sacramento; Texas's is Austin; Florida's Tallahassee and Pennsylvania's Harrisburg. These are all political decisions, not effects of uneven socio-economic city development. Motives were mixed, but basically rooted in eighteenth- and nineteenth-century varieties of fear of and hostility to big private interests, power and/or unruliness.

Urban-rural conflicts have been a constant of US politics since then, refuelled by White suburbanization and the Blackening and Browning of metropolitan cities.[8]

The Southern location of the US capital brought one feature of settler city characteristics to the fore: racism. The great African American intellectual and community leader Frederick Douglass gave a lecture on 'our National Capital City' in the hopeful years of the mid-1870s, after the military defeat of the slave-holding South, in which he spelled out what the Southernness of Washington meant before the Civil War's outcome:

> Sandwiched between two of the oldest slave states, each of which was a nursery and a hot-bed of slavery . . . pervaded by manners, morals, politics, and religion peculiar to a slave-holding community, the inhabitants of the National Capital were from first to last, frantically and fanatically sectional. It was southern in all its sympathies and national only in name. Until the war, it neither tolerated freedom of speech nor of the press.[9]

Slaves made up a fifth of Washington's population in 1800, and the Capitol Building was partly constructed by slave labour.[10] By 1860, Blacks made up 18 per cent of the city, most of them freed.[11] Washington, until recently, was never a major port of immigration, and immigrant communities left less impact on the capital than on many other settler-state cities. There were a few, though: The German Schützenfest became the city's second festive event, after the Fourth of July, and the Societá Culturale Italiana donated a statue of Garibaldi to Congress.[12]

The Natives had been killed or expelled, and in 1853 the major figure of Native ethnic cleansing in the first century of the United States, the military hero and president Andrew Jackson, was honoured by the nation's first equestrian statue.* But the African American issue soon returned, after the Emancipation decade following the Civil War. From

---

* Kirk Savage, *Monument Wars: Washington, D.C., the National Mall, and the Transformation of the Memorial Landscape*, Berkeley: University of California Press, 2009, 78ff. The statue of George Washington, decided by Congress in 1783 'to be executed by the best Artist in Europe', was never made (Rubil Morales-Vázquez, 'Imagining Washington: Monuments and nation-building in the early capital', *Washington History* 12(1), 2000: 14).

about 1880 until the New Deal, the situation of African Americans steadily deteriorated, politically and legally. Washingtonians were somewhat less badly off than people of colour in other Southern cities: there were no lynchings in Washington, streetcars and public libraries stayed open to all races and in the entertainment district of U Street Northwest, where Duke Ellington once lived, there was an inter-racial 'contact zone'. But much racial apartheid descended upon the city, upon its neighbourhoods – although not as strictly as according to the South African Group Areas Act – its schools, its restaurants, its theatres and cinemas and its employment structure. President Woodrow Wilson – who would soon be selling slogans like 'national self-determination' and 'a world safe for democracy' – reintroduced the racial segregation of federal office facilities for the few African Americans still allowed there.[13]

To the White rulers of the state and the capital, Negro Washington was largely a 'secret city', having no part in the city's official layout and monumentality. It did develop a centre of its own though, outside the city centre, of course, in the Northwest quadrant around Howard University – put up in 1867 by the Freedmen's Bureau, the Howard Theatre and the jazz and entertainment district around U Street. In 1900 African Americans constituted a third of the population of Washington, a larger share than in any other big US city. Since 1957, until recently, they have made up the majority, which, together with legal desegregation of neighbourhoods and schools, started a massive White flight to the suburbs and about four decades of financial plight and drastic social deterioration of the remaining city.

Architecturally, Washington has maintained a sober, modern – in the Jeffersonian sense – style, keeping neoclassicism for important buildings with a public role, like the Supreme Court or the US Chamber of Commerce, abstaining from modernist iconography and keeping skyscrapers at bay through height-control laws.

Over time, an extensive iconographic programme has been deployed. Most imposing are the monuments to the two most famous presidents of the two established parties of the nation – so established that you publicly register your membership in one or the other – Abraham Lincoln of the Republicans and Thomas Jefferson of the Democrats. While more stylish, to Euro-American taste at least, the large quasi-religious monuments to these political leaders have hardly any contemporary near equivalent outside Pyongyang. A huge marble Lincoln has since

1922 been sitting in a Greek temple across the Reflecting Pool at the western end of the memorial Mall, while a bronze Jefferson of triple human height has stood since 1943 in a Roman pantheon across the Tidal Basin south of the Mall, at the end of a not-quite-straight axis from the White House via the Washington Monument. The Lincoln and Jefferson Memorials were the self-celebration of 'the generation that took pleasure in the mean triumph of the Spanish-American exploit and placed the imperial standard in the Philippines and the Caribbean', in Lewis Mumford's comment on the first memorial.[14] The Roosevelt Memorial of 1997 is very different, a pedagogical historical landscape about the issues of Franklin Delano Roosevelt's four presidential periods.* Currently, a Frank Gehry (biographical landscape) design for an Eisenhower homage is on hold, because of opposition (from his descendants and conservatives) to its perceived insufficient solemnity.

A contemporary visitor to Washington is struck by something which probably would have surprised both Washington and Jefferson: the military character of the city. Across the Potomac is the world's largest military building, the Pentagon, started in 1941, and a military-cum-national cemetery, Arlington Cemetery, with its iconic Iwo Jima Marine Corps War Memorial of victory in the Pacific. In the centre of the public city is the imposing building of the Department of Veterans Affairs, and in the Southeast until recently a Navy Yard and the headquarters of the US Navy, now with their 'adult entertainment' environs redeveloped. On the Mall are three memorials to the veterans of the Vietnam War, one to those of the Korean War and, since 2004, a grandiose monumental layout to the 'Victory on Land, Victory at Sea, Victory in the Air' in all the theatres of World War II. Only in Moscow is there anything similar.† More specific to Washington is a 2007 Goddess of Freedom hailing

---

* The most comprehensive overview of Washington urban iconography is probably James Goode's *Washington Sculpture: A Cultural History of Outdoor Sculpture in the Nation's Capital*, Baltimore: Johns Hopkins University Press, 2008.

† The military visibility is sustained by the post-Cold War military and security build-up; a large share of generous government contracting has gone into the Washington economy. The constant wars of the United States after the end of the Soviet Union are a boon to the Washington economy and to the income of its elites. Annie Lowrey, 'While most of America struggles, its capital thrives on government cash', *International Herald Tribune*, 12 January 2013; James Galbraith, *Inequality and Instability: A Study of the World Economy Just Before the Great Crisis*, Oxford: Oxford University Press, 2012.

the 'Victims of Communism', organized by an anti-Communist activist of Ukrainian background, Dobriansky, and financed by Jesse Helms, Grover Norquist and others of the US far right.[15]

The secessions of Canada, New Zealand and Australia were rather like a young adult leaving home than a divorce. Canadians let Queen Victoria choose their capital in 1857. In a five-city race, including two major Québec cities, Québec City and Montréal, and two Ontario cities, Toronto and Kingston, Ottawa emerged as the winner. It was centrally located in the Canada of that time, at the confluence of the Ottawa River and two other rivers and at the border of Anglo-Protestant and Francophone/Irish-Catholic Canada; it was no plausible rival to the commercial centres of Toronto and Montréal. But it had little population weight, and the ratifying Parliament vote was narrow, sixty-four to fifty-nine.[16]

The 'dominion' status of the White settlements of the British Empire was ambiguous. They were territorial units in which ethnic/national balances and power blocs mattered, but their state sovereignty evolved gradually, finally inscribed as the legislative independence of the Dominions in the Statute of Westminster in 1931. In 1929 it was the British Privy Council which finally settled a contentious issue in Canadian politics: are women persons? The Supreme Court of Canada had said 'no', but the supreme imperial court graciously declared 'yes'.*

The new capital rapidly got a towering Parliament building on Barrack Hill, built in neo-Gothic style and out of local sandstone, soon turning from its original beige colour to a sombre dark grey. Unlike Washington and Canberra, the city grew without any grand plan. In 1884 a leading politician of the time, Wilfrid Laurier, wrote: 'Ottawa is not a handsome city and does not appear destined to become one either'. About a decade later Laurier became prime minister, and as such he established an Ottawa Improvement Commission, with a view to making Ottawa the 'Washington of the North'.[17]

Twentieth-century planning has focused largely on bringing out the natural beauty of the city on hills by the rivers. But towards the end of

---

* The issue had come to the fore because only persons could be nominated to the Canadian Senate. (See Susan Munroe, '10 Firsts for Canadian Women in Government', *About.com*, 21 May 2015, canadaonline.about.com.) In 2000, the five Alberta women who had brought the case were commemorated on Parliament Hill with a nice ensemble of statuary depicting them at an informal gathering.

the century, it also developed a new political awareness, giving rise to a distinctive spatial layout and monumentality quite different from that of the imperial capital south of the border. Ottawa did not become a Federal District, but in 1958 the National Capital Act gave special planning powers to a National Capital Commission. One of its results was the Confederation Boulevard, a route, based on existing streets, connecting in a central loop Parliament Hill, the governor-general's residence and, across the river, the Québec city of Hull – renamed Gatineau in 2000 after an amalgamation – manifesting the confederate unity of multi-national Canada. A noteworthy outgrowth of Westminster parliamentary courtesy is that Ottawa has an official residence for the leader of the opposition, for which the National Capital Commission is responsible.[18]

Ottawa monumentality is not militaristic, although there is a huge central commemoration of World War I, with World War II and Korean War additions. The antidotes to the Washington battle monuments are the abstract Canadian Tribute to Human Rights (1989) and the Reconciliation and Peacekeeping Monument, or 'Peace Tower', of 1992. Instead of the Caesarean Washington presidential monuments, Ottawa sports a set of modest tributes to its leading politicians on Parliament Hill.

The capital of New Zealand is named after the successful British commander in the Napoleonic Wars, the (first) Duke of Wellington. It was chosen by the settlers as the colonial capital in 1865, for its location on the Cook Strait between the North and South Islands, out of fear for the secession of the latter. Auckland, in the north of the North Island, was then the capital and has remained the economic and population centre of New Zealand.

Rich Australia had capital ambitions, but found it had to handle the rivalry between New South Wales, the oldest settlement with its main port capital of Sydney, and nouveau riche Gold Rush Victoria, fielding Melbourne as a major capital contender. Like Washington, but unlike Ottawa and Wellington, Canberra was built from scratch in a designated rural area, in New South Wales but 'not within 100 miles of Sydney'. While a site was being determined and built up, it was decided the capital of the federated Australian colonies should be in Melbourne.[19]

The Australian Commonwealth and its first parliament came together in 1901, and in 1908 agreed upon an area called Yass-Canberra as the future capital site. The planning went out for international competition in 1911, which was won by an American architect of the Prairie School, Walter Burley Griffin. It was a great design of monumental axes and spatial proportions, but made with an explicitly democratic layout in mind. There was a 'land axis', from Capitol Hill and the government district across a built lake made from a dammed-up river, to the city and a hill behind it, and a crossing 'water axis'. The main building of the government district was to be the Parliament, flanked by residences of the governor-general and (on its right side) the prime minister, with ministries below. At the top of the hill was not to be a building of political power but a 'Capitol' of the people, 'for popular reception and ceremonial, or for housing archives and commemorating Australian achievements'.[20] The residential part of the city was laid out according to garden-city ideas.

Like L'Enfant's great plan for Washington, Griffin's suffered for decades from the pettiness and parsimony of politicians – and from the Depression of the 1930s. In the 1950s interest was revived, and the planners found that the Griffin plan could not be improved, but needed implementation.[21] With its ample use of natural space and its low-rise, unpretentious architecture, Canberra has managed to be at the same time monumental and popular. Its 1988 Parliament building has become a democratic icon, partly built into Parliament Hill, with a sloping grass lawn on its back on which citizens could walk and play (at least before 2001), with a low-slung front of modernist columns, dominated by a huge national flagpole.[22]

Canberra also features, most prominently, one of the strangest monuments in the world. The land axis from the flagpole and Parliament across the lake continues into the ANZAC Parade, a ceremonial military parade ground (laid out in 1965) ending in a huge part-Egyptian funeral War Memorial (of 1941), later embellished by commemorations of later imperial wars in which Australia voluntarily participated, like the Vietnam War.

It is not the World War I memorial that is so extraordinary, but the ANZAC myth and its iconographic domination of Canberra. 'ANZAC' refers to the Australia New Zealand Army Corps, which volunteered to fight for the British Empire in World War I. Its main exploit was a disastrous attack on the Ottoman Empire, two oceans and a continent away, at Gallipoli in 1915. On grounds beyond reason, this military adventure and bloody defeat has become a 'baptism of fire' of Australian and New Zealand national manhood, annually commemorated on 25 April.[*]

Pretoria had been the capital of the Boer Republic of Transvaal, which the British Empire had finally subdued after a gruesome war. In 1910 it was to become the main capital of the British-Boer Union of South Africa, but sharing functions with British Cape Town almost 1,500 kilometres away, as the site of Parliament and Bloemfontein, the capital of the other Boer Republic, the Orange Free State, allocated the Supreme Court. Pretoria, named after a Boer commander and conqueror, kept its Boer insignia, the republican *Raadzaal*, becoming a provincial assembly, in the *Kerkplein* with equestrian statues of Pretorius Senior, the founder, and Junior, a Boer president, with the Boer president Kruger standing in another central square.

The new White settler union got its own monumental executive, on a hill on the outskirts of the city. Herbert Baker, one of the Empire's leading architects, designed a huge, Roman-inspired building, of two wings with dome-capped towers, connected by a semi-circular colonnade, symbolizing the union of the two settler nations, and with a classical amphitheatre in front of its centre, for political rhetoric.[†] After World War II, Pretoria got its second landmark monument, the Voortrekker (Pioneers) Monument commemorating the Boer exodus in the 1830s from what they perceived as the too 'negro-friendly' British-ruled Cape Colony, and a local Boer victory over the Zulus. It is a huge (40 metres tall, wide and deep) granite building with references to Egyptian temples as well as the Halicarnassus Mausoleum, surrounded by fifty-four ox-wagons in stone, and containing a Heroes' Hall and a Cenotaph Hall.

---

[*] The ANZAC legend got a big push from the 'embedded' official war correspondent Charles Bean and has been promoted with the full force of the Australian government since the early 1920s as a nationalist-cum-imperial narrative. It was reinvigorated after the mid-1990s by the conservative Howard government and is explicitly connected with the new Australian adventures into Afghanistan and Iraq. See Alastair Thomson, *ANZAC Memories: Living with the Legend*, Clayton, Australia: Monash University Publishing, 2013, especially chapters 5 and 8.

[†] Herbert Baker had been the protégé of Cecil Rhodes and had a very developed sense of empire. Design for the Union Building had originally included a locus for the Natives. Even that was too much for the South African government, but Baker's idea of it is also an eloquent example of settler ideology: Outside the building Baker suggested a small place for Native gatherings 'where the Natives, without coming into the Building, may feel the majesty of Government' (Vale, *Architecture, Power, and National Identity*, 78; Sonne, *Representing the State*, 199ff).

Pretoria was a White Afrikaner city, although by 1950, 132,000 'Europeans' were served by 25,000 native domestic servants.[23] In 1994, however, the racist settler state crumbled and South Africa mutated into a democratic ex-colonial state, an epochal popular moment to which we shall return below.

Iberian Secessions

The ethno-cultural context and the political process of Latin American nation-states seceding from their Hispanic and Lusitanian motherlands are quite varied. However, in contrast to the states of the British secession, their new nation-state capitals are all former imperial centres. This reflects a different pattern of settlement, more directly empire-organized – like, later, British India and French West and Central Africa. Adventurers, of course, abounded: from the original Spanish South American conquistadors to their explorers of North America and the Brazilian *bandeirantes* going west, but religious dissenters, racist purists (like the Boers) and convicts were marginal and/or discrete.

Iberian colonization was urban-based. The first thing the conquistadors did after conquering a territory was to found a city. The cities of Hispanic America were laid out according to the rules of the imperial Leyes de Indias of 1573, in a grid pattern with four straight streets radiating from a central Plaza Mayor. After the plaza, the main buildings should start with the church or monastery – close to but preferably not directly in the plaza, rather by an access of its own – and then the royal house of power, according to the city's rank in the imperial hierarchy, and the *cabildo* (municipal council). The sites around the main plaza should not be left to private individuals but preserved for the state and the Church, though merchants' houses and stalls could be allowed. They were often used for a bishop's palace and sometimes for an office of the Inquisition. The founder's mansion had a right to be around and other principal settlers could be allocated central plots, but for the rest, settlers' sites were allocated by lot. The Plaza Mayor, also known as Plaza de Armas (as a parade ground), was usually the central market, with rows of shops and stalls; nearby there should be military barracks, a hospital and a prison.[24]

Brazilian urbanism was originally less centrally regulated, and Rio de Janeiro, although of sixteenth-century vintage, had been the colonial capital for only half a century when the Napoleonic Wars in Europe instigated the national issue in Ibero-America.

However, while there was an important urban continuity, national independence in Hispanic America was established through very convoluted politics and only after protracted, devastating wars. The process started with the fall of the imperial monarchy at home, through a forced abdication of the Bourbon king and a Bonapartist usurpation of the throne. But Napoleon's reach never crossed the Atlantic, except for the Caribbean islands. From the Americas the events must have appeared confusing as well as disturbing.

In August of 1808 a pack of issues of the *Gaceta de Madrid* arrived in Quito, telling, at the same time, of the uprising at Aranjuez, Spain, through which the prime minister of King Carlos IV had been fired and his son Fernando VII ascended to the throne; the son's abdication in favour of his father; the latter's transfer of the Crown to Joseph Bonaparte; the French occupation; and the Spanish insurrection against it.*

Legitimate imperial rule was suspended. In this situation the municipal councils, the *cabildos* of the major cities, came to the fore. National independence was not yet in the mainstream. Cabildo power ranged from electing a new viceroy in Mexico to 'revolutionary councils' (*juntas*) claiming temporary governmental power in the name of the legitimate king.† Hispanic America thereby became implicated in the convoluted vicissitudes of Spanish politics for the next twenty years. Anti- and post-Napoleonic Spanish politics added another conflictual dimension: liberalism or absolutism?

The first moves toward independence in Hispanic America began in 1808, upon news of the lapse of a legitimate monarchy. The final decisive battle against the Spanish imperial army took place in Ayacucho, Peru, sixteen years later. Callao, the port city of vice-regal Lima, surrendered

---

* Demélias, *Invención Política*, 197. The viceroy of New Spain got the news earlier, in June 1808 (Alfonso Vázquez Mellado, *La ciudad de los palacios: Imagenes de cinco siglos*, Mexico City: Editorial Diana, 1990, 128–9).

† Ibid., 129–30. The first such revolutionary juntas established themselves in Chuquisaca and La Paz (Bolivia) and in Quito (Ecuador) in 1809 (Demélias, *Invención Política*, 190), somewhat misleadingly giving rise to Bolivian and Ecuadorian bicentenary celebrations in 2009. A classic overview of the Hispanic American independence revolutions is John Lynch, *The Spanish American Revolutions, 1808–1826*, New York: W. W. Norton, 1976.

only in January 1826. In Mexico the wars of independence started in 1810, under the leadership of a priest, Miguel Hidalgo, and succeeded only in 1821 under a defected imperial general, Agustín de Iturbide. The Mexican vice-regal capital was not a centre of the strivings and struggles.

The two decades of almost incessant sub-continentally inter-connected wars laid waste to much of American society and fatally fractured its military and political elites, issuing into decades of post-independence coups and civil wars. By 1855, Mexico, for instance, had had fifty governments in thirty-four years of independence, eleven of those governments headed by General Antonio López de Santa Anna, a burlesque, tragic-comic figure who lost Texas, California and the other north-western territories to the United States.*

These wars did not destroy, or even much damage, the major cities. Earthquakes, such as in Lima, were much more destructive. Urban colonial continuity was not broken, but the political turmoil delayed the nationalization of the colonial capitals.

The ethnic configurations and conflicts characteristic of settler states differed in the Iberian countries from the British ones, in particular before the later waves of mass immigration. Whereas the British mainstream was dichotomous – either you are 100 percent White or you are non-White – the Iberian view and practice was hierarchical: White, less White, a little White, non-White. There were African slaves and ex-slaves in Hispanic America, but not that many, and in some areas, like Uruguay, they were killed off as cannon fodder in the independence wars. Surviving *Afrodescendentes*, as they are now called, were usually barred from Hispanic American citizenship, like in the United States before the Civil War. The most significant groups were Spanish-born *peninsulares* (or, pejoratively, *gachupines*), American-born (more or less) White Creoles, Mestizos and Indians. Centuries of ethnic intercourse had made Hispanic America a third Mestizo, a fifth White, half Indian and 4 per cent Black.†

The size and the cultural weight of the Native population in Hispanic America induced some respect among the colonial conquerors,

---

* Vázquez Mellado, *Ciudad de los palacios*, 162ff.
† Lynch, *Spanish American Revolutions*, 29n. Lynch is relying on von Humboldt. Simón Bolívar stated in his important speech at Angostura in 1819: 'We are not Europeans, we are not Indians, but a middle species between the aborigines and the Spanish' (quoted in ibid., 39).

particularly in Peru, and most of the new nation-states took them into account. In both Mexico and Peru, independence meant an abolition of the special legal status of Indians – subordinate but also protected and locally autonomous – into national citizenship.

Hispanic American independence, and Mexican independence in particular, was not exactly a straight settler secession. The popular nationalist movement in Mexico was launched by two rural priests, Miguel Hidalgo y Costilla and José María Morelos, one Creole, the other Mestizo, under the banner of the dark-skinned Virgin of Guadalupe and to the call of 'death to the *gachupines*'. In the final Act of Independence (of 1821), reference is made to 'the Mexican nation, which for three hundred years [i.e., since the colonial conquest] has had neither its own will nor free use of its voice'.* The Mestizos were, of course, descendants of the settlers and part of the settlements created by the conquering Europeans, societies very different from colonized indigenous communities, in the Americas as well as in Africa and Asia. But *mestizaje* has been a very important part of Mexican national rhetoric, imagery and urban iconography, at least until World War II.†

Brazil was part of the American slavery belt (from Washington to Rio de Janeiro), abolishing slavery only in 1888. However, it operated Black and White relations in a hierarchical Iberian way, meaning that if you were a light-skinned, non-enslaved mulatto/a, you were on your way up.

Mexico City, built on the Aztec metropolis Tenochtitlán, was the prime city of Hispanic America. On the eve of the beginning of the wars for independence, the city had about 135,000 inhabitants, the largest of

---

* D.A. Brading, 'Social Darwinism and Nationalism in Mexico', Susana Carvalho and François Gemenne (eds), *Nations and Their Histories*, New York: Palgrave Macmillan, 2009, 112. That is, the insurgent Creole nation was itself in some sense related to a pre-Columbian Mexican nation. This link was either absent or less significant in the other Iberian secessions, except Peru.

† The most frequent iconic image used by the early nationalists of Mexico referred back to pre-Spanish symbolism: an eagle on a *nopal* cactus with a serpent in its beak (Enrique de Florescano, *Imágenes de la Patria*, Madrid: Taurus, 2005, chapter 3). In 1925, José Vasconcelos, minister of education and in the 1920s and 1930s an important ideologue of the Mexican Revolution, published a book, *La raza cósmica* (The Cosmic Race), arguing for an 'Iberoamerican mission', based on his experience of miscegenation, to lead humanity into a higher, aesthetic civilization, constructed by beautiful people of all the 'four contemporary races, the White, the Black, the Red, and the Yellow', constituting a 'cosmic race' (José Vasconcelos, *La raza cósmica*, Mexico City: Espasa Calpe, 1925).

the hemisphere. Half of them were White, a fourth Indian, a fifth Mestizo and some 10,000 were what was then called 'mulattos'. It was a uniformly planned city of baroque palaces, surrounded by artisanal and shopkeepers' neighbourhoods with an Indian periphery.* Its enormous, austere, horizontal sixteenth-century Vice-Regal Palace was the grandest building of the colonial Americas, 197 metres long. To its right side on the Plaza Mayor was the exuberantly baroque cathedral. Mexico was the capital of New Spain, the richest and the most unequal of the *Indias*, as the Americas were called in imperial Spain.[25]

The palace later became the National Palace, originally housing the two legislative chambers and the ministries as well as the president. Now it functions partly as a museum, with great Diego Rivera murals of national history, and occasionally as a ceremonial public building. The presidential residence, after some time in Chapultepec Castle, has been located somewhat off-centre since the mid-1930s. The cathedral is still in use.

The large plaza in front of these buildings was once intended to house a grand independence monument, at the equestrian site of the Spanish King Carlos IV. This was an initiative of the perennially unlucky Santa Anna in 1843. In the end there was no financing and no power to complete it; only the pedestal or *zócalo* was completed. But the name has stuck: the central public place of current Mexico, the central gathering place of all protest rallies and national celebrations, is the Zócalo. There is no national monument there, only a big flagpole flying a gigantic national banner.

However, the true nationalization of Mexico City came later, with a national liberal period known as the Reforma, after Mexico defeated a bizarre European imperial adventure by Napoleon III to install a Habsburg prince as Emperor of Mexico on the basis of unpaid Mexican debt. The national iconography was laid out in a monumental programme of the late nineteenth century along the Paseo de la Reforma (previously del Emperador/Emperatriz), running northeast from the huge castle park at Chapultepec Castle. The iconographic cast included a large roster of liberal and classical national politicians, military men and intellectuals, with three major stars: Miguel Hidalgo, 'Father of the

* Serge Gruzinski, *Histoire de Mexico*, Paris: Fayard, 1996, chapter 11. An interesting narrative around the colonial and early independent palace city is given by AlfonsoVázquez Mellado, *La Ciudad de los palacios*, Mexico, Diana, 1990.

Nation' at the feet of the Column of Independence, topped by Winged Victoria, later known as the Angel of Independence; second, the last Aztec king, Cuauhtémoc – as a majestic statue, but with a *bas-relief* depicting his torture by the Spanish; and finally Cristóbal Colón (Columbus) as a peaceful navigator bringing Christianity to the Americas. Mexico does not monumentalize its conqueror, Hernán Cortés. Also standing by an abstract neoclassical semi-circle, is the great, diminutive (137 centimetres, or about 4 feet 6 inches) liberal president during the years around the French imperialist interlude, Benito Juárez, to my knowledge the first Indian president in the Americas.*

Mexico City is one of the best cities to see the historical layers of urban formation. There is the Aztec and Mexican capital, the lacustrine layout of which can still be enjoyed in the southern lake area of Xochimilco, viewed from the large, visible archaeological excavations, from the central Templo Mayor to the Plaza of the Three Cultures, and experienced through the deep knowledge on display in the most stunning anthropological museum of the world. Imperial splendour is centred on the Zócalo, where the colossally horizontal Vice-Regal Palace was given a third floor by President Plutarco Elías Calles in the 1920s. Further north, alongside the sixteenth- and seventeenth-century Basilica de Nuestra Señora de Guadalupe, dedicated to the patron saint of Mexico, a huge new modernist one was added in the 1970s. Mexican nationalism, a third layer of the city, did not find its urban and iconographic form until the last decades of the nineteenth and the first of the twentieth century, under the liberal quasi-dictator Porfirio Díaz. This was when Paseo de la Reforma was made the parade street of the city and when the Avenida de los Insurgentes, referring to the classical nationalist rebels, was laid out as the main north-south thoroughfare of the city – originally as Avenida del Centenario, reflecting the focus on upgrading the capital for the coming centenary of 1910.

The revolution of 1910–17 is another stratum of Mexican urban geology. It started under the modest slogan of 'Effective suffrage and no reelection' – reflecting the particular political problematic of the settler

---

* That Juárez could make it to the top of Mexico, first as a Supreme Court judge and then as an elected president, tells us something of the open interstices of Ibero-America, for which the United States waited for more than a century. But his was an extraordinary individual experience, as an orphan benefiting from a Franciscan's discovery and patronage of his impressive talent.

nations: the main issue is not, as in Europe, 'What rights should the people have?' but 'Who are the people?' as well as respect for their rights. Nevertheless, it became the most epic story of the twentieth-century Americas. In today's Mexico City, the most original enduring visible effects are perhaps the indoor public murals of Diego Rivera and José Orozco, the outdoor ones of the Políforo Siqueiros of culture and Juan O'Gorman's at the Central University Library. Furthermore, they also include a recycling of an unfinished parliament building into a (sepulchral) Monument to the Revolution and the Petroleum Fountain, commemorating the nationalization of oil in the 1930s by President Lázaro Cárdenas.

However, it was also after the revolution, including during its most radical period in the 1930s, that Mexico got (most of) its current polarized pattern of neighbourhoods, segregated between, on one hand, 'stupendous splendour' in California Colonial style, and, on the other, colonias proletarias without potable water, sewage or paved streets, both built by private developers. Mexico City expanded in a particular way, through new urban neighbourhoods, colonias, sometimes mixing upper-class mansions with middle-class apartment buildings, but seldom mixing the middle and popular classes. Decent working-class housing came onto the public agenda, but there were too few resources and too little political energy devoted to it for much of an impact.[26]

Conservative, liberal, revolutionary – Mexico has always been an executive country. After their early location in the national executive palace, the legislative chambers were rehoused in modest colonial palaces in the city centre. With the Centenario festivities in mind, the Porfiorato regime launched a project for a new, more grandiose Legislative Palace. The revolution put a stop to the building. Only in the 2000s did the Senate build itself a proper building.

Under Cárdenas, capital accumulation was largely restricted to private residential land and building. After World War II, capital power became more public, signalled in 1956 by the Torre Latinoamericana, at the time Latin America's tallest building (built for an insurance company). The most recent globalist layer of Mexico City will be treated in the 'Global Moment' chapter below.

Lima was the second vice-regal capital of Hispanic America; its late-eighteenth-century population of 64,000 was less than half of Mexico's. Spanish Lima was intensely royalist – 'the City of Kings' – and

Catholic, full of religious buildings and street processions, 'an immense monastery, of both sexes', as one commentator wrote in the seventeenth century;[27] another, in the early nineteenth century, found it misty with incense. It was here that the empire had its ultimate core of loyalists, led by a forceful viceroy. It also had a White and Mestizo population fearful of Indian rebellion, which had materialized as a large-scale event during the late eighteenth century. A significant minority of the city's inhabitants sailed off with the last Spanish troops. On the other hand, like the Mexican Creoles, the Peruvian Creoles included their pre-Hispanic culture and royalty in their pedigree. Colonial Lima was painted in Indian costume and monarchical chronologies were created, starting with Inca rulers and continuing with Spanish kings. An Indian nobility had been re-established, educated by Jesuits and living in the city.*

Peru had no independence heroes of its own, and independence was first proclaimed by José de San Martín in 1821, at the head of an army originating in Argentina, and finally won by Simón Bolívar, arriving in Ayacucho in December 1824 with an army from Colombia. Social change was slow after independence, with both African slavery and Indian tribute – in spite of San Martín's proclamation that the Indians were Peruvians – remaining in force for some time. Some of the mid-nineteenth-century national republican changes to Lima were toponymic, substituting national geographic names for religious ones in the centre.[28]

When a national monumentality programme was initiated in the late 1850s, financed by the short guano boom, it featured first Bolívar, in Plaza Bolívar (formerly the Plaza de la Inquisición) in front of a Congress built earlier, and Columbus (Colón). San Martín returned as a monumental hero only for the centenary of 1921.

After the end of the guano boom and a disastrous war against Chile, followed in the late nineteenth century by a recovery under an 'aristocratic republic', urban development took off during the Oncenio, the eleven years of the authoritarian, more middle-class presidency of

---

* There is some very interesting iconographic literature on colonial Lima and Peru: see Karine Périssat, *Lima fête ses Rois*, Paris: Editions L'Harmattan, 2002; Pablo Ortemberg, *Rituels du pouvoir à Lima*, Paris, EHESS, 2012. James Higgins's *Lima: A Cultural History*, Oxford: Oxford University Press, 2005, p.96ff, also has a noteworthy section on the Enlightenment 'Society of Lovers of the Country' and their conception of the Inca-Spanish succession.

Augusto Leguía. Wide avenues were opened up, named after the president and progress; sewage and piped water were installed (by a US company). The centre of the city began to move to a new, neoclassical Plaza San Martín, with the Liberator on horseback above a colossal marble pedestal, and an international luxury hotel, Bolívar. The country finally got a Legislative Palace, a national pantheon (out of a converted church), an Inca Museum of Archaeology and, off centre stage, a somewhat downsized replica of the huge Brussels Palace of Justice. The bourgeoisie showed off its wealth and power in imposing corporate buildings, such as those of *El Comercio* newspaper and the insurance company Rimac (named after the river of the city), and in their ostentatious elite clubs, the Nacional in Plaza San Martín and the Unión in the Plaza Mayor. The buildings around the latter were rebuilt or repaired from the 1920s to the 1940s (after the 1940 earthquake), including two beautiful neocolonial buildings in yellow sandstone, with loggias and Moorish carved wooden balconies (the City Hall and the Union Club), as well as the cathedral, a boastful colonial-style Archbishop's Palace and a neo-Baroque Palace of the President.*

An extensive iconographic programme was launched in connection with the centenaries of 1921 (the Republic) and 1924 (the decisive battle against the Spanish). As so often in the settler capitals, alongside national founders and heroes it included a number of gifts from ethnic immigrant communities. In Lima's case the gifts included the 'Worker' sculpture by Constantin Meunier from the Belgians, a statue of the Inca Manco Cápac from the Japanese and a museum of Italian art from the Italians. The Washington monument and square signalled the president's admiration of the United States and his eagerness to attract US capital.[29] As part of a Hispanist conservative reaction, an equestrian statue of Francisco Pizarro, the conqueror of Peru and the founder of the colonial city, was placed in the middle of the Plaza Mayor in 1935.

Originally, the vice-royalty of Peru included all South American Hispanic America – and the Philippines – but in the late eighteenth century, the Spanish crown created two new vice-royalties: New Granada, centred on Santa Fe de Bogotá and comprising today's Colombia, Venezuela and Ecuador; and La Plata, with Buenos Aires as

---

* Colonial Lima never had a grand Vice-Regal Palace of the Mexican type, and by the time of independence it was clearly run down (Higgins, *Lima*, 35).

its capital, including today's Argentina, Uruguay, Paraguay and Bolivia. In 1810 the two new vice-regal capitals were in the hands of new revolutionary powers, although not yet of independent nation-states.

National Buenos Aires got a uniquely rapid demographic start, thriving on its trade with Britain and the revenue from its customs. Under the slogan 'to govern is to populate', Argentina was actively promoting a policy of building a nation by immigration. The city population, which by independence in 1816 was 46,000, had by the census of 1869 increased to 187,000, half of it foreign-born.[30] However, the political structure of the nation remained violently contested until 1880, when a certain balance between the coast and the interior was established by separating the city of Buenos Aires, as a federal entity, from the big (and also rich) province of Buenos Aires.

Remodelling of the Gran Aldea (big village) started in the 1860s, when the modest vice-regal fort was renovated, expanded and painted pink, which gave the presidential office the name it still holds today, Casa Rosada. The building originally included both ministries and legislature. From the 1870s, Florida became the street of *porteño* elegance. However, the main reshaping took place after 1880, directed by a local follower of Baron Haussman, Torcuato de Alvear, as presidentially appointed *intendente* of the city. Under him, the modern political centres were laid out: the Plaza de Mayo in front of the Casa Rosada, by uniting the previous Plaza 25 de Mayo (after the revolution of 1810, before that the Plaza Mayor) and Plaza Victoria, and by opening up the Avenida de Mayo, leading up to a Washington-like Congress.

In the decades around 1900, the population of Buenos Aires exploded, from 187,000 in 1869 to 664,000 in 1895 and to 1,576,000 in 1914, half of whom were foreigners.[31] Unsurprisingly, Buenos Aires was not settling down as a successful and prosperous national capital. The centenary festivities of 1910 were held under a state of siege in the midst of massive strikes (which were repressed) and targeted killings by anarchists.[32] The city was dominated by an immensely rich oligarchy of commercial landlords-cum-merchants, who built neo-Baroque palaces for themselves around Plaza San Martín of a size and opulence this writer has not seen since the Saint Petersburg of Catherine II. At the other end of housing were the notorious *conventillos*, tenement houses, where families lived in single four-by-four-metre rooms without kitchens and mostly without running water.[33] The repressed labour movement had strong, militant anarchist and anarcho-syndicalist currents.

Like similar celebrations everywhere in Latin America, the centenary in Buenos Aires was an occasion of ambitious efforts at urbanistic upscaling and iconic celebration. Settler culture got a new centre: the opera and music theatre Teatro Colón, of hemispheric fame. The various immigrant communities – German, French, Italian, Spanish and others – organized monumental tributes to the capital of their new homeland, though only the French managed to get theirs ready in time.[34] The city also commissioned a sculptural ensemble called 'Song to Labour', but put it up only afterwards, in 1921. It shows a curious group of naked workers seemingly pulling a big stone, with great effort and ending in success.[35] Apparently, it is still a rallying point on May Day. Like Meunier's 'Monument to Labour' in Brussels (now virtually abandoned), the Buenos Aires 'Song to Labour' has no class or movement referent, but its triumphant end pose points to competitive sports instead of the serene piety of Meunier's work.

After World War I, Buenos Aires got a more middle-class character, politically expressed by the Radical Civic Union, a middle-class politics without the urban impact of the coeval Lequía government in Lima. The ostentatious *ancien régime* palaces of the oligarchy have become public buildings, from the foreign ministry to an officers' club. But Argentina never became a hegemonic middle-class society, with two political parties competing peacefully within a narrow, pre-defined field. The radical middle class and the privileged old right had already fallen out by 1930, and the Radical government was ousted by a military coup. The ensuing 'Infamous Decade' of military rule and massively fraudulent 'elections' developed several 'pharaonic' projects for Buenos Aires, most of them unrealized. Its major urban footprint was the opening of 'the broadest avenue in the world', the Avenida 9 de Julio, and its gigantic obelisk for the quadricentennial of the foundation of the city in 1536.[36]

To Buenos Aires's very particular popular moment, in the form of post–World War II Peronism, and to its more conventional global moment, we shall return below.

Bogotá, the fourth vice-regal capital of Hispanic America, was a provincial town in a mountainous region with bad communications in an economically little developed realm between the two centres of the empire. Towards the end of the eighteenth century the city had no more than 13,000 inhabitants. However, it had two religious colleges of higher learning – the national congresses later assembled in the chapel of the ex-Jesuit college – as well as a small Enlightenment milieu, and played a major part in the official botanical exploration of South America. The city has been referred to as 'the Athens of the South'.

Post-colonial Colombia had a difficult birth and got its major outline only in 1830, after Ecuador and Venezuela broke away from Gran Colombia (formerly New Granada). In the nineteenth century the country was riven by eight nationwide civil wars, fourteen local wars and two international wars. Bogotá developed slowly in violent, conservative aristocratic Colombia. By mid-century, central Bogotá was still without sewers, piped water or paved streets.[37] It had about the same number of inhabitants, 40,000, in the 1870s as it did at the final establishment of Colombia in 1830.* It became a major city only in the twentieth century, when its growth rate was explosive. From 1905 to 1951 its population increased more than sevenfold, and from 1951 until 2016 its population has multiplied ten times, reaching about eight million.[38] Cundinamarca, the provice around Bogotá, has been part of the coffee boom since the late nineteenth century. Later Bogotá became the industrial and the financial as well as the political capital of the country, and for all its violence, now under some control, it has offered escape from the persistent mass violence in the countryside. It is spread out on a high plateau (more than 2,500 metres above sea level), with mountains to the east. Apart from its official buildings, Rogelio Salmona's modernist redbrick architecture and the occasional colonial construction, its business centres, its small British-looking enclaves, and the gated and/or guarded upper-middle-class apartment complexes in the northeast, Bogotá today looks like a vast agglomeration of small towns from the 1950s, comprising two- or three-storeyed, more or (usually) less rundown buildings. Kennedy, a populous lower-middle-class area, bears witness to the fading but

---

* Wilhelmy 1952, 157ff; Lynch, *Spanish American Revolutions*, chapter 7; Almadoz (ed.), *Planning Latin American Cities*, 36, on nineteenth-century population. Its centenary in 1910 was organized under conservative auspices, with a major part played by the Church, emphasizing a deferential daughter-mother relationship to Spain (L.C. Colón Llamas, 'Representar la nación en el espacio urbano: Bogotá y los festejos del Centenario de la Independencia,' in Margarita Gutman and Michael Cohen (eds), *Construir Bicentenarios Latinoamericanos en la Era de Globalización*, Buenos Aires: Infinito, 2012, 328).

enduring US alignment. The large popular district in the south, Ciudad Bolívar, is not a slum, and testifies to collective urban mobility. But at the Bogotá city boundary all urban services in the metropolitan area end.

The power centre is still around the colonial Plaza Mayor (now Bolívar), but its buildings have had to be rebuilt several times due to earthquakes and fires, and the, not very impressive, cathedral is the only point of historical stability. Unplanned changes had already started in 1827 when the Vice-Regal Palace was destroyed by an earthquake, inaugurating a century and a half of temporary presidential accommodation. The current one was inaugurated in 1979, an upgrading of a building from 1908 on the site of the house of the great Colombian Enlightenment figure Antonio Nariño. The presidential Casa Nariño is behind, and slightly below, the Capitolio (Congress), initiated in 1846 and completed in 1926, a heavy neoclassical construction without a cupola, which has a seemingly commanding presence in the plaza. In front is the more modern Palace of Justice, twice severely damaged by urban violence, in 1948 and in 1985. On one side of the Plaza is the rather austere cathedral and the archbishop's palace, and on the other is the City Hall, a long, horizontal French nineteenth-century-style building from the early twentieth century, originally a commercial market.

Except for some liberal and anti-clerical moments, when some buildings of the rich Church were nationalized and secularized – like in Lisbon and Madrid – Colombia has been a predominantly conservative nation, and as late as the early twentieth century the cathedral was Bogotá's agora of political discussion.[39] Its old but circumscribed Enlightenment tradition has been reproduced, though, for instance in the White City (University City) of the 1930s, followed by a series of universities after World War II. The country's famous modernist architect, the late Rogelio Salmona, has in current times been commissioned to provide the city with several impressive buildings of cultural institutions: for instance, the Virgilio Barco Library, a modern kind of palace of learning, and the characteristically inviting Centro Cultural Gabriel García Márquez, close to Plaza Bolívar.

In a way unqiue for Latin America, political conflict in Colombia has been largely structured around a two-party system of liberals and conservatives, both led by wealthy oligarchs, going back to the 1820s, with allegiances transmitted through family inheritance to a not insignificant extent until today. Long civil wars have continued to plague the country in the twentieth century, usually won by the conservatives. The communist FARC guerrillas grew, in 1964, out of remannts of the liberal guerrillas in the Violencia, with capital V, which erupted after the assassination of the progressive and non-elite Liberal presidential candidate Jorge Eliécer Gaitán in 1948.

In Bogotá the murder caused the most massive and violent urban riots in the history of the Americas. Among the buildings destroyed were the Palace of Justice and the central railway station, which led to the end of railways in Colombia. Another effect of the Bogotazo was the flight of the middle and upper classes from the city centre, mainly to the northeast of the city and to the Andean slopes. This means that a few blocks from the political centre of the country are some of the most dangerous, dilapidated streets of the city, the worst one known as the Bronx.* A visitor to the Plaza Bolívar today is reminded of the destruction of the Palace of Justice in 1985, in a mysterious, non-revolutionary guerrilla operation crushed by military storming, killing not only the *guerrilleros* but also the judges of the Supreme Court.†

Chile was part of imperial Peru, so Santiago was no vice-regal city but the seat of the general-captaincy of Chile and of a high court, a Real Audiencia. By Independence, in 1817, it was a rather poor outback area of the Iberian settlement. However, Chile and its capital can claim some special interest, because it was arguably the first Hispanic American nation-state to consolidate after the convulsive secession, and in routing the Peruvian-Bolivian alliance in the War of the Pacific (1879–81) it demonstrated its capacity to punch above its weight.

The national consolidation was conservative, oligarchic and Catholic, and coalesced in the 1830s after the liberal liberator–hero (Bernardo O'Higgins, Chilean-born of Irish descent, illegitimate son of a Peruvian

---

* I am grateful to local friends who kindly took me around or introduced me to different aspects of Bogotá, among them Juan Luís Rodrígues, who showed me the great architecture of Salmona, Ricardo Moreno who took me to various popular neighbourhoods, and Maria José Álvarez, who shared with me her research on the city periphery. A handy historical context of the city development is Ricado Arias Trujillo, *Historia de Colombia contemporánea*, Bogotá: Universidad de los Andes, 2011.

† A moving story of the still not fully clarified event is given by the current Colombian minister of justice, Yesid Reyes, whose father, the Supreme Court chief justice was shot dead, with a bullet not used by the M-19 guerrillas, in *El Tiempo*, Bogotá, 8 November 2015, 10.

viceroy) had been forced to abdicate in 1823. The social basis was the rich landowners and the import/export businessmen of the Central Valley, soon to be sustained by huge mining rents.* This regime was remarkable, for its time and place, for two main reasons. First, it created an institutionalized polity with regular parliamentary and presidential elections ('managed' from above, true, by the executive). Second, it succeeded, throughout the nineteenth century – not in the twentieth – in subordinating the military to civilian rule.†

Like all the Hispanic American capitals (except Buenos Aires and Montevideo), Santiago is not a port city. It was founded on the insignificant Mapocho River in 1541, for half a century sharing its central role of the 'Nuevo Extremo' with Concepción a good 400 kilometres to the south. In 1800 it had something like 18,000 inhabitants, swelling to 50,000 by the end of the independence wars. Chile was not a big receiver of immigrants, but the country urbanized rapidly. In 1865 the capital had a population of 115,000, in 1900 of 300,000, and it became a city of a million in 1941.[40]

Santiago was built according to the imperial rules around its Plaza de Armas from the 1540s on, but the public architecture bequeathed to the new nation was late-born, from the last half-century of the empire. The cathedral, the fifth church on its site, was from the mid-eighteenth century, the city hall from 1789. The court, which also housed the captain-general, was late eighteenth century. Most inherited public buildings were designed by an Italian architect, Joaquín Toesca, or his disciples. Toesca then built the more impressive La Moneda Palace some blocks southwest of the Plaza de Armas, which was not only a mint but also included bureaucratic offices, a *bodega* and a chapel.[41] After first using the Royal Court Palace, Chilean presidents moved into La Moneda in the 1850s.

---

* The Chilean oligarchy has demonstrated striking staying power in the twentieth and early twenty-first centuries, which is probably unique. Many of the nineteenth- and early-twentieth-century presidential and politically prominent families are still around in the foreground of politics, business and culture, e.g., Bulnes, Edwards, Errázuriz, Larraín, Montt, Riesco.

† An interesting *laudatio* to the Chilean nineteenth-century conservatives is J. Samuel Valenzuela, 'Class relations and democratization: A reassessment of Barrington Moore's model', in Miguel Angel Centeno and Fernando López-Alves (eds), *The Other Mirror*, Princeton, NJ: Princeton University Press, 2001. A brief classical Marxist alternative is Marcos Kaplan, *Formación del estadio nacional en América Latina*, Santiago: Colección Estudios Internacionales, 1969.

The conservative character of the state was expressed in the prominent mid-nineteenth-century Archbishop's Palace in the Plaza de Armas and, above all, in the iconographic sequences of public homage. The first national monument, decided in 1837 and inaugurated in 1860, celebrated Diego Portales, the businessman who – as minister of the interior, external relations and war and the navy – was the strongman of the state-formative regime of the 1830s. The liberal Bernardo O'Higgins, later remembered as the *padre de la patria* (father of the fatherland), died in exile in Peru and was officially rehabilitated only in the late 1860s. In 1872 he got a prominent equestrian statue, sixteen years after a monument to the commander who deposed him.[42]

The institutionalist orientation of the Chilean state has an interesting correspondence to the early infrastructural priorities of capital-city planning, pushed primarily by liberals like O'Higgins and, in the 1870s, Benjamín Vicuña Mackenna. The former laid out the first part of the new main street of Santiago, the Alameda, as an agora-promenade, with benches, fountains, cafés and provisions for civic information. It has been extended, widened and given a due official name which nobody uses: Avenida Libertador Bernardo O'Higgins. It runs straight east-west but functions more like Vienna's Ringstrasse than the Champs-Élysées, through its public institutional buildings, including the state and the Catholic universities, the military headquarters and the Presidential Palace, with the government complex of the early-1930s Civic Quarter around it and the Citizenry Square in front of it.

Benjamín Vicuña Mackenna is the most famous of Santiago planners; he governed only for three years, but his immediate successors continued his work.* He was the first of the great Latin American city planners inspired by Baron Haussmann, followed by Alvear in Buenos Aires, Francisco Pereira Passos in Rio and others. In his concern with streets, promenades and public space, Vicuña Mackenna was an eloquent, focused, nineteenth-century republican modernist – before twentieth-century CIAM modernists wanted to turn city streets into automobile highways: 'After his house, where he spends a third of his

---

* For a history of Santiago planning, see F. Pérez Oyarzún and J. Rosas Vera in Almadoz (eds), *Planning Latin American Cities*. Both before and after Vicuña Mackenna, there were several French architects active in Santiago (and the decades of 1870 to 1900 have been called 'those French years' by Gonzalez Errázuriz). A major impact was also made by the Austrian Karl Brunner, who laid out the Civic Quarter.

life, nothing interests man more than the street, where he passes two-thirds of his life'.[43] In today's Santiago, Vicuña Mackenna's imprint is most visible in the Cerro Santa Lucía, a central rocky hill turned into a much-beloved public promenade space with a historical scenography of monuments. His plan also included a vast modern sewage system.

The conquistador and city founder, Pedro de Valdivia, is in the Plaza de Armas, but his statue was an early 1960s gift of Francoist Spain. Conservative Chileans seem to have had a somewhat less subservient stance to the motherland than their Colombian *compadres*. The indigenous issue is still a wound kept open by the militant Mapuche people of the south, but like the settlements of British secession, post-dictatorial Chile came to recognize the other side of the conquest in a monument to the indigenous peoples in 1992.

There is no space here to follow the establishment of all the other Hispanic American capitals, from the colonial beauty of central Quito to the post–World War II Yankeefied ugliness of Caracas. I shall return to some of them in the context of popular and global moments, and I shall enter into Havana in connection with the urban coming of Communism. Before leaving the capitals of the Hispanic secession, we should note an exception to the rule of national capitals rising from previous imperial centres: the legal centre of Upper Peru, as today's Bolivia was then called, was Chuquisaca, the seat of the Royal Audiencia (Court) of Charcas, not far from the silver wealth of Potosí, once the largest city. Under the name of Sucre, after one of Bolívar's most able commanders, it became the capital of Bolivia. It still has a special constitutional status and was used for the Constituent Assembly of 2007, but with mineral wealth shifting from silver to tin further north, and after a regionally fractured civil war, the Bolivian capital was in the 1890s relocated to La Paz, also an old American city, founded in 1548.

The capital foundations of Brazil are not only 120 to 150 years apart, they were at the opposite ends of their own epochs. Rio de Janeiro started out in 1808 as the temporary dynastic capital of a European king in exile, the Portuguese king fleeing from the Napoleonic armies in a convoy of the British Royal Navy. Under his son, Brazil was in 1822 proclaimed a monarchical nation-state, based on slave labour and presided over by a titled aristocracy. In other words, Rio was the capital of the most traditionalist of all the settler secessions, British and Iberian. In 1960, the government of Brazil moved to Brasília – at that time, and even today, the most modernist capital city ever built. On both cities there are extensive, separate literatures which need no repetition here. What we have to do is to try to capture their manifestation of national power and, without dabbling too far into the dense *floresta* of Brazilian history, the bridge between these two polarized national moments.

Rio was never much of a state vitrine. Unlike Salvador/Bahia in the northeast, Rio was not built as a colonial capital, but as a fortified regional outpost. With the shift of the gravitation of the Brazilian export economy, it was made the capital in 1763. In 1799, the city had 43,000 inhabitants, a fifth of them slaves. The arrival of the Portuguese royal court, about 8,000 people, was an enormous boost, and by the time of independence the city had a population around 70,000, half of them slaves or domestic servants.[44] The king was taken aback by the appalling quarters of the governor-general, in a swampy, insect-infested area by the harbour. Some extensions were made and another floor added, but the shabbiness and the climate stayed. A partial solution was a hilltop summer mansion donated by a rich merchant. This set something of a Rio pattern of executive buildings. After the end of the monarchy the President was housed in two aristocratic palaces bought by the state, first the Itamaraty Palace (later Foreign Office) and the Catete Palace. The republican Constituent Assembly in 1891 assembled in Quinta da Boa Vista, the mansion once given to the king. Before the Chamber of Deputies got its semi-neoclassical building in the late 1920s, it was located in the Monroe Palace, initiated as the overloaded Beaux-Arts Brazilian pavilion at the Saint Louis World's Fair of 1904, then shipped back to Rio and reassembled under the name of the US president for the occasion of the Pan-American Conference before being recycled as a national Congress building.

Between the Congress of Vienna and Brazilian independence, Rio was the official capital of the United Kingdom of Portugal, Brazil and the Algarves, and in late 1815 a set of French artists and architects, easily available because they were associated with the now fallen Napoleonic Empire, were invited to Rio. The architect Auguste-Henri-Victor Grandjean de Montigny had the most impact, in spite of the fact that most of his projects were never carried out; he did build and found the first school of architects in the Americas.[45]

Under its two emperors, Rio grew, educated itself, grappled with its tropical diseases and gradually evolved towards a wage society; slave trading was abolished in 1850 and slavery itself in 1888, but neither emperor had much interest in projecting imperial power. The republic (from 1889), on the other hand, became increasingly aware of regional competition from Buenos Aires, for immigrants as well as for international capital and prestige.

In the first decade of the twentieth century Rio joined the late-nineteenth-century Haussmann admirers from Mexico to Buenos Aires in a major overhaul of the central city and sanitary system. In Rio the key figure was the prefect Francisco Pereira Passos. Rio's equivalent to the Avenida de Mayo was the Avenida Central, a thoroughfare running Southeast from the centre and opened in 1906 after a series of brutal demolisions and evictions. In 1912 its name was changed to the current Avenida Rio Branco, in memory of a major political figure of the dying Brazilian aristocracy.

Like its Hispanic American sisters, Rio substituted a variety of individual – but all historical – architectural styles for the strict uniformity of the Parisian boulevards. It issued in a new cultural district with a fine arts school, national library, the Municipal Theatre (paying homage to the Parisian Palais Garnier) and Cinelândia, a cinema quarter (in 1908!). Politics was somewhat secondary, but not absent. What started being built as the Archbishop's Palace became the Supreme Court upon completion; the Monroe Palace was placed here; the square in front of the Municipal Theatre was dedicated to and monumentalized by the second president, Floriano 'Iron Marshal' Peixoto, and to the right of the theatre, the Municipal Council was soon erected.[46]

The presidential capital-city programme which Pereira Passos was appointed to implement focused on immigration and capital, not on tourism.[47] But in 1912 Sugarloaf Mountain became accessible by cable car, and in 1917 construction started on the Copacabana Palace Hotel, emulating the Negresco Hotel in Nice.

At midnight on 21 April 1960, a bell rang in Brasília, the same bell which in 1792 had rung the execution of Tiradentes, the first fighter for the independence of Brazil. Now it announced the ceremonial inauguration of the new capital of the nation. The city was illuminated, a message from Pope John XXIII was read and a religious communion and benediction of the city were given.[48]

This was not secularized Europe, but the elaborate thirty-six-hour ritual should not let us forget that what was inaugurated was an avant-garde of capitals. The city itself was planned by Lúcio Costa as a 'sign of the cross',[49] and the initiation of construction in 1957 was celebrated by a Mass on the same day as the Mass Pedro Álvares Cabral organized in 1500 to celebrate his discovery of Brazil.*

The contrast between the tropical languor of Rio and the dashing daring of Brasília is stunning. How did the same country manage to move from one to the other in little more than half a century?

The twentieth century unleashed a new economic dynamic of Brazil, away from the land-rent economy of slave-worked plantations and mines to entrepreneurial coffee cultivation and processing, using wage-labour and investing in manufacturing. This dynamic became increasingly concentrated in São Paulo. Its Avenida Paulista, opened in 1891, became the main street of the country, and its Week of Modern Art in 1922 was the launching-pad of artistic modernism in Brazil.

Brazil never lived by the frontier myth of the United States, but it was, like the US, a country of continental proportions with the mystique of unexplored wilderness. Parts of the Brazilian elite developed a notion of cultivating and civilizing the largely uninhabited interior of the country. Already in 1891 the Republican Constitution stipulated an ultimate goal of moving the capital to the interior.

Here we have a new societal dynamic and a vague geo-cultural goal. But this is not enough. The politics have to be specified, and the cult of the interior has to get a vanguardist architectural push.

The entrepreneurial Paulistas had no interest in a new capital, but they were not running the country's politics, having been violently defeated in 1936. The political dynamic of Brazil derived from the presidencies of Getúlio Vargas (1930 to 1945 and 1951 to 1954): statist, anti-oligarchic and developmentalist. Although he was not a chosen successor, the 'populism' of Vargas was the political formation and base for Juscelino Kubitschek, the president who built Brasília. It was probably not without significance that JK, as he became known, had been mayor of Belo Horizonte, itself a daring political construction of the nineteenth century as the new capital of the rich state of Minas Gerais

---

* The date chosen, 3 May (actually Cabral's second Mass), had an interesting meaning, because then, in contrast to the first on 26 April, no Natives had been present. In 1957 a delegation of Indians from the region were invited and paid their respects to the president. When the modernist capital was inaugurated, no Natives were invited (Vidal, *De Nova Lisboa à Brasília*, 268ff, 280ff).

and where JK in the early 1940s pushed radical urban modernization. Brasília was a monument to presidential developmentalism.[50]

A crucial part of Brasília was Brazilian architecture. It developed early, because, as noted above, imperial Brazil initiated architectural formation in the Americas. In the 1920s Brazilian architecture started to embrace modernism. Lúcio Costa, an extra-curricular disciple of Le Corbusier, became head of the Belas Artes School in 1930. Through public commissions, modernism soon became a national style of Brazilian architecture. A world-pioneering modernist building was the Ministry of Education and Health in Rio in 1936, designed by Costa and a team including Oscar Niemeyer and the landscape architect Roberto Burle Marx, also active in Brasília later. As mayor of Belo Horizonte, Kubitschek put forward Niemeyer to create a luxury tourist area in Pampulha, the most remarkable part of which is its stunningly original modernist church. US curators acknowledged the extraordinary achievements of Brazilian modernism in the exhibition *Brazil Builds* at New York's Museum of Modern Art in 1943.[51]

The crucial contextual factors mentioned above coalesced, quite contingently, in Kubitschek's 1955 presidential campaign. He was running, on the basis of the heteroclite Vargas coalition, for thirty objectives of fifty years of development in five years. Building a new capital was not among his thirty goals. Only in the course of the campaign trail did it emerge as a 'synthesis goal'.[52]

Kubitschek won the election, then turned naturally to his old collaborator from fifteen years back, Oscar Niemayer, who had left the directive plan (Plan Piloto) to an international competition (won with an artistic sketch by Lúcio Costa), but kept the role of main architect. Kubitschek made Brasília his life's project, but left almost all design matters to Niemeyer and Costa while recruiting an able entrepreneur, Israel Pinheiro, to run the state construction company. The uniquely trusting relationship between the powerful Brazilian president in the midst of a large-scale national developmentalist decade (with 80 per cent growth from 1956–61) and the world's most creative architect at that time – who was basically given a blank cheque for deploying his extraordinary creativity – created Brasília, *the* city of twentieth-century modernism.

What is the power message of Brasília? First of all, that Brazil is a nation committed to radical change and development – but without indicating what kind of change and development, apart from a belief in automobiles and their possession of cities.* Costa's plan sketch was basically aesthetic, and honoured as such. Niemeyer was a card-carrying Communist and his commitment to democracy is manifested in the balance of the three powers, executive, legislative and judiciary (clearly dominated by the legislative), in Praça dos Três Poderes ('Three Powers Plaza'), but his buildings principally display a plastic creativity, with few, if any, political indicators.

The residential area plan did include an egalitarian vision of uniform 'super-blocks', oriented inwards to a social life away from the streets, which were left to cars according to Le Corbusier modernism. Contrary to the explicit stratification of New Delhi or Islamabad, the residential 'super-blocks' of Brasília were originally intended to house government employees of all kinds, although Costa hinted at the possibility of some social 'gradation' by amenities. *Favelas* were to be avoided, even on the outskirts and in the surrounding countryside.[53] However, little thought was given to housing the workers from afar who were building the city. Temporary encampments were put up for them, meant to be destroyed once the capital was standing.[54] The capital was meant for government functionaries, the president insisted.[55] This was not only naïve but contradictory. Brasília was launched as a grand project of developing the almost empty interior of the country. To the extent that the project was successful, vast migrations would occur. And they did, attracted by the opportunities of the city construction and pushed by the devastating 1958 drought in the poor Northeast. Novacap, the powerful state construction company of Brasília, tried to stop the wave of desperate migrants by erecting police barriers on the access roads – but in vain.[56] A set of informal satellite towns grew on 'invaded' land around the city of the Plan Piloto before the latter had been inaugurated. By the end of the twentieth century, their population amounted to three fourths of the whole Federal District's.

The naïve or myopically aesthetic vanguardism of the Brasília project could flourish under the protection of a trustful president, delegated generous wide powers by his party coalition in Congress. But the stark realities of Brazilian inequality and fragile democracy soon caught up. The succeeding short-lived presidencies of Jânio Quadros and João Goulart stalled the

---

* Auto traffic was planned to flow freely, with neither street crossings nor traffic lights. Many thanks to my architect friend Frank Svensson, who took us around in his car.

Brasília project and did not reside there. Then there was a military coup in 1964. It was actually the military regime which sealed the fate of Brasília, in a positive as well as a negative sense. It decided the capital issue by moving there and continuing construction. It also presided over upper-class private appropriations of most of the lakeshore, originally meant to be accessible to all. Marketizing the apartments of the designed city in addition to accelerating economic inequality made the Federal District more unequal than the country as a whole.[57] In 1970, the per capita income gap between Brasília proper and Ceilândia, the poorest of the satellite cities, was equivalent to four times the minimum wage; in 1976 it was thirty-one. In the oldest satellite city, Núcleo Bandeirante, the jump was from two to twenty-three times the minimum wage.*

Nevertheless, half a century later, it is clear that Brasília has been a sort of success, as a thriving metropolis, a strong pole of regional economic development and a full-scale monument of architectural modernism – but also as a showpiece of Brazilian inequality.

The Capitals of Secession

It took several decades, usually more than half a century, for the capitals of the seceding settler states to get their national form. There were two reasons for this. One was the economically difficult construction of new capitals under competing political bipolarity in the new nations out of the British Empire. Pretoria was an exception to the lag, the former capital of a defeated and disappeared nation-state. The other reason was due to the travails of constituting nation-states in Hispanic America, long convulsed by civil wars. Chile was here an exception, with an early conservative establishment, strong enough to send its liberal national liberator, Bernardo O'Higgins, into exile. Rio de Janeiro could thrive on being the site of the imperial Portuguese court in exile and of the new Brazilian nation. Although the main urban municipal governments, the *cabildos*, of Hispanic America had initiated the national uprisings, once

---

* S.F. Netto Gonzalez, 'As formas concretas da segregacão residencial em Brasilia,' in A. Paviani (ed.), *Brasília em questão*, Brasília: UNB, 1985, 92. The wealthiest were concentrated in the two illicitly appropriated lakeshore areas, where in 1997 two-thirds of the residents had a family income of more than forty minimum salaries (Brasilmar Ferreira Nunes, *Brasilia: A fantasia corporoficada*, Brasilia: Paralelo 15, 2004, 106).

the nation-state was proclaimed they were, like all the secession capitals, under the thumbs of national parliaments and governments.

The new capitals imported their architectural styles from Europe, neoclassicism (in particular for public buildings) and nineteenth-century French Beaux-Arts and historicist eclecticism; neocolonial Spanish styles, as in Lima, came only later in the twentieth century. Occasionally they added a significant legislative accent, as in Washington, Bogotá, Montevideo, Brasília and Canberra, with a signal of popular power over the legislative.

But more striking is the brash assertion of national pride and power in several of the new capitals. There are the spectacular temples to Lincoln and Jefferson and the large and lavish war victory monumentality in Washington; the ANZAC Parade ground in Canberra with its seemingly endless celebrations of participations in imperial wars overseas. The late-nineteenth-century Mexican layout, in the Paseo de la Reforma, of the triumphs of liberal nationalism has no European equivalent. In Buenos Aires, the main avenues are wider and the equestrian statues are higher than anywhere in Europe. The governmental Union Building of Pretoria has no European match, nor does the monumental recentring of Lima to the new Plaza San Martín.

The White Dominion volunteers for the British imperial wars and the Hispanic *paseos*, statues and theatres to 'Colón' illustrate the reproduced ties to the motherland. Such ties were reciprocated when London in 1921 accepted the Virginia gift of Washington in Trafalgar Square, or when the Spanish government donated a 'Moorish Arch' to the new Leguía Avenue as a gift at the centenary of the Peruvian secession.

The specific ethnic issues of the settler capitals developed along two lines. One was the integration of the permitted immigrant communities, which proceeded quite well across enduring cultural diversity – by immigrant-language newspapers, for instance – and ethnic competition for jobs and positions. The ongoing integration in diversity was expressed in the typical ethnic-community mobilizations for gifts to the city on occasions of celebration, as well as in citywide celebrations of ethnic landmark events.

The other ethnic issue, how to relate to slavery, ex-slaves and Natives, was much more difficult. To this day, it remains a sore spot in Washington, which is half Black and since the mid-1970s under African American home rule but subject to budgetary supervision by Congress, which is mostly White and conservative. The race issue is much less articulated in Brazil than in the United States, but given the much larger proportion of the non-White population – about half, according to self-identification – it has more explosive potential, and the core of Brasília is very White. The Natives were not dying out, even in the British secessions, where they were denied civic rights. The centres of the Hispanic Empire – as well as, more explicitly, their national successors in Mexico and Peru – did recognize pre-Columbian America, in part even seeing themselves in a historical line of succession to it. However, the Native question was not just symbolic. It was also, and above all, socio-economic. The export- and foreign investment–oriented capitalist market and land and mining rent-based development did not give Natives much of an economic chance. But, while not part of the national foundation, the Natives have returned as part of a popular moment distinctive of the settler capitals.

4

National Foundations: Nationalizing Colonialism

About half of all current United Nations member states emerged from European colonial rule, not counting states that seceded from European settlements which I have dealt with in the previous chapter. Emancipation from European colonialism is the most common route to a modern nation-state. It had better not be mistaken for a uniform background. In the early twentieth century, the British colonial administration distinguished more than forty categories of overseas territories of the British Empire.[1] However, for our purpose of understanding something about the capital cities of post-colonial nation-states, we have to find some common denominator.

The ideal typical modern colony is, first, an overseas territory with a population of a quite different culture than that of the ruling country. In other words, typical colonial rule is rule from a long distance, geographically as well as culturally. Second, colonial rule is based on force, but very significantly also on the claimed cultural superiority of the colonial ruler, which is also deployed as a military, administrative and technological force. Third, part of this claimed and deployed cultural superiority gradually becomes recognized by part of the colonized population. Fourth, colonial emancipation derives its basic dynamic not (primarily) from counter-claims to cultural superiority or even equivalence, but from internal contradictions of the ruling culture – *inter alia*, its notions of freedom, equality, people/nation, education, merit – and from discriminatory access to it.

The above fits most of the largest ex-colonial nation-states: India, Indonesia, Nigeria, Egypt. But there are outliers. One is the group of former slave or coolie labour colonies, where the Natives were killed off but the European plantation owners in the end had to surrender to descendants of their slaves and serfs. Haiti, at great cost, opened this escape road, which is now characteristic of the Caribbean. At the other end from the mainstream is Korea, once a colony of Japan, which jump-started modernization, thereby gaining an upper hand, but was not that culturally different. Here we have to sail by most of the Caribbean (except Havana), but attention will be paid to Pyongyang and Seoul.

At independence, all ex-colonies that could do so first stayed with their colonial centres as national capitals. In Botswana and Mauritania this was impossible, because where the capital of the former had been was now another nation. New capitals developed rapidly, without much distinction: Nouakchott, little planned and ostensibly unequal between its skyscrapers and informal popular housing, in Mauritania; Gaborone, in Botswana, more gracefully as a dispersed and more proportional savannah veld city. Pakistan opted very soon for building a new capital, Islamabad, with the help of an international modernist planner and architects, followed, more cautiously, by Sri Lanka, designing a new political centre, Sri Jayawardenepura Kotte, adjacent to the real central city, Colombo. Hastings Banda of Malawi had South Africans build him a new, more ethno-politically suitable capital, Lilongwe, largely a ministerial hilltop and an elite garden city, outside a local township.

In the mid-1980s, the founding president of Côte d'Ivoire, Félix Houphouët-Boigny, announced that his native inland village, Yamoussoukro, would be the new capital of his country. The project survived his death and the end of the cocoa boom, but it has not (yet) displaced the metropolitan lagoon capital, Abidjan. Julius Nyerere wanted to create a new capital for Tanzania, Dodoma. Dodoma has also survived and has even been upgraded by Chinese aid, but it is still an outback, a temporary though recurrent parliamentary site, unostentatious and human-scale, like Nyerere himself. Abuja, on the other hand, has made it as a fully functioning political capital of Nigeria, with a design somewhat resembling Islamabad and Brasília, but without any of the dash of Burle Marx, Costa and Niemeyer or the planning rigour of Constantinos Doxiadis.

Almost all of the inherited colonial capitals of sub-Saharan Africa were colonial creations, as ports, forts, government sites. By their independence, they all had attracted a sizeable native population, with their vernacular architecture, and were largely beyond colonial planning. These post-colonial metropolises, like Abidjan, Accra, Dakar, Kinshasa, Lagos, Luanda, Nairobi and so on, had no indigenous urban tradition of their own – which pre-colonial Africa did not lack, for example in West African Benin and Ife.

The situation in North Africa and Asia was the opposite. Most of the colonial capitals, later recycled as national capitals, were ancient indigenous cities: Algiers, Tunis, Cairo, Damascus, Baghdad, Delhi, Dhaka, Hanoi, Seoul and Yangon. All had their own indigenous traditions of architecture and city layout. Kuala Lumpur and Singapore were imperial creations and so were, but very far back, Batavia (now Jakarta) and Manila.

The colonial capitals bequeathed to the new nations had a characteristic duality, between the rulers' area, in African French referred to as the *ville*, and the *cité* of the natives. In India this was expressed in the addition of a British imperial New Delhi to the Mughal capital of (Old) Delhi. A Belgian colonial exhibition in Brussels in the 2000s explained the planning rule: at least 400 to 500 metres of separation (i.e., beyond the flying range of mosquitoes), with a vertical dimension, Europeans on top. This urban duality of rulers and ruled was the poisoned chalice colonialism left to its successors. But, as many of them were trading ports, the colonial capitals, from Manila to Dakar, were at the same time multi-ethnic cities. The Chinese, for instance, were an inherent part of Manila and Batavia, and all over West Africa were Levantine traders.

The ex-colonial nation-states inherited both the territorial principle of sovereignty and their actual territories. The latter were, as a rule, delineated in quite arbitrary ways, ignorant and insouciant of cultural and ethnic boundaries and connections. Wisely, most ex-colonial nations accepted the arbitrariness as a historical legacy; when they did not, as in South Asia's Partition or the Biafra secession, bloody mayhem ensued. However, the ex-colonial nations varied culturally. A few were in fact culturally homogenous or hegemonic, whereas others had to develop a new *modus vivendi*, very often by adopting the language of the colonizer as the official national language or, as in India, as the officious *lingua franca* of the elites.

Korea, Vietnam, Southeast Asia (except for Singapore) and the Arab world, from Iraq to Morocco, are culturally and linguistically homogenous or countries of indigenous cultural hegemony, able to build anew on the basis of a national native culture. South Asia and, in particular, sub-Saharan Africa, on the other hand, have to find their inter-cultural connectors.

South Asia

New Delhi was the jewel in the crown of the British Empire, 'the setting for the grandest living on earth'*, the confluence of the modern wealth and power of the British Empire and the memory of the opulence of the Mughal Empire and the Hindu maharajas. The central axis of the new Delhi, built alongside the old, was the Kingsway, a long, wide processional avenue running from an All-India War Memorial Arch to the majestic, if stylistically rather bastard, Vice-Regal Palace on top of Raisina Hill. Around it was a spacious, leafy garden city of white mansions and bungalows, socially graded by size and by distance to the palace.

After decades of struggle, mostly if not always non-violent and including imprisonment of national leaders, Independence was finally negotiated among gentlemen – Lord Mountbatten, Jawaharlal Nehru and the Muslim League leader Muhammad Ali Jinnah, whose demand for a separate Pakistan was the most contentious issue. Indian independence was declared on 15 August 1947 – not in imperial New Delhi but from the Red Fort in Old Delhi. While marking a distance from the British Empire, the location had its own irony: The Red Fort was what remained of the imperial Mughal palace after the British destructions upon crushing the Sepoy Mutiny of 1857.

The Indian nation-state moved into colonial New Delhi, with some ritual cleansing: first toponymical, gradually also monumental. The statue of George V at the end of the processional way was taken down only in 1968. Gandhi's proposal to turn the Vice-Regal Palace into a

---

* In the 1930s, the viceroy was served by 6,000 servants (David Cannadine, *Ornamentalism: How the British Saw Their Empire*, Oxford: Oxford University Press, 2001, 56).

hospital was not followed. It was just renamed Rashtrapati Bhavan (Presidential Residence) and got a national resident. Kingsway became Rajpath (roughly a republican translation) and used for Republic Day and other ceremonial processions. Queensway became Janpath (People's Way). A later renaming of the commercial centre of New Delhi, Connaught Place, into Rajiv Chowk (after the assassinated prime minister Rajiv Gandhi) does not seem to have stuck in daily practice.[*] The World War I Memorial was kept, under the name of India Gate; a campaign to surround it with commemorations of the nationalist Quit India movement during World War II was thwarted. Plans to change the layout of space and buildings were all rejected in the end.[2] The area is still, in municipal planning, referred to as the Delhi Imperial Zone and is the only urban area protected from new development.[3] Fortunately for a parliamentary democracy, there was a legislative building in the area, added on as a post–World War I recognition of political changes, not far from the centre of power but clearly showing a belated after-thought in the layout. In 2000 it was supplemented by a Parliament Library, rather characteristic of post-colonial India: respectful of the large imperial building and at the same time manifesting a creative and indigenous modernity.[†]

Jawaharlal Nehru governed independent India as prime minister for almost two decades and, though he sometimes had to accommodate other prominent figures of the ruling Congress Party, he dominated national politics. He was high-caste with an elite British education, and his leadership habitus has probably contributed to national India's continuing chasm not only between rich and poor but also between a great – often very progressive – prosperous, world-class intelligentsia and mass illiteracy. However, he was a democratic socialist, not seeing himself as a national successor of emperors and viceroys. The Imperial Palace on the hill was left to a powerless, symbolic president. For himself, Nehru chose Flagstaff House, renamed Teen Murti Bhavan,

---

[*] In 1980 toponymical politics was institutionalized with the setup of a State Names Authority. On Delhi toponymy and monumentality I am indebted to a report prepared for my research project by professor Anand Kumar of JNU and two his students, Ramesh Singh and Sarada Prasanna Das.

[†] Cf. Rahul Khanna and Manav Parhawk, *The Modern Architecture of New Delhi*, New Delhi: Random House India, 2008, 174ff. It was built by one of India's most distinguished architects, Raj Rewal.

the mansion of the imperial commander-in-chief. The building did not become an institutional residence, but after Nehru's death (in 1964) a kind of memorial, with a memorial library added.

Nehru was very interested in and knowledgeable about architecture, and he played an important part in the post-colonial search for a national architecture and a national urban planning. At first, this did not much concern Delhi, which, above all, was facing the effects of Partition. A large part of its Muslim elite was fleeing to Pakistan, and large numbers of Hindus and Sikhs were fleeing into Delhi from there. Settling and caring for the hundreds of thousands of refugees became the prime task. Beyond the immediate urgencies, though, the crucial question of architecture and city planning was preoccupying not only the architects of the country but also the prime minister, the state chief ministers and the public works departments of all major cities.

There were two main alternatives, not polarized and irreconcilable but distinguishable: revivalism, borrowing freely from India's broad repertoire of pre-colonial cultures and styles, including Mughal, Hindu, Sikh and Buddhist; and post-imperial modernism. Independent India had a roster of architects trained abroad by the masters of modernism, such as Walter Gropius, Erich Mendelsohn, Frank Lloyd Wright and Louis Kahn, and very much inspired by Le Corbusier and Oscar Niemeyer.[4]

Nehru was a social modernizer, so he was favourably inclined to the modernists, including supporting the invitation of Le Corbusier to plan Chandigarh, the new capital of Indian Punjab after the old pre-Partition one, Lahore, had been allocated to Pakistan. He did not object to the hierarchical layout of Chandigarh, but he did stop its planned overtowering governor's palace[5] and supported Otto Königsberger's egalitarian design of the new capital of Orissa, Bhubaneswar.[6] Sometimes Nehru intervened in the design of individual buildings, insisting on Rajput traditionalist features on Delhi's first five-star hotel, the Ashok, for instance.[7] The architecture of independent Delhi has been led by public buildings for research, culture and state corporations and development agencies, and the modernist concrete tower of New Delhi City Hall (completed in 1983) is a governmental exception.

Delhi is sometimes called a city of monuments, but those of national Delhi are dwarfed by the heritage of the Mughal and British emperors: the castles, mosques and tombs of the former and the Imperial Zone of the latter. The national shrine is the Raj Ghat, the park-embedded cremation ground of the Mahatma Gandhi on the riverbank, and the adjacent cremation grounds of Nehru, Indira Gandhi and some other high dignitaries. Political naming is also remarkably frequent in Delhi, centred around the Nehru-Gandhi dynasty, from Indira Gandhi International Airport to Jawaharlal Nehru Stadium and Jawaharlal Nehru University.

Delhi city planning has turned out woefully deficient, with about a third of all housing stock and perhaps up to half of the population in illegal settlements, 'unauthorized colonies' or squatter settlements by the end of the twentieth century.[8] The power of the Indian state is severely limited. The planned areas have largely continued the inherited colonial pattern of 'colonies' for particular occupational groups or income strata. This legacy includes colonies of government employees, organized by salary rank after the example of the British Raj,[9] and an explicit military presence in the city, as the Defence Colony, the Air Force Colony and the Cantonment Board administering the military neighbourhoods (the 'cantonments').

However, on national terms, Delhi has been a very successful capital, even more so than Brasília – although it has been called 'the city nobody loves'.[10] Not only has it succeeded Lahore as the cultural capital of northern India, it has become the national capital of culture, arts (except, of course, film) and media and a major hub of higher education, particularly in the humanities and social sciences. Though still second to Mumbai, Delhi has also become a major business and industrial centre. In 1991, a third of Delhi employment was in industry.[11]

Pakistan had no colonial capital to nationalize. Lahore was the historical centre and the socio-culturally prime city of the region that in 1947 had become West Pakistan. But in the intense geopolitics after Partition it had the vulnerable disadvantage of sitting just twelve miles from the Indian border. Karachi was a thriving colonial port and the obvious short-term solution. The new state was put up there and desperately tried to find room for its civil servants – who sometimes had to make do with tents – in a city suddenly overwhelmed by refugees from India. Discussions of building a new capital started early, but in the first round pro-Karachi opinion prevailed. A city plan for the government was developed, as well as for a central monumental mausoleum (actually built) to the Father of the Nation, Ali Jinnah, who had died in 1948. But the military dictator (from 1958), Ayub Khan, wanted to move away from the humid-hot climate, the business corruption and the unruly masses of Karachi. He decreed the site of the new capital should lie on an inland high plateau in the north, adjacent to the army headquarters at Rawalpindi, which in 1959 was elevated to interim capital.

In 1960, the capital to be constructed was given the name 'city of Islam', Islamabad. The Pakistani military and, even more, its advisors on planning and architecture were almost all modernists. There was never a question of resurrecting some traditionalist Islamic city.* The commission for the master plan was given to Constantinos Doxiadis, a Greek modernist planner and theorist of human settlement – 'ekistics' – of global reputation and the leader of a major firm that was particularly active south of the Mediterranean, from Accra to Baghdad. Doxiadis's work on Islamabad was roughly coeval with Le Corbusier's on Chandigarh and Costa's and Niemeyer's on Brasília, with which the former had many similarities: the large geometric divisions of residential areas, a dominant central axis of an enormous avenue, an urban focus on the concentrated political power district at one end of the city, etc.

The Islamabad plan had some special features. Doxiadis saw himself as a scientist; he had none of the aesthetic interests and monumental concerns of the others. The main monument of Islamabad is the Faisal Mosque, an angular, modern structure with four slender minarets built by a Turkish architect on the initiative of Zulfikar Ali Bhutto to commemorate the meeting of the Organization of the Islamic Conference in 1974. While Costa's Plan Piloto was deliberately designed for a delimited bureaucratic capital, Doxiadis was equally deliberately planning for a 'Dynametropolis', a growing city, thus avoiding the Brasília pattern of a designed city surrounded by informal satellites. He even stressed that you had to build a city from the bottom up, starting with housing for the builders.[12] In practice, however, what he did was to begin by designing housing for low-rank civil servants, whereas the building labourers had to find shelter on their own, wherever they could.[13] Islamabad housing

---

* On the building of Islamabad, apart from my own observations in 2004, I have relied on Z.D. Kwaja, *Memoirs of an Architect*, Lahore: Ferozesons, 1998; Nilsson, *New Capitals*; and Orestes Yakas, *Islamabad: The Birth of a Capital*, Oxford: Oxford University Press, 2001.

was from the very beginning based on the governmental pay scale. In Islamabad there is, in contrast to Brasília and Chandigarh, a cultural centre (peripherally) within the district of power, starting out with a national library and a museum.

The Pakistani Capital Development Authority wanted non-monopolistic modernism, and, with varying emphasis, some attention to tradition – usually Mughal style. From early on, it was made clear that as a master planner Doxiadis would not be considered as an architect of major buildings. Many stars of architectural modernism were considered and invited: after Chandigarh, Le Corbusier was out of the game, to local collegial regret. Walter Gropius, Marcel Breuer and Kenzō Tange turned down invitations. Arne Jacobsen and Louis Kahn had their projects rejected.[14]

In the end, a malleable US architect, Edward Stone, designed the two key buildings, the presidential and the parliamentary: two white horizontal edifices, the parliamentary one slightly higher and longer than the other. Upon the demand of a new general chairing the Development Authority, Stone took out the traditionalist elements demanded by a previous government.[15] In my opinion, the only remarkable building of the 'Administrative Sector', at least from the outside is a creative modernist building – the Supreme Court by Kenzō Tange (who later agreed to contribute) – which might be sited anywhere in the modern world.

Pakistan has hardly lived up to its claim to be the Land of the Pure, with its national history full of coups d'état and military violence from above and sectarian violence from below, as well as endemic corruption. But Islamabad bears witness to Muslim modernism, which was once part of the mainstream of Pakistani nationalism. Islamabad is an indicator of Pakistani potentialities but not a predictor of national outcomes.

Southeast Asia

Dutch colonialism was run by Calvinist merchants of the Dutch East India Company and of the United Provinces republic. Dutch Batavia reproduced the sober lack of ostentation of Amsterdam. Unusually for a colonial city, it had a city hall on par with the governor-general's residence. A progressive chief town planner and architect of the Dutch East Indies, Thomas Karsten, submitted in the 1930s a restructuring plan for the political centre and its surroundings, which would have reoriented the latter around a new city hall.* But then the war and the Japanese came. With the latter, the city got its pre-colonial name back (in adulterated form): Jakarta.

The Indonesian nation-state was not born by consensus after belated colonial resignation, as in India. Independence was proclaimed on 17 August 1945, upon news of Japan's surrender. But soon British troops arrived, and in their wake the Dutch. In Jakarta there developed a dual-power situation, with Indonesian nationalists running the indigenous city from City Hall and the Dutch the colonial quarter from their Office of Municipal Affairs.[16] In July 1947, the Dutch felt strong enough for a *reconquista*, which they called a 'police action'. But the national republic stayed put, and after two years of low-intensity war and constitutional intrigue and under US pressure, the Dutch recognized the independent republic in December 1949.

Indonesia was the first example of victorious rupture with colonial rule, which did not prevent it from recycling the colonial city. The (powerful) president moved into the governor-general's residence villa, renamed Istana Merdeka (Independence or Freedom Palace), in Merdeka (Independence) Square (formerly the Koningsplein), with recycled or new buildings of the state around it. Indonesia emerged as a nation-state with a ravaged economy, a massive flight from the countryside into the capital and a sharply conflict-ridden and unstable polity set to govern a huge ethnically and culturally diverse archipelago. Early national Jakarta suffered from overcrowding, poverty and a dramatic lack of urban services of all kinds.

Sukarno was the first president and from 1958 to 1965 the almost unlimited leader of the country. By training he was an engineer, with a stint of architectural practice before becoming a professional politician. Like Nehru he was a modernist, intensely committed to making Jakarta a modern capital of a modern nation, 'a beacon of the New Emerging Forces' of the world, and with his greater powers Sukarno made a larger impact on Jakarta than Nehru did on Delhi. A major difference was that

---

* Abidin Kusno, *Behind the Postcolonial: Architecture, Urban Space, and Political Cultures in Indonesia*, New York: Routledge, 2000, 55. Abidin Kusno has written extensively on Jakarta, elegantly combining architectural and social perspectives. See also his *The Appearances of Memory: Mnemonic Practices of Architecture and Urban Form in Indonesia*, Durham, NC: Duke University Press, 2010.

Sukarno was a militant leading a ruptural nation-state. Nationalist symbolic politics was to play a larger role in Jakarta. The two main manifestations of this are the national monument, Monas, in the middle of Independence Square, and the Irian Jaya Liberation Monument, opposite the Treasury building.

Monas refers back to the pre-Muslim, pre-colonial Hinduist high culture of Java in the form of a 137-metre-high marble *lingam* (penis) topped by a square platform with a gold-coated flame, and a *yoni* (vagina) at its base. Whatever their sexual connotations,* they are ancient symbols of life, virility and fertility still revered in India. The Monas conveys an abstract, assertive nationalist force, owing nothing to more than three centuries of European colonialism.

The other assertive monument commemorates the takeover in 1963 of Irian Jaya (Western New Guinea), which the Dutch had kept in 1949. It depicts a heroic, muscular male breaking his chains and shackles on top of a high, rectangular cement frame. As far as I know, Sukarno did not have any monuments erected in his own honour, and the current tranquil double statue of Sukarno and Mohammad Hatta, his vice-president and-rival, is of a later date, as is the giving of their names to the capital airport.[†]

Sukarno pushed several buildings as signals of modernity, most immediately with a view to the Asian Games in 1962 and the anti-Olympic 'Games of the New Emerging Forces' in 1963 at the new Gelora Bung Karno (Brother Sukarno) Stadium. All colonial names of streets and squares were removed, and an axial north-south through-boulevard was laid out and named after two heroes of the struggle for independence: the pre–World War II nationalist politician Mohammad Husni Thamrin and General Sudirman, commander of the nationalist army.

---

* Sukarno was a notorious sexual predator and sexual imagery probably came to him easily, but that is largely beside the nationalist point. Pre-Islamic Hindu-Buddhist mythology is also monumentalized in other forms in Jakarta, including in the dioramas of national history at the base of Monas. On Monas, see Gerald McDonald, 'Indonesia's Medan Merdeka: National identity and the built environment', *Antipode* 27:3 (1995): 270–93. A classic overview of Jakarta's national symbolism is by the Dutch anthropologist Peter Nas, 'Jakarta, City Full of Symbols: An Essay in Symbolic Ecology', *Sojourn* 72 (1992): 175–207. It was the author's first major contribution to the field in a life-long career largely focused on urban symbolism.

† The posthumous monumentalized reconciliation of Sukarno and Hatta has some resemblance with that of Mao and Liu Shaoqi in Beijing.

On the boulevard is the Hotel Indonesia, with its huge 'Welcome' statue outside, as well as the city's first department store and its first clover-leaf road crossing. Sukarno dreamt of a city of skyscrapers that would over-shadow Singapore.

Indonesian nationalism is explicitly multicultural, and it is notewor-thy how prominent Hinduist motifs were in the first nationalist iconography. In the city centre there was not only the National Monument but also a dynamic and colossal statue of Hanuman, the monkey god from the classical Indian epic Ramayana. The tradition continued after Sukarno with a big monumental ensemble of Arjuna, a figure of the other classic Hindu epic Mahabharata, on his war chariot drawn by a long team of horses, outside the twin modern towers of the Bank of Indonesia. Sukarno was also quite active in the planning of a national Independence Mosque (Masjid Istiqlal) near the Independence Square, a big modern building with an Arabic dome designed by a Christian architect, but it, like the Monas, was completed only in the 1970s, half a decade after Sukarno's rule. A Parliament building also came later, in the same area as the stadium.

Little was done for the social problems of the city, which were huge, if not comparable to the abject misery found in some of the big Indian cities. A new, post-colonial form of urban dualism, characteristic of Jakarta, started under Sukarno and has expanded much since: a system of elevated highways for (upper-)middle-class motor traffic roaring beneath, to the sides of and past popular neighbourhoods or *kampung*. These highways, the recent high-rise super-blocks along them and the perennial traffic jams on them are good sites for a melancholy contem-plation of what the Jakarta architect Jo Santoso has called the 'five layers of Jakarta': the pre-colonial Javanese city, the Dutch colonial city, the modern national capital, the globalized mega-city of Suharto's 'New Order' and the fifth layer, dearest to Santoso's heart, the *kampung*, the base for a sustainable city.[17]

The counterpoint to the Jakarta Monas is the National Monument of Kuala Lumpur, the capital of Malaysia, a state with which Sukarno launched a *konfrontasi* in the early 1960s: a pointless, self-diminish-ing political theatre reminiscent of Mussolini's, whose ridiculous idea of 'living dangerously' Sukarno quoted or repeated. But it is history, not theatrics, which counter-poses the two monuments. The muta-tion of the imperial British Malaya peninsula into the nation-state of

Malaysia was a peculiar variant of the negotiated, non-ruptural path out of colonial subservience. Under the sovereignty of the British Empire, Malaya was governed by a layer of Malay royalty and aristocrats ruling Malay peasants. Colonial tin mines and rubber plantations were worked by imported and/or immigrated Chinese and Tamils and the Asian business sector was run by Chinese. Modern Malay nationalism, as proudly remembered in the museum house of Malaysia's first prime minister, Tunku Abdul Rahman, started in 1945 with a petition and a campaign against a British proposal to provide equal citizens' rights to the Chinese, who had provided the resistance to the Japanese occupation.

A visitor to the National Monument in Kuala Lumpur, officially designated but less centrally located than its Jakarta counterpart, might think she is standing in front of a replica of Washington's Iwo Jima Marine Corps War Memorial. She would not be mistaken. It was actually made by the same sculptor who created that monument, Felix de Weldon, whom Tunku Abdul Rahman invited to make something similar. Half folded, the Malaysian flag held by the hero on top (the *Tunku* as a young man) looks like the American flag. This is a monument to heroes, but of what? Not of independence, nor of the nation. The frontal dedication is 'to the heroic fighter in the cause of peace and freedom'. On another side we are enlightened as to what peace and freedom: from 'the Emergency'. That was the euphemism the British gave to their more-than-decade-long war against a Communist anti-imperialist guerrilla force that in the end was brutally defeated mainly because of its increasingly narrowed Chinese ethnic base. At the bottom of the monument lie two dead Communists.[18]

The 'National' Monument of Malaysia actually celebrates the last victorious imperial war in Asia, of which the Malay princes – *tunku* could be translated as 'prince' – were the main local beneficiaries. Malaysia is still a rotational monarchy, among nine sultans, but their role is mainly symbolic and the Malay aristocracy is no longer in charge. In Kuala Lumpur this is manifested in the city's more recent landmark, the Petronas Towers, perhaps the world's most striking monument to national state capitalism. It is the headquarters of the state-owned oil company Petronas, built by César Pelli under the direct supervision of then–prime minister Mahathir Mohamad, a radical middle-class nationalist, very different from the aristocratic elite.[19]

Seoul had a special colonial trajectory – like Cairo starting after a thwarted effort at reactive modernization – and was special in its exceptional relationship to its colonial power. After all, Korea and Japan were both offshoots of Sinic civilization, and its educated elites had both been brought up on the same Confucian classics in the same Chinese ideograms.

Partly inspired by the Japanese Meiji Restoration, Korea attempted from the 1880s a reactive modernization from above, but its internal as well as geopolitical situation was much more vulnerable than that of khedival Egypt. Korea was officially subordinate to the Chinese emperor, who still had more clout in Korea than the Ottoman sultan had in Egypt. On top of that came the increasingly aggressive Japanese and Russian predators. In 1894 a massive peasant uprising, the Tonghak Rebellion – comparable to if not identical with the Chinese Taiping Rebellion a generation earlier – was on the verge of toppling the Korean monarchy. The monarchy called for help from China, which came and crushed the rebellion, but enticed Japan to intervene. The Japanese routed the Chinese army, and in the peace treaty, the Chinese had to accept Korean independence.

The Korean king then made himself emperor – thus equal to the Chinese and Japanese – of a realm now called the Great Han Empire. A modern-style nationalism emerged, and in 1896–7 the country's first national monument, a simple Paris-mirroring Independence Arch, was erected. It is still standing, looking somewhat pathetic but also striking in its modesty, off-Broadway in central Seoul. But Japan then defeated Russia too, and in 1910 it formally annexed Korea. A Korean nation-state came about only after 1945.

Some urban modernization of Hanseong, as Seoul was then called, had begun before colonial rule – the city wall had been torn down, and there had come some street widening, some street lighting, trams, a shining Christian cathedral on a hill. But the city, renamed Gyeongseong (Keijō in Japanese), a part of Gyeonggi Province and in particular its centre, was radically transformed under Japanese city planning and construction. A vast street improvement programme, modelled after Tokyo's, was launched, and a set of landmark institutional buildings: an imposing city hall, a similarly massive Government-General building in front of a former royal palace and an official residence for the general governor behind and above the latter. The centre became largely

Japanese, with Japanese shopping streets and residential areas, and by the mid-1930s a quarter of the population was Japanese.[20]

Japanese colonialism shared its cultural arrogance and repressive surveillance with other colonial powers, but it also had some special features. After a relatively tolerant bi-cultural period in the 1920s, Japan went for a serious – instead of French-style token – assimilation, trying to make Korea and Koreans Japanese, 'to integrate Korea into Japan'. Of course, this had a strong repressive side to it, including forcing Koreans to adopt Japanese names. But the other side was unique socio-economic development. By 1945, more than half of all Korean children were enrolled in elementary school, up from 15 per cent in 1930.[21] Seoul quadrupled its population after 1910, passing the million mark in 1942 and becoming a significant industrial city, with a fifth of its employment in manufacturing by 1937.[22] Manufacturing contributed 39 per cent of the Korean national product in 1939, and almost half (46 per cent) of Korean exports to Japan.[23]

Japanese colonial rule generated an intense nationalist resentment among Koreans which persists until today. At the same time, however, *sub rosa*, Japan has also functioned as a concrete model of economic development to Korea, because the cultural matrix of departure was rather similar and because the original Korean attempt at reactive modernization was only about twenty years later than Japan's.

Pre-modern Asian polities were more explicitly patrimonial than European ones. Countries often had no name of their own but were referred to by some name given by a dynastic founder, referring to the dynasty and its rule. Korea was known in East Asia as Choson (sometimes transcribed as Joseon), a name decided in 1394 by the Chinese emperor, to whom the new Korean dynasty had submitted two proposals. The Chinese envoy to Korea in 1898 carried a letter on behalf of 'the Great Emperor of the Great Qing'.* A new concept corresponding to the European 'nation' emerged in East Asia at the end of the nineteenth century, composed of two Chinese characters: *min* for people, and a second denoting family or clan. Together they became *minjok* in Korean,

---

* The name Korea derives from an earlier dynasty, Koryo, and Han of the short-lived 'empire' (1896–1910) to another old kingdom in the south of the peninsula (Andre Schmid, *Korea Between Empires*, New York: Columbia University Press, 2002, 74–5; see also chapter 5).

minzu in Chinese and *minsoku* in Japanese, denoting a new social phenomenon: nation.[24] There was an ancient word, *kuk* (or *guk*), which could mean state and which was now revived.

The modern Korean nation started out, inauspiciously, as a declaration of a self-proclaimed government in exile in Shanghai in 1919.* Its real birth after the Japanese defeat in 1945 was difficult and painful. An early September 1945 proclamation by a National Conference of a Joseon [Korean] People's Republic was not recognized by the United States, whose troops landed soon afterwards and put southern Korea under US military rule. The Allies agreed to put Korea under five-year trusteeship by the four big powers: the United States, the Soviet Union, China and the United Kingdom. Emerging Cold War tensions soon made this impracticable and the country was divided between an American South and a Soviet North. Korean nationalists became bitterly divided among themselves, not only between the right and the Communists, but also between intransigent and synthesizing currents.

In 1948, after elections boycotted by the left and the pan-Korean nationalists, the Republic of Korea (Taehan Min'guk) was declared, assuming the name of the 1919 Shanghai 'provisional government' in exile.[25] Its leading figure was a conservative expatriate from that era, known in the West as Syngman Rhee (later Korean historians referred to him as Li Seung-man). Then, in 1950, civil war between the Communist North and the South broke out, which immediately became a protracted international war because of US intervention, followed, as usual by a trail of allies, which then provoked a massive Chinese counter-intervention. (Stalin's Soviet Union supported the North materially but stayed out of the war.)

After World War II and liberation, the South Korean capital got its third name in the twentieth century, Seoul, which literally translates to 'capital'. During the Korean War (1950–53) it changed hands several times and the city was largely destroyed, above all by US bombing. Half of its housing stock was damaged and almost a third became uninhabitable. The population halved from its size of 1946, to 600,000.[26]

Anti-colonial changes started directly after the Japanese surrender, and the large Japanese population left. The Shinto shrine was burnt.

---

* It was called Taehan Min'guk, as South Korea is still called today. Taehan Cheguk, the 1897 Empire of the Great Han, became the Republic of the Great Han (Schmid, *Korea Between Empires*, 254).

Gyeongseong Imperial University became Seoul National University, and a number of neighbourhoods got new names. The Meiji Theatre became the Sigonggwan. Probably unique among ex-colonial nations, an official cultural campaign was also unleashed in South Korea in 1949: 'Make a Clean Sweep of Japanese Manners'. Fully in line with ex-colonial practice, the residence of the colonial governor-general became the presidential residence, named the Blue House after its roof tiles. The sombre headquarters of the colonial government was used for ministries, then from 1985 for some years as a museum, before finally being dynamited in the new millennium. The central colonial city hall was turned into a Seoul city hall, recently and elegantly overshadowed by a modern addition.

The first monument built in liberated Seoul, in 1955 and 1956, fêted President Syngman Rhee in a colossal ensemble claimed at the time to be the largest statue in the world – 24 metres with pedestal – erected on the site of a former Japanese Shinto shrine.[27] Seoul was then in competition with the Communist Northern capital, Pyongyang, and a personality cult was part of it. The Sejong Centre (1974–78) on the central axis of Seoul, named for a fifteenth-century king, was built in emulation of the Pyongyang Grand Theatre, with a hall large enough to seat a huge National Conference for Unification.[28] Rhee was toppled by an urban uprising in 1960, and his statue with him. Perhaps the second monument (of 1968), and in any case the currently most central one, is the stern, armoured figure of admiral Yi Sun-shin, a classical hero of sixteenth-century resistance to Japanese invaders, whose iron ship is Exhibit A at the National Museum.

Korea and Seoul were not allowed to modernize on their own terms. Their enduring and monumentalized anti-colonial bitterness bear witness to that. On the other hand, to a European, Seoul and Tokyo share some fundamental features: a dynamic capitalist modernism combined with a deeply rooted sense of a long national history, a manifest concern with national cohesion and an avoidance of extreme socio-economic polarities. Intimate knowledge and direct experience of the Japanese model of rapid economic development and post–World War II privileged access to US markets made possible a uniquely successful ex-colonial national development. By the first decade of the twenty-first century it was clear that this development had made it possible for Seoul to master the enormous post-colonial rural influx into the capital. (In 2007, a Korean colleague kindly showed me the 'last slum' of Seoul, a small shanty neighbourhood in the south-eastern periphery.) The process took its time of trial and error. Under the 1960s and 1970s developmentalist regime of General Park Chung-Hee, several 'slum clearance' evictions were launched, capital immigration was restricted and a new capital was envisaged.* But resources were emerging for some positive solutions. Peripheral high-rise housing for the popular classes started in the 1960s. Its often low quality did not stigmatize it, and from the 1970s better-quality high-rises, with individual apartment ownership, built by private developers and not by a public corporation, as in Singapore, became standard middle-class housing in Seoul.[29]

Seoul is a blatantly capitalist city – the only capital, as far as I know, with a public monument to stock-trading operations, the Trillion Tower sculpture in the plaza by the tall Trade Tower, which celebrates the first day of trillion-won trading. But in spite of its current 'global city' aspirations, to which we shall return later, it is also a profoundly national city, the capital of a national community that does not 'transcend' class and gender inequality and conflicts, but is strong enough to matter materially to the privileged and the powerful.

The North Korean capital Pyongyang will be looked at later, in the chapter on Communism.

The Arab World

Virtually the whole Arab world, from Morocco to Iraq, has had an especially convoluted path to a nation-state (save perhaps Algeria, with a straighter colonial experience). Some Arab countries haven't made it at all yet. Saudi Arabia and the Gulf monarchies are still patrimonial states. Lebanon is more an uneasy confederation of religious communities

---

* On the back burner after Park's assassination, the idea of a new capital remained on the agenda. It was stopped by the Constitutional Court in 2004, with the notable motivation that 'since the public has come to recognize Seoul as its permanent capital, the tradition and custom related to this recognition are the equivalent of constitutional provision'. Here quoted from Moon Chang Keuk, 'Maintaining Seoul as our capital', *Korean Forces* 12(6), November–December 2004. In the 2010s, a less ambitious administrative annex city began construction.

than a nation-state, and the national character of Iraq, Jordan and Syria is a recurrently reopened question. The convolution of the mainstream Arab experience derives from a long – in the case of Egypt, about a century and a half – period of complex power games between a foreign prince (the Ottoman sultan), local princes and European predators posing as 'protectors', after World War I as having a 'mandate' from the League of Nations, games into which nationalist forces came to intervene belatedly. The slow emergence of national Cairo bears witness to this.

Egypt was part of the Ottoman Empire, to which it paid tribute and respect. It was ruled by a *wali*, who by the nineteenth century was basically autonomous but needed the formal sanction of the sultan. The country was shaken up by an invasion by Napoleon Bonaparte in 1798 and by an active French modernizing immersion into the culture of the country, with several commanders publicly converting to Islam. The French provided inspiration and advisers to a forceful Ottoman commander Muhammad Ali, who in 1807 usurped the governorship of Egypt, embarked upon a successful military upgrading of Egypt and got the sultan to acquiesce to hereditary suzerainty by Muhammed Ali's descendants. While successful in its own terms, this was not a reactive modernization construction of a nation-state. Egypt stayed patrimonial, under a foreign, Turkic dynasty, surrounded by a similar court.

The new, Europeanized city of Cairo was not (in the beginning) built by colonial powers, but by the Ottoman *wali*, Muhammed Ali's grandson Ismail, who ruled from 1863 to 1879. Buoyed by the Egyptian cotton boom, due to the northern blockade and, later, war dislocations of Southern US cotton to the United Kingdom, Ismail bought the Persian title of *khedive* from the sultan and built a new Cairo, with the able help of Egyptian engineer-planner equivalents (and contemporaries) of Torcuato de Alvear and Benjamín Vicuña Mackenna: Ali Pasha Mubarak and Mahmoud al-Falaky Bey. The centre of the city was moved west, to the east bank of the Nile (now regulated, with the swamp drained), away from the old locus of power, the Citadel on the Muqattam Hill. For himself Ismail had the huge Abdeen Palace put up, a horizontal two-storey building in a style reminiscent of French classicism and Viennese Baroque. The centre of the new city, Ismailiya, was Maidan Ismailiya, today's Maidan Tahrir (Tahrir Square). 'Egypt is no longer part of Africa.'

It is part of Europe', the ruler announced in 1867.* The Paris Exposition, his close relationship with the then-empress of France and the coming of the Suez Canal (in 1869) added to the frenzy.

Extravagance and European loan sharks forced Ismail to abdicate. Various 'risk deductions' meant that Egypt had to service, at more than 10 per cent interest, notional loans of £77 million while de facto borrowing £50 million.† Another *khedive* followed, and colonial Cairo continued to expand. But the British had acquired control of the Suez Canal, and a defeated nationalist uprising brought Egypt under British armed control, centred on a former Ismail palace, Qasr al-Nil. Cairo developed as a cosmopolitan city for the upper and upper-middle classes. Exclusive clubs were built on Gezira Island, new suburbs were generated by foreign developers, an international consortium built a garden city south of Maidan Ismailiya and the Belgian Baron Empain built Heliopolis in the north. Among the locals, Jewish bankers and Greek shopkeepers played a prominent role. 'Cosmopolitan' in this case mainly meant non-Egyptian, although at the consuming side it included the largely Turco-Circassian pasha stratum.

Egyptian nationalism was inspired by the Japanese victory over Russia in 1905 and by the aspirations opened by World War I. Like in India, the British faced a nationalist mass mobilization in Egypt in 1919, which they repressed but from which they learnt to negotiate. In 1922 Britain ended its 'Protectorate' of Egypt, and the 1923 Egyptian Constitution proclaimed that 'Egypt is a sovereign state, free and independent'.[30] That was a pious aspiration; according to a 1922 treaty, which the Constituent Assembly had accepted by a narrow majority, Britain kept the right to have military troops in Egypt, control of the Suez Canal and control over 'Anglo-Egyptian Sudan' and foreign jurisprudence was still to be applied in Egypt by 'mixed tribunals'. Unspoken in the treaty was Britain's de facto power, used most blatantly in 1930 and in 1942, to veto undesirable governments.

In 1947 the British evacuated their central Qasr al-Nil barracks (but not all their troops from Egypt), and in 1949 the mixed tribunals

---

* Trevor Mostyn, *Egypt's Belle Epoque: Cairo and the Age of the Hedonists*, London: Tauris Parke, 2006 (1989), 44, gives a lurid picture of Cairo's colonial *belle epoque*.

† Ibid., 120. The *dey* of Tunis was brought down in largely the same way, and the Ottoman and Qing Empires had a similar experience.

disappeared. In 1953, after a military coup in 1952, Egypt got its first native ruler since the Pharaohs, Muhammad Naguib. His compatriot successor, Gamal Abdel Nasser, nationalized the Suez Canal in 1956, whereupon Britain, France and Israel invaded Egypt to get the Canal back to the former, with a view to crushing uppity Arab nationalism on the top of the agenda of the two latter powers. Under rare American-cum-Soviet pressure, this project backfired. The Egyptian nation-state was consolidated.

The particular history of Arab nation-state development meant most immediately that the alien colonial city the nation appropriated was largely a city built by Europeanized local princes. After the 1952 revolution,* the distribution of palaces to the new national rulers was not about colonial buildings *sensu stricto*, but local royal and princely palaces. The republic made Ismail's Abdeen Palace and Farouk's Koubbeh Palace into presidential palaces; princely Tahra was added as such, whereas the Council of Ministers and the Foreign Ministry moved into other palaces of the deposed royal house.[31] In the main square, Tahrir (Liberation) Square, there is no representative public edifice – only a hulk building of bureaucratic agencies. There were massive toponymical changes in central Cairo, substituting revolutionary events and nationalist heroes – and Pharaoh Ramses – for royal names.[32] There was less of new monumentality. A statue of Nasser was planned for Tahrir, but after his disastrous military defeat in 1967 this was no longer conceivable, even though the people's publicly demonstrated loyalty kept him in power until his death in 1970.[33] His successor, Anwar Sadat, built a monumental complex to the Unknown Soldier in commemoration of his semi-victory against the Israelis in 1973.

Nasser's Cairo meant a plebeian nationalization of the city; the division of the centre between the colonial city and the indigenous city,

---

* It became a national revolution in its consequences, but it started as a military plot by a group of officers, most immediately concerned with protecting themselves against monarchical repression after having won the election to the executive of the Officers' Club. They had originally no political programme and initially handed over government to a politician of the old elite. The monarchy was kept, with Farouk forced to abdicate in favour of his infant son. A revolutionary dynamic soon started, though, with land reform and tough negotiations with the British about their remaining troops in Egypt. In 1953, the monarchy was abolished and political parties banned. By late 1954 Gamal Abdel Nasser had emerged as the supreme leader.

along Ibrahim Pasha (now Republic) Street, became blurred. But the Third World division between the formal and the social spheres of the city has remained, with some improvements to basic services under Hosni Mubarak. By the late 1980s, for the first time a majority of Cairenes had running water and (official) electricity, while most of those still living in the unplanned popular quarters of the city did not.* Almost two thirds of Cairenes were living in 'informal housing' in 2006.[34]

Algiers was, like all of North Africa east of Morocco, officially part of the Ottoman Empire, but de facto largely independent under a local ruler, a *dey*, and also a notorious harbour of Mediterranean corsairs. It was invaded by France in 1830 and subjugated after prolonged, fierce resistance. The French developed Algeria into a settler colony. In spite of its Arab and Turkish origins, Algiers became a European-majority city. In 1926, 212,000 people lived in the city agglomeration – an increase from about 30,000 in 1830, – of whom 156,000 were Europeans. *Intra muros* there were 45,000 Natives and 67,000 European settlers. The Natives were concentrated in the traditional *casbah.*†

A bloody and bitter war of independence started in 1954, when Algiers had almost 600,000 inhabitants. The city was a major battlefield and the *casbah* a core of the insurgency. Through a massive use of torture of prisoners, French paratroops won the Battle of Algiers of 1957, commemorated in Gillo Pontecorvo's famous film. In the end, however, the Natives won the war, and in 1962 Algeria became an independent nation-state – not a very happy or democratic one though, even if a large oil rent has kept popular discontent within bounds most of the time. In the early 1990s actual (secular) army rule was challenged by Islamists,

---

* The sewage system was upgraded at the same time (Susanna Myllylä, 'Cairo – A Mega-City and Its Water Resources', paper presented at the Ethnic Encounter and Culture Change conference, Joensuu, Finland, 19–22 June 1995, org.uib.no/smi/paj/ Myllyla.html; Max Rodenbeck, *Cairo: The City Victorious*, New York: Vintage, 1998, 224, 244ff). Rodenbeck, a great, sharp-eyed journalist, also tells us that at least some part of the old Turco-Circassian upper class have survived the revolution, with both their wealth and their orientalist decadence (ibid., 305–6).

† Le Corbusier, who in the early 1930s worked on a self-commissioned plan for Algiers, had an orientalist admiration for the *casbah*, which he wanted to preserve as a touristic landmark under an elevated road-bridge connecting the two European quarters, the heights south of the *casbah* and the Marine Quarter by the bay. This plan never became reality. Zeynep Çelik, *Urban Forms and Colonial Confrontations: Algiers under French Rule*, Berkeley: University of California Press, 1997, 42, 70 (population figures).

first victorious at the polls and then defeated by ferocious repression. During the Arab Spring of 2011, Algiers was rather quiet, due mainly to the trauma of the 1990s but also to some regime openings.

Algiers has not (yet) found its proper role in this corrupt and violent context. Various plans for upgrading the mythical but – in terms of space and urban services – very disadvantaged *casbah* do not seem to have gone very far in practice, and the recent Grand Alger plans do not appear to have a good grasp of the demographic influx.*

However, symbolically – and fully legitimated by its history – Algiers is a master example of a ruptural ex-colonial capital. The central Place du Gouvernement, originally a nondescript open area in front of the palace of the Ottoman *dey*, has become Place des Martyrs. The huge statue of the Duke of Orleans, which destroyed the vista of the main new mosque, has been removed. The late-1920s functionalist government palace has been occupied by the powerful Ministry of the Interior, while the presidents of Algeria reside in a pre-independence Moorish villa in El Mouradia, south of the city centre.

The Place Bugeaud, named after the French conqueror, has been renamed Place de l'Émir-Abdelkader, after the leader of the resistance to the French. A martial statue of the latter, with drawn sword, has been substituted for the former. Colonial rulers disappeared from street signs, replaced, in Arabic and in French, by leaders and heroes of the War of Independence. Settlers Street (Rue des Colons) became Rue des Libérés.[35] The new landmark of the city is the Mémorial du Martyr, a 93-metre-high sculptural concrete ensemble of three connecting palm leaves (perhaps inspired by the Azadi Tower in Tehran), with three soldier-statues at their base, on the southern heights of Algiers.

Africa

The colonial legacy of African nation-states and capitals is strong – and quite varied. The ex-colonial powers have all bequeathed their language to the new nations as their official means of national communication as

---

* In 1962, after the colonial exodus, Algiers had about 500,000 inhabitants; by 1998, three times that many (Hammache, 'Concentration et étalement urbain à Alger', in Ali Hadjiedj, Claude Chaline and Jocelyne Dubois-Maury (eds), *Alger: Les nouveaux défis de l'urbanisation*, Paris: L'Harmattan, 2003, 116ff.

well as their legal and administrative models. Sub-Saharan Africa did have a pre-colonial urbanization, along trade routes to and from the Sahara, like Timbuktu, Ife, Oyo in Yorubaland (in today's Nigeria), port cities on the Indian Ocean and Great Zimbabwe in the south, although of a delimited kind, and very little in the vast central interior.[36] In Lingala, the lingua franca in Kinshasa and surrounding areas, there is no proper word for city. *Mboka* means 'village' and *mboka ya mundele*, meaning 'White man's village', refers to a city.*

Most of the capital cities are colonial foundations. By exception, Ouagadougou, Burkina Faso, has an indigenous background, as capital of the fifteenth- to eighteenth-century Mossi polity. The colonial constructions were usually given local names, which have survived. European names have fared worse. Fort-Lamy in Chad has become N'djamena; Léopoldville in the Democratic Republic of the Congo was rechristened Kinshasa, one of the few initiatives of the dictator Mobutu Sese Seko surviving his ignominious end; Santa Isabel has become Malabo as capital of Equatorial Guinea; Salisbury in Zimbabwe is now Harare; Lourenço Marques in Mozambique is today's Maputo. But Brazzaville in the Republic of the Congo has kept the name given to it, as a future colonial trading station, by the Société de Géographie de Paris in honour of its founder, the explorer Pierre Savorgnan de Brazza. In 2006, Congo's post-'socialist' government put up a mausoleum to de Brazza with a huge statue, portraying him rather more like a pilgrim, with a wanderer's staff, than as an aristocratic colonial officer. Few ex-colonies have persevered with moving their capitals: only Malawi (from Zomba to Lilongwe) and Nigeria (from Lagos, a kept Portuguese name referring to the lagoon site, to Abuja) went the whole way, while Tanzania (from Dar es Salaam to Dodoma) and Côte d'Ivoire (from Abidjan to Yamoussoukro) never completed the switch. Botswana, Mauritania and Rwanda have had to build capitals. Equatorial Guinea is currently building a new capital, Oyala, with a planned inauguration in 2020.†

---

* T. Trefon, 'Hinges and Fringes: Conceptualizing the Peri-Urban in Central Africa', in Francesca Locatelli and P. Nugent (eds), *African Cities: Competing Claims on Urban Space*, Leiden: Brill, 2009, 16. In Mozambique I have also heard a similar expression referring to the colonial cities.

† In March 2015 the Egyptian government suddenly announced plans to build a new capital '12 times the size of Manhattan' just east of Cairo (*International New York Times*, 17 March 2015, 20).

The urban inheritance of the colonial rulers has everywhere been overwhelmed by post-colonial urban migration explosion and socio-economic crises, but is still discernible: the British garden cities, from Accra to Nairobi and Harare; the representative French *centres-villes*, most elaborate on the *plateaux* of Dakar and Abidjan; the Portuguese division of *cidade baixa and cidade alta* ('low city', 'high city'); and the sturdy German church and administration buildings from the brief German rule before World War I.

Politically, the birth of African nation-states is much more polarized between historical alternatives than Asia, illustrated above by Jakarta and Kuala Lumpur. Colonialism was buried in South Africa only after the settler state had imploded, leaving a colonial inheritance, and had to be fought to death in Portuguese Africa and almost in Zimbabwe. At the other end, French West Africa produced national fathers – Félix Houphouët-Boigny of Côte d'Ivoire, Léopold Sédar Senghor of Senegal and a host of lesser figures – far surpassing Thomas Macaulay's dream of British enculturation of India: 'a class of persons African in blood and colour but French in tastes, in opinions, in morals, and intellect.'* In 1958 all the main political leaders of French Africa, save Sékou Touré of Guinea, campaigned in a referendum, successfully, for a 'no' to independence and 'yes' to a French-African Community – to little avail, as a rising tide of nationalism soon forced the same leaders to ask Charles de Gaulle politely for independence, which he graciously granted in 1960.[37]

True, the French had invested much more in their assimilation project. The first of the famous 'Four Communes' of Senegal got full municipal rights in 1872. Since 1848 they had had the right to elect a deputy to the French National Assembly; after 1914 that deputy was always an African.[38] Two such deputies, Blaise Diagne and Léopold Senghor, also became government ministers. So did Houphouët-Boigny, from 1957 to 1959, during the Algerian war; he had been elected to the French National Assembly from Côte d'Ivoire in 1945.

Accra was the first fully national capital of sub-Saharan Africa through the independence of Ghana (formerly called the Gold Coast) in 1957. Ghana's was basically a negotiated independence. Dependent

---

* The quotation is a paraphrase of Thomas Macaulay's 'Minute on Education in the Council of India', 2 February 1835.

parliamentary government had been established by the British after
World War II, and the election of 1951 was won by Kwame Nkrumah,
in prison for subversive agitation. After some hesitation the governor-
general set him free and asked him to form a government, and upon
successive electoral victories by Nkrumah and his party, Her Majesty's
government declared that Ghana would be independent by 6 March
1957.

The capital was at the time one of the largest Black African cities, with
a population of 377,000 in 1960, without any central monumentality.[39]
The old Danish slave-trading fort which housed the British governor-general was largely hidden from view. The city and the country were
riding on a world cocoa boom – soon to crash. Already, in 1923, an
imperial White Paper had concluded that 'segregation of Europeans and
Asiatics is not absolutely essential', and in Accra the European Quarter
and enclaves were mainly separated by economic barriers.[40] The business district was, of course, dominated by European firms, but did also
include a number of African ones. The electrifyingly charismatic leader
of Ghanaian(-cum-pan-African) nationalism, Nkrumah, had his political base in Accra and, like Nehru and Sukarno, took a very active and
important part in changing the existing cityscape.

Although an avowed socialist, formed in British left-wing and
anti-imperialist milieux, Nkrumah rather early showed tendencies to
megalomania. In 1956, as Chief Minister of the still-British Gold Coast,
he had a huge bronze statue of himself erected outside the legislative
assembly. He actively promoted architectural office modernism in
Accra, but his main urbanistic interest was monumentality. A new
national parade ground was laid out, Black Star Square, with a Roman-
type Independence Arch and, at the opposite end of the square, a
modern arch with an elevated monumental presidential dais from which
to look at the mobilized masses and receive their admiration. A modern
State House was built, although Nkrumah personally preferred either
the suburban colonial Flagstaff House or Christiansborg Castle, the
governor-general's old Danish slaving fort. Plans and funds for a new
parliament building were diverted to an exuberant building for the 1965
summit of the Organization of African Unity. The former was built later,
in the apt symbolic form of an Ashanti stool (a symbol of authority). The
1958 town plan's proposal to turn the non-urbanized, swampy coast-
line, a fishermen's base, into a touristic promenade was thus thwarted

and the proposal to expand the city's green open space from the gardens surrounding a few public buildings was ignored.[41] As a typical colonial city, Accra also has an ethnic issue; it is the original site of the Ga people, whose land rights and customs are in friction with modern notions of individualist property rights and multi-cultural cosmopolitanism.[42]

Nkrumah was toppled by the military in 1966, and an officially proclaimed iconoclasm succeeded the previous hagiography. The Black Star Square was abandoned and left decaying. Nkrumah was resurrected in the early 1990s, by the new military government of Flight Lieutenant Jerry Rawlings, who had a monumental mausoleum created with a new statue. By 2008, Black Star Square had not been fitted into contemporary democratic Ghana. Directly, Nkrumah's downfall matched the style of his career. But he was representative, rather than unique, of the first generation of African national leaders, many of whom began to fall to military coups in the mid-1960s, many of whom became megalomaniac and virtually all of whom were both victims of and contributors to economic collapse.

The nation of Nigeria is almost caricaturally colonial. It derives its name from a London *Times* journalist who later married the colonial governor, and in 2014 it celebrated the centenary of the imperial unification of the North and the Southern coastal colonies.* Its colonially inherited (in 1960) national capital was Lagos (locally called Eko), a Southern port city. Nigerian independence was a very amicable affair. The Northern conservative prime minister, Alhaji Sir Abubakar Tafawa Balewa, in his independence speech, paid 'tribute to . . . successive British Governments' and referred to 'all our friends in the Colonial Office'. He also addressed 'the representative of those who have made Nigeria': 'Representatives of the Regional Governments, of former Central Governments, of the Missionary Societies, and of the Banking and Commercial enterprises'. One other actor contributing to the making of Nigeria was also represented on the square, but remained un-named – the people.[43]

Lagos was a controversial capital, and had been for decades. It was pronouncedly excentric in a large, multi-ethnic and multicultural

---

* Flora Shaw was an extraordinary female journalist in the Victorian patriarchal world and the colonial editor of *The Times*. Her piece on substituting Nigeria for the Royal Niger Company Territories appeared in *The Times* on 8 January 1897. In 1902 she married Frederick Lugard, the governor-general of the unified colonial Nigeria from 1914 to 1919.

country, in which the North could not be marginalized as an underdeveloped backwater. It was the most populous part, with a well-developed
and well-preserved Muslim power structure – Nigeria was, after all, the
showcase of imperial indirect rule. In spite of this and Lagos's taxing
tropical climate, the British stuck to Lagos. One of the reasons given by
the new governor-general, Sir Hugh Clifford – a professional imperial
administrator whose career included postings on the Malacca Straits
and in Trinidad – is remarkable:

> This is a function [of government] which [we] can hardly hope to
> fulfil unless the principal operations of the Government are carried
> on in the midst of the most active life and thought of the country,
> whence it is able to maintain the closest touch with every section of
> the community and where its activities are exposed to the closest
> scrutiny and criticism.*

The later national rulers, civilian and military, who moved the
Nigerian capital to a new site, Abuja, obviously did not agree with Sir
Hugh but they had other, heavier reasons. In the parliamentary jockey-
ing for power in colonial Nigeria of the 1950s, the status of Lagos became
a bone of contention. Although multi-ethnic and multi-cultural –
including an Afro-Brazilian quarter – Lagos was largely a Yoruba city in
Yorubaland, which was then the Western Region. The Yoruba-dominated
Action Group wanted to keep the rich port-revenue-generating city as
part of its region, and as a price for it was prepared to accept a move
of the capital. The other, larger Southern party, the National Council of
Nigeria and the Cameroons (NCNC), rooted in Igboland in the Eastern
Region but also politically majoritarian in Lagos, wanted to separate the
city from the Western Region as a federal district. At the time of independence, the latter was the situation.

The architectural framework of Balewa's independence speech corresponded well to its rhetorical content. It was held at a new square (since
named after him) laid out by a private developer near the National

---

* *Lagos Weekly Record,* 14 February 1920, quoted in W. Adebawi, 'Abuja', in Bekker and
  Therborn, *Power and Powerlessness,* 87. Imperial enlightenment did not exclude the
  development, from the early 1920s, of a European reservation in Ikoyi on the eastern
  part of Lagos Island (L. Fourchard, 'Lagos', in ibid., 67).

Assembly in the elite Ikoyi district, originally reserved for Europeans, of Lagos Island. It has a multiple-entrance gate, seemingly to fight off evil spirits through four fierce horses on their hind legs, and topped with seven eagles with spread wings. For the occasion a new Independence House was built on the square, a twenty-three-storey office building in standard corporate International Style. There is also an Arch of Remembrance commemorating the Nigerians who died for the British Empire in the two world wars.

It soon became clear that the national government could not cope with the demographic pull of Lagos and its chaos-creating effects of over-crowding and congestion, aggravated by its geography centred on the islands of Lagos and Victoria, with under-developed connections to the swampy mainland areas. The haughty conservative elites of the North were not comfortable in the nation's capital and received no respect from the Southern 'rabble'. The bloody, ultimately suppressed Igbo 'Biafra' secession of 1967 to 1970 put national integration and consolidation on top of the agenda. After a rapid investigation, the military ruler Murtala Mohammed announced a move of the capital to the centre of the country in 1976. In 1991 the capital move to Abuja was officially announced.[44]

The new capital is publicly referred to as the 'Centre of Unity', and Nigerians may proudly tell you that this is the most developed part of Nigeria. Globalized town planning was recruited: an Anglo-American consortium, Doxiadis, and Kenzō Tange, who finally designed the central city. The formal outcome is something similar to Islamabad, without anything of the design or architectural flair of Brasília. Like in both its predecessors, the focus of Abuja is on the (east-north-eastern) edge, where the Three Arms Zone is located, dominated by a green-domed National Assembly but also including a presidential compound and the Supreme Court. Behind this display is a back-up of military and police barracks. In front of the zone is the Eagle Square. Then, following the functionalist canon of capital design, there are a Ministerial Zone, a Cultural Zone and a Central Business District.

As a manifestation of Nigerian modernism, Abuja has proved an attractive success, and it is aiming to become a 'world-class city' with a corresponding high-rise skyline.[45] Its national-unity function has been questioned, but nurtured. The city first built a grand mosque, resented in the Christian South, but after lobbying it was followed by an ecumenical Christian cathedral. Like Brasília, the modernity of Abuja proper contrasts with the unserviced satellite towns. In this sense, Abuja is yet another example of the powerlessness of Third World cities.[46]

The street toponymy of Abuja exhibits an extreme ecumene, which should probably be interpreted as expressing a fashion for history-conscious post-ideological policy. Not only are all the military dictators of Nigeria – even the most despicable and corrupt, like Sani Abacha – commemorated in street names. In eastern Abuja you find Winston Churchill, Josip Broz Tito and Mao Tse-tung side by side, all leading up to Malcolm Fraser (the right-wing Australian prime minister). Jimmy Carter joins Charles de Gaulle, and Vladimir Lenin takes you to John F. Kennedy.*

The major cities of French sub-Saharan Africa were Dakar, Senegal, the capital of French West Africa; Abidjan, Côte d'Ivoire, growing rapidly on cocoa and coffee; and Brazzaville, Congo, the capital of French Equatorial Africa. All were colonial creations, but each had a distinct history of its own. Dakar was the biggest of the nineteenth-century autonomous communes, conveying French citizenship on its official residents. Abidjan was an economic upstart. Brazzaville was the main entrepôt of equatorial trade and gained political renown as the locus of a Gaullian conference on the future of the French Empire in 1944.

Dakar was the centre and the model of French colonial development and urban planning.[47] It elected an African mayor in the 1920s, Blaise Diagne, who a decade later became a minister of colonies. Nevertheless, it had a distinctive colonial layout, with a Europeanized hill promontory plateau of business and administration, clearly demarcated from the low-lying indigenous *medina*. From around 1930 Dakar was also pioneering a new colonial style of architecture, 'Sudanese' (*soudanais*), inspired by the famous Mosque of Djenné in today's Mali. Dakar's Cathedral of the African Memory actually looks more like a mosque than a Catholic cathedral, although it also shares chracteristics with the Hagia Sofia in Istanbul. A couple of major hospitals and the gate of the major market are clearly echoes of Djenné. The idea seems to have been similar to a British conception in India, of stylistically demonstrating a

---

* Brunel, *Brunel Abuja City Guide*, 2nd ed., Abuja, 2007. Less surprisingly, there is further east an African quarter remembering Nelson Mandela, Kwame Nkrumah, Thomas Sankara and others.

continuity between the current European empire with the old empires of the region at their zenith of power and glory.[48]

The national leader and first president of Senegal, Léopold Sédar Senghor, great poet of Négritude and member of the Académie Francaise, was an astute politician. In 1959, somewhat before the majority of the thoroughly Frenchified African leaders, he understood that time was rapidly running out for formal colonial empires, however dressed up as 'Community'. Himself a Catholic, Senghor built his national power base through skilful alliances with the powerful Muslim Mouride brotherhood. One of the few new monumental buildings of independent Dakar was a new central mosque.

Like other new national leaders, Senghor was actively interested in urban planning, but primarily for maintaining French regulations; the colonial city centre had just changed inhabitants, including the president of the republic succeeding the governor-general. Outside the core centre, an Independence Square with a tall obelisk was raised – in Avenue General de Gaulle. The central monument to the Senegalese Tirailleurs (riflemen), valiant colonial troops in both world wars, was of course maintained, with the addition of their 'defence of the "Free World" ' – presumably in Korea – but without any line of commemoration of the unknown number of them shot dead by French soldiers in the autumn of 1944 for protesting against undisbursed wages and other maltreatment.*

Senegal has had its spells of authoritarian rule, but not of military dictatorships, megalomaniacs or untrammelled red-meat capitalism. This, and the planning foresight of the French, may explain why the main demographic expansion after independence has not produced the kind of slums you find in Nairobi or Kinshasa. The satellite city of Pikine – with more than a million inhabitants in 2006 – is certainly under-serviced in its ubiquitous sands inland from Dakar proper, but it is an organized city of elected *arrondissement* governments with some resources (largely thanks to foreign donors) for local development.

In the 1970s, Senegal was hit both by the global oil and commodity crises and by an extraordinary drought in the Sahel region. The cultural vigour and centrality of Dakar could no longer be maintained, in spite

---

* The story of the protest massacre I owe to the conversation of French Africanist historian Odile Goerg.

of its International Fair in impressive Africanist modernism.* Economically as well demographically, the city was overtaken by Abidjan, the capital of Côte d'Ivoire, from the air a shining agglomeration with a centre of white (moderate) high-rises set in a lagoon. Its plateau is smaller than Dakar's but more beautifully located.

The founding father of the Ivory Coast, or Côte d'Ivoire as it now wants to be called even in English, Félix Houphouët-Boigny, had a French education and an African chief's authority. He was the leading Francophone African politician of his generation, the head servant of the French Empire. He was also a successful planter and businessman, and Côte d'Ivoire in the 1960s and 1970s had something of the same capitalist flair as Kenya. National Abidjan was also the most French of African cities, full of French bureaucrats, businessmen, restaurants and *boulangeries*. Like other colonial cities, Abidjan had been racially and economically segregated, more sharply than many because of its topography of easy demarcation. This stratification was reproduced after independence in the formal, planned city. Abidjan was divided into a set of autonomous communes, similar to the Parisian *arrondissements*, with their own revenue base and budget. Given the socio-economic division of the city, that meant that in 1990 the per capita budget of the most prosperous commune (excluding the plateau, with its tiny population), Abobo, was sixteen times larger than that of the poorest, Attécoubé.[49]

In the 1980s, Houphouët-Boigny wanted to make his native village, Yamoussoukro, the capital of the country. The star piece of the new capital was to be a Catholic basilica – in a country at least half Muslim – in a style and with an arcaded forecourt similar to Saint Peter's, but much larger: the largest church in the world. It was consecrated by a fellow conservative, Pope John Paul II, in 1990. The basilica is the end focus of the city, corresponding to Three Powers Plaza in Brasília. There are secular public buildings, including a parliament, a politicians' hotel and an airport. There is a kind of city of a quarter of million on a vast grass expanse in the centre of the country, and several institutions of higher learning built by modernist French architects. But the capital project seems to have been put on the back burner for the time being,

* Singled out for well-deserved architectural praise in M. Herz (ed.), *African Modernism*, Zurich: Park Books, 2015, 192ff.

after the death of its author (in 1993) and the succession crises.* The
lustre of Abidjan was also peeled off by civil wars around the millennium, while Dakar is recovering a good deal of its former centrality to
Francophone Africa.

On opposite banks of the Malebo (formerly Stanley) Pool are the
capitals of the two Congos, the least democratic of which is currently
officially called the Democratic Republic of Congo (DRC), while the
mostly less authoritarian, chaotic and violent one is simply known as the
Republic of Congo. The latter and its capital, Brazzaville, are much
smaller than the DRC and its capital, Kinshasa, which was until 1966
Léopoldville and until 1960 Belgian.

The two cities should not be carelessly lumped together. Though
both have had their share of popular impoverishment, violence and
dictatorship, they have had quite different historical experiences: colonial, post-colonial and transitional. Brazzaville followed the amicable
path of separation from the empire, including voting 'no' to independence in 1958. South of the river in Kinshasa, independence was
precipitated by anti-colonial riots in January 1959. Although Belgium
accepted independence, the anti-colonial resentment shocked the
Belgians and their NATO allies, leading to the US-organized murder of
the Congo's first prime minister, Patrice Lumumba. But nationalist
resentment ran even in the veins of the 'West'-oriented local rivals of
Lumumba, who were accomplices in his murder. By the mid-1960s
Lumumba was officially rehabilitated as a 'national hero' and the road
to the airport changed from Leopold III Avenue to Avenue Patrice
Lumumba. The main street of the centre had already been turned into
Boulevard du 30 Juin (Independence Day) from Boulevard Albert I
and Place du Trône into Place de la Nation. Colonial statues were
swiftly removed and have not returned. The DRC exemplifies a ruptural
national transition.

The interconnections and interchanges between the two river capitals
should not be ignored, however. As national capitals in difficult times,
they have provided sources of provision and migration outlets for each
other, and they share important aspects of modern urban culture, like

---

* The basilica is well analyzed from an architectural perspective by Nnamdi Elleh,
  Architecture and Power in Africa, Santa Barbara, CA: Praeger, 2002; less so the capital
  project.

popular music (Cuban-inspired rumba and jazz) and vibrant fashion display.*

Kinshasa poses some particular challenges to any meaningful analysis of capital cities and nation-state power. In a very apt formulation, the Congolese state has been characterized as an 'absentee landlord'.[50] The great anthropologist of the city Filip De Boeck has said that 'Kinshasa seems to a large extent to have unhooked [*dégagée*] from its architecture', and that 'all forms of planned and controlled urbanization stopped immediately after independence'.[51] Between 1960 and 2000, Kinshasa's population multiplied twelve-fold[52] – i.e., in forty years of virtually permanent economic and political crisis. No urban planner and no national government could be expected to cope properly with that. By comparison, in sixty years of predominant boom from 1871 to 1930, Chicago increased tenfold.[53]

All African capitals had an explosion of immigration after independence. Colonial Africa was very under-urbanized in comparison with the rest of the world. In 1955, about 6 per cent of the population of sub-Saharan Africa (excluding South Africa) was urban,[54] while around 16 per cent of the Third World population as a whole (excluding China, North Vietnam and North Korea) was.[55] One reason for this was that all the colonial powers – Belgian, British, French, Portuguese – did their best, though always less than fully successfully, to keep the Africans out of the cities beyond necessary domestic workers and some labourers and industrial workers, in principle as guest workers only. This, of course, enhanced the urban attraction of White opportunities once the colonial apartheid system broke down at the moment of independence.

To the lucky few Africans with an urban permit, this flood of migrants opened lucrative opportunities, which also boosted demand. In the case of Kinshasa, a Congolese historian has noted three special mechanisms of interest.[56] One was aspiring politicians recruiting voters from their tribes by allocating public urban land to them. Another was traditional

---

* Gary Stewart, *Rumba on the River*, London: Verso, 2000; Wim Cuyvers et al., *Brakin*, Maastricht: Lars Muller Verlag, 2006; G. Tati, 'Brazzaville', in Bekker and Therborn, *Power and Powerlessness*, on Brazzaville. While not all the same and less unequal, the Brazzaville-Kinshasa relation has some affinity with that of Montevideo and Buenos Aires. In August 2010 there were two official boats a day from Kinshasa to Brazzaville (or vice versa), at prices difficult for popular *citadines*.

chiefs of the urban and peri-urban areas using their customary land rights to sell urban plots. Third, local district mayors and similar functionaries sold public interstitial terrains, like 'football land, steep slopes, vegetable plots, sidewalks' for migrant plots. However, the main reason for the particularly massive rural exodus in the Congo has no doubt been the ravaging of the countryside by incessant civil wars and marauding militias.

Enormous rural migration to a city without real industrialization or significant formal-services growth is, of course, testimony to a failed state, incapable of providing security of life or protecting livelihood in the countryside. However, the citations from Kobia and De Boeck were written in the early 2000s against the background of the catastrophic 1990s, after Mobutu's disastrous rule of the 1970s and 1980s, the big-city riots and lootings in 1991 and 1993, the lesser looting of 1992 and the internal war of 1998.

By the second decade of this century, Kinshasa appears to function rather like an ordinary big African city, which means badly but not beyond the pale. The state displays a network of *maisons communales* and *bureaux de quartier*, often painted in the blue and red colours of the nation, although not much activity was going on in the one I visited. State monumentality has been restored, refurbished and expanded. The big former governor-general's palace has become the Palace of the Nation, the official presidential residence. In front of it is the mausoleum of the murdered President Laurent-Désiré Kabila (father of Joseph), and nearby are the Supreme Court and the ministerial quarter, slightly shabby but accessible. A second monumental centre has also been built by the Chinese in view of the fiftieth anniversary of the nation, with an eight-lane Boulevard Triomphal, a new Martyrs' Stadium and a renovated Palace of the People for the elected National Assembly. The two first leaders of the country, President Joseph Kasavubu and Prime Minister Patrice Lumumba, have statues.* The university has started to operate again, but for the students it is quite complicated to get to/from the huge south side campus to the centre of the city (buses exist, but not many, and no direct ones). There is little new formal civilian

---

* I visited Kinshasa in August 2010, and have followed the city on and off since then on the Internet. An overview of the monumental politics of independent Congo is given by Isidore Ndaywel è Nziem, *Nouvelle histoire du Congo*, Kinshasa: Le Cri, 2008, 670ff.

architecture,* and the central roundabouts are still unpaved – although in 2015 they were provided with surveillance cameras – and surrounded by dilapidated streets. The humanitarian and military agencies of the United Nations maintain their own special, securitized *quartier*.

The grand monumental complex which Mobutu started but never completed at an interchange known as L'Échangeur, thought to be intended as a monument to independence, is still a ruin, like the Congolese nation-state. But its concrete tower has become *the* landmark of the city, limping on, like the nation, in spite of everything.

East Africa was turned to the Indian Ocean, which at the time of European colonialism had become a less economically and culturally dynamic channel than the Atlantic. Its slave trade was with Arabia, which had much less demand than the plantations of Euro-America. African nationalist politics developed later in the east than on the West Coast, although it caught up rapidly around 1960 and had some specific dimensions.

Kenya, in contrast to all West and Equatorial Africa, had a White settler problem, demographically much weaker than in Rhodesia/Zimbabwe, but nevertheless significant on the fertile high plateau around Nairobi and in the city itself. Europeans ran the city council in the 1950s. The imperial 'Master Plan for A Colonial City' of 1948 Nairobi was not explicitly racist, but it took the racialized functional division of the city for granted and basically ignored the African housing issues.[57]

All three countries of British East Africa had a socio-economically significant Asian trading minority, on the middle rung between the British rulers/settlers and the Africans. The Indian Bazaar was a central area of colonial Nairobi. After national independence, the situation of the (mainly Indian) Asians deteriorated, and in Uganda they were (in principle) all forcefully deported by the military dictator Idi Amin. Anti-Asian animosity, discrimination and persecution hurt the East African economies, particularly Uganda's, but it also delayed national intellectual development, as many regional scholars and intellectuals were of Asian background. However, this context did not prevent the

---

* An international, London-based consortium, Hawkwood Properties, has since 2009 been building an upscale 'River City' (Cité du Fleuve) on an island in the river. From promotional materials, most of the villas and apartment buildings look like a rather mediocre middle-class suburb by Latin American or European standards.

architect of Indian descent Anthony Almeida from playing an important role in the national modernism of Dar es Salaam.*

East African politics harboured much stronger pre-colonial features
than West African. The Mau Mau Rebellion in Kenya of the 1950s,
driven by settler encroachments on Kikuyu land and denied access to
Nairobi, was the last pre-modern, proto-nationalist movement in Africa.
It was ferociously repressed by the British. In Uganda, the pre-colonial
kingdom of the Baganda people was reproduced inside the colonial
framework. After independence, the role of the *kabaka*, the king, has
been hotly controversial. The current, more or less elected government
has invited him back from exile, and the capital, Kampala, now includes
not only the royal compound but also an area around it under the juris-
diction of the *kabaka* and his council – a kind of African Vatican City,
but of a worldly, ethnic power.

Nairobi is the undisputed capitalist hub of East Africa and the main
UN centre in Africa. By African standards it is well organized, upgraded
by a post-millennium boom. The city centre sports fancy public transport, functioning public telephones (in 2006, before the mobile era),
even a few decent public toilets. Its monumentality is modern and
sophisticated, with the Kenyatta International Convention Centre as its
landmark, a round, lid-covered tower beside a low-rise stone pavilion
capped by a conic roof.† Jomo Kenyatta, the first president and the Father

* ArchiAfrika Projekt, *Modern Architecture in Tanzania around Independence*,
  conference proceedings (Dar Es Salaam, Tanzania, July 27–29, 2005), Utrecht:
  ArchiAfrika Projekt, 2005. Dar es Salaam also has some pieces of sturdy German
  architecture, a respectful reconnection with a pre–World War I colony. Ernst May,
  who after his stint in the Soviet Union in the early 1930s went to Africa to escape the
  Nazis, has left an exquisite mosque on the University of Dar es Salaam campus, and in
  the 1970s West Germany built and financed a new Faculty of Engineering (Antoni
  Folkers, *Modern Architecture in Africa*, Amsterdam: Sun, 2010, 170ff).
† The Convention Center has an interesting history, vividly illustrating the important
  role of contingency in city building. It was originally meant to be the headquarters of
  the ruling KANU party, but when the World Bank decided to hold its first meeting in
  Africa (in 1973) in Nairobi the unfinished party HQ was deemed the only respectable
  venue. For the purpose, the tower was tripled in height and the auditorium vastly
  expanded. It was designed by a Norwegian architect, Karl-Henrik Nöstvik, on loan
  from the Norwegian aid agency to the Kenyan Ministry of Public works, who
  recommended him to Kenyatta. There is a national and international consensus that
  Nöstvik produced an inspired work, but he does not seem to have built anything
  remarkable either before or since. Cf. Shadi Bahbaran and Manuel Herz, *Nairobi
  Kenya*, Basel, Lars Müller, 2014, 127ff.

of the Nation, is seated patriarchally on an elevated chair in the middle of the government district. In the vast African savannah, Uhuru (Freedom) Park is a metaphorical monument based on the example of Kenyatta.

It fits the starkly capitalist character of Nairobi that the city includes two of the largest slums of Africa, Kibera and Mathare,[58] manifesting not the racial-colonial but the economic-social dualism of untrammelled capitalism. All the failed, often brutal slum-clearance projects testify to the futility of dealing with popular (migration) demands negatively. And the slums are not just negations of decent human housing; they have their own complex economics and sociology. Kibera was originally a settlement of Nubian colonial soldiers, whose descendants drew profits from letting to Kikuyu migrants from the 1950s on. There is a certain parallel to the Rio *favelas*, originally settled by soldiers of Northeastern Brazil's Canudos war of the late nineteenth century.[59] Kibera today is not only a vast informal city of slumlords and their tenants – less of auto-constructions – but also a differentiated agglomeration with its own services, including a radio station.[60]

Dar es Salaam is a big bustling port city; in comparison with Nairobi it still lives up to its name, Haven of Peace, although it has recently heated up economically. After smashing the Mau Mau Rebellion, the British acquiesced in East African independence, and neither Tanzania nor Uganda really had to struggle. The national leader of Tanzania, Julius Nyerere, was a socialist counterpoint to Nkrumah in Ghana, personally modest but with national ambitions hardly less grand than Nkrumah's pan-African dreams. There is no personality cult in Dar, only a fountain-cum-obelisk, Uhuru Torch, to commemorate independence.

Nyerere's project of regrouped *ujamaa* (independence) village socialism was more concrete than Nkrumah's plans for a socialist industrial Ghana, but both failed. In 1970 Nyerere also launched a project for a new capital city, inland and more central: Dodoma. It is a plan very characteristic of Nyerere and his rule, and very different from contemporary Abuja. Dodoma was planned and has been built as a provincial African city: low-rise, poly-centric, non-monumental. A modest parliament constitutes the political centre. The only monumental building is the building of the then-ruling and only party, shining white on a hill outside of the city. (Now it is a conference centre.) After the fall of Nyerere the project was largely suspended, but never quite abandoned.

With better economic times after 2000 it was taken up again, and a construction company of the Chinese People's Liberation Army promised to build a new and larger Parliament within a year. It did. Today, regular parliament sessions take place in Dodoma, the city's administrative functions are being extended and Nyerere has got his unwanted statue. But Dar continues to be the real capital.

Alongside Nairobi and Dar es Salaam, Kampala appears like a post-colonial hill station, with a central parliamentary compound but without much national iconography, and socially rather sedate in spite of its two decades of violent political conflict (1966–86). On a short visit, I found no traces of Ernst May's years from 1945 as planner of Kampala, but he did with some success push for African urban housing.[61]

The southern ruptural capitals of Harare and Maputo, formerly Salisbury and Lourenço Marques, had a very different colonial formation: one the savannah garden city of British settlement, the other the more concentrated, vertically divided port city of the Portuguese. Both countries had to fight with arms for their independence. Currently, both countries are taking the capitalist road, after initially making the opposite choice, but their urban toponymy reveals two different anti-imperialist options. Maputo still bears witness to a universalist Marxist-Leninist orientation, with central streets commemorating not only Lenin but also Mao Tse-tung, Kim Il-sung and so on. Harare's streets, on the other hand, are all African: Julius Nyerere, Samora Machel, Kenneth Kaunda, Robert Mugabe (not for the principal street) and Zimbabwean nationalist figures.[62]

The Ex-Colonial Fate

The ex-colonial nations all had to cope with nationally alien capitals, founded or centrally transformed by alien powers and with the enduring duality between the ex-colonial and the indigenous city, manifested in architecture, building quality, street layout and service provision. The extremes of colonialism were usually reproduced urbanistically in a national divide between a tiny political (or politically connected) elite and the popular masses. Upon independence, many ex-colonial countries continued the capitalist path of their former masters, but their capitals rarely built any sizeable bourgeois, not to speak of popular, neighbourhoods. The indigenous class of capital was too small, and it hardly ever managed to produce any sizeable areas of decent, well-serviced popular housing, for lack of economic resources, focused leadership and competent management. There have been urban improvements in recent times, but they have not been able to keep pace with the challenges of urban immigration.

With urbanization, slum populations are growing (except in North Africa), in 'developing nations' from 650 million in 1990 to 883 million in 2012; however, the share of the urban population living in slums is going down, from 46 to 33 per cent, which is more significant, as pre-urban rural housing can be worse than an urban slum. A noteworthy singular case of slum development is Iraq, where, thanks to George W. Bush and Tony Blair, the slum population quadrupled from 2000 to 2012 and its urban share tripled, from 17 to 53 per cent. Generally speaking, slums are most prevalent in poor countries: about 60 per cent of the urban population in sub-Saharan Africa, a third of South Asia's and a quarter of Latin America's.[63] It is normally more prevalent in smaller cities than in larger ones and capitals. Exceptions to this are Dhaka in Bangladesh, La Paz in Bolivia and Manila in the Philippines, countries which also have larger slum populations than their surrounding regions.[64]

In urban semiotics, the new capitals were anxious to display their modernity while also, from the Malay Archipelago to the West African Sahel, willing to recognize the urban authority of pre-colonial chiefs and rulers. Monumentality was largely modern, but almost always had to incorporate pre-modern, pre-colonial motifs. The stark socio-economic duality and hierarchy of the colonial city was maintained virtually everywhere, although the personal vanity of the new national rulers varied enormously, mostly in Africa: between, on one hand, Sékou Touré and Julius Nyerere and, on the other, Nkrumah, Houphouët-Boigny and Mobutu. The explosion of urban immigration overwhelmed almost all the ex-colonial capitals. Only Seoul, riding on tremendous economic success – on exceptional Japanese colonial foundations – has been able to cope successfully. The result of all this has been fragile and contested national power spanning extremely polarized societies and capitals – not only in resources but also in language, family and religion.

5

National Foundations: Reactive Modernization

By the mid-nineteenth century, European and US imperialism were threatening all the rest of the world. Most of Africa and large chunks of Asia were conquered and subjugated. There were a few exceptional cases of successful resistance, however, of pre-modern realms embarking on historically updating transformations of their own and managing to stave off at least the worst imperialist encroachments. These changes came from above, from sections of the traditional elite, who alone had the means to acquire adequate knowledge of the new military, technological, economic, political and cultural challenges of the world. This was the reactive modernization route to modernity.

'Reactive modernization' refers to socio-political transformations towards a conception of political rule at least decisively dependent on, if not necessarily legally or ideologically deriving from, the nation, brought about from above, in a context of acute external threat. Constitutions and civic rights to vote, for instance, were originally fought for by popular forces from below, but on this route to modernity they were launched from above in order to withstand threatening external assaults by US and European imperialism. The crucial idea learnt from the predators was that the strength of a polity was not reducible to its weapons technology but derived from the commitment of its population. This commitment and cohesive force seemed to derive from institutions like constitutions, citizen equality before the law and rights of political participation, all sustained by public education.[*]

Japan is the paradigmatic example, first threatened by an assault of the US Navy in 1853; in 1868 embarking upon radical, rapid and successful change; and, a generation later, becoming an imperialist predator itself. Several other attempts failed: above, we noticed how Korea and Egypt were forced into colonial subjection. China was a semi-failure, which we shall deal with in the chapter on Communism. Most failures were due to external pressure, military or economic, but occasionally internal reaction was crucial.

Reactive modernization is radical change from above. Popular forces appear here driven not by social ascendancy but by fear of social and cultural decline and of the unknown. In East Asia this was less of a problem, as there was no dominant autonomous religion whose clerics could whip up popular anger. Confucianism, the prevailing moral discourse of China and Korea, was secular and emperor-centred. The huge, and horribly repressed, peasant rebellions of the mid- to late-nineteenth century in China and Korea, the Taiping and the Tonghak Rebellions, did not constitute anti-modernist reaction. On the contrary, they were egalitarian peasant uprisings, modernized by imported religious syncretism. Confucianism had weakened in Japan, but was richly compensated by empire-loyalist Shintoism. Siamese Buddhism may have had more potential of autonomy, but ancient Hindu-Buddhist notions of kingship bound it to the court. In Tokyo and Bangkok, modernization was wrapped in the aura of monarchy, to which there was no religious alternative. The main dangers in East Asia were dynastic and court intrigues, which in a vulnerable geopolitical context proved fatal in Korea and thwarted Qing attempts at modernization in China, although the Middle Kingdom turned republic did escape full colonization, just barely.

The situation was different in the Muslim world, where the clergy of a universalist salvation religion could speak to the masses in a religious idiom of protest, as their Christian colleagues did successfully against Guiseppe Garibaldi in the Kingdom of Naples and, at least with violent

---

[*] This process of citizenship and citizens' rights from above first became clear to me during a global comparative study of the history of the right to vote, 'The Right to Vote and the Four Routes to/through Modernity', in Rolf Torstendahl (ed.), *State Theory and State History*, London: Sage, 1992, 62–92.

significance, against the Mexican Revolution in the 1920s and 1930s. Modernizing rulers of the Muslim world faced this problem again and again, from Sultan Selim III in Istanbul in 1807 to the Afghan Communists of the late 1970s and early 1980s and Reza Shah Pahlavi in the Tehran of 1979. The Afghan modernizing king Amanullah, having survived one tribal revolt with the help of the Soviet Air Force, was chased from his throne in Kabul in 1929, just before Albert Speer was to come to help him rebuild the city. Instead, Speer became Hitler's architect.[*]

Though Japan is the model case of reactive modernization, it was not alone. On a more modest level, Siam (today's Thailand) also made it, helped by Franco-British rivalry. The Ottoman Empire failed, due both to domestic reaction and external assaults, but out of it came the Turkish Republic, successfully modernizing from above a new capital out of a previous provincial backwater. Persia was also luckier than its eastern neighbour, again helped by intense inter-imperialist rivalry, in its case between Russia and Britain, and in the end less successful than its north-western neighbour, modernist model and ancient rival. Abyssinia (today's Ethiopia) was, with Afghanistan, the only country able to resist an armed colonial assault, decisively defeating the Italians at Adwa in 1896. In 1935 it did succumb to a fascist Italian attack, including aerial bombardments and mustard gas, and Addis Ababa still has some colonial traces of it. But in 1941 a British army drove out the Italians and the emperor returned. In this chapter we shall primarily look into Tokyo, Bangkok, Istanbul and Ankara, but we shall also cast a glance at Tehran and Addis Ababa.

The capitals of reactive modernization have some common characteristics, deriving from their distinctive history. They are all rooted in urban structures and cultures very different from the European and the latter's pre-modern vista of avenues, *piazze*, royal monuments and open-front residences. At the same time, their modernization involved massive imports of European examples. A kind of urban duality ensued, but not, as in the colonial cities, based on racial segregation. The whole project of reactive modernization was to 'modernize' in order to preserve

---

[*] Speer was invited as part of a German team of architects. Albert Speer, *Inside the Third Reich*, New York: Simon & Schuster, 1995, 42. The Communist project of modernization of the late 1970s and early 1980s faced the same reaction, but was brought down only with the help of Saudi money, Pakistani secret services and US arms.

(the most important aspects of) tradition, which included habitation practices of patron-client proximity instead of class segregation. These capitals all changed from above, by powers already in existence, with no significant positive input from below.

Tokyo

Modern Japan began with the Meiji *ishin* of 1868. *Ishin* is usually translated as Restoration (in this case of imperial power), but the Meiji Restoration did not have the restorative implications of the British 'Glorious Revolution' of 1688. It abolished the whole feudal structure of the country and aimed at a cohesive nation capable of resisting the external threats. Did it create a nation-state? On this question there is room for controversy. Popular sovereignty was explicitly enshrined only in the constitution of 1947, imposed by General MacArthur and the US occupation. The crucial question is the position of the emperor.

The Meiji Constitution of 1889 was promulgated in the name of the emperor and countersigned by his government. It did proclaim imperial rather than national rule. Its first article stated: 'The Empire of Japan shall be reigned over and governed by a line of emperors unbroken for ages eternal'. Article IV gave sovereignty to the emperor: 'The Emperor is head of the Empire, combining in Himself the rights of sovereignty and exercises them according the provisions of the present Constitution'.[1]

Meiji Japan was not a Euro-American type of nation-state, but it was much inspired by it and it did become part of the new global family of nation-states, functioning like a constitutional national monarchy. The emperor did not derive from the people but from the Sun Goddess, and only in 1946 did Emperor Hirohito renounce having a divine character. In practice, this hardly meant more than that the Japanese emperor was roughly equivalent to the invocations of God in Euro-American constitutional politics and warfare. The Meiji emperor was not absolutist, bound not only by a constitution but by powerful oligarchical institutions like the Privy Council. Nor was the 'empire of Japan' his personal possession. The 'Restoration' was never driven by the emperor himself – fifteen years old at the time – but in his name by a set of aristocrats and gentry. Their project was the creation of a nation and a state able to stand up in international imperialist storms.

The capital of pre-modern Japan was Edo, by the mid-eighteenth century the largest city in the world, with a population well above one million. It was a major commercial centre, but above all the site of feudal power. It was dominated by the huge castle of the Shogun, surrounded by the hierarchically scaled palaces and gatehouses of the *daimyo* lords with their samurai retinue. The powerless emperor resided in the millenarian capital of Kyoto.

The new modernization was announced in Kyoto by the teenage emperor in a proclamation of amazing globalist radicalism in the imperial Charter Oath of 1868 that all of Japan's actions 'shall follow the accepted practices of the world . . . Knowledge shall be sought out throughout the world so as to strengthen the foundations of imperial rule.'[2]

The Restoration renamed Edo as Tokyo, the Eastern Capital, for reasons not quite clear but implying a new concern with national integration. The immediate effects of the new order were pretty disastrous for the city, as the lords and their huge retinues now were free to leave. The city's population descended to half a million, recovering only by the end of the 1880s. Abandoned *daimyo* palaces were turned into public buildings and foreign embassies and, after a fire in the dilapidated Edo Castle, an imperial residence for sixteen years.[3]

For all their imperial exhortations, the modernizing rulers were little interested in creating a new national capital. Their first priority was a foreign show-window of Japanese bourgeois modernity. The Ginza commercial area was rebuilt, after a fire in 1872, into a Westernized shopping quarter. The Mitsubishi conglomerate built 'London Town' somewhat later, also in new brick. The main symbol of modern Japan and the swinging Tokyo of the 1880s was the Rokumeikan, an upper-class dancing hall and entertainment palace in Italianate style, conceived by Foreign Minister Inoue Kaoru and built by an English architect, Josiah Conder.[4]

A new Imperial Palace was started only in 1884, inaugurated in 1889, built in traditional Japanese wood but with Western interior décor in its audience chambers. (It was rebuilt in stone after World War II.) It is much smaller than the old Shogun castle, an 'empty centre' (Roland Barthes) hidden in a big park. But before settling on Tokyo as the imperial seat, the Meiji rulers put the emperor, with a huge retinue, on popular display throughout the realm. The emperor also toured the country after the 1945 disaster.[5]

The Tokyo rulers rejected most of the orientalist projects of invited German and other foreign architects, opting for modern buildings within the Western repertoire by the European-informed Japanese architects like Katayama Tōkuma, who built the Versailles-inspired crown prince palace in Akasaka, and Tatsuno Kingo, who, after a stint of European studies of banking buildings, built the Bank of Japan, the majestic domed Tokyo Station and, in part, the Diet Building, with its Anatolian Halicarnassus tower.[6]

From 1878, urban services of water and sewage were mandated, and urban planning powers were extended in 1919. However, Tokyo has remained an under-planned city, without any street-planned homogeneity of houses and façades, but at the same time socially cohesive and well serviced. Part of the original layout remains: inside the Yamanote subway line is the old High City, and east of it the old popular Low City. Historical fires, earthquakes, US bombings and a Japanese tradition of discontinuity have made Tokyo a strikingly unhistorical city, although a few Meiji monuments remain, like the statue of the medieval imperial loyalist warrior Kusunoki Masashige and the bronze *torii* of the Yasukuni Shrine to the war dead.

Bangkok

Bangkok became the capital of Siam in 1782, after the Burmese had destroyed the classical capital Ayutthaya, further upstream on the Chao Phraya River. Siam, now Thailand, was an offshoot of Indic civilization; the kings of the current Chakri Dynasty are officially called Rama, at the time of writing Rama IX.[*] Even more than Edo, Bangkok was a waterborne city, on the eastern shore of the river amid countless streams and canals. Commoner housing was usually either floating or built on stilts, and there were floating markets.[†] Siam managed to survive under a

---

[*] According to the late Benedict Anderson, who should know, the dynasty is of Sino-Thai (Teochew-Thai) origin ('Riddles of Yellow and Red', *New Left Review* 97, January/February 2016.)

[†] See Davisi Boontharm, *Bangkok – Formes du commerce et évolution urbaine*, Paris: Éditions Recherches, 2005, 126ff, 167ff. A Thai architect, Sumet Jumsai (*Nam: Cultural Origins in Siam and the West Pacific*, Bangkok: Chalermnit Press, 1988) has developed a civilization philosophy out of the 'water-borne traditions' of the Western Pacific area.

couple of modernizing kings, such as Mongkut (Rama IV, 1851–68) and, in particular, Chulalongkorn (Rama V, 1868–1910), between British Burma to the west and French Indochina to the east. The official name of Bangkok (City of Angels) is the longest of any in the world.* Siam was a tributary to China until 1853 and an absolutist monarchy until 1932. A bloodless civil-military coup preserved the monarchy in a nation-state, renamed Thailand – 'land of the free'.†

Modernization was much narrower in Bangkok, as well as in Siam, than in it was in Tokyo and Japan, in its socio-political base and in its scope of change. Architecturally, it was first expressed in royal palace construction, where it can be followed from the traditional Siamese palace in the grand palace and temple area on Rattanakosin Island by the river, via a mixed early-1880s palace built by British architects, with European-style walls, windows and porticos under Siamese roofs topped by Hinduist *mondop* spires, to the 1890s inland Dusit Palace, built with imported Italian marble in Italian neo-Renaissance style by Italian architects.

Between the two palace compounds, Bangkok's (still) main avenue, Rajdamnoen (Royal Procession Road), was laid out, the 3.2 kilometre stretch of which has the map form of a high-backed chair. On the 'seat' part, the national regime put up a huge, abstract Democracy Monument in 1940 commemorating the regime change of 1932, an ensemble full of number symbolism: four wings of freedom around a shrine topped by a bronze cast of the Constitution. Since 1934 an annual Constitutional Celebration Fair has been held in Rajdamnoen, in memory of the victory of the Democracy Movement in 1932, and the military prime minister

---

* It is given a monumental stone inscription of its own, south of the city hall, and it runs 'Krung Thep MahaNahon Amon Rttanakosin Mhinthara Aythaya Mahadilokphop Noppharat Ratchatani Barirom Udom Ratcchaniwet Maha Sathan Amon Piman Awathan Sathit Sakkathatthiya Witsanukam Prasit' (Bangkok Metropolitan Administration, *Bangkok, Bangkok*, 2001, 10).

† The coup was organized by a small group of young radicals educated in France, who formed a People's Party. It had two main leaders: a civilian socialist, Pridi Banomyong, and a military nationalist, Pibul Songkram. When they fell out, the latter won and became prime minister in 1938. As such, he allied Thailand with Japan and had to flee when Japan was defeated. Thailand escaped being treated as an enemy because of a resistance movement organized by Banomyong, who had been regent for the king, still at a Swiss school during the war, and who now became prime minister. His rule was brief, though, as he was accused of being involved in the mysterious death of the king, whereupon he had to run into exile. Pibul returned to power in 1947 and was deposed in another military coup ten years later.

Pibul Songkram wanted the monument to be 'a centre of all things progressive'. Princely palaces along the avenue have been turned into public buildings.[7]

In 1957, a right-wing military coup put an end to the nationalist-democratic era and staged a monarchist urban iconography full of huge portraits of the king, which persists to this day, through the oscillations of Thai politics between brief periods of democracy and longer ones of military governments, with the royal court manoeuvring behind them.

The non-colonial character of Bangkok is manifested in its still-living indigenous cultural institutions and traditions, royal[*] and others, alongside its Westernized lowlife of fast food, cheap drinks and prostitution. (During the Vietnam War, Bangkok became a US military brothel.) Streets and expressways have now covered many of the canals, largely ending the old water city, but the traditional founding city pillar is still enshrined in the original palace and temple compound, although its cosmological connectivity may no longer be believed in. Due to US and Japanese investment after World War II, metropolitan Bangkok has become a major industrial assembly hub and an economic watershed of Thailand, overwhelming the national economy.

From Istanbul to Ankara

The Ottoman Empire was in a sense part of Europe – not only because all the Balkans were under Ottoman rule, but because it was part of the European system of power alliances, with varying allies (and enemies), France, Britain and Russia among them, and in the early eighteenth century it was eagerly courted by Sweden. For gender and religious reasons, it was never – unlike Russia – part of the European dynastic intermarriage network. From the early eighteenth century, it was obviously a decaying big power, en route to becoming a former one. By the time of the French Revolution, it had dawned upon the sultan and members of his court in Istanbul that the empire was falling behind, at least militarily. Reaction quelled military-specific changes in 1807, but

---

[*] Around 2008 I noticed people laying flowers and bowing to the equestrian statue of King Chulalongkorn (Rama V), as to a divine icon.

in 1839 a broader reform movement asserted itself, remembered as the Tanzimât. A key figure was Mustafa Reşid Pasha, a former ambassador to Western Europe who became grand vizier (prime minister). The Tanzimât launched the upgrading of Istanbul, largely concentrated on the medieval Genoese merchant centre on the Galata peninsula, north of the Golden Horn. The attempt at European-type modernization dualized the city in a colonial direction. In Istanbul proper, south of the Horn, the modest street widening and neighbourhood openings which actually took place happened only after city fires, while Galata and in particular around the *Grande Rue* (today's *Istiqlal*, 'Independence') of the Pera area (now Beyoğlu) developed into a cosmopolitan, Euro-Levantine city.[8]

The Ottoman Empire had collapsed by the end of World War I, and Istanbul was occupied by the Allied victors. Soon after, the Greeks landed an army in Smyrna (now İzmir) with the aim of capturing a large chunk of Anatolia. The Turkish, post-Balkan, post-Arab rest-state was on the verge of extinction. The routing of the Greek invaders and the rescue of the Fatherland provided general Mustafa Kemal Atatürk, who already as the victorious commander of Gallipoli (see the section on Canberra above) had proved his extraordinary military capability with a special aura among Turks, expressed in the title Gazi (a leading fighter for the Islamic faith).

The first new capital of the twentieth century, Ankara, was proclaimed by a National Assembly in 1923. A Turkish Grand National Assembly had met there already in 1920, and the town seated the headquarters of the Turkish army (under Mustafa Kemal) in the decisive War of Independence against the Greeks. Istanbul was very vulnerable to naval enemies, had just been occupied and was the city of the ignobly defeated, old-fashioned Ottoman Empire. Ankara was in the middle of the Anatolian heartland of the new Turkish Republic.

It was not laid out from scratch, like Brasília, Canberra or Islamabad; it was similar to Astana, an outback provincial town, becoming the Kazakhstani capital out of Soviet Akmolinsk/Tselinograd. Angora (Ankara) wool had lost out to British imperial imports and industrialization in the nineteenth century, and the city's population had declined from 45,000 in 1700 to 28,000 in 1920. But it had a railway connection, though no electricity, and was listed in the 1915 Baedeker Guide to Constantinople.[9]

The new republican government of what was now very much a nation-state was very explicit about its urban task in 1925: 'To build in Ankara a set of government worthy of an advanced state, by outfitting it with the necessary infrastructure, sanitary and scientific dwellings and other essentials of civilization is one of the most vital duties of our government'.[10]

German and Austrian planners and architects were invited to lay out the new capital on a drained swamp, alongside the old city around the Citadel. Because of its gradual development out of a pre-existing city, the modernity of Ankara does not display the ostentatiousness of Islamabad or Brasília nor the innovative urbanism of Canberra. But because it is not an old capital, like Tokyo or even Bangkok, it does have a predominantly internationally modern outlook, including CIAM zoning, but with its own distinctive iconography.[11]

The necessary new public buildings of Ankara had been preceded by a 1917 local headquarters for the Committee of Union and Progress (CUP), the secretive military-civilian organization that had more or less been running the empire since 1908, especially during the war. (Mustafa Kemal came out of its Saloniki branch.) It was built in a Westernized, orientalized style, contemporarily referred to as the National [or Ottoman] Architectural Renaissance, and retrospectively as the First National Style. The style had developed in Istanbul during the Tanzimât period and came to characterize the new capital in the 1920s, including the new Grand National Assembly (after the first CUP provisional), ministries, the Ankara Palas (a hotel for state guests) and the first bank buildings. (One of the earliest new streets laid out was Banks Avenue.)

In the 1930s, having consolidated its power, the Kemalist regime embarked on a radical programme of secular and Soviet-planning-inspired social transformation. The new urban plan, by the German planner Hermann Jansen, was part of this, as was the design for the 'government quarter', including a parliament by the Austrian Clemens Holzmeister, who also built the Ministry of Defence, other heavyweight ministries and Atatürk's new presidential villa in the suburb of Çankaya. The villa is a two-storey, light pink modern residence without any representational pomp and in 1932 succeeded an extended vineyard house which had been Kemal's Ankara headquarters since 1921 (and during the War of Independence). The famous German expressionist architect Bruno Taut was in town for a while, but was kept on to design some school buildings and the Faculty of Humanities of the new university.

The National Republican Architecture of the 1930s turned its back on anything orientalist or ornamentalist and developed a heavy monumentalist modernism akin to that favoured by Italian Fascism. Holzmeister's National Assembly and Atatürk's memorial, the Anıtkabir, by a new generation of Turkish architects, are the most telling architectural examples, both completed only after World War II.* Monumentally outstanding is the Security Monument of 1935, a huge ensemble the centerpiece of which features two giant nude muscular warriors, representing the police and the gendarmes, providing security. It was made by Anton Hanak and Joseph Thorak, who also worked for Hitler and Speer, invited by Holzmeister.†

While not given to narcissistic personal ostentation, Kemal was very much concerned with political iconography. As early as 1925, an Austrian sculptor was commissioned to make a Victory Monument in Ulus (Nation) Square, then central to the city. Featuring Atatürk on horseback upon a six-metre pedestal, it was erected in 1927. In the same year, at least two other statues of Atatürk went up, by an Italian sculptor. There developed a tradition for a number of institutions to have a specific Atatürk monument in front of them. A late one is 'Atatürk and the Constitution', set up outside the Constitutional Court in 1995.‡ Until the current mildly Islamist (though increasingly authoritarian) regime, the political personality cult in late-twentieth-century Turkey was second only to that of the Kim family of North Korea. The Atatürk cult survived a split of the regime after World War II, when a secessionist group formed a Democrat Party, which governed from 1950 to 1960.

Like all other serious, uninterrupted capital constructions of the twentieth century, Ankara has grown fast, into a metropolis of millions.

---

* The stone-paved path, with its stone lions, up to the Anıtkabir has an unexpected resemblance to the path to the Ming tombs north of Beijing.
† The monument and its park, in front of the Interior Ministry, were later referred to as Güven, meaning *trust* or *confidence*, including self-confidence, and alludes to an Atatürk quote.
‡ The broader architectural context is provided by Bozdogan, *Modernism and Nation Building*, and by Türkoglu Önge, 'Spatial Representations of Power', and a useful historical backdrop is Toni Cross and Gary Leiser, *A Brief History of Ankara*.

By 1955 it had become Turkey's second city in terms of population. Istanbul stagnated for decades, losing most of its Greeks and Armenians as well as its civil servants, and also suffering from the decline of Black Sea trade after the Russian Revolution. In 1950 its population was below that of 1918. But in recent decades it has taken off again, more than another ex-capital, Rio, always in the economic shadow of São Paulo.

Tehran

Tehran is not a beautiful ancient city of Persian Islamic civilization, like Isfahan or Shiraz. It is the thirty-second capital of Persia, selected in 1786 as the seat of the Qajar Dynasty, pushed into exile in the early 1920s. The city developed concentrically around the Arg, the citadel-palace complex of the shah with the Bazaar in proximity, as a very traditional West Asian city of walled-off, inward-oriented houses, without open public spaces and with narrow lanes and alleys instead of streets. Like pre-Meiji Edo but unlike imperial Beijing, Tehran had no carriages or carriage traffic until the mid-nineteenth century.[12]

Pressures and impulses for change started in the second and third decades of the nineteenth century, with military defeats to the Russians in 1813 and 1827 and British imperial missions, as well as offers of study. But Persia was far off from then-central Europe. The Paris Exposition of 1867 was attended by the deeply impressed Khedive Ismail of Egypt and the Ottoman sultan, but not the Persian shah. There was, however, a modest Persian handicraft pavilion and a small official delegation, and the breath of Haussmannian Paris was, in filtered form, gradually to be felt also in Tehran.

The first Persian modernization effort, by Amir Kabir from 1848 to 1851, was as unsuccessful as most of the contemporary European revolutions. His more conservative and long-lived successor Naser al-Din did not stop change, though, and during his reign the first actual modernization of the city began, with carriage-carrying streets and Euro-orientalist buildings as well as European-type equestrian statues of the shah.*

---

* My impressions of historical Tehran are partly taken from the rich collection of photographs assembled by Yahya Zoka and Mohammad Hassan Semsar, *Tehran in*

A Persian nation-state did not emerge in this first wave of urban modernization. The Constitutional Revolution of 1906 to 1908 was the starting point of the former and was brought about by a broad coalition, including traditional bazaar businessmen as well as modern nationalists. Its focus was in part anti-imperialist; protests against the shah's concession of a tobacco monopoly to British interests had been a dress rehearsal. Then came the revolutionary wave in Russia in 1905, sending imported food prices soaring in Persia and causing a major economic crisis.

One of the four key demands in the protest movement, which ended in a revolution, was for the dismissal of the Belgian director of the customs administration. For the first time, the slogan 'Long live the Nation of Iran' (*Mellat-I Iran*) was shouted in the streets of Tehran.[13] Dynastic absolutism was done away with, but the revolution issued into a very fractured polity, always under external threat. While a landmark of national history, the revolution itself does not seem to have had much of an urban impact, although an erratically functioning electrical illumination was introduced in 1908. It did institutionalize a municipality of Tehran in 1910, and with it a first spate of urban regulations.*

In 1921 the commander of a Cossack Brigade, deployed in Persia under the Anglo-Russian semi-colonial regime, staged a military coup. Through skilfully manoeuvring civilian politics while expanding his military base, Reza Khan managed to get himself elected shah by the National Assembly in 1926. In the footsteps of Kemal Atatürk, he set out to transform Iran from above.

A grid plan of broad avenues was imposed on Tehran; like in Europe about seventy-five years earlier, new peripheral boulevards replaced the demolished city walls. An urban edict of 1939 required city houses to have at least one storey opening to the street instead of walling

Illustration, Vol. 1, Tehran: Serwush Press, n.d.; M. Marefat, 'The protagonists who shaped modern Tehran', J. Scarce, 'The role of architecture in the creation of Tehran', and Gurney, 'Transformation of Tehran', all in Adle and Hourcade (eds), *Téhéran Capitale Bicentenaire* (Paris – Téhran, Institut francais de recherche en Iran, 1992).

* Royal Tehran had an appointed vizier surveilling the most basic matters, but it was the shah and his court who ran the city. There was an ancient Persian tradition, documented at least as far back as Emperor Darius, that when big building projects were being envisaged by the shah, master builders – today's architects – from all over the realm were invited to submit proposals. This happened also in the late-nineteenth-century reign of Naser al-Din (Marefat, 'Protagonists,' 100).

themselves off. A set of European-educated architects, French, Russo-Georgian, cosmopolite Armenian and, soon, returned Iranians produced a set of modern public buildings, apartment houses and private residences. They were often more innovative in their mixing of Iranian motifs and international modernism than prevailing pre–World War II Japanese architecture or the Second National Style of Kemalist Turkey, both more subservient to what was then the international canon.[14]

Politically, on the other hand, the national character of Pahlavi Iran remains open to doubt. In August 1941 the country was invaded by the new British-Soviet alliance for not being reliably anti-German. The deeply unpopular Reza Shah, on the verge of being deposed, abdicated in favour of his son, Mohammad Reza, who after a nationalist surge in 1953 was reimposed on the country by the US Central Intelligence Agency (CIA), which had taken the British imperial baton. The short-lived dynasty ended ignominiously to a complex popular revolution in 1979. Behind the latter were many grievances and forces, but among the urbanistic ones was a plan to turn the national metropolis of Tehran into a vast *banlieue* of a new Versailles, a new Royal City at the extreme north of the area, a new Shahestan Pahlavi, servilely planned by the British consultancy Llewelyn Davies International.[15]

Originally, in 1979, the Islamic Republic of Iran proclaimed itself an Islamic rather than a national state, open to all Muslims. De facto, though, it is seen as an Iranian nation-state with a minoritarian, schismatic version of Islam, Shia, in a tense neighbourhood of mostly Sunni Arabs.

Today, the two-shah Pahlavi Dynasty has left at least two major legacies to Tehran. The most important is the north-south divide – started by providing land for military officers and higher bureaucrats in the north – between a prosperous, largely secularized north (of Enqelab Street), at the foot of the impressive Alburz Mountains, and a pious, popular and largely, if not always, poor south, where the Bazaar and the Khomeini memorial mosque complex are. The second is the impressive, abstract central city roundabout landmark in white marble, launched as an imperial Shahyad (King's) Tower, celebrating, in 1971, 2,500 years of imperial Persia. Since the Islamic Revolution it has been known as the Azadi (Freedom) Tower.

Addis Ababa

Ethiopia remained, by and large, an imperial patrimony until the ill-fated revolution of 1974, although its 1931 Japanese-inspired constitution constituted an important step in a national direction.* Its last emperors did defend and modernize their country, against high odds and in a hostile colonial context. For these reasons, Ethiopia and Addis Ababa have a special place in African consciousness, and Addis has been chosen twice as the capital of Africa, by the Organization of African Unity in 1963 and by the African Union from 2001. This special role is always based on the non-colonial history of the country and the city.

Addis was also a recent, late-nineteenth-century capital, made more permanent largely due to the importation of fast-growing Australian eucalyptus trees, which prevented the usual desolation (of forests cut to firewood) around the imperial cities. Like Rome, it was built on hills, where the lords resided, with their retainers and clients beneath. The enormous compounds of the many imperial palaces still leave their imprint on the city. Although now rapidly disappearing, the territorially non-segregated habitation has survived until the present day. In the summer of 2014 one could still find a small, informal 'slum' area in the middle of the central Churchill Avenue. The 2002 Addis Ababa Development Plan claimed that 'social mixity and land-use mixity . . . can be cited as the unique character of Addis Ababa'. The Italian Fascist plan aimed explicitly at exactly the opposite. With its current Chinese-led globalization and 200 high-rise towers on the drawing board, Addis seems to be heading in a direction closer to the colonial vision than to its own multicultural social history.[16] However, today's Addis also includes the largest recently built neighbourhoods of middle-class (and probably also popular) housing that I have seen in Africa north of the Limpopo River.

---

* Sometime in the 1940s or perhaps 1950s, Ethiopia's most distinguished modernist intellectual civil servant and, for a short time, cabinet minister, Täklä-Häwaryat, had a conversation with Emperor Haile Selassie, cited in the introduction to his unpublished autobiography, in which Selassie said: 'You keep on saying 'Ethiopia', but Ethiopia is nothing without me . . . I am her destiny. Do not imagine that Ethiopia will exist without me.' (Bahru Zewde, *Pioneers of Change in Ethiopia*, Athens: Ohio University Press, 2002, 170).

While Asmara in Eritrea is a museum of Fascist Italian modernism, the colonial remnants of the much shorter colonial occupation of Addis are few, consisting mainly of the Mercato, the now huge informal market.

The modern landmarks of Addis are late, built in anticipation of the arrival of the OAU, in the Emperor's words, 'with a view to make this "great village" a city and a true great capital': Africa Hall, for the United Nations Economic Commission for Africa, and, more originally, a monumental city hall, on the crest of a ridge at the top of Churchill Avenue. A special modernist compound was erected for the OAU, recently enhanced by new buildings for the newly resident African Union, financed by the Chinese. After the fall of the empire, Haile Selassie's residence, the Jubilee Palace, was renamed the National Palace and put to government use, currently by the weak federal president. The great Menelik Palace was taken over by the revolutionary Derg and is now occupied by the key power-holder, the prime minister. A parliament building has existed since the 1930s, but is now being replaced.

The Marxist-Leninist iconography of the 1974 revolutionaries has been taken out – in spite of the fact that the victorious guerrillas were themselves originally Marxist–Leninist – but their militant monument in memory of the Somali war survived. A small private museum to the victims of revolutionary repression has been put up in a corner where the rallies take place.

The National Foundations and Their Capitals

The nations of the world were born not only in very different times but also in very different ways. There were the European patricide (or gentle paternal marginalization), the settler divorce (including the White Dominions moving out of the parental home), the mutinies in the colonial classes of 'Enlightenment' and 'evolution' and the preventive imitators of reactive modernization.

The ensuing capital cities all got lasting birthmarks from their nations. The domestic process of nation-state formation in Europe – except for the ex-Ottoman Balkans – meant a long continuity of urban form and architecture. National capitals needed a lot of new buildings – parliaments, courts, ministries, operas, concert halls, museums, universities, railway stations – but they were virtually all built according to the existing European repertoire of styles and forms, fitting them well into the pre-national urban landscape. Quite often, nation-states just recycled existing buildings for national use: convents and monasteries, aristocratic townhouses, minor royal palaces. The capitalist character of the national capitals, while anchored in specific institutions – banks, stock exchanges, luxury stores and hotels, even occasional business districts – was inscribed in much larger bourgeois cities of grand apartment buildings or townhouse complexes. The old burgher institutions of urban government were extended, even if vigilantly supervised in the capital cities, and manned by members of the new capitalist class, who also developed their own urban sociability of arts patronage, charity and entertainment, a bourgeois 'civil society' outside politics and economics in which women also participated.

The new capitals of the secessions from the British Empire were all more or less built from scratch, without any traditions of their own, constructed as they were for reasons of post-imperial settler balance and compromise. They were rather small politico-bureaucratic centres, with Washington and Pretoria, furthermore, living on top of racial oppression.

The Latin American capitals were former imperial centres, rather young by European or Asian standards but mostly around three centuries old, well endowed with Baroque churches, aristocratic palaces and old institutions of higher learning. Their polities, the *cabildos*, had played a key role in initiating the independence process. However, except for Brazil, the divorce proceedings had been lengthy, violent and disruptive, with almost two decades of incessant war, often followed by decades of civil and international war. The built environments of the capitals were little damaged by this violence, but their social patterns were.

The settler states defined themselves as 'club' nations – in contrast to the European 'language and historical culture' nations – and all set out to recruit desirable members. New immigrant communities came to leave their impact on all the capitals, providing their own monuments as gifts to the latter and structuring urban sociability. Latin American cities were also changed by the impact of expatriate foreign capitalists.[17] The commodities boom of the second half of the nineteenth century and the first decades of the twentieth – from gold to guano, coffee to copper, wool to wheat and later also oil – and US industrialization created enormous fortunes in the New World. The ensuing capitalist cities and societies were brash and brazen, pioneering the skyscraper and indulging in competitive private residential monuments for which size and expensiveness were the decisive criteria. New World capitalism was a capitalism of the super-rich, recently fortunate, rather than of a historically evolved bourgeoisie. In Latin America, the urban model of this elite was the Paris of the Second Empire, before Latin Americans shifted their admiration to New York, Chicago and Miami.

The ex-colonial nations define themselves by colonial politics, by the territorial boundaries of their former colonial powers, however contingent and arbitrary. Their capitals had all been shaped by colonial duality, between the city proper of the colonizers and the settlements of the natives. This duality has been reproduced virtually everywhere – Seoul being the single big exception – albeit with variable mutations. The ex-colonial city has been nationalized by the rulers of the new state, while the settlements have been enormously expanded by massive post-colonial rural migration. The typical ex-colonial capital remained extremely polarized in style, layout and services. The capitals of reactive modernization, on the other hand, have maintained good parts of their traditional hierarchical integration and still exhibit some sense of cultural continuity and evolution, in spite of their large-scale architectural modernity. Bangkok and Tokyo, in particular, convey a combination of distinctive, non-European urbanity with imported styles of building and street behaviour.

Upon their very different national foundations, the capitals of the world have faced their popular and global challenges.

6
People Rising:
Popular Moments in Modern Urban History

Most nation-states, and their capitals, have had a rocky ride through modernity, challenged from the inside as well as from the outside. While some traces have been obliterated, it is intrinsic to cities and to human settlements in general to leave layers of history alongside as well as beneath their present.

Instead of long narratives of urban evolution, this work focuses on a few crucial moments of modern world city history. In the previous part, I treated the founding moments of nation-states and their capitals. In this chapter I shall first try to grasp the rise of the subalterns of the nations and of elite challenges by other popular forces: the 'rebellion of the masses', as the conservative Spanish philosopher José Ortega y Gasset put it. Subsequent chapters will deal with moments after the foundational.

Two particular kinds of politics have shaped specific periods of urban history. Fascism and military dictatorships have constituted extreme responses to perceived popular threats. Communism, on the other hand, was an extraordinary form of political power coming out of popular uprisings. Finally, we have the current global moment of transnational finance capital and accelerated global exchange. We shall look at it from the angle of attempts at a globalized, 'world city' urbanism, and as changes in urban power.

The 'nation' of the nation-state can take on different colourations, from national-imperial in Britain and France to White-popular in the United States. Everywhere, however, the 'nation' has comprised or been represented only by an 'elite', defined by class, race/ethnicity and gender. Subsequently, this exclusive nation has been challenged and changed, or at least eroded. In some countries and cities, there came a ruptural popular moment of national history and city development.

The moment of the popular tolled when the subalterns of the nations entered the front stage as interlocutors of the elites: when their voices could be heard about their conditions, concerns and aspirations and when their specific cultures were recognized and made visible. It has happened at different times in the world, and it has taken different forms, leaving variable impacts.

The popular moments have had two primary *roots*: the social ascendancy of subaltern forces and rebellions rising from cultural change – even though the former certainly had an important cultural component of a changed collective identity, and the latter a strengthened socio-economic base for raising demands. The moments have manifested themselves in urban power relations in two *forms*: one institutional, using the institutions of national and city government to deal with popular concerns; the other centred on popular movements and their protest action. While there is a significant correlation between the roots and the forms, they can be empirically as well logically independent of each other.

We shall first look into some examples of entries of the people in the form of institutional changes to urban power and politics and of institutional cultural accommodation to a rise of the previously excluded and despised. The ascent of the people has taken very different forms amongst the capitals of different national foundations.

European Working-Class Municipal Socialism and Welfare-State Urbanism

As a distinctive phase of urban development and experience, a popular moment emerged most clearly in Europe – against the background of the latter's class-structured bourgeois nation-states and national capitals, but also because of the pioneering centrality of the Industrial

Revolution to European national societies and cities.* Industrialization drew hard and eminently visible class lines.

While an awareness of the social challenges of rapidly growing industrial cities spread in the nineteenth century among the ruling elites as well as among the new breed of social investigators, there was no sustained popular moment before the end of World War I, which finally ended the remaining *anciens régimes* of Europe and opened up at least male universal suffrage. The Parisian revolutions of 1830, 1848 and 1871 brought the masses to the fore, but their popular dimension was more a blink of history than a popular entry into urban politics and processes of change.

The popular moment in Europe was, above all, that of the working class and the labour movement. The century from the Paris Commune (of 1870–71) – the fear of which inspired the German welfare state[1] – to about 1980 was the working-class century in social history, recognized as such even by enemies of the socialist labour movement, like Pope Leo XIII in his 1891 Encyclical *Rerum Novarum* (On New Things) or the racist nationalist who led the 'National Socialist German Workers' Party' to power in Germany. The working-class century was Euro-centric, centred on (if not confined to) European trade unions, labour parties and working-class cultural and leisure organizations. Through emigration to the Americas and later through the Comintern, European labour inspired workers, intellectuals and peasants around the world, most importantly in China and Vietnam.

'Municipal socialism' was originally a pejorative British label for what were in fact mostly left-liberal policies of urban public services, sanitation, water, sewage, schools, libraries and so on.[2] In the late nineteenth and early twentieth centuries, the new salience of urban services in rapidly growing and industrializing cities became a manifestation of a new social landscape where the working classes had taken up a sizeable place, although their voices were still low or little articulated.

Capital cities, with their consolidated social establishments, were usually not in the forefront, where you would rather find mid-sized

---

* There was no direct connection to the medieval 'plebeian city' in Italy of the twelfth and thirteenth centuries, which Max Weber discussed in his *Economy and Society*. But there may be a significant parallelism in the clear class structuration of the Western European medieval city, with their absence of clan *Geschlecht* power, and of very significant ethnic and religious divisions (Max Weber, *Wirtschaft und Gesellschaft*, Berlin: Köln, 1964, chapter 9, section 7).

industrial cities, like Ghent, Belgium – the (liberal) origin of publicly subsidized unemployment insurance run by the trade unions – Roubaix, France, socialist already from the 1890s, or Sheffield, Britain, from 1918.³ Working-class eruptions in capital cities, like Paris in 1848 and 1871 and Saint Petersburg in 1905, had been brief and in the end repressed, their enduring effect largely confined to class memory.

In some countries, like Germany and Sweden, popular municipal weight was held back longer than in national politics because of a much more unequal municipal voting system, but after the end of World War I that was no longer possible.

In Amsterdam on the eve of World War I, a new urban era began to be prepared. Already in 1912, the Dutch housing campaigner, later city building inspector, Ary Kepler had dreamed in public about 'beautiful workers' dwellings' as 'monuments to [the working-class] struggle'.⁴ After World War I, this programme was implemented in Amsterdam under the alderman for housing, the left-wing Social Democrat Wibaut, with the help of the modernist Amsterdam School of architecture and the politicized working-class housing associations.

The paradigmatic example of municipal socialism was Vienna from 1920 to 1934: 'Red Vienna', sustained by a stable Social Democratic majority and its fiscal autonomy as a state (*Land*) of its own in federal Austria. It is most famously remembered for its centrally located social housing complexes: 'super-blocks' of apartments usually six to eight stories high, with vast courtyards taking up half or more of the settlement. They often had a monumental entrance or portal, open to the street. The complexes comprised collective services of many kinds: maternity clinics, health centres, day-care centres, schools, laundries, shops, pubs without alcohol, sometimes a restaurant, libraries, meeting rooms, labour-movement offices and post and social-insurance offices. The settlements each had a name, mostly after figures of the Austrian, German and other European labour movements (Jaurès, Matteotti), but one was called George-Washington-Hof. The flagship of Red Viennese housing was Karl-Marx-Hof, of 1,400 apartments with 5,000 inhabitants, and a courtyard the size of a public square, which it had actually been before the settlement was built around it. At the entrance were masts, on which red banners were hoisted on May Day and during other major working-class events.

While refraining from vanguardist architectural modernism, the buildings themselves were testimony to the political control that the urban poor of Vienna had acquired over the shape and use of space in their city. The ring of working-class settlements around the outer edge of the centre was proudly called 'the proletarian *Ringstrasse*', counter-posing itself to the great late-nineteenth-century constructions of the imperial bourgeoisie.

The Austrian Social Democrats developed ideas of a socialist city while drawing upon the big city (*Grossstadt*) conception of the pre-war Viennese architect Otto Wagner.[5] They remained hemmed in, though, limited to an exceptional municipality in a very conservative nation-state. Their 'General Architecture Plan' was, for various reasons, never adopted, and control of urban land was never achieved. In fact, Austria lacked an effective 'eminent domain' expropriation legislation, a crucial legal basis for Haussmann in Paris. Instead, the city and its architects employed great ingenuity in making use of odd, underdeveloped land for their famous settlements. Karl-Marx-Hof, for instance, was built in an area between a commuter train station and a sports stadium, incorporating its public square into the settlement.[6] The Austrian Social Democrats did not have the power to build a Berlin Stalin/Karl-Marx-Allee, and there was no love lost between Communism and Austro-Marxism, but there is clearly a certain affinity between Karl-Marx-Hof and Karl-Marx-Allee based on a common heroic socialism and an idea that only the best is good enough for the working class.

Red Vienna succumbed, after street-fighting with live ammunition, to Austro-Fascism in 1934, which immediately abolished public-housing construction. However, it has not been erased as a form of urbanism, still visitable and still a thorn in the side of the local bourgeoisie.*

Berlin was the first capital of the world in which a working-class party gained an electoral majority, in 1903 capturing five of the six Reichstag seats, though not the old city centre. The restrictive municipal franchise did not allow a Social Democratic city council majority, though. Mainstream party support for the German war and different stances in

---

* Sometime in the 1990s I was in Vienna for an academic congress, and a city tour was an optional extra. The first priority of the group was Karl-Marx-Hof. Our guide, a middle-aged bourgeoise, reluctantly allowed our tour bus to get there, but she steadfastly refused to enter or to say anything about it, apart from it being a prime example of socialist clientelism, where you could only get a flat if you had a party card.

the revolution which ended the Kaiserreich then split the party into three, which together were weaker than the pre-war SPD and no longer majoritarian. The Weimar Social Democrats elected a liberal as mayor of Berlin. At the same time, they took great pride in their city policies, in cooperation with left-liberals, above all its social, educational and cultural policies.[7]

Weimar Germany had several cities with Social Democratic or more middle-class progressive governments which created architectural history by aligning themselves with avant-garde architects of the time: Bruno Taut, Walter Gropius, Ludwig Mies van der Rohe and others. Frankfurt and Stuttgart, rather than Berlin, were in the urbanistic front rank. But Weimar Berlin also had its popular moment of modernist housing settlements designed by vanguard architects for trade-union building cooperatives, with flat-roofed, low-rise apartment buildings in an urban lawn-green landscape rather than lined up in straight street rows. One was named after the trade-union leader Carl Legien, whereas the best known, Siemensstadt (mainly designed by Hans Scharoun), still standing, carries the name of the employer.

In London there was no unified city government, and its interwar spells of popular upsurge were initially concentrated in the poor eastern borough of Poplar, where in the early 1920s radical Labour councillors and Poor Law Guardians broke legal budget rules to help the poor and the unemployed, and to pay modest living wages to employees. For this they were sent to prison, but continued to test the limits after their release. In 1934 Labour won a majority of the vote for the London County Council and expanded social housing, health care services and municipalized public transport. The leaders of the LCC and of Poplar Labour, Herbert Morrison and George Lansbury respectively, had both been conscientious objectors to the World War mobilization, and the LCC cut school links to the military and celebrated Commonwealth instead of Empire Day.[*]

France before the 1920s was constrained by vigilant prefectural control later somewhat loosened.[8] Paris was mostly under right-centre

---

* Their biographies offer interesting introductions to the times: B. Holman, *Good Old George*, Oxford: Lion, 1990, and B. Donoughue and G.W. Jones, *Herbert Morrison*, London: Weidenfeld and Nicolson, 1973. Owen Hatherley makes a passionate and strong case for the London Labour tradition, focused on the LCC but covering the field into 2020, in *Red Metropolis*, London: Repeater, 2020.

national government control, so popular influence was largely limited to the working-class belt around it. Most important and most radical and ambitious in social, fiscal and cultural policies, less so in housing, was the northern industrial suburb of Saint-Denis, with a Socialist majority from 1892 and after World War I a Communist stronghold.* In Copenhagen the Social Democrats became the largest party in 1903 and could elect the primary of the city's nine mayors. The former craftsman Jens Jensen became a popular representative of the sociological change of Danish politics, but his consensual administration constituted no new urban regime, although during the war the city made good use of its prescient land purchases for public housing and for braking private-development prices.[9]

London had its most flamboyant popular moment in the first half of the 1980s, when a left-Labour Greater London Council, charismatically led by Ken Livingstone, fought for a city of popular multiculturalism – sexual as well as ethnic and religious – and for a regeneration of industrial and port jobs, against not only a hostile central neoliberal government under Margaret Thatcher but also a 'world city' concept financed by transatlantic capital. The city council was then housed across the river at the Westminster Parliament and sent unwelcome, transparent messages about the rising rate of unemployment to Parliament. The main urban battlefield was the eastern Docklands: how to regenerate them after the closure of the historical docks? The outcome of the battle was a decisive victory of global capital, which I shall treat below as a crucial stepping-stone in the arrival of the current global moment.

The labour movement also built for itself, for the *Arbeitervereine* in Germany and Austria – in particular Austria – buildings seen by its leaders as 'houses of struggle', 'fortresses of solidarity'.[10] In Belgium and France they had a less militant accent and went under the name of

---

* On Saint-Denis, there is an incredibly detailed three-volume *thèse de doctorat* by Jean-Paul Brunet (*Une banlieue ouvrière, Saint-Denis 1890–1939*, Lille, 1982). On French municipal socialism, there is an overview with a Socialist Party focus by Aude Chamouard: *Un autre histoire du socialisme*, Paris: CHRS Editions, 2013. Saint-Denis was the base of one of the most dynamic inter-war French Communists, Jacques Doriot. In the 1930s he refused to follow the party's turn to Popular Front tactics and was expelled from the party, but stayed in local power in Saint-Denis. In 1936 he founded a new party, increasingly pro-Nazi, which kept the upper hand in Saint-Denis, providing Neville Chamberlain with a street in gratitude of his surrender at Munich (Brunet, *Banlieue ouvrière*, 1429).

Maisons du Peuple (Houses of the People), a concept also prominent in Italy and Scandinavia. Most of these buildings were functional halls for meetings and socializing, sometimes including residential apartments, without monumental ambitions. But a few had such ambitions, such as the Art Nouveau Maison du Peuple built by Victor Horta in Brussels and the *Arbeiterheim* in the Vienna neighbourhood Favoriten.

The second institutional popular moment in Europe came after World War II, the moment of building welfare states.* Basically, the welfare states meant a national recognition, extension and ideological de-mobilization of municipal socialism. The last aspect was most visible in the difference between inter-war and early post-war Vienna, between the working-class fortress of Karl-Marx-Hof and the suburban Per-Albin-Hansson-Siedlung, with its long rows of *Heimatstil* non-detached, two-storey family houses. It is an eloquent expression of the turn of the SPÖ from militant Austro-Marxism to consensus-seeking Scandinavian social democracy.†

As a constructor, the welfare state made at least three significant contributions to the built environment. The largest was to assume a national public responsibility for housing – not only for the poor, not only for the clearance of slums, but for all the non-rich, the middle as well as the working class. The French pre-war designation of public housing, HBM, meaning 'cheap housing' (for the cheap classes), was in 1950 changed into HLM, 'housing for moderate rent', aiming at the (lower) middle class as well. A massive state-municipality-financed housing programme ensued, particularly around Paris.[11]

In Britain, 'council housing' remained for the working class and below, in contrast to Scandinavia.‡ Ironically, the progressive ideology

---

* To my knowledge, the welfare state has not yet been given a full architectural history. But a good, wide-ranging contribution is Lisbeth Söderqvist, *Att gestalta välfärd* [Giving Form to Welfare], Stockholm: Forskningsrådet Formas, 2008.

† Per Albin Hansson was between 1932 and 1946 the Social Democratic prime minister of Sweden, who provided substantial relief aid to Austria after the war. Hansson commisioned the building of the Swedish welfare state. See the excellent comparison of postwar with inter-war Vienna by Eve Blau: 'From red superblock to green megastructure: Municipal socialism as model and challenge', in Mark Swenarton, Tom Avermaete, and Dirk van den Heuvel (eds), *Architecture and the Welfare State*, New York: Routledge, 2014.

‡ An older Swedish colleague of mine who got a British professorship in the 1960s told me of the shock of his new colleagues in answer to their question of where he planned to live: 'Oh, I suppose I will look for some municipal housing.'

behind the dismal practice of British public housing seems to have inspired the world's most extensive and successful public-housing construction in a capitalist economy: that of Singapore, where in 2009, 82 per cent of the population lived in publicly built (but individually owned) housing.[12] In Western as well as in Eastern Europe (in the Khrushchev era and after), this public commitment to urban housing led to huge suburban settlements of apartment buildings of highly variable quality and natural surroundings, as a rule not properly maintained, but widely maligned for the consequences of the social problems they tended to concentrate.[13]

Second, welfare states promoted and sustained a large number of efforts at communitarian social planning. 'Neighbourhood planning' was actually a 1920s American idea of the New York planner Clarence Perry, which was incorporated into the Soviet *mikrorayon* concept and practice. Nevertheless, after World War II, new suburban communities, deliberately not conceived as separate satellite towns, became showcases of Scandinavian welfare modernism, in particular Vällingby in Stockholm and Tapiola in Helsinki. Breaking with the pre-war CIAM orthodoxy of separating 'zoning', they were built according to the Swedish 'ABC' concept (*A*rbete/work, *B*ostad/dwelling, *C*entre).* Paris, by contrast, maintained a clear demarcation between the city and the *banlieue*, where the *grands ensembles* were built. Later, the French came to adopt the post-war British idea of 'new towns' (outside London, by a green quarantine) and created a set of new satellites around Paris. In the 1980s and 1990s, the Catalan architect Ricardo Bofill was allowed to add some flair – or, one might say, some Socialist Realist extravagance – to

* Work provision was never quite adequate in these suburbs, particularly for women, while nevertheless displaying a noteworthy ambition. The Swedish architectural professor Helena Mattsson ('Where motorways meet: Architecture and corporatism in Sweden 1968', in Swenarton, Avermaete, and van den Heuvel (eds), *Architecture and the Welfare State*, 159ff) has drawn attention to the variations of the planned post-war Stockholm suburban centres. An early one, Årsta, opened in 1953 and was designed by Uno Åhrén, a leading Social Democratic ideologue of Functionalism in the 1930s. The Årsta centre has a strong cultural accent of library, cinema and theatre, and has been criticized as commercially underdeveloped. Vällingby opened a year later, designed by the CIAM modernist Sven Markelius, paid more attention to the interests of shoppng and consumption as well as to culture. In September 1968, in southern Stockholm, a new suburban centre, a belated example of a period about to end, Skärholmen, opened at the intersection of three motorways, with the largest parking area of the city and mainly devoted to private consumption.

the housing estates of a couple of them, such as Cergy-Pontoise and Saint-Quentin-en-Yvelines.

Third, welfare states have been concerned with overcoming social polarization – through taxation and social transfers, above all, but also by means of planning for 'mixed development' (Paris), for 'affordable housing' alongside market housing for the well-heeled or, more ideologically, for an 'open society' (Amsterdam).[14] How far welfare-state urban de-segregation has gone is very difficult to measure comparatively. Just to take two examples. The typical Swedish welfare-state housing estate is not a US ghetto of the poor. However, its internal distinctions are very clear to its inhabitants: flats for rent for low-income people, condominiums for aspiring, skilled working-class and middle-class people and family houses for the arrived middle class. Some recent London mixed buildings have separate entries for the market-rate tenants, who are provided with concierge services, and for those who cannot afford more than what is 'affordable' and have to wait for quite some time for any housing service.

One might expect that generous welfare states, like those of continental North-west Europea, should have less socially segregated cities than other capitalist countries. There is undoubtedly a tendency in that direction, but comparisons are difficult and measurements fragile. Concluding an anthology on segregation, Kumiko Fujita has made a bold attempt at comparing urban inequality, combining residential segregation and urban life chances in a qualitative, non-metrical ranking.[15] Among eleven cities, she ranked Beijing, Istanbul and São Paulo as 'highly separate and unequal', followed by 'moderately separate and unequal' Budapest and Paris. At the other pole she placed Taipei and Tokyo, where people were 'living together and equal'. Copenhagen, the only strong welfare state capital in her sample, she assessed as less segregated than the first five mentioned, but more so than than Athens, Hong Kong and Madrid, where people were living 'together but unequal'. Dealing with the current Global Moment below we shall come back to the issue of segregation and another, somewhat more recent, dataset.

The popular ascendancy had an *iconographic* aspect, too, ushering ordinary people and their leaders into the monumental cityscape. It was often a long, uphill slog, even when the reference was only to work and the individual worker without any hint of class struggle. The Belgian sculptor Constantin Meunier was a pious Catholic, politically conservative, but all his life he was concerned with the dignity of working men

and women. For the last ten years of his life, he was working on a monumental ensemble in honour of labour – not of the working class. It was
never put up in his lifetime: only in 1930 (twenty-five years after his
death), and out of the centre of Brussels. It is a peaceful ensemble of
working men of different occupations and a maternal figure, on top of
whom, on a low column, is a sower. Currently, it looks abandoned and
unkempt in the Laeken district, from which one has a good view of the
shining business towers at a distance.

Inter-war Vienna housed some labour movement commemorations. The most important was the Monument to the Republic, near
Parliament, an austere modernist ensemble of three oblong stone
pillars covered by a horizontal stone beam with a dedication to the
founding of the Republic in 1918, with busts of three labour leaders in
front. It was taken down by the Austro-fascists after 1934 but was
resurrected in 1948.[16]

Since World War II, labour and labour leaders have been incorporated into the urban iconography of the Nordic capitals. A major one is
the large sculptural bronze relief ensemble in Stockholm, focused on the
founding leader of Swedish Social Democracy, Hjalmar Branting. The
grand new City Hall of Oslo commemorates, along with Nordic myths,
its building workers, a common practice in Communist Europe that still
survives in places such as in Warsaw's Constitution Square. Already, in
the inter-war period, Nordic capitals had their labour-movement
areas, around a square of which trade unions and other working-class
organizations had their buildings: Norra Bantorget in Stockholm, where
the Branting monument stands, Hakaniemi Square in Helsinki and
Youngstorget in Oslo, the most concentrated, where the Social
Democratic Workers' Party and its newspaper also had their offices.*

In the Netherlands, Amsterdam came to pay belated homage to the
firebrand anarcho-socialist first leader of the Dutch labour movement,
Domela Nieuwenhuis. The famous February 1941 strike, called by the
Communist Party against a Nazi anti-Jewish pogrom, is remembered by
a realist statue of a dock worker. The most spectacular labour monument in a capitalist capital is in Dublin, where the 1913 strike leader Jim

---

* Some years ago the anti-tax and anti-immigrant Progress Party, currently in
government together with the traditional right, provocatively bought itself an office
building in the square.

Larkin has been standing since 1979, still agitating, in the main O'Connell Street.*

The most moving of all working-class remembrances in Europe is probably the monument in Helsinki to the Reds fallen in the Civil War of 1918 or starved to death in the White concentration camps after the war. It was put up in 1970 on a wooded hill near the Olympic Stadium, but is visible only to those who know where to search for it: a rough, torn, slightly folded, damaged-looking concrete wall with sculptured reliefs of harrowed humans on one side and a poetic dedication by the left-wing modernist of the period, Elmer Diktonius, to the 'graves of heroes'.†

The Helsinki monument was erected as part of a final reconciliation process of the late 1960s between victorious White and defeated Red Finland. Its most loaded moment was when President Urho Kekkonen walked the Long Bridge from his (modest) Presidential Palace in bourgeois Helsinki towards the working-class district and labour movement centre of Hakaniemi to meet leaders of the workers' movement.

London, Paris and Rome have never found any significant place of homage to the labour movement – outside their graveyards: the Highgate Cemetery, where Karl Marx is remembered, and the Père Lachaise cemetery, where the militants of the Paris Commune were buried, and after them many people on the left. The same is basically true of capitalist Berlin, where Mies van der Rohe in the 1920s built an expressive grave monument in East Berlin in honour of Karl Liebknecht and Rosa Luxemburg, later reconstructed after the Nazis destroyed it. Herbert Frahm, better known as Willy Brandt, was indeed a labour militant and became a Social Democratic leader. But he would hardly have survived in monumental form if he had not been mayor of the city and federal chancellor. Post-Franquista Madrid does remember its classical labour leaders – Pablo Iglesias, Largo Caballero and Indalecio Prieto – but not in any very iconic way. Ironically, the labour movement is more prominently present in the iconography of Washington, where there is a big

---

* After a long, rebellious life-course, including a spell of Communism, Larkin did enter into more respectable Irish nationalism, but he is monumentalized not as a patriot but as a trade-union agitator. The initiative to the monument came from the trade-union movement, which is not particularly strong in Ireland. No other Western European capital has paid such a symbolic tribute to a working-class militant.
† On my first visit I was shown the way by my colleague J.P. Roos.

statue to Samuel Gompers, the anti-socialist, skilled workers' leader of the American Federation of Labor.*

American 'Populism' and Racial Rehabilitation

Settler states and cities were racially defined, by the marginalization, subordination or exclusion of Native people, slaves and descendants of slaves. Popular moments in the settler world were most distinctively moments of racial rehabilitation, recognition and inclusion of the subaltern, marginalized 'races' – often meaning not much change of urban power, but at least a kind of ruling accommodation to different cultures. However, the New World of conquest and immigration also became the homeland of 'populism'.

The political system of the newly independent settler states was in most cases more open and less firmly anchored in the social structure (at least for periods) than those of the European nation-states. In Latin America in the nineteenth and early twentieth centuries, tumultuous pathways to power could be found by plebeian strongmen, including Mestizos and others of mixed heritage. In big North American cities, though not in Washington, plebeian 'political machines' captured city power through electoral mobilization of ethnic blocs.

Twentieth-century national politics in the Americas developed populism, a 'rabble-rousing' anti-establishment political rhetoric, which – if and when in power – usually meant substantial benefits to ordinary people, but not popular power. Populist regimes were typically run from the very top by a charismatic leader governing clienteles rather than a citizenry or a self-organized republican people, and usually within the confines of 'dependent' capitalism. For this reason, for its limited capital-city impact[†] and because its political analysis requires much extra space, American populism, however interesting, is not as

---

* Canberra got a 'National Workers' Memorial' in 2013, an abstract set of pillars in King's Park by Lake Burley Griffin. It has no connection with the historically strong Australian labour movement, but is dedicated to the victims of work accidents and work diseases.

† In the United States, but not in Latin America, populism was mainly rural and Western.

such treated here as a popular moment, although we shall occasionally encounter it below.*

Race after the British Empire

While African Americans made up a high proportion of the Washington, D.C. population by US standards, they never constituted more than a third of the city's population until the 1950s. Then White suburbanization started a decline of D.C.'s White population, while the Black population continued to grow. From 1960 onwards, Washington has had a Black majority. African Americans began to appear in official Washington about two centuries after independence, after they gained the right to vote in the South. Congress granted the city home rule in 1973 and in November the first mayor was elected. At first there was continuity: the elected mayor, Walter Washington, who was African American, had previously been the appointed city commissioner.

Political change came in 1979, with the election of civil rights activist Marion Barry, a share-cropper's son and a very colourful and controversial politician who was elected four times. He opened up municipal jobs to African Americans, attracted investors for downtown office development and provided summer jobs for youth, house-buying subsidies and food programmes for the poor elderly. In his first term he also introduced budgetary and accounting rectitude into the city's notorious financial mess. His three later periods reverted to the old messy practices, though, and his administration was mired in corruption. The capital establishment had many reasons to loathe him, and his increasingly erratic personal life gave it a chance. In a Cold War spy-thriller-like operation, on the eve of the electoral campaign in 1990 he was framed by the FBI, which hired a woman to invite him to her hotel room and offer him drugs, video-taping the event, whereupon the police broke in. Barry had to stay out of the election, but in 1994 he was elected for a fourth term.

---

* Populist leaders in the Americas may be seen as a series of colourful figures, starting with William Jennings Bryan, three times defeated US presidential candidate for the Democrats around the previous turn of the century, and in Latin America including Getúlio Vargas in Brazil, Carlos Ibáñez in Chile, Juan Peròn in Argentina, Juan Velasco Alvarado in Peru, and, as the last in the row so far, Hugo Chávez in Venezuela. Remarkably, many were military men; of the list just mentioned, only Bryan and Vargas were not.

Barry's career and achievements have a striking resemblance to those of many ex-colonial leaders: a charismatic, radical ethnic leader promoting ethnic development while also trying to please external business and investors, becoming increasingly dissolute in power and finally leaving a cesspool of corruption, police thuggery, public debt and social underdevelopment – while until the end retaining a bedrock of supporters who never forgot that he had stood up for his people.[*]

In the 1970s and 1980s, middle-class Blacks also began to move out of the shrinking city, and since 2011 the African American proportion of the population has dipped below 50 per cent, but in a city now demographically growing. The fractured Black Democratic politics succeeding Barry has not produced any significant social reform programme and would have had little chance to implement it if it had tried, indebted and under hostile Congress budgetary tutelage as the city is. But the current mayor has called her 2016 budget 'Pathways to the Middle Class', with no explanation.

There was, of course, no role for African Americans according to the vision of the 1902 Park Commission for the 'beauty and dignity of the national capital', in the midst of White racist reaction.[†] The Freedmen's Memorial of 1903, financed by African Americans, off centre in the city's South-east quadrant, was above all a monument to White magnanimity, portraying a tall Lincoln holding his blessing hand over a Black man crouching at his feet, shackles broken. Since 1974 Lincoln has faced a more respectful little statue ensemble in honour of the African American educator Mary McLeod Bethune.

In the 1980s and 1990s, US racial iconography started to change significantly. The two more conservative Vietnam War memorials added to the famous non-heroic Memorial Wall, put up in 1984 and 1993, both included obvious African American warriors. In 1998 an African

---

[*] Marion Barry got a seemingly fair, informative obituary in the *Washington Post* on 23 November 2014 by Bart Barnes. For analyses of his administration, see Howard Gillette, *Between Beauty and Justice*, Philadelphia: University of Pennsylvania Press, 1995, chapter 10, and Harry Jaffe and Tom Sherwood, *Dream City: Race, Power, and the Decline of Washington, D.C.*, New York: Argo-Navis, 1994.

[†] Wolfgang Sonne's *Habilitation* (professorial qualification thesis) gives a good architectural overview without any attention to the political context, and hastily labels a country which had a smaller proportion of male citizens with rights to vote than the German Reich a 'consolidated democracy' (Sonne, *Representing the State*, chapter 2).

American Civil War Memorial was unveiled. In 2001 an officious African American Heritage Trail of (often very generously defined) African American landmark sites in the city was laid out.* Martin Luther King Jr. got a full memorial statue on the Mall in 2011. An African American Museum finally opened in September 2016 on the Mall, in an original, Yoruba-inspired building by the London-based African architect David Adjaye, and American Indians at last got official recognition in a museum in 2004 (by a Canadian Indigenous architect), eleven years after the (federally financed) Holocaust Museum.†

The poor Black areas of the city are mainly in the Southeast across the Anacostia River, but also to be found north of S Street Northwest; they are mostly invisible to congressmen and think-tankers as well as to casual visitors.

Canada was the first of the ex-British settler states to acknowledge, belatedly, the rights of the Natives, who got some land rights in the Constitution of 1982. In its Museum of Canadian Civilization in Ottawa-Gatineau, the country was also the first of the British Empire secessions to pay full official respect to its indigenous population. Unlike later recognitions in Wellington, Canberra and Washington, the Canadian museum is not a Native niche. It brings Indigenous peoples into the centre of Canadian history. Its ground-floor Grand Hall is wholly dedicated to showing 'the rich cultural heritage of the aboriginal peoples of Canada's West Coast'. Alongside it is the First Peoples Hall, highlighting native cultural diversity. Only later, upstairs, do you reach the Canada Hall of Immigration.

Until the 1970s, 'Keep Australia White' was national policy ; it was the first programme plank of the Australian Labour Party. Then the tide turned (under a new Labour leader) and the Aborigines began to stir, including pitching an 'embassy' tent outside Parliament. Australia has been more reluctant in recognizing its Indigenous people than Canada, but in 2001, on the occasion of the centenary of Australia's federation, the new Australian National Museum included an architecturally ambitious

---

* Currently it has been renamed 'From Civil War to Civil Rights', and an African American woman working at Tourist Information in April 2016 did not know of any African American Heritage Trail.

† On monumental Washington see Savage, *Monument Wars*. There is in Washington also a federal agency called the American Battle Monuments Commission, proudly inscribed in the World War II Memorial of 2004.

annex building of 'Australian Aboriginal and Torres Strait Islanders Studies'. In the same year a large commemorative ensemble in the Parliamentary Triangle by Lake Burley Griffin was started, Reconciliation Place. It is a claim to settler-native reconciliation, including symbolic recognitions of Aboriginal country origin, land rights and leaders. This is the most comprehensive and prominent case of latter-day symbolic recognition of native peoples by settlers. It derived from the National Capital Authority and strong national opinion, but not, it seems, from the right-wing Howard government in power at the time.

New Zealand was unique among the settler states of the British secession in having to pay some recognition from the beginning to the Maoris – a relatively large, well-organized people with fighting traditions – who were granted delimited land rights and a recognized minor place in the settler polity according to the 1846 Treaty of Waitangi. Wellington has always been a White settler town. In 1998 an iconic, albeit not exclusively, Maori-centred national historical museum opened: *Te Papa* (Our Place). A popular moment had arrived in Wellington.

In the early 1990s the whole racist settler state of South Africa imploded, and Pretoria turned into the ex-colonial capital of Tshwane.* The South African economy and society have not (yet) had a very successful human development. But its radical regime change has been handled with impressive, unique skill. There was transitional violence, but the old and new political elites managed to keep it on the margins, or at least from penetrating the core of the polity – even after the racist assassination of the very popular and influential Communist leader Chris Hani.

The city of Tshwane represents this process very well. Until the 2016 election it has been governed by the African National Congress. The inner city is now mainly Black – from lily-white on my first visit in 1991 – and bears the name of a (possibly mythical) Tswana chief, Tshwane, who now stands in front of, but together with, the settler leader Pretorius, who gave the city its previous name. The massive governmental Union Building, built by the British imperial architect Herbert Baker for the two wings of the settler union, the Boers and British, is still there in its imposing (now presidential) presence, but

---

* White opponents challenged the name change in the courts and in 2015 it was suspended due to some improper decision procedures, but the name change is likely to return officially.

between its parapet and the equestrian statue of the Boer general Louis Botha, the first prime minister of South Africa, is now a larger-than-life, relaxed, informal statue of Nelson Mandela. The new capital is much larger than the old one, extending across open quarantine fields and industries in order to include outlying Black 'townships'.

The Boer shrine on the outskirts, the impressive and symbolically highly charged Voortrekker (Vanguard) Monument, is not only left untouched, it has been classified as a national, but not state-owned heritage site. In 2009, it received an additional 'Remembrance Wall' inscribed with names of members of the South African armed forces fallen on duty (defending apartheid) between 1961 and 1994 – an extraordinary gesture of defiance, and of reconciliation.* On another hilltop, at a distance across the highway, a symbolically elaborate Freedom Park has been laid out, connected by road to the Boer monument, in 2011, on Reconciliation Day.

Freedom Park opened in 2007, with additions continuing after that. It is the most elaborately deliberated and original symbolic ensemble in modern history, perhaps ever. It is based on Indigenous knowledge systems. Tribal elders, traditional healers and (indigenous) anthropological Africanists were extensively consulted and crucially involved in the design. The layout is a symbolic landscape based on African principles and expressed in concepts of African languages. It has three main parts.

The first to be constructed and the most distinctively African is *Isivivane*, a sacred place where the spirits of the fighters for freedom rest. It is demarcated as a circle by eleven boulders: one for each of the country's nine provinces, one for the nation as a whole and one for the international community contributing to the struggle against racism and apartheid.

Then-president Thabo Mbeki questioned the monument's abstract anonymity, and a new section was built, *S'khumbuto*, a Garden of Remembrance, including a Wall of Names of identified victims of wars in South Africa, from pre-colonial wars and colonial genocide and slavery to apartheid repression, and a Gallery of Leaders. The latter are divided into three categories of descending size: South African, continental and world leaders who have contributed to African freedom. The still-open list

---

* When the end of apartheid was coming, the Voortrekker monument was privatized into the control of an Afrikaner cultural organization (Annie Coombes, *Visual Culture and Public Memory in a Democratic South Africa*, Durham, NC: Duke University Press, 2003, 33), hence the defiance. Reconciliation was on the part of the government, which tolerated it and declared the whole ensemble a national heritage monument in 2011.

currently (as of 2014) mentions four names in the third category: the African American scholar and activist W.E.B. Du Bois, the Jamaican back-to-Africa politician Marcus Garvey – who notoriously collaborated with White racists for his scheme – Che Guevara and Toussaint L'Ouverture, the leader of Haitian independence. The South African gallery is ecumenical and includes – alongside defunct historical ANC leaders from Luthuli to Tambo – the founder of the ANC's rival Pan-African Congress, Robert Sobukwe, nineteenth-century Zulu warrior-kings, two White anti-apartheid militants (Bram Fischer and Helen Joseph) and, upon second thought, two Boer commanders from the Anglo-Boer War, De Wet and De la Rey.*

//hapo, a Khoisan word meaning 'dream', is the third major component of the Park, located in a boulder-shaped edifice. It is a museum of African cosmology as well as history, starting with the origins of the Earth, its peopling and the world of ancestors, going through colonialism, industrialization and urbanization up to contemporary nation- and continent-building. No wonder one international architectural competition and one art competition chose no winners because entries did not understand the cultural context properly. Instead, the organizing committee turned to local architects and artists with very specific guidelines.[†]

Latin America: La Raza, populism and urban reform

Racial rehabilitation started much earlier in the principal capitals of Iberian succession. As noted in the chapter on national foundation, the new states of Mexico and Peru did not see themselves as exclusively settler states and included pre-Columbian motifs and connections in their iconographies and master narratives. In the 1850s, the great liberal Benito Juárez, a Zapotec Indian, became a Supreme Court judge and in the 1860s president of Mexico.

---

* A first list of twenty-four names was announced in 2009 and may be found at politicsweb.co.za. By 2014 there were thirty-seven names (A. Oliphant et al., *Freedom Park*, Pretoria, 2014, 43), and additions can be identified at archivalplatform.org. Far from all are on display at the Gallery of Leaders, and in early September 2016 there were no Boer commanders and only one international figure, Che Guevara.

† There is an informative, well-illustrated official guidebook: Oliphant et al., *Freedom Park*. It is quite helpful, but no proper substitute for a full historical treatment. From my own visits and kind informants, it seems that the park has not (yet) become a major site of pilgrimage or tourism, although school classes are regularly taken there.

In the 1920s and 1930s there arose a wave of native cultural recognition, particularly in the two old imperial vice-royalties, Mexico and Peru, both centres of major pre-Columbian polities. It went under the name of *indigenismo* and involved a major cultural revalorization of indigenous culture, which had never been as obliterated or marginalized there as in Anglo North America, despite the continued exploitation of Indian peasants.

The Mexican Revolution was a popular eruption of epic proportions, but its final outcome was a socially ambiguous regime of the victorious warlords. The most dramatic popular revolutionary moment of Mexico City happened in December 1914, when the city was held by the two radical commanders, Emiliano Zapata and Pancho Villa, and their popular militias, but it turned out to be brief and inconsequential. However, the ensuing revolutionary governments were very committed to the education of Indians and Mestizos and to a nationalist, anti-colonialist conception of history in which the Indians, not the conqueror-settlers, had centre stage. This was conveyed to the public by government-commissioned public murals in the National Palace, schools and other public buildings. The long-time minister of education, José Vasconcelos, elevated the Mestizos into a 'cosmic race' of universal significance.[17]

A monument of racial rehabilitation was inaugurated in Mexico City in 1940, at the end of the reign of the most progressive of the presidents out of the Mexican Revolution, Lázaro Cárdenas, a reaffirmation of non-settler Mexican-ness in the form of a *Monumento a la Raza,** with Mexican ethnicity represented by an Indian pyramid topped by an eagle. However, it should also be underlined that alongside official respect and, by Cárdenas, communitarian Indian land rights, inequality, White domination and discrimination continued in Mexican society, aggravated after the end (with Cárdenas in 1940) of the domestic progressive legacy of the 'Institutionalized Revolution'.†

Peru got its first president of Indian descent, Alejandro Toledo, only in 2003. He did not turn out to be a very effective one, but he did remove

---

* Literally 'Monument to the Race', but *la Raza* has very special connotations in Hispanic America. Most often it refers in a cultural way to Hispano-American people. The celebrated Day of *la Raza* is October 12, when Columbus landed in the Caribbean. In the Mexican monument, *la Raza* is basically synonymous with the Mexican people, represented by an Aztec pyramid.

† In foreign policy, some autonomy from Washington dictates has been maintained. Mexico did not go along with the US blockade of Cuba, for instance.

The Reichskanzlei, rebuilt for
Adolf Hitler by Albert Speer,
finished in January 1939.

The official residence of the West German Bundeskanzler in the provisional
capital of Bonn. Designed by Sepp Ruf, finished in 1964.

The Chancellor's Office in
reunified Berlin by Axel
Schultes in 1997–99.

The Union Building in Pretoria, built in preparation for a joint settler state in South Africa shared by its two White settler groups: the Boers and the Anglos. Designed by the imperial architect Herbert Baker, completed in 1913.

Never colonized, Siam was modernized from above in reaction to foreign threats. The first new royal palace, for Rama V, also known as Chulalongkorn, was completed for the centenary of Bangkok in 1882. Combining imported European elements, it was designed by a British architect, incorporating traditional Siamese roofing

Malaysia's National Monument in Kuala Lumpur, inaugurated in 1966. Inspired by the Arlington Cemetery Marine Corps monument, its designer, Felix De Weldon, adopted the imperial narrative of the colonial war: an 'emergency' caused by Communists.

Korean Admiral Yi Sun-Sin, who beat Japanese invaders in the late 1500s, commemorated here in celebration of anti-colonial heroism, 1968.

Replacing colonial conquest with anti-colonial resistance: Emir Abdel Kader, leader of the armed Algerian resistance to French occupation, replacing a statue of the conquering general taken back to France in 1962.

Karl-Marx-Hof in Vienna, the flagship of municipal socialism. A complex of 1,400 apartments with amenities that include a dental practice, maternity clinic, post office, library, shops and meeting rooms. Built by the city of Vienna in 1926–30, architect Karl Ehn.

Influential protest movements constitute another kind of popular moment in urban history. The most innovative, and an important source of international urbanist inspiration, was the Dutch Provos of Amsterdam in the mid-1960s.

African-American Civil War Memorial in Washington, D.C., recalls the participation of African-American soldiers in the Civil War, remembered since 1998.

The South African settler state crumbled and was succeeded by a new post-colonial nation. The Isivane part of the South African Freedom Park on the outskirts of Pretoria/Tshwane is where the spirits of the freedom fighters rest. The boulders represent the nine provinces of South Africa, the nation as a whole, and the international community which supported the struggle against apartheid and settler rule. It was designed by groups of architects guided by traditional healers and Africanist anthropologists. This part opened in 2004, on the tenth anniversary of democratic, post-colonial South Africa.

The early Soviet Union was a world centre for avant-garde architecture, which frequently found expression in workers' social and cultural clubs, such as Rusakov Workers' Club in Moscow, designed on a trade union commission by Konstantin Melnikov in 1927.

Moscow architect Lev Rudnev designed the Palace of Culture in Warsaw to mimic the style of post-WWII Moscow high-rises, but utilizing Polish ornamental motifs. Exemplifying Stalinist Socialist Realism, it was built by Soviet workers and given to Warsaw in 1955. It endured the fall of Communism and survives now in an environment of corporate capitalism.

Canary Wharf in East London, built by and for foreign global capital. In the centre, One Canada Square, a commercial office building designed by the Argentine-American Cesar Pelli, completed in 1991, is flanked by two financial buildings.

Part of the new skyline of Jakarta, where fourteen buildings taller than 210 metres went up in the boom years of 2005–15, mainly funded by local private developers.

Tokyo City Hall, designed by Kenzo Tange, 1991, for the Tokyo Metropolitan Government, a major player in the globalization of Tokyo.

Presidential Palace, Ak Orda
(White Camp), 2004, built by the
Mobetex Group.

Bayterek Tower, 2002, designed by
A. Rustembekov, S. Bazarbayev,
and B. Torgayev. Visually, it refers
to a national folktale about a
golden egg (the sun), laid in a tree
by a mythical bird, which is
devoured by a dragon each winter.
In the nearer background is the
headquarters of KazMunaiGas,
the state gas company, and in the
far central background is the top
of the Khan Shatyr (Royal
Marquee) shopping and
entertainment centre, designed by
Norman Foster and built by a
Turkish firm, opened in 2010.

Peace and Reconciliation Palace,
by Foster + Partners, completed
in 2006. Intended as a world
centre of ecumenical religious
encounters.

the conquistador Pizarro's statue from the main square of Lima and flew a rainbow Amerindian flag over the presidential palace. Between the two world wars there was a significant *indigenista* movement in Peru, spearheaded by two formidable political intellectuals-cum-leaders, the Indoamericanist Victor Raúl Haya de Torre and the heterodox Communist José Carlos Mariátegui. Neither managed to get power, nor, as far as I know, to leave any significant imprints on the city of Lima. There was also in 1920s Peru a paternalist state *indigenismo*, and the liberal semi-dictator Augusto Leguía proclaimed himself 'Protector of the Indian Race'.[18] An odd part of the mood outside the White oligarchy was a donation to the city by its Japanese residents of a statue of the Inca Manco Cápac, given a central location, which Toledo often used as a background to his campaign speeches.[19]

Lima was historically the stiffest and most conservative of the former vice-regal capitals, arguably of all the Hispanic capitals of the Americas. But it came to change radically in the 1960s and 1970s, when the city's population almost tripled, from 1.6 million in 1961 to 4.6 in 1981, through immigration from the Andean areas. City politics did not change much, with weak finances and mayors always under presidential pressure, even if now elected. From 1983 to 1985 a United Left city government was in office, trying social change. It was blocked in its efforts to distribute land rights to popular residents and in instituting popular participation, but its Glass of Milk programme for school children was very popular.[20] In this century there has been at least one more progressive mayor, elected as an independent, but no attempt at any municipal socialism.

However, what has happened has been a major cultural change. The old White Creole culture of Lima has been swamped by that of the Andino immigrants. The latter's *chicha* culture and, particularly, its music have acquired popular hegemony. This is a music very different from the Europe-inherited Creole one and with lyrics that demonstrate a historic cultural shift.

There are three noteworthy themes of the predominant *chicha* songs: class/ethnic pride, modernism and nationalism. My English and my poetic talents are not sufficient for translating the Spanish lyrics idiomatically, but let me give you a few examples of literal translation:

Soy un cholito cantor	I am a little Indian singer
Me gusta ser como soy	And I like what I am.
No tengo dinero	I have no money
soy un pobre obrero . . .	I am a poor worker . . .
trabajo con amor y con calor	I work with love and fervour
por ver grande a mi patria.	to see my fatherland great.
Nosotros los cholos no pedimos nada	We Indians don't ask for anything
pues faltando todo, todo nos	as we lack everything, everything
alcanza	will reach us.
El pueblo va despertando	The people are awakening
el día va amaneciendo . . .	the day is dawning . . .
mire tu pueblo hermano	look at your people, brother
ahora de tí depende . . .	it depends on you . . .
no comas más tu pobreza	don't eat your poverty anymore.
Soy muchacho provinciano . . .	I am a provincial boy . . .
No tengo ni padre ni madre . . .	I have neither father nor mother . . .
Sólo tengo la esperanza de progresar.	I only have the hope of advancing.[21]

To my knowledge, this proud modernist plebeian culture of Lima may be unique. Anyway, it conveys a very distinctive contribution to the meaning of popular moments in urban history.

Peronism was, and is, a national movement of populist origin, with remarkable staying power, but its power was initiated by a mass demonstration in Buenos Aires on 17 October 1945, crucially organized by Trotskyist cadres (and other heterodox militants) of the labour movement in support of Colonel Perón, then labour minister of a fractured military government. While in power Peronism did include a push for popular housing, especially in Buenos Aires,[22] but it has to be remembered as a contributing factor to racial rehabilitation in a very White European city. The White middle class of Buenos Aires was immediately scandalized and horrified by the masses of darker-skinned workers marching into the city centre, like 'an invasion from another country'. Peronist economic and political development promoted the Mestizo population of the interior of Argentina. Its supporters were known as the *cabecitas negras*, the 'little blackheads' or, simply, *negros*.[23] In 1955

Perón was ousted from power, only to return as a ghost in the early 1970s, when chaotic right-wing Peronism paved the way for one of the worst military dictatorships in the hemisphere.

The egalitarian moment of South America, when from 2002 to 2012 the hemisphere went against the inegalitarian headwinds of the rest of the world,[24] had a strong ethno-racial dimension in the Brazilian *Bolsa Familia* and education programmes and the popular 'missions' of the Chavista Venezuelan government. In the increasingly polarized politics of Brazil and Venezuela in 2015 and 2016, the ethnic divide became very visible in the street demonstrations and rallies, overwhelmingly White on the right-wing side, clearly much more pigmented on the left.

Bolivia, like South Africa, left settler statehood altogether. Its 2009 constitution defined Bolivia as a 'plurinational' state, with a number of collective rights granted to Indian communities. The transformation of a deeply inegalitarian formal democracy with a history of a Mestizo class revolution (in 1952) into a largely Indian plurinational democracy was less of an upheaval than the abolition of apartheid – although it was driven forward by epic urban protest movements against the privatization of urban services such as gas and water, issuing into decisive presidential elections. But in terms of reducing economic inequality, the new Bolivia has been much more radical and successful than democratic South Africa.[25]

Urbanistically, the new dispensation is illustrated by the state-initiated cable car connection (of 2014) between the Indian city of El Alto ('The High', at 4,000 metres) with the settler capital La Paz some hundred metres below. But the latter has always had its Indian women traders, and I have not noticed any major capital city change. The glitz of a decade of more than 5 per cent annual economic growth is more visible in La Paz, while the former still perceives itself as poor and a victim of corrupt municipal government – until 2015, when the officialist mayor was outvoted and later landed in jail.

Indian protest movements and claims against the settler states have become significant in large parts of Latin America, from Chile to Guatemala to Chiapas in southern Mexico, as well as in the northern United States and Canada. Their struggles have always been hard and are often repressed. Their rallies and demonstrations have been visible in several capitals, Quito and La Paz particularly, but their movements are mainly rural.

In Brazil and Brasília, racial rehabilitation has been minor, even in comparison with Ottawa, Canberra and Wellington, although Oscar Niemeyer was asked to build an Indian museum in Brasília. Brazil, the largest slave importer of the Americas, still has no proper slavery museum, but one of Afro-Brazilian history was opened in São Paulo during the Lula government. The Workers' Party governments of Lula and Dilma did finally accept racial discrimination as a public issue, above all by introducing affirmative action in higher education. In spite of its national myth of 'racial democracy' (Gilberto Freire), the Brazilian political elite is still much more racially exclusive than that of the United States.*

Popular urban reform

Several capitals of the settler world have had left-of-centre or maverick progressive city governments, even in backwaters of social progress like Central America: San Salvador, for example.[26] But in the past working-class century, no capital city had the organized labour base for municipal socialism of the classical European type.† While Latin

---

* Brazil has no equivalents to, say, Thurgood Marshall, Colin Powell, Condoleezza Rice and Barack Obama. It seems that it is mostly foreign observers who have noticed that the unelected government coming into power after a farcical parliamentary-judicial coup in April–May 2016 is not only all-bourgeois but also all-White and all-male. On the other hand, the racial gap of life expectancy is much smaller in Brazil than in the United States, one year versus four and a half in 2010, respectively (Therborn, 'Moments of equality', 22, with references).

† Immigrants of German descent established one in the Midwestern US city of Milwaukee, finally succumbing to the characteristic New World issue of race. Milwaukee in 1910 was an industrial city with a big working class of largely German origin – familiar with Germanic working-class movements – run, like most American cities at the time, by a clientelistic 'political machine', representing and protecting crony capitalism. In the election that year the Socialist Party managed to forge a winning coalition on anti-corruption, the main concern of the honest middle class, and labour issues (Richard W. Judd, *Socialist Cities*, Albany: SUNY Press, 1989, 22). In the increasingly hostile climate of the capitalist United States, this coalition, made up of labour and sections of the middle class, maintained itself in Milwaukee for five decades, with two stints of opposition (in 1912–16 and 1940–8), until 1960, when mounting anti-Black racism drove the last Socialist mayor not to seek re-election. Clean, practical, efficient government focusing on public utilities and sanitation – chided as 'sewer socialism' by Socialist Party rivals – along with education, housing, and other public services and amenities kept the coalition winning. For further references, see www.wisconsinhistory.org.

American urban politics has had populist aspects, even setting the tone and the agenda in the Caracas agglomeration under Hugo Chávez, successful people-oriented urban politics has been more popular than populist: that is, driven not by the radical anti-establishment rhetoric of a charismatic leader, nor by a European-type class movement, but by a loose coalition of different social forces outside the national establishment, from middle-class sectors to workers and the self-employed of the large 'informal' economy.

Politically, the most successful left city-reform governments have been those of the Broad Front in Montevideo, Uruguay, which has governed the city since 1990, paving the way for a Broad Front presidency in 2005, and which is still in office. Honesty, efficiency and cautious moderation have characterized the Front governments of both city and nation. Urban services, from street lighting and garbage collection to day-care centres, have been extended.[27]

As its name suggests, the Front is a diverse coalition, in constant dialogue but also firmly directed by exemplary (non-rhetorical) leaders, including the soft-spoken family-doctor type Tabaré Vázquez, its first mayor and its first and third president, and the avuncular ex-*guerrillero* Pepe Mujica, its second president. Mujica set a Franciscan example of personal modesty and simple living, but his government refrained from any radical policies of equalization, although the country did take part in the South American moment of equality. After ten years of Broad Front national government, Uruguay is still more economically unequal than any European country.[28]

The most ambitious and comprehensive capital city government of social reform was the Mexico City government led from 2000 to 2006 by Andrés Manuel López Obrador (AMLO), as the peak of a long record of progressive city government (under persistently neoliberal national rule) since 1998. Two formidable secretaries of the city (whose population is equivalent to that of the three Scandinavian countries put together), health secretary Asa Cristina Laurell and social secretary Raquel Sosa, aimed at a system of European-type universal social rights.

AMLO himself may best be described as a nationalist republican; he played his part in following the complex Scandinavian-model game by making development deals with big capital at the same time as pushing social reform. AMLO managed to cooperate with Mexico's richest tycoon, Carlos Slim, on historical centre renovation while also negotiating a solution for the street vendors of the area and with Paul Reichmann (of Canary Wharf) about global sky-scraping; promoting flyover motorways; and hiring the brutal former mayor of New York, Rudy Giuliani, as a consultant – while inspiring his reform secretaries to social boldness. The Native issue was not prominent in the AMLO government, nor was it absent. Southern urban expansion was legally delimited not to encroach on Native rights, for instance.

The social policies of the AMLO government evolved in tandem with large-scale inventories of the social situation of the population and involved several big new programmes. Biggest and most popular was probably the launch of modest universal pensions for people above seventy. After two years, 400,000 seniors were enrolled in the scheme, which also included free medical check-ups. It was financed by 'Republican Austerity': a 15 per cent salary cut for the chiefs of government and all higher managers and a drastic restriction of perks like representation, travel, cars, private medical insurance, etc., with total savings of $300 million. Another programme provided free health care and medicine to people not covered by the complicated health insurance in place. By 2006, 854,000 families had their medical and health care costs paid for by the new system of citizens' rights.[29] The Social Secretariat developed care and assistance for almost 200,000 disabled persons and launched a special programme for single mothers. In order to function as intended, all these programmes required large efforts to identify and contact the people eligible, many of whom were marginalized or excluded from mainstream society. Students of the health and social secretaries, both university professors, were enlisted to help.* The city pension system was soon so successful that it was later adopted by a right-wing national government.

A further lasting achievement was a special kind of participatory budgeting. For local community purposes, the city government functions like an academic research council, where neighbourhoods can apply for money to better the amenities of their locality. If

---

* Asa Cristina Laurell has given good factual accounts of the health and social policies of the López Obrador government in the articles cited above. My knowledge has been enriched by several interviews and conversations with her, with Raquel Sosa and with several Mexican colleagues outside of the government.

approved, the projects are provided with technical expertise and accountants from the city. Examples I saw included a playground for children, an athletic field and a pathway along a brook in the neighbourhood.

Mexican politics is much more brutal, vicious and violent than Uruguayan (under civilian rule), not to speak of Scandinavian. In spite of the great popularity of his city government and, especially, its social policies, Andrés Manuel López Obrador was stopped in his 2006 presidential bid by a professionally developed, hateful campaign as 'a danger to Mexico (*un peligro para México*)', allegedly crowned by electoral fraud.

Urban change in Bogotá has been not so much *by* the people as *for* them, initiated by unaffiliated maverick mayors. But the innovations of the latter do deserve mention in a popular context. Antanas Mockus – former rector of the National University and mayor from 1995 to 1997 and 2000 to 2003 – managed to instil a 'civic culture' (*cultura ciudadana*) into this big unruly capital of a country soaked in violence, political as well as criminal. He did it through a series of pedagogic stunts and symbolic events, including enlisting mimes as traffic police and trading toys for guns at Christmas.[30]

Mockus's successor, Enrique Peñalosa, changed the urban infrastructure, above all with a bus system, Transmilenio (later imported into Santiago, Chile, with less skill and success). Transmilenio runs in separate lanes and is organized like an above-ground subway. It is a very convenient mode of urban transport – as far it goes, which is not quite up to the challenges of the metropolis's needs. In 2015 Peñalosa was re-elected mayor and promised further expansion. In between, Bogotá was governed by the left, without very much success. Its momentum was interrupted by a corruption scandal; once back on the political track, its attempts at tackling inequality and bad popular housing ran into conflicts with the overly mighty real estate interests of developers and middle-class sectors.

Ex-Colonial Elitism and Twenty-First-Century Reform Coalitions

The anti-colonial movements were all popular, but virtually all of them ended up installing post-colonial elites in the very same mansions and bungalows the colonial elites occupied. Most post-colonial politics has not provided much space for ordinary people.

Conceptions of anti-colonial people and nations and their liberation movements change overtime, adding other currents to those created by the post-colonial ruling elite. India and Delhi are central examples. In the course of the 1990s, when the Congress Party was out of office, leaders and 'martyrs' of the violent struggle against the British were officially commemorated in Delhi. (The Congress campaigns under Gandhi and the Nehrus had been non-violent on principle.) In 1995, Shaheed (Martyrs') Park paid homage to the Punjabi revolutionary Bhagat Singh and two of his co-conspirators, executed by the British in 1931. The (once) left-wing Congress leader Subhas Chandra Bose, who during World War II formed an Indian National Army (INA) fighting with the Japanese in Burma, was honoured in 1998 in statue form, with his honorific title Netaji ('respected leader'). Other INA officers were also remembered, as well as commanders and princes who fought against the British in 1857. The decade was strongly dedicated to memorials, including one dedicated to prominent Dalit ('Untouchable') leaders as well as figures of the Hinduist far right.*

Also in Cameroon, the defeated armed popular struggle for independence by the Union des Populations du Cameroun in the late 1950s and 1960s was rehabilitated in the 1990s. Other cases have been more socially ambiguous because the previously unrecognized belonged to pre-colonial elites, like J. B. Danquah, of local royal descent and brought up in post-Nkrumah Ghana, or Mohammad Hatta, now put up alongside Sukarno in Indonesian iconography.

At the end of the day, a recognition of other voices in the nation's history does not quite amount to a popular moment. Nor is an ascendancy of new social forces into power easily detectable in the ex-colonial zone. At a state level, the rise of Dalits in India would count.

However, there are at least two significant and recent examples of popular urban change: in Jakarta from 2012 to 2014 and in Delhi in 2014 and, after a setback, from 2015. They are important moments of urban reform with noteworthy similarities to Latin America, although in different political contexts and with different social dynamics. In both Jakarta and Delhi, like in Montevideo and Mexico City, we are talking about non-elite reformist mayors elected by the populace and

---

* Two then-students of prof. A. Kumar at JNU, Ramesh Singh and Sarada Prasanna Das, compiled a list for me of monumental and toponymical changes in Delhi.

by segments of the middle class: Joko Widodo, known as Jokowi, in Jakarta and Arvind Kejriwal in Delhi.

Jokowi was a inconsequential entrepreneur outside the political establishment and an outsider to Jakarta, having previously been a very popular reform mayor of another important Javanese city, Surakarta (or Solo). He was elected governor of Jakarta against the incumbent, as a known successful reformer attracting both middle-class and popular voters but also with some backing in the complex hinterland of Indonesian party politics. In office, he introduced health insurance, education support for poor students, transparent merit recruitment to the city bureaucracy, a public transit programme to tackle Jakarta's notorious traffic congestion (not very effectively) and a populist style of governing, regularly visiting popular communities in an accessible way. His two-year stint as metropolitan governor was successful enough, buoyed by considerable fiscal powers, to win him the presidential election in 2014. His collaborators in the city continue to run, but there is hardly any organized popular basis to sustain it. The succeeding governor has also a popular style, but as a Christian of Chinese descent he has come under Islamist attack. New elections are due in February 1917.

The current chief minister of Delhi, Arvind Kejriwal, is a former tax official who became fed up with the omnipresent system of corruption in India. His original base was an anti-corruption movement organized along Gandhian lines of exemplary leadership by Anna Hazare, who hesitated to support Kejriwal's entering the game of electoral politics. Kejriwal's triumph, especially his first in December 2013, was due to a kind of coalition politics which may constitute one of the most realistic left-wing strategies of the twenty-first century. It had two pillars: middle-class revulsion at political and bureaucratic corruption and poor people's demand for respect and social support. The Hazare movement brought in middle-class anti-corruption resentment. The Rickshaw Drivers Association, 80,000 strong, provided the core of popular mobilization. Its demands focused on respect and an end to police harassment. But the main issues of broad popular mobilization were free electricity and water (up to a certain level) for the poor. Kejriwal's Common Man Party, running against – by Indian stand-ards – a relatively progressive and only moderately corrupt Congress administration, captured the wealthiest constituency of Delhi (the former colonial New Delhi) as well as most of the constituencies reserved for the so-called backward castes.

Governing Delhi has been a rough ride. In early 2014 Kejriwal resigned, as he could not get his full anti-corruption programme through the city council. In 2015 he won a new election, though with reduced middle-class support. There was an obscure conflict between Kejriwal and a number of prominent left-wing intellectuals of the party, ending with the expulsion of the latter. However, the promises to the poor seem to have been kept. They are getting a basic amount of electricity and water for free.[*]

Reactive modernization from above and anti-modernism from below

Modernization from above, in its inherited elitism, is not only deeply non-popular, it is particularly prone to meeting popular anti-modernism from below. The 1979 Islamic Revolution in Tehran is the most dramatic and far-reaching example in recent times. For sure, the populace of Tehran had excellent, rational social reasons to rise against the Shah's 'modern' city, where 80 per cent of the city budget went to the privileged northern part.[31] And there were genuine popular-progressive forces active in the first phase of the revolution. But the stage had been set against the latter, and the astute ruthlessness of Ayatollah Khomeini decided the outcome.

Popular anti-modernism was most successfully aroused in religious terms, and the militant salvationist religions of Christianity and Islam were most forceful in this respect. In Europe, modernism rose from below and Christian popular reaction hardly became prominent anywhere. But it did exist at the time of the French and the coeval nationalist revolutions and wars: in French Vendée, in the peasant mobilization against the Dutch Batavian Republic – reverently painted by Constantin Meunier – and even in fighting for the Neapolitan Bourbons – as well as for God, of course – against nineteenth-century Italian nationalists. The Ottoman sultans were repeatedly pushed back

---

[*] Arriving in Delhi shortly after Kejriwal's first victory, I scanned the lively Indian press, and since then I have kept bombarding friends among former students and colleagues for information.

from modern reforms by an angry Istanbul populace, as was King Amanullah in Kabul in 1929. Fifty years later, the Afghan Communists had to confront a similar popular reaction: 'Can you think, these Communists want me to send my daughters to school!' as an outraged Afghan tribal leader told an Indian friend of mine.*

In Japan there was no salvationist clergy around to speak reaction to the people, and Siamese Buddhist monks were too tied to the monarchy to try. Nor has there ever been much progressive popular influence. Japan might be said to have had a popular moment in the very first years of the post-war American occupation, with well-meaning New Dealers and a singular Japanese-speaking feminist† on General McArthur's staff, successfully inserting women's rights into the Japanese Constitution. But after the devastating US bombings, rubble clearance and basic reconstruction were the overwhelming urban tasks. And then the Cold War broke out, and anything popular was 'Communist'.

Post-war Tokyo has had a share of urban protest movements, in the end defeated, against the building of Narita Airport and against the city's woefully inadequate coping with homelessness, for instance, but it has only had a brief, rather ineffective stint of progressive governance, in the 1970s. Bangkok, whose city governments have all been well-heeled and not very effective, has, to my knowledge, had none. However, we shall later briefly revisit Bangkok as a site of urban revolution and counter-revolution.

Urban Rebellions

Popular moments may also come out of urban protest movements, among which we are here only concerned with urbanistic ones affecting the shape of the city and with city-moulded movements changing the nation-state. There have been many of them, mainly after World War II,

---

* This US-orchestrated and Saudi-financed anti-modernist movement in Afghanistan and its final victory, cheered by all the liberal media of the West, was the breeding ground and the *rite de passage* to adulthood of contemporary Islamist jihadism and terrorism. Special thanks for the latter should be given to Jimmy Carter's security adviser Zbigniew Brzezinski, who was the first to lionize and support the former.

† Beate Sirota, born in Vienna and raised in Tokyo before the war. See Göran Therborn, *Between Sex and Power*, New York: Routledge, 2004, 93.

but the prevailing literature is predominantly movementalist – i.e., mainly interested in the mobilizations, demands and battles of the movements, and not that much in their urban or state effects.* Here we shall take a look at three kinds of urban popular movements of signifi- cant impact. They differ widely. One is a movement of claims, another of protest and veto and a third is an insurrection or revolution. Their geog- raphy tends to be specific and varied. The claims movements are Latin American in particular, although with wider Third World ramifications. The most successful urban protest movement, so far, was North Atlantic, situated in the very core of developed capitalism. The third is distinc- tively semi-peripheral, mainly Eurasian and North African.

Poor people's claims to the city

The oldest still-existing urban popular movements are probably those claiming poor people's rights to urban living. The *favelas* of Brazil go back to 1897, when veterans of a national army suppressing an armed rebellion in the Northeast of the country left unpaid occupied land on a hill in Rio, which, for reasons still disputed, they named Favela Hill (Morro de favela). In spite of demolitions during the attempt to Haussmannize Rio, official prohibition in the Construction Code of 1937 and efforts at relocations into 'proletarian parks' in the early 1940s, the favelas have remained and expanded.[32] The original Favela Hill (Morro da Providencia) is now an open-air museum.

All over Latin America a pattern of land occupation for self-built urban housing in barren areas, usually public, in or most often around

---

* The grand contribution on urban movements is Manuel Castells's *The City and the Grassroots* (Berkeley: University of California Press, 1983), to which he has added many others, including the recent *Networks of Outrage and Hope* (London: Polity, 2012). In his first work Castells makes, among other things, a major analysis of squatting movements of popular housing. But, typically of the genre, his concluding chapter on 'The Social Significance of Contemporary Urban Movements', concentrates on their possible role in contemporary and future politics – without any intimation of their possible part in future urban developments. Similarly, David Harvey's recent *Rebel Cities* (London: Verso, 2012) is much more focused on the rebels than on the cities, and on rebels' effects on the latter. In his main scholarly work, *Paris: Capital of Modernity* (New York: Routledge, 2005), Harvey is, of course, one of the world's most distinguished urban scholars.

big cities, has established itself: de facto a poor people's claim to rights to the city. At least in some places it has been ritualized and semi-institutionalized as a route to collective urban mobility. The Peruvian language acknowledges this in calling these settlements *pueblos jóvenes,* young neighbourhoods.

In an ideal-type story, a group of families – this is not individual youth squatting, as in recent Europe – usually from the same rural origin, will assemble in the early morning on a selected site with one or more national flags as a sort of symbolic shield and start constructing housing shacks on it. Unless driven away, after many years the settlements will be recognized by the city. Cement may be offered for building better houses. Later water and electricity may be connected, schools may be built, streets may be paved. This unplanned urban development could be linked to populist politicians and regimes interested in popular votes, and to a whole informal economy of squatting, developers and building workers for hire.[33]

These are stories I have heard and seen in Bogotá, Lima, Mexico City and Rio, cities where informal squatted settlements are tradition, although accelerated in the 1960s, and very significant: 60 per cent of the population of Mexico City, around 40 per cent in Lima and Caracas, 30 per cent in Rio and 25 per cent in Bogotá around 1990.[34] The stories probably exist on other continents, but I have not heard them in the cities I have visited.* The ex-colonial cities of Africa and South Asia and their squatters have had fewer resources and less capacity to upgrade their massive informal slums, and many slums are not self-built but set up by slumlords and let out, as in Nairobi's huge Kibera, originally built by Nubian war veterans. However, India has recently launched a National Urban Renewal Mission and Kenya a Slum Upgrading programme.[35] And there has been self-organization, since 1996, including a tri-continental Slum Dwellers International, strongest in Kenya and India.

Squatting settlements, even in the exceptional cases of successful collective mobility, always start as sub-standard housing, 'slums' by the

---

* Nor do such stories of collective squatting, upgrading and mobility occur in recent literature on urban 'informality', as in Ananya Roy and Nezar Alsayyad, *Urban Informality: Transnational Perspectives from the Middle East, Latin America, and South Asia,* Lanham, MD: Lexington Books, 2004, and Huchzermeyer, *Cities with Slums: The Informal City Reader,* Johannesburg: SACN, 2014.

UN Habitat definition. It should be underlined that slum dwelling is, first of all, a denial of full rights to the city, an indicator of the city's urban power being incapable and/or unwilling to provide adequate services for all its inhabitants. We have seen above how the number of people living in sub-standard housing is increasing.

However, informal land occupation and self-construction are also claims of rights. In at least some experiences they have, moreover, been vehicles of collective social mobility. Squatting is an assertion of popular power in the face of an abdication of official power, upon the cooperation of which poor people's rights to the city, to urban services, ultimately depends.* Outside Latin America, bulldozing and mass evictions have been the most extensive power response to poor people's housing needs: a million evictions in military Rangoon in the mid-nineties, half a million in 'reform' Jakarta from 2001 to 2003, and 700,000 in Robert Mugabe's Harare in 2005.[36] In the 1970s the Argentine military junta kicked off the trend, expelling almost 200,000 poor people from the city of Buenos Aires.[37]

Challenging the car city

Popular moments of urban history have also surged because of informal civic protests gaining traction and power, although mainly veto power. One major target of such protest movements consists of plans to build motorways cutting through central cities – plans for realizing the 'Futurama' city General Motors envisioned at the New York World's Fair in 1939.† The projects were a truly northern transatlantic plague, launched from the 1950s to the 1970s in a large number of big cities – like New York and London – and small ones, like my old little Swedish university town of Lund. In the 1950s, Western European urban and traffic planners had become infatuated with the expressways through

---

* The fundamental aspect of inequality and denial is the focus of Mike Davis's justly acclaimed *Planet of Slums*, London: Verso, 2006. An upbeat journalistic counterblast is Doug Saunders, *Arrival City*, New York: Vintage, 2010, focusing on transitions and individual mobility.

† A picture of it can be found in Christopher Klemek's excellent architectural history, *The Transatlantic Collapse of Urban Renewal*, Chicago: University of Chicago Press, 2011, 51.

Chicago and Los Angeles, and a spate of officious reports followed enthusiastic travelogues. The 'car-friendly city', or simply the 'car city' – the title of a celebratory urban-planning conference in Stockholm in 1956 – was the new slogan of European urban modernism, in Germany, the United Kingdom (as in the Buchanan Report of 1963) and the rest of the sub-continent, from Scandinavia to Italy.[38]

In most places these projects of city planners and private developers were stopped by public protest movements, occasionally with Machiavellian high-level supporters, such as in Washington, D.C., with some help from the Nixon administration.*

Starting in the late 1950s and gathering momentum in the 1960s and 1970s, there arose an intercontinental urban cultural rebellion. Its hardest edge was against the 'motor city' or 'car city', tearing apart the existing urban fabric for the benefit of fast motor traffic to sprawling suburbs. The movement derived its strength from its cultural and political ecumenism, uniting conservationist conservatives, poor ethnic neighbourhoods threatened by demolitions and displacement, young people in need of affordable central-city housing and radical democrats calling for participatory democracy and civic rights to the city.†

The first major battle was in Greenwich Village, New York City, where Robert Moses, arguably the most vicious and racist of urban planners, wanted to bisect Washington Square with a motor thoroughfare. The victorious resistance was led by a remarkable amateur urbanist, more conservative than radical: Jane Jacobs, who afterwards wrote a very thoughtful and influential book on American cities.[39]

The Greenwich Village victory over motorist modernism was very inspiring to other US cities. Washington, D.C. had its own battle, above all against the powerful congressmen then ruling the capital. The key issue was a proposed Three Sisters Bridge across the Potomac River as part of a Potomac River Freeway, which would entail razing a number of African American dwellings. The idea of building the bridge was first

---

* J. Schrag, 'The federal fight in Washington D.C.: The Three Sisters Bridge in three administrations', *Journal of Urban History* 305 (2004): 668–73. President Nixon, as a pragmatic, non-ideological conservative crook, played a positive role in finally winding down the freeway with its crucial bridge and unlocking funding for the Washington Metro.

† The first good study of this, though largely limited to the United States, the United Kingdom and West Germany, is Klemek, *Transatlantic Collapse of Urban Renewal*.

concretized in 1960, in the plan of the D.C. Highway Department. Civic protests were voiced early in official public hearings. The controversy turned into a bitter political conflict later in the 1960s, when key members of Congress declared they would refuse any funding for a Washington Metro unless the bridge was built; public protesters were arrested. After more than a decade of political and legal wrangling, the project was finally stopped – and its provisional beginnings washed away by a storm.[40]

The cultural change or rebellion was mainly confined to North America and north-western Europe, although sometime in the late 1960s White Pretoria, without rebellion, abandoned a plan to rip up the city with motorways.* The movement arose where the car had already become a nuisance of mass consumption, in north-western Europe just barely. It did not, until much later, reach Southern Europe, Eastern Europe or Africa, Asia and Latin America, where a private car was still a popular aspiration. In Paris in 1959, the city council rejected a motorway loop inside the city, but the ringway around it, the Boulevard Périphérique of 1962, constituted what an eminent urban historian has aptly called a 'concrete moat' between the city and the *banlieue*.[41] In Britain a 'Homes Before Roads' movements developed over the course of the 1960s, and in 1973 Labour gained the upper hand in the London election under the banner of 'Stop the Motorways'.[42]

The most colourful and, internationally, the most culturally influential of these movements of urban rebellion was that of the Amsterdam Provos (from 1966 on), who worked on a number of fronts, including a pioneering boost of city cycling. They mainly operated as squatters in empty buildings, setting off a significant international movement of youthful squatting, from Italian 'social centres' (still existing) to the Copenhagen 'Free State' of Christiania, a remarkable neighbourhood (on ex-military land) of extra-legal survival for decades and counting. The idea of young people squatting – so different from Third World family occupations of unused land – has even spread to post-Communist Europe, as a 2015 visit to Warsaw revealed.† An enduring urban effect of the Provos was the preservation of the Nieuwmarkt neighbourhood, threatened by – you guessed it – a motorway.[43]

---

* Here I am indebted to my South African colleague and friend Alan Mabin.
† Thanks to my Polish publisher, Mikolaj Ratajczak.

In terms of urban politics, the example of the 1960s and 1970s battle of Stockholm, relatively little known internationally, merits some attention. The context was a major reconstruction of the core of the city of Stockholm, as usual demolishing sub-standard popular housing, easing traffic and providing more office space. The ultimate focus of the battle was very specific: felling or preserving the elm trees in Kungsträdgården, a central city square, for the building of a new Metro station. De facto, of course, the conflict was much wider: about house demolitions, street widening and, perhaps above all, civic say in urban planning. The conflict was basically non-violent, in a Swedish manner, but the line-up was noteworthy.

In defence of the elms and for a different city conception was a loose convergence of bourgeois intellectuals, journalists, some young politicians, left student radicals and the middle-class urbanistic 'Alternative City' activists, and against was a Social Democratic–led compact of all the mainstream political parties. At this time, Social Democracy was still a working-class cadre movement, so the embattled Social Democratic leader of the collective mayoralty enlisted the party apparatus to get support resolutions from workplaces and local trade unions. The support resolutions did come in, but they did not change the new urban balance of power. Classical working-class politics was ebbing out, even in Sweden, beginning in the capital. The 'City '67' plan was substantially scaled down and the elm trees survived – without hindering a new Metro station.[44]

The cultural rebellion against the motor city scored a number of local victories, with enduring effects. Even more importantly, it asserted the effective rights of a public say in the town planning process, a demand backed up intellectually and politically from many sides – including that of Jane Jacobs in the United States, the empirical urban sociology of Paul-Henry Chombart de Lauwe and Henri Lefebvre in France, and the 1968 British parliamentary Skeffington Committee.[45]

The protest surge of the European popular moment has resided, but it remains a non-negligible aspect of Western European urban politics. Berlin and Hamburg, for example, are now officially proud of their once violently contested neighbourhoods, which still include occupied buildings and list them among city 'highlights', like Berlin's Kreuzberg or Hamburg's Schanzenviertel. Brussels got a big participatory injection after the Parisian riots in May 1968. Most European capitals still have their watchful and occasionally riotous popular movements. Berlin has a powerful institution of referendum, which in May 2014 stopped any construction at the former Tempelhof airfield. East Berlin had not been allowed that contentious tradition, which has contributed to the final political go-ahead for rebuilding part of the Wilhelmine royal palace in the former Marx-Engels-Platz (now Palace Square) of central East Berlin. While currently hardly qualifying as a popular moment of urban history, civic influence on urban development has not disappeared, as the Berlin example illustrates. Rather, it has spread, often involving innovative progressive architects as well as neighbourhood activists. It can even be found in some locales of Moscow.[46] Institutional power, like personal, is no longer absolute.

Urban equality of the bicycle with, and perhaps even in some respects primacy over, the car has become public policy in many European capitals. In London it has been pushed by the Conservative mayor Boris Johnson. Paris seems to be most ambitious, first out (after the Amsterdam Provos) with public bicycles, and currently building a bicycles-only expressway through the city.

Outside the North Atlantic and appended areas, institutionalized popular participation in urban planning and development – as well as bicycle paths – is mostly contested terrain, but even contestability is an advance of global urbanism. Urban movements continue, most often focused on housing issues, and I have had students write about them in Istanbul and Beijing, among other places. The 2011 Occupy movement added a remarkably global dimension to anti-capitalist protest, so far without much effect, alas.

The Unexpected Return of Urban Revolutions

At the end of the nineteenth century, Friedrich Engels put forward a bleak view of the present and the future of urban revolutions in a preface to a new edition of Marx's analysis of the 1848 revolutions, *The Class Struggles in France, 1848 to 1850*. While not excluding that urban fighting might play some role in future social transformations, Engels pointed to two main reasons why 'the mode of struggle [*Kampfweise*] of 1848 is in every respect obsolete'. First, the military had become much stronger, and much more lethally armed. Second, 'an uprising with which all popular strata sympathise will hardly [*schwierlich*] come back; in the class struggle all the middle strata will never group themselves around the proletariat so exclusively that the party of reaction around the bourgeoisie almost disappears'.[47]

Engels's *Spätstil* (late-style) evolutionary conception of social change was challenged in 1917 Russia, where both victorious revolutions, February and October, were urban. However, after that, urban history proved him right for at least sixty years.

Then the world changed again. Our contemporary era has seen a number of successful urban revolutions, from Tehran's Islamic Revolution in 1979 and Manila's People's Power in 1986 to Kyiv's Maidan in 2014. The implosion of Eastern European Communism included several moments of urban revolution: in Dresden-cum-Berlin, in Prague and Bucharest in 1989 and in Moscow in 1991. This century has seen successful revolutionary upheavals in Belgrade, Kyiv, Tbilisi, Bishkek and Bangkok, among others. Buenos Aires in December 2001 might also be counted, as a vast protest wave, middle-class and popular, against a literally bankrupt neoliberalism which drove President Fernando de la Rúa to resign. In spite of its popular slogan – *Que se vayan todos* ('They should all go', meaning the whole political establishment) – the movement was almost immediately canalized into the other established sector of Argentine politics, Peronism, and its still-functioning legislative institutions.*

'Revolution' is here used as a concept of urban, not of social, history. It refers here to urban popular movements of street protest succeeding in toppling a sitting national political regime, usually by forcing its leadership to resign.

In its rapid international diffusion, the Arab Spring of 2011, with its centres in Tunis and Cairo, resembled the Europe of 1848, to which it was often compared. However, the revolution most similar to the one in which Engels took part was probably the Kyiv Maidan – that is, as a form of uprising, not in its social and political content. It was partly armed and successfully defended its barricades and occupied city space against repeated attacks by the police.

---

* De la Rúa was a Radical who had unwisely continued the unsustainable neoliberal economic policies of his predecessor, the right-wing Peronist Carlos Menem. Police repression had left several dead, and De la Rúa gave up when his beleaguered presidency was denied any parliamentary backup by the Peronists. The crisis ended with a turn to the more progressive wing of Peronism, and the presidential election of its then-little-known candidate Néstor Kirchner, who turned out to be an effective president.

The geopolitics was of course different, almost the reverse of 1848. Leaders of Euro-American reaction, from John McCain to Jarosław Kazcyński to minor figures like Swedish foreign minister Carl Bildt, lined up applauding the insurgents, and a top State Department official came feeding them. The outcome, and the meaning, of 1848 would have been different if the politicians of the Holy Alliance had come along cheering and if the Tsar's chargé d'affaires had handed out blinis to the barricade fighters.*

Now, Engels's first reason for the obsolescence of urban revolutions – a stronger military – according to his own argument needs not necessarily be decisive. As he wrote, even in 1848 it was not the fire-power but the willingness of the soldiers to attack the insurgents which was decisive. His second reason holds only on the assumption that a mass rally of the people can only group around the working class. Adapted to later, more volatile class alignments, the core of the revolutionary analysis of the old 'General' of 1848 has shown itself surprisingly relevant to recent urban upheavals: passivity of the repressive forces and massive rallies of heterogeneous social forces, in which the alignment of the middle strata has been crucial. Like the successful revolutions of 1830 and 1848, the outcome of the Kyiv Maidan was decided by the refusal of the army and large contingents of the police to defend the government.

The recent revolutions have all been socially ambiguous in their intentions as well as in their consequences, an effect of being driven by broad, heteroclite coalitions and convergences of short-term interests. The Kyiv Maidan involved the broadest convergence ideologically, from liberals dreaming of EU prosperity to rabidly anti-Russian nationalists to fascists and Nazis. The latter were a small minority but a crucial one, providing the streetfighters and snipers who fought the vacillating regime to exhaustion.

None has been a working-class revolution, nor have any of the unsuccessful ones been. Instead, there has usually been large and influential

---

* As might be expected about an event so eagerly supported by the major powers of the North Atlantic, the mainstream reporting and literature is very ideologically overdetermined. An exception is Richard Sakwa, *Frontline Ukraine*, London: I.B. Tauris, 2016. Also informative is the early documentation put out by supporters of the uprising: Claudia Dathe and Andreas Rostek (eds), *Majdan!* Berlin: Edition fotoTAPETA, 2014.

middle-class participation, of businesspeople as well as professionals. Students and unemployed youth have generally been very active in the streets and squares, workers most of the time less so.

The adversary, even when elected, lacked constitutional democratic legitimacy because of fraudulent or rigged elections.* The reason France came close to a revolution in 1968 was that the Fifth Republic had been set up on the shoulders of a coup – or rather a mutiny of the colonial army in Algeria, the tenth anniversary of which was the starting point of the mass movements of protest. Secondly, the incumbent government was obviously incompetent, unsuccessful and/or blatantly corrupt. Internally it was ideologically hollowed out, often personally exhausted and very often ailing at the top. More robust and brutal regimes resisted and fought back. If the third condition for a successful revolution was absent, they succeeded, as in Kwangju, South Korea, in 1980, Caracas and Beijing in 1989 and Syria in 2011.

The trigger of the protest movements varied and was usually quite contingent. Its dynamic interaction with the ruling regime – of demands, rejections, new demands, repression, concessions, etc. – also varied. However, there was a decisive factor common to them all. The protests turned into regime-changing revolutions because, at the crucial moment, the repressive forces – the military in particular – refused to back up the regime. In Tehran in 1979 and Manila in 1986, where the People's Power revolution had actually started as a small military conspiracy before mobilizing masses of people against the corrupt president and his latest rigged election, important military units ultimately defected to the insurrection.[48] In Paris 1968 there was a moment when de Gaulle disappeared and went to consult his commanding generals, especially the most brutal of them all, the parachutist General Massu. Reassured of their preparedness to intervene, De Gaulle returned to Paris and made his famous 'I do not resign' speech. Game over, and the Gaullists went marching up the Champs-Élysées.

The Occupy and Indignados movements of the latest financial crisis faced regimes with dubious popular credentials kowtowing to capital interests, but nevertheless with a constitutional legitimacy not seriously disputed. Because of that, there was never any doubt that the whole

---

* That was not the case with De la Rúa's election in Argentina; his resignation had a constitutional exit, from the executive to the legislature.

police force would defend the regime and, if need be, so would the military.

Cities of power can, then, under certain circumstances, turn into cities of revolution through tenacious, resilient mass appropriations of urban space, of main avenues and squares. Radical ideas of whatever kind circulate more rapidly in big cities, and the site of government provides an obvious target of protest. But urban institutions have, in most cases, been spectacularly absent, from the confrontation as well as from the revolution. There are few equivalents to the nineteenth-century Paris Hotel de Ville or Commune.

Why, then, this recent propensity to revolution? There seem to be two major reasons. On the side of revolution, there is the growth of a large, volatile middle class – overcompensating for the decline or stalling of the working class, very different from the sedate European bourgeoisie and the traditionalist bazaar traders, often linked to a large student milieu and currently hooked in the virtual community of social media. These middle strata, in contrast to their bourgeois predecessors, constitute a potential for democratic urban street protest and are on some crucial occasions capable of rallying sectors of the precariat and the unemployed.

In the post-Soviet countries, these middle strata are also particularly cultivated and have a lot of organizations trained and financed by the US government and by private US and allied donors. Their activity and involvement are relatively well known in the cases of Belgrade in 2000; in the so-called Colour Revolutions of Ukraine, Georgia and Kyrgyzstan; and in the Maidan uprising.[49] According to the State Department official in charge of the Ukraine, Victoria Nuland, the United States has invested more than 5 billion dollars in pro-US promotion since 1991.* That is an enormous sum, corresponding to 4 per cent of Ukraine's GDP in 2014. While this greatly compensates for the lack of middle-class revolutionary parties or movements of the classical-left type, it had better not be taken as politically decisive. The many failures and defeats of the Comintern and of revolutionary Cuba in trying to promote revolutions should teach us that exporting revolution is a very difficult trade.

On the regime side, the twentieth-century ideological edges – anti-Communism/Communism, fascism/anti-fascism – have been

---

* Officially labelled 'pro-democracy', of course. Sakwa, *Frontline Ukraine*, 86.

blunted. When these polarities were paramount, unarmed or little-armed revolutions stood no chance. Fascism was defeated in 1945, but the Cold War soon resurrected the Communist/anti-Communist divide. Anti-Communist uprisings were put down in Eastern Europe. In the Americas Marxism was 'not negotiable', as Henry Kissinger declared: as demonstrated by the doctrine of the coup against the Popular Front government in Chile and of US interventions in Central America. Towards the 1980s the Cold War was thawing – in spite of a fatal US attempt to play a card of Islamic fundamentalism against modernizing Communism in Afghanistan. The revolutions of Tehran, Manila and Cairo owe a significant part of their success to gentle US nudging out of the Shah, Ferdinand Marcos and Hosni Mubarak. Mikhail Gorbachev made it clear to the Communists of Eastern Europe in the 1980s that if they got into trouble with their own people, the USSR would not intervene. And the corrupt post-Communist regimes of Ukraine, the Caucasus and Central Asia no longer have any patron to turn to, with the possible exception of the current Ukraine regime, in which the United States and European Union have invested much as a pawn against Russia.

The third element of the current revolutionary equation – corrupt, incompetent regimes – is much more a constant feature of political history than a novelty. But there seems to have been an aspect of twentieth-century ideological senility, whether of Communism, post-Communism not injected by neoliberalism or Arab secular nationalism.

The urban effects of these revolutions have been mainly symbolic. The People's Power monument in Manila was arguably the most authentic, expressing the joyful victory of the people.[50] The abstract Shah monument in Tehran has been turned into a freedom monument, and in popular southern Tehran a big memorial mosque complex has been raised in memory of Ayatollah Khomeini. The Ukrainian 'Orange Revolution' launched a large-scale project of nationalist iconography and narrative, and the military which ended the Arab Spring in Egypt has used the people's Tahrir Square for a redacted monument to the victims of the anti-Mubarak protests. The Islamic Revolution in Iran has been exceptional in its brutal, puritanical regulation of urban living, dress codes and rigid gendering of space.

Even when successful, urban revolutions have their limitations, which Marx analyzed more than 150 years ago in *The Eighteenth*

Brumaire of Louis Bonaparte. They tend to represent a particularly volatile segment of a national society. In the Arab Spring, the unrepresentative
nature of the capital appeared in the Islamist electoral victories in Egypt
and Tunisia. The nationalists of western Ukraine conquered Kyiv but
were blocked in large parts east of the Dnipro. The (predominantly if
not exclusively) right-wing Yellow Shirts of Bangkok have learnt that
they cannot (in the foreseeable future) win a democratic election, which
is why they want to abolish universal suffrage for elections limited to 'us,
who are educated, and who know what is right or wrong'.

None of the 'revolutions' we have talked about here has been or even
attempted to be a social revolution. Nor was the restoration of capitalism a public aim of the anti-Communist upheavals in Prague, Bucharest
and elsewhere. The revolutionary movements have been socially broad
and heterogeneous while narrowly focused on the political regime, and
with political effects often short-lived or delimited even when
successful.

Egypt, the first prize of the Arab Spring, is back to a new version of a
well-known military authoritarianism. Both the Orange Revolution in
2005 and the Maidan of 2014 left the Ukraine with similar, corrupt
oligarchic regimes. The country has moved closer to Europe but hardly
closer to European prosperity, and in some respects further away from
European freedom.* In the Philippines, People's Power led back to the
oligarchic power of the Aquinos and other landowning dynasties,
including, after some quarantine, the once-ousted Marcos family. True,
the Shah's regime is gone forever in Iran, but whether the people have
gained anything economically and socially is questionable.

However, this bleak academic conclusion is not the whole truth. The
urban revolutions, the failed as well as the briefly successful ones, were
popular movements of generational imprint, moments of challenge to

---

* The former government party was forcibly dissolved in the West, the Communist
party has been banned and it has become a crime to criticize the World War II
Quislings and Mussolinis of Ukraine or to 'sympathize with the separatists of the East'.
A few years ago, before the division of the Ukraine, I was sitting on a summer night
by the Black Sea in Crimea with a Kyiv academic summer school. We were talking
about what features of our countries we could be proud of. Few Ukrainians saw
anything in their country to be proud of. But one person had an answer: 'In the
Ukraine you can say and you can read whatever you want'. By 2016 that is no longer
quite true.

rotten powers, moments of mass movement, of collective strength and community: 'festivals of the oppressed', as Lenin said. The recent urban revolutions remind us that even twenty-first-century cities are not reducible to global business services, luxury consumption and privileged 'creativity' or, alternatively, slum misery. At some moments, cities can turn strangers into a people, consumers into citizens. And the participants will remember: a *soixante-huitard* (a participant in the 1968 aborted revolution) will remain one for the rest of her life as much as a *quarante-huitard* (a participant in the 1848 European revolution) will, and so will the protagonists of People's Power in the Philippines of 1986 and of the Arab Spring of 2011.

The Plural Popular Moments

There have been many popular moments in modern history when elite establishments have cracked or broken. We may even say that over the long run there has been an evolutionary trend towards wider popular inclusion in national societies and more participation in national polities. This trend, uneven and irregular as it is, has in large part been driven by the socio-economic ascendancy of the working class, of women, of subordinated and downtrodden races or ethnic groups and of a new middle class.

People rising has taken many forms, and above I have only hinted at a few of them, from institutionalized social reform to urban insurrections via non-institutionalized movements, such as squatters claiming a right to urban living and alternative-culture movements against building cities around cars and motorways.

Popular moments have their social geography related to that of the national foundations. Institutional social reform developed in Europe as 'municipal socialism' and later as welfare states, but there have also emerged differently composed reform coalitions in Latin America and elsewhere. Racial rehabilitation has been the distinctive task of the descendants of conquerors and settlers, who set up their nation-states on the base of racial exclusion, marginalization and/or subordination. In two countries, South Africa and Bolivia, this rehabilitation has led to a reconstitution of the nation-state as post-colonial and multi-ethnic. Autonomous popular movements have had difficulties developing in post-colonial countries – although urban riots have erupted, against rigged elections as well as IMF policies – where the anti-colonial liberation movements have tended to define themselves as 'the people'. But we have seen inspiring urban reform movements recently getting into power in major post-colonial capitals such as Delhi and Jakarta. Reactive modernization from above runs the risk of facing popular moments of traditionalist reaction, particularly in countries with numerous clergy who are autonomous from the state. Communist as well as monarchist regimes in the Islamic world have been confronted with this, as are currently the heirs of exhausted secular Arab nationalism.

Urban revolutions or uprisings have staged a remarkable comeback, broadly based socially, albeit with a middle-class core, and politically narrow. They are spread more widely than the medieval and nineteenth-century revolutions, largely confined to Europe, but concentrated in what world-systems analysts would call the 'semi-periphery' of the world, outside the centre of consolidated electoral democracies – whose constitutional legitimacy remains intact – but also of the poorest parts, where violence is less controlled and restrained.* Such uprisings have been at least temporarily successful because of the ideological de-polarization and aging of the world, which has made governments less militant and the police and the military more reluctant to defend them.

Peoples' insurrections, protest and claims movements and peoples' reforms all mean that the cities of power also have the potential of cities of opposition and power change. At the end of this book, I shall approach the question of the urban future of the people.

---

* Possibly foreshadowing more urban revolutions in Africa, the October 2014 civil movements in Ougadougou (capital of Burkina Faso), initiated by popular musicicans, forced the president to resign instead of taking extra-constitutional measures to prolong his power. In September 2015, popular street mobilizations quelled a coup that had blocked that year's election.

7
Apotheosis of Power:
Fascism and Kindred Dictatorships

Fascism has a special place in any study of modern power. It was the High Mass of a cult of power, violence, war, leadership and imperialism. Its urbanistic ambitions measured themselves in relation to those of the emperors of ancient Rome and the Pharaohs of Egypt, although it is true that they had also learnt something from the Paris of the Second French Empire. Any serious look at modern cities of power will have to give some particular attention to the capitals of fascism: Rome under Mussolini and Berlin under Hitler. Though part of national trajectories, these urban times cannot possibly be subsumed under a generic concept like nation-state capitals.

Fascism has had many admirers and followers, to be duly recognized in proper contexts and who may all be seen as belonging to a tribe of chauvinistic, violent, anti-egalitarian authoritarians. However, in terms of regimes, I think it is most fruitful to understand Italian Fascism and German Nazism alone as proper fascist regimes because of their predominant modernism: political, economic and cultural. They defeated or outwitted their original conservative allies, the Salandras and the Hugenbergs, while in Hungary, the Baltics, Romania, Portugal and Spain it was the other way around. Not everybody will probably agree with that, but nobody would dispute that Mussolini's Rome and Hitler's Berlin were the most important fascist capitals.

While briefly taking stock of ambitions or achievements by some kindred right-wing capital rules of the first half of the twentieth century, we shall also pay some attention to the most violent military regimes of the last third of the previous century: the rulers of Jakarta, Buenos Aires and Santiago de Chile.

Mussolini and the Third Rome

Rome is the only ancient power centre of Europe, although both London and Paris may boast of some ancient Roman archaeology. As such, Rome has almost always had a deeply ambiguous status in Italian modernity. Attracted by its ancient aura, the Italian nation-state made the city its capital, but it retained even on the eve of World War I a widespread negative image as a parasitic, venal city of priests, bureaucrats and prostitutes.[1] At the same time (and often in the same persons, from Mazzini to Mussolini), it was the 'eternal city' of ancient glory. The fascists were, of course, bent on pursuing the second track. The fascist takeover of power took the form of a northern March on Rome in 1922, where the Blackshirt militias, after a few days of skirmishes in the San Lorenzo working-class district, were welcomed on the steps of the Vittorio Emanuele monument by the mayor and the municipal council *in pleno*.[2] The king offered the prime ministership to Mussolini:

> The first phase of the national revolution is completed. The parliamentary oligarchy is shattered [*spezzata*]. The democratic ideology, the ideology of the individual and of humanity, of the stomach and of the cloud, is knocked over [*rovesciata*].[3]

Rome thrived under fascism, growing much faster than the big industrial cities of the North: Milan, Torino and others. In 1931 it became a city of a million, and during the twenty years of fascist rule its population more than doubled.[4] This development should first of all be seen as an indication of the centralization of power and resources into the capital.

Rome's imperial history provided a decisive backdrop to all fascist endeavours of urbanism, which were mostly improvised and ad hoc. The City Plan of 1931 did not regulate much. For all its ostentatious cult of the Leader – *il Duce* – fascism, as little as any actually existing dictatorship, did not correspond to the liberal Cold War notion of 'totalitarianism'. Mussolini was surrounded by different forces and inter-ests, and he often changed his mind. For most of the fascist era the appointed governorate of Rome was run by members of the old nobility of papal Rome, although there was a brief mid-1930s *intermezzo* of a particularly dynamic, intellectual and aggressively violent fascist cadre, Giuseppe Bottai.[5]

Fascism created its own power centre in Rome, at some distance from royal and parliamentary Rome. It was centred on Palazzo Venezia, an imposing edifice, formerly the Venetian embassy to the papacy. After the demise of Venice it was inherited by the Austrian empire, from which the Italian state seized it in 1916 as a booty of war. In front of it was a square on which the masses could be rallied; in view of it was the huge Vittoriano monument with its Altar to the Fatherland and, under fascism, a relatively discreet relief to the Unknown Militant (of fascism). Nearby was the Campidoglio, the hill centre of the government of Rome, with a beautiful square laid out by Michelangelo and a red granite tomb commemorating the Fallen of Fascism. After taking power, the fascist Grand Council met in Palazzo Venezia, and in 1929 Mussolini moved his offices there. From the balcony of the palace he made his notorious speeches.

In an early programmatic speech in 1924, Mussolini put the tasks of fascist Rome into two categories: 'necessity', first of all housing (of which not much positive was achieved), and communications; and *grandezza*, liberating the city from medieval ugliness and 'creating the monumental Rome of the twentieth century'.[6] In contrast to Hitler, Mussolini did not keep one court architect for his capital but surrounded himself with several favourites, mainly of modernist inclinations. Marcelo Piacentini, who successfully recycled himself into a post-fascist, post-war architect, was *primus inter pares*. The most gifted is usually held to be Giuseppe Terragni, a true fascist believer who made the famous modernist Casa del Fascio in Como and the key part of the Tenth Anniversary of the Fascist Revolution exhibition in 1932. The striking modernist Palace of Italian Civilization at the Esposizione Universale Roma (EUR) was designed by yet other architects, a group headed by Giovanni Guerrini.

Modern *grandezza* was pursued by three main means. One was a series of brutal Haussmannian demolitions of houses and neighbour-hoods in the old city in order to enhance the solitude of landmark buildings – *giganteggiare in solitudine* – to widen streets and to build

some new thoroughfares. In characteristic fascist fashion, the inhabitants had no choice but to be deported to new suburban *borgate,* the first
of which were just shacks without water or electricity, far away from the
artisans' traditional livelihoods.[7] The most devastating of these demolitions was the destruction of the *borghi* neighbourhoods in front of Saint
Peter's Square to open up the grand entry to the Vatican, the Via della
Conciliazione, referring to the 1929 Concordat between Mussolini and
Pope Pius XI.

Second, several spectacular secular roads and places were laid out:
the Autostrada del Mare (Sea Highway); the Via dei Trionfi, used for
military parades until World War II put an end to Italian triumphs; and
the Foro Mussolini, with its obelisk to the *Dux.* In the mid-1930s, at the
crest of the regime's self-confidence and popularity, these central
representations of power were to be focused on a palace to the Fascist
Party, including its martyrs and exhibitions of its achievements: a
Palazzo Littorio (referring to the ancient lictor and fascio). This was
meant to be an extremely important monument of the regime to itself,
and therefore location as well as style were hot issues. Another urbanistic aim, of resurrecting and reconnecting to the ancient might of
Imperial Rome, first seemed to point towards a palace site near the
Colosseum and the imperial fora. However, it was soon realized that it
was difficult, and probably impossible, to erect some modern grandeur
in that context without debasing the majesty of the ancients. It was then
decided to move the building to the new Foro Mussolini. A rather flat
design of pompous modernism was selected and built. But during the
war, the Fascist Party rapidly lost centrality in the regime – although its
Grand Council remained powerful enough to depose its own dictator in
1943, without being able to launch a successor – and the Palace of
Fascism became the Ministry of Foreign Affairs of the Italian nation-
state and has remained so until the day of this writing.*

Third and most ambitious of all was the planning of a new centre of
Rome, in the southeast, around a World Exhibition planned for 1942
and the twentieth anniversary of fascism. It was known then as E42 and

---

* The story of the planning of and the competitions of designs for the Palace of Fascism
is vividly narrated by Paul Baxa (*Roads and Ruins: The Symbolic Landscape of Fascist
Rome,* Toronto: University of Toronto Press, 2010, chapter 5), who for some reason
does not bring his story up to the completion of the construction.

now as EUR. A good part of its monumental modernism was built before the project was stopped by the war. It is clearly modernist and clearly monumental, but it is by no means megalomaniac, as were Speer's designs for Hitler.

Twentieth-century fascism was unashamedly imperialist. Mussolini solemnly proclaimed the Italian empire from his balcony at Palazzo Venezia on 9 May 1936, on the basis of the conquest of Addis Ababa and, as it turned out, the rather short-lived victory of Italian mustard gas. The Via dell'Impero, across the ancient fields of Roman archaeology, had been inaugurated already in 1932 in its trajectory from Piazza Venezia to the Colosseum, and then further prolonged in 1934.

The bi-millennium of Augustus in 1937, with an excavation of his mausoleum, focused on the rediscovery of his – or rather the Roman Senate's devoted homage by way of an – Altar of Peace, in the very clear sense of an imperial peace heavy-handedly imposed on the provinces of Gallia and Spain. Mussolini was explicitly presented as the contemporary Augustus.

While some liturgical loci of fascism and some toponymies of the city were changed soon after 25 July 1943, when Mussolini was deposed by his own comrades of the Fascist Grand Council, much of fascist Rome survived. In August 1943 the Foro Mussolini became the Foro Italico, and from July 1944 the altar to the Fallen Fascists on Campigoglio was removed and streets to Hitler and to Italian Fascist iconography disappeared.[8] However, fasci (Roman *littorio*) and fascist-era dating (from 1922) have remained in post-Fascist Rome. On 17 April 2015 there was a brief debate, raised by the president of the Chamber of Deputies, about whether the seventieth anniversary of the defeat of fascism might not be the proper occasion to take out the obelisk devoted to Mussolini *Dux* in the Foro Italico. The question did not even come to a vote before being buried.[9]

Fascism's two major urban interventions remain the main road across archaeological Rome, once Via dell'Impero, now more historically Via dei Fori Imperiali, and the grand access to the Vatican, the Via della Conciliazione, both of which were laid out on the basis of devastating urban and archaeological demolitions.[10] The Via della Conciliazione was completed in 1950; EUR was resurrected in view of the 1960 Olympics and has been continued to be renovated and upgraded ever since into its current status as a major centre of business and administration, somewhat similar to Paris's La Défense, but in an older style of modernism. Even the Augustan Altar of Peace has been revived, now encased in a stylish transparent building by Richard Meyer, replacing the surprisingly similar but much more modest construction Morpugno once built for Mussolini, which was meant to be temporary.

The main change, apart from the growth of the city, is perhaps that Palazzo Venezia and its below-balcony piazza have lost centrality. But that had already happened before the ultimate fall of Mussolini.*

Italian Fascism was vicious and violent, a major source of inspiration for Hitler and an object of admiration for large sections of the European bourgeoisie, including editorialists of the London *Times*, at least until its uppity late-imperialist assault on Abyssinia. But Mussolini was more bluster than butcher, and he did leave an amazingly lasting imprint on the 'eternal city'. For this, there seem to be two different, but probably more confluent than competing, explanations: one urbanistic, the other political.

Urbanistically, Mussolini, his architects and his political advisers basically all agreed that Rome was an ancient city to which respect and restraint were due, particularly if you wanted to build a future of empire and power on the basis of ancient glory. At the same time, it was clear to anti-fascists as well as to fascists that papal Rome had decayed and that national Italian Rome had not done much about it. One way or the other, Rome in the 1920s was a city in urgent need of modern hygiene, services and opening up of traffic and communication. Fascism clearly contributed to this overdue infrastructural upgrading.

Second, fascist urbanism has also survived for political reasons. While the speaker of the Italian Chamber of Deputies in April 2015 had to retract the suggestion that the obelisk to Mussolini should perhaps be removed, we know what would have happened to the mayor of a small town in Bavaria defending keeping a monument to Hitler as a 'historical memory' – he or she would have been hounded out of office in less than a week. Post–World War II Italian politics and culture never saw any sustained reason to investigate critically or reflectively reject and transcend the mind-set and practices of fascism. It took a long time in West

---

* At his oratorical peak, in 1936, Mussolini delivered twelve speeches from the balcony of the Palazzo Venezia, followed by ten in 1937, diving to three in 1941, zero in 1942 and one in 1943 (Vidotto, *Roma contemporanea*, 203).

Germany. Lest we forget, for example, that the lawyer who wrote the Nuremberg Laws, Hans Globke, was a key trusted adviser to Konrad Adenauer, the long-time chancellor, and that a high officer of Nazi espionage, Reinhard Gehlen, became the head of West German anti-Soviet espionage. But over time, there was an impressive German clean-up of the fascist past. Nowhere else was there such a preoccupation with 'democratic construction'.[11] In Italy there has been very little washing the black out of the past; on the contrary, there has even been explicit whitewashing of Mussolini.[12]

From Berlin to Germania

Hitler was obsessed by the idea of constructing a capital corresponding to and representing his dreams of power, the power of a great German Reich and of the world. Capital construction was second only to his drive for imperial power. Existing Berlin was from this perspective much below standard. It was not a great metropolis like Vienna or Paris – the latter especially was Hitler's yardstick – to start with. His sketches for the new Reichshauptstadt (Capital of the Reich) centred on emulating and overtaking the Champs-Élysées, but soon his ambitions grew. The task of his favourite architect, Albert Speer, became to plan for 'World Capital Germania', 'comparable only to ancient Egypt, Babylon, and Rome'.[13]

While Mussolini had spoken of 'necessity' as well as *grandezza*, Hitler had a dandyish aesthete's complete lack of interest in mundane issues of everyday urban living.* Housing construction stalled in Nazi Berlin.[14] But Nazism meant a heavy intervention of the most brutal kind into the everyday lives of one part of Berlin's population: its 160,000 Jews. Ultimately, virtually all had to flee abroad or were deported to their deaths. But before that, famous Jewish properties were seized, such as the publishing houses Ullstein and Mosse and department stores such as Wertheim and Tietz. According to Speer's right-hand man Wolters, these added up to 23,765 properties. In the orchestrated pogrom of

---

* True, some Nazis had, such as Hitler's first deputy Rudolf Hess, but his influence was already waning, and according to the Führer, Hess had no taste (Speer, *Inside the Third Reich*, 127).

November 1938, thousands of Jewish shops were destroyed and most of the synagogues burnt down.[15] By decree, Jews were prohibited from living in the proximity of governmental areas, driven out of apartments in planning areas and prohibited from renting housing from Germans. A police order of 28 November 1938 banned Jews from entering any theatre, cabaret, cinema, concert hall, museum or sports ground and from using any street in the government quarter.[16]

Modern traffic and communication attracted the German as well as the Italian fascists. The Tempelhof Field, still used for Nazi May Day parades in 1933 and 1934, was turned into an airport, an *Autobahnring* around Berlin was built as a 'high priority' even after the beginning of the war and spokesmen of the regime took pride in the busy traffic of Potsdamer Platz.[17]

Weimar Berlin was Europe's, perhaps the world's, biggest industrial city with 4.2 million inhabitants on the eve of the Nazi takeover and almost half of its working population in industry. Before World War I the Social Democrats had a majority in Berlin's parliamentary elections, which were held under universal male suffrage, but not in city politics, run under the auspices of a three-class franchise. After the war, the bitter divides between right-wing Social Democracy, left-wing Socialists and Communists prevented any proper municipal socialism in Berlin. The city was not a Nazi stronghold, although Goebbels's ruthless leadership did give them a substantial following. The 'Capital of the Movement' was Munich, and the masterfully choreographed Nazi Party rallies took place in Nuremberg.

The 'thousand years' of Nazism were actually only twelve, and for the last three of those the regime was mainly fighting for its life. The main impact of the Nazis on Berlin could be seen in the ruins of their devastating defeat. Here, however, from a perspective of fascist city-making, we shall look at two things: first, actual changes during the nine years of autonomous Nazi governance, and second, Hitler's and Speer's plans for 'World Capital Germania', intended to be completed by 1950.

The first manifestation of Nazi urbanism in Berlin was political mass theatre. It started on the evening of 30 January 1933, when torch-carrying uniformed Nazi battalions marched the streets of central Berlin to the sedate Wilhelmstrasse (Berlin's equivalent to London's Whitehall) and the chancellor's office, where Hitler could appear only at a window – because there was then no balcony – and through the Brandenburg Gate. A star performance was May Day 1933, turned into a Day of

National Labour, in which the trade unions were lured to participate –
before being dissolved the day after. Central squares such as Lustgarten,
before the Nazis more a park than an open square, and Wilhelmsplatz
were refurbished and paved to function as rallying-grounds, the latter
for listeners to the raw voice from the soon-to-come balcony on the new
Reichskanzlei.

Construction focused on the governmental quarter in and around
Wilhelmstrasse. Probably by accident, the first big project to get started
(in May 1934) was the extension of the Reichsbank, after the last open
competition in which Walter Gropius and Mies van der Rohe took part,
without success, after Hitler's decision. The result is a kind of monumentalist modernism, a long, heavy, five-storey horizontal with a sober,
unornamented façade. To be expected from the new regime, three other
buildings were planned for the area: a colossal Ministry of Aviation
replacing the old Prussian Ministry of War, representing the power and
narcissism of Hermann Göring more than German air transport; the
Ministry of Propaganda and Popular Enlightenment, i.e., Joseph
Goebbels's ministry; and a new Chancellery for Hitler, built by Speer,
who also had a hand in the alteration and enlargement of the press office
of the Weimar Republic to fit the needs of Goebbels. While the
Reichskanzlei was completely destroyed by the war victors, the
Reichsbank and the ministries survived and have had an important
post-war recycling: first in Communist East Berlin, with the Bank as
Central Committee building and the Aviation Ministry as the Council
of Ministers, and thereafter in reunified Berlin as new federal ministries,
including the Foreign Office. For the 1936 Olympics, a big stadium was
built, which still survives.

Albert Speer was appointed Inspector-General of Buildings for the
Renovation of the Capital in January 1937, a new position especially
tailored for him, although the title echoed the position of the great
Prussian architect Karl Friedrich Schinkel about a century earlier. It
made him the master architect of Berlin, directly under Hitler, subordinate neither to the Nazi leader of the Berlin district, Goebbels, nor the
new Nazi mayor, an old Party member who had financial doubts about
the grand projects of Hitler and Speer.

Another remaining change to central Berlin was a contribution to a
planned grand East-West Axis through the huge Tiergarten park:
moving the Prussian Victory Column of 1864–73 from outside the

Reichstag to a roundabout on the avenue through the park, ending in a West Berlin square renamed Adolf-Hitler-Platz (now Theodor-Heuss-Platz after West Germany's liberal first president).

Iconographically, Nazi Berlin was full of swastikas: on public buildings, on pylons, on banners. But there was little new classical political monumentality. One exception could be found in the inner court of the new Reichskanzlei, where there were two huge torch-carrying male bronze nudes symbolizing the Party and the military (Wehrmacht). Toponymical changes were few and did not target major streets or very important squares. Adolf-Hitler-Platz was significant but hardly prominent. Hermann-Göring-Strasse succeeded Friedrich Ebert (a Social Democratic Weimar president) and was more or less part of the governmental quarter, but not a key address. There was also a street to Horst Wessel, a Nazi martyr of the early 1920s.

However, even renovated and monumentalized, Berlin was not enough for Hitler. For his coming Teutonic empire from Norway to northern Italy and for coming German world domination he envisaged a new capital, Germania, for which much of central Berlin was to be torn down. In 1937 Speer was entrusted with making detailed plans, to be realized by 1950. Speer and his office made lots of design models, which Hitler inspected, fascinated. Some demolitions were made but hardly anything was built, and in spring 1942 Speer persuaded Hitler to suspend works on it, concentrating construction capacity on the war effort.

The new Reichskanzlei and the Germania plans are the best examples of German fascist building. The former was finished for the New Year reception of the diplomatic corps in 1939; the second existed only in models carefully kept hidden from public view and shown only to Hitler's closest companions, probably because their gigantomania might be politically embarrassing. Speer's aged father, who was also an architect, was shown the models. His reaction was: 'You've all gone completely mad'.[18]

Before the future there was the present, though: the complete inadequacy, in Hitler's view, of the existing Chancellery or any alternative to it. From 1935 the regime began to subtly and discreetly force out the firms in Voss street, near the old Chancellery in Wilhelmstrasse. In early 1938 Speer received the order to have a new building or, rather, a new extension ready in one year. 'The cost is immaterial', Hitler told him.[19]

The size and the façade, in monumental granite with a two-storey high portal of modern stone columns, of the new part were constrained by the old one, so the manifestation of power was concentrated in the interior. It started with a long, sombre court of honour leading up to another huge stone portal, from which the visitor had to ascend an outdoor staircase, pass through seventeen-foot-high double doors and continue across two reception halls before reaching the pride of the proprietor and his architect, a 480-foot Marble Gallery, twice as long as the Hall of Mirrors at Versailles. Hitler was delighted: 'On the long walk from the reception hall they'll get a taste of the power and grandeur of the German Reich.'* Here is a brilliant exemplification of several of the elements of an architectural 'grammar of power', as the Norwegian architect and theorist Thomas Thiis-Evensen has formulated them: the heaviness and the closure of the building, the size of the portals and the doors and, above all, the distance of the courtyard and the Marble Gallery.[20]

This Chancellery was only meant to be temporary, while waiting for Germania. When Hitler presented his vision of the new capital, not yet called Germania, in late 1936, it contained three key ideas. First, a *Prachtstrasse* (Street of Magnificence) running north-south through central Berlin – inspired by but, of course, meant to surpass the Champs-Élysées – 130 yards wide. Second, a huge Triumphal Arch, 400 feet high. Third, a domed meeting hall with standing room for 150,000 people: in Speer's plan the interior volume of the Great Hall would be sixteen times the size of Saint Peter's, and the structure would be taken from the Roman Pantheon.[21] The dome was to be crowned by a German eagle – no longer holding a swastika in its claws, Hitler told Speer in the summer of 1939, but a globe. The hall would be surrounded by water, expanding the Spree River into a lake, and on the southern side of it would be the central plaza, Adolf-Hitler-Platz, with a new Chancellery and the Führerpalast. Nearby would be military and governmental buildings.[22]

In the hall and in the Triumphal Arch we see an accentuation of another element of the architectural grammar of power: height. A model photograph shows the Brandenburg Gate and the Reichstag, which

---

* Speer, *Inside the Third Reich*, 158–9. Mussolini's office at Palazzo Venezia in its Renaissance *Mappamondo* (Map of the World) hall, with a mosaic floor twenty metres long, was also up to fascist standards.

Speer but not Hitler wanted to raze, completely dwarfed by the hall.[23] On the other hand, along the Grand Avenue there were to be no skyscrapers[24] – presumably they were still too modernist for the imperial monumentality which governed the design. Stylistically, Germania largely followed the Second French Empire, avoiding the modernist current of Italian fascism – manifested in the EUR – which Hitler abhorred. Symmetry, a sixth item on Thiis-Evensen's list, does not figure prominently in Speer's self-account, although the court of honour of the Reichskanzlei is laid out symmetrically.

Fascism was obsessed with the idea of manifesting its power impressively and intimidatingly. At first sight it may be surprising how much of this concern by supposedly very nationalist regimes was directed at impressing foreigners, diplomats, visitors and tourists, and carried out with keen eyes on foreign cities to emulate and surpass. On New Year's Eve 1925, Mussolini spelt out his ideas about Rome: 'In five years Rome should appear marvellous to all the peoples of the world'. In early 1939 Hitler rejoiced in how the distances and size of the new Reichskanzlei would show Germany's standing in the world.[25] But one should not be surprised: fascism saw itself as competing in a worldwide imperialist game. As Speer had learnt already in 1939, for Hitler the globe was more important than the swastika, and the peak of Mussolini's power was his proclamation of the Italian empire.

Grand avenues were central to fascist urbanism: the Roman Vie dell'Impero, flanked by the Via de Triomfi; the North-South Axis of Germania; and before that the western breakthrough of Berlin's Charlottenburger Chaussee (today's Strasse des 17 Juni), and the de-lindification of Unter den Linden in order to make room for pylons and flagpoles. They were, of course, not for strolling. The flâneur was a distinctively non-fascist urbanite, but the streets were not only for parades of marching Black- or Brownshirts: they were also meant for motorcades and automobile traffic. Speed, motor traffic and aviation were part of the fascist cult of modern power, and urban thoroughfares; traffic hubs; motorways around, into and out of cities; and airports were key parts of the fascist urban agenda.*

---

* The great architectural historian and theorist Spiro Kostoff once summed up Mussolini's Rome as 'traffic and glory' (Baxa, *Roads and Ruins*). Two of the most prominent fascist leaders were avid aviationists: Italo Balbo and Hermann Goering.

By comparison, rallying squares were secondary and largely there already, as with the Piazza Venezia and the Tempelhof Feld, but sometimes were refurbished for a new purpose, like Lustgarten and Wilhelmsplatz in Berlin.

The central buildings of power changed with the political regime into renovated buildings, such as the Palazzo Venezia, or extended-cum-renovated, such as the new Reichskanzlei. The whole existing capital was considered inadequate to the new power: the Italians built the E42 or EUR, intended as a new centre of Rome, while the Germans planned for 'World Capital Germania'.

Fascist ideology had a few simple core tenets: virulent nationalism, a macho Social Darwinism – which in Nazism included anti-Semitism – imperialism and, crucially for its success, a preparedness to learn from its older, main enemy, the Marxist labour movement (in mass organization and in attention to social issues). For the rest, the top leaders were quite pragmatic – among their inner circle Hitler and Goebbels made fun of the Aryan mysticisms of Rosenberg and Himmler – and occasionally ruthless. Ernst Röhm was one of Hitler's four *Duzfreunde* (those who could use the intimate German form of *you* to him), but when he insisted on replacing the military with the SA militia, he was killed off. Fascism had its leaders and its party insignia, but neither founding fathers, great pioneering thinkers nor canonical texts. Nor did it have much history, although it did have some 'martyrs'. All this meant limitations on possible fascist iconography. It did have national history, but its nation-states already had their formative moulds. An imperialist reading of national history was a way out. Italian fascism naturally reached back to the Roman empire, giving it a concrete twentieth-century colonial form after the conquest of Ethiopia. Nazism saw itself as the successor of the medieval Holy Roman Empire and the Wilhelmine Reich. While it kept its world-domination ambitions under wraps, Nazi Germany did set up a Colonial Ministry.

The party symbols, the fascio and swastika, were lavishly displayed and so were Leader portraits, but rarely in stone. Italian fascism dated its buildings according to its own calendar, starting in 1922, as well as according to the Christian one. National monuments were already in place from the earlier nation-state, and the fascist capitals hardly got any new ones. The ambitious attempt, through the bi-millennial anniversary (in 1937) of the Augustan Peace Altar, to claim Mussolini as the modern successor of Emperor Augustus soon turned ludicrous in view of the unstoppable decline and descent of the Duce. The Nazi cult centred on Nuremberg, not on Berlin. Speer got an assignment for a gigantic future rally-ground, capable of gathering 400,000 people. Writing about it long afterwards, in his post-prison memoirs, Speer goes on at some length about how the field and its surrounding buildings would surpass in size and volume the Roman Circus Maximus, Persepolis and the Cheops pyramid.*

There was no proper fascist style of construction apart from the architectural grammar of authoritarian power. A heavy, stone-faced modern monumentalism may be said to be a common characteristic of mainstream fascism in Rome as well as Berlin. But whereas Hitler had a nineteenth-century abhorrence of strict, post-ornamentalist modernism, Italian fascism included a pure-blooded modernist (in Italy known as rationalist) current. One of the most dedicated fascists among Italian architects, Giuseppe Terragni, belonged to it. As might be expected, the fascist leaders and urban planners were all admirers of Baron Haussmann and his practice of ruthlessly demolishing popular neighbourhoods.

Financially, the fascist capitals were both what today would be called public-private partnerships – but for the anachronism of calling the secretive fascist state 'public'. Two-thirds of the Grand Avenue of Germania was to be reserved for private business buildings.[26] Rome had a general plan (in 1931) which had been discussed in public and some of the big fascist projects were debated publicly, such as the location and the style of the Party headquarters, Palazzo Littorio, but others became known only when they had been decided. Speer's models for Germania, on the other hand, were hidden even to most Nazi dignitaries, and its enormous costs were hidden under a scheme of 'creative accounting'. To what extent did fascist Rome and Berlin also manifest capitalist power? A brief first answer would be: at least as much as pre-fascist Rome and Berlin.

The 1931 general plan of Rome counted on future peripheral land-rent speculation; its stipulations were anyway soon overwhelmed

---

* Ibid., 112ff. Like Germania, it was never built, but Speer did contribute to the ground in the late 1930s.

by private interests, 'particular' plans and ad hoc political interventions.[27]

In Berlin, elbowing out and outright expropriating Jewish capital was for private 'Aryan' benefit. Hitler was full of admiration for the ethnic Germanic capitalist Amann, who succeeded Ullstein in dominating the German media.[28] The big (non-Jewish) industrialists and bankers of Berlin all kept their property and thrived in the rearmament boom. During the war they had to follow the political directives of war production – as had their US and British counterparts.

Modern Military Dictatorships

Classical fascism did produce a set of themes of modern authoritarian urbanism, but hardly a blueprint. In this section I shall make a brief overview of the urbanistic exploits of some of fascism's latter-day grandchildren: military dictatorships of one kind or another. While they have usually included explicitly neo-fascist currents, the main heirs have learnt from the pragmatic opportunism of the classical leaders as well as from their defeats. But before that, I shall take a look at a contemporary cousin of classical fascism, Franco's Spain.

In the second half of the 1930s, Spain was the hot battlefront between fascism and anti-fascism. Workers and progressive intellectuals from all over the North Atlantic world volunteered for the International Brigades, defending the Spanish Republic, while the fascist powers sent troops, tanks, and air squadrons to the fascist side. In March 1939, Generalísimo Francisco Franco's troops marched into Madrid, the defeated capital of a defeated republic. The victors did consider moving the capital out of 'disloyal' Madrid and the new leaders investigated the possibility of Seville, but discarded it. In 1938 a congress of architects assembled in Franco's command city, Burgos, to plan the fascization of Madrid: The city should stop looking at Paris and take in the examples of El Escorial and Toledo. A new political centre should hold up a *fachada imperial* (imperial façade) carried by three main buildings: El Alcázar, a medieval fortress rebuilt into a royal palace in the eighteenth century; the Cathedral, a then-unfinished construction just south of the former, started in the late nineteenth century; and a new headquarters for the Falange Party. This trio was meant to represent the Fatherland, religion and modern fascist power.[29]

Most of this part stayed on paper. The World War II bulletins soon made it obvious that fascism proper was a losing horse, and the regime reinforced its military-conservative-clerical character. The new Party building was never built, and the royal palace remained unused. In the early 1950s even the idea of an 'imperial façade' was destroyed by two large private commercial buildings, supported by the appointed mayor: the Torre de Madrid and Edificio España. Private capital was asserting its part in the conservative coalition. The Puerta del Sol hub, from where the Republic had once been proclaimed and which the Franquistas denounced as a 'plinth of corrupts where Marxism circulate[d] comfortably', survived.

But other sides of the plan were implemented. The north-eastern entrance to Madrid still includes the Triumphal Arch built for the entering Franquista troops. Coming that way, you pass the Ministry of Aviation, a kind of military Escorial. Further east, the fascist plan of 1944 took over the 1929 idea of a major street prolongation to the north. At the time it was known as Avenida del Generalísimo; today it is the Paseo de la Castellana. Under the Republic it was meant to be mainly an avenue of state public construction, representing the republic and democracy. The new zoning made it part of the 'special or political-representative' zones. A big complex of new ministerial buildings was completed. With the coming of democracy, murals were created to recognize historical socialist leaders, yet the complex also had the dubious merit of keeping the last equestrian statue of Franco in Madrid, until the Socialist Zapatero government of the mid-2000s. However, the several aristocratic palaces demolished after the war were replaced by big business buildings, and from the 1970s the northern end of the Castellana became the favourite site of Spanish financial capital.

The Spanish Civil War was an almost three-year, very bloody combat of intense hatred and bitterness. The main monumental achievement of the Franco regime is a grave monument, the Valley of the Fallen (Valle de los Caídos), built originally by republican prisoners from 1941 to 1959 in the mountains north of Madrid. Above all, it is a representation of the Catholic credentials of the regime. Beneath a huge cross is a large mountain crypt which the pope in 1960 graciously promoted to a basilica, and the complex also includes a Benedictine monastery. The iconography is overwhelmingly Catholic. Four huge figures in the basilica represent the military: the army, the navy, the air force and 'their respective militias'. Franco is buried there, but as head of state. The only explicitly fascist part, as far as I have noticed, is the tomb at the foot of the altar of José Antonio Primo de Rivera, the founder of Spanish fascism, the Falange.*

A proposal by a Zapatero-appointed historical commission to neutralize the monument into a national site of mourning for the Civil War dead on both sides was rejected by the right-wing Rajoy government elected in 2011. On the other hand, the radical city government elected in 2015 has announced a plan to take out the remaining Franquista toponymy in Madrid, where streets still commemorate fascist Civil War generals, many other Franquistas (numbering far over a hundred) and the 'Fallen of the Blue Division', which took part in the Nazi invasion of the Soviet Union.[30]

Franquismo had to evolve out of the mid-1930s of fascist glory. Later-born dictators had learnt the verdict of history in 1945 well before taking power. In more aspects than one, the brutal military dictatorship of Chile (1973–89) was the most innovative. In a ceremony in front of a recently raised 'Altar of the Fatherland', General Augusto Pinochet made a speech on 11 September 1975 which, in bravura and honest truthfulness, equalled the declaration by the slave-owners and merciless hunters of 'Indian savages' in 1776 that they held it 'self-evident that all men are created equal': 'Today, in front of the world, Chile lights the flame of liberty. It is doing so in the belief of being the vanguard of light and hope in a world aimlessly wandering in darkness.'[31] The four members of the military junta then carried torches to light the flame in a huge elevated stone bowl across the street from the bombed-out Presidential Palace. The junta let the latter decay and moved into a new, modern building nearby, built under the Salvador Allende government for an UNCTAD conference, and renamed it Edificio Diego Portales after the conservative strongman of 1830s Chile. After a big fire in 2006, the building was radically refurbished and turned into Centro Cultural Gabriela Mistral. The Presidential Palace has been restored and is in democratic use again, while the military 'flame of liberty' has been extinguished in the layout of a Square of Citizenship.

---

* Franco's and José Antonio's are the only named tombs. The official visitors' guide is Sancho, *Visitors' Guide: The Holy Cross of the Valley of the Fallen*, Madrid: Editorial Patrimonio Nacional Madrid, 1996.

During the Chilean Popular Unity government, local fascists' graffiti often referred to 'Jakarta'. What they had in mind was the massacre of hundreds of thousands, perhaps a million, Communists – all unarmed – by the Indonesian military and its egged-on thugs in their taking power in 1965 upon a botched coup attempt by a group of junior officers. While Himmler would have admired the brutal 'hardness' of the Indonesian generals and their subordinates and Islamist civilian followers, there were hardly any fascists in Jakarta in 1965.

The founding myth of the 'New Order' in Jakarta was enshrined in a new monument: the Crocodile Pit. It is a huge ensemble in the south-eastern part of the city dominated by a large exemplar of Garuda, the national mythical bird of the country, with open wings, more awe-inspiring than a Nazi eagle. Beneath, standing on a podium with an anti-Communist frieze, are full-size statues of the seven officers killed by the mysterious and inept first coup-makers, the martyrs of the New Order and the rationale for the vengeful massacres of civilian Communists and alleged sympathizers. Behind them is a hole, referring to the disused well into which the bodies of the seven officers were thrown – but there is nothing to see there. The monument of 1969 was supplemented in 1981 by a propaganda museum of the regime, the 'Sacred *Pancasila*' [the founding principles of the nation], and in 1990 by a 'Museum of PKI [Communist Party] Treason'.

The second nationalist monument of the regime was more peaceful: the Beautiful Indonesia in Miniature Park, commonly known as the Mini. It is a large folkloric park showing the architecture and the culture of the big, diverse country.[32] The idea is similar to Skansen in Stockholm almost a century earlier, but the Mini has an aristocratic grandeur – in big replica mansions – absent from Skansen and its modest, authentically original peasant and artisan cottages.

At the political summit, *Pak* Suharto, 'father of development', succeeded *Bung* Karno, Brother [Su]karno, brother of the revolution. Capitalist development was the drive of the Suharto regime, and not without success, in spite of its cronyism and massive corruption. Around the Thamrin-Sudirman north-south axis, office towers and shopping malls overtook the state emblems of the Sukarno era. Economically and socially the regime was clearly modernist: banning pedicabs from the streets of the capital, expelling the poor as much as possible from the centre and building elevated highways across the city, flying above the *kampung* neighbourhoods of the people. The development has been characterized, not uncritically, as the end of 'urban involution' and the 'breakthrough of urbanism'.[33]

However, the culturally conservative nationalism typical of right-wing military regimes also flourished in Jakarta alongside its globalist business modernism. Sukarno, an anti-imperialist nationalist and architecturally an international modernist, had been pointing to 'New York and Moscow' – in fact, more to the latter. The architects of the New Order explicitly did not want Indonesian cities 'to be the same as . . . New York, Los Angeles, and Washington'.[34] The impact of nationalist architecture in the jungle of capitalist development was limited, but it does exist: for example, the restored Demak Mosque, more akin to an Asian pagoda than to a West Asian mosque, and the main building of the University of Indonesia.[35]

While not quite matching Hitler and Speer in architectural mega-lomania, there is a recent capital which more than matched them in secrecy and clearly surpassed them by actually implementing the military rulers' dream of a new capital. This is Naypyidaw, since 2006 the official capital of Myanmar. Its foundations had been built in total secret in the geographical middle of the country. There had been rumours of some new military centre, but no more. On the morning of 6 November 2005 convoys of military trucks started to move north from the ex-colonial capital of Yangon, and the day after, the Minister of Information announced a 'new administrative capital', 'to ensure more effective administration of nation-building activities'. No name was given. Only on 12 July 2006 did a leading general declare that 'Naypyidaw will become the nation's capital in accord with the new constitution to be adopted'. Myanmar's capital was given the ancient name for 'capital' – *naypyidaw* – a word used for the seats of pre-colonial kings.*

The reasons for the move are still shrouded in mystery, but the most plausible explanation is military security from the potentially unruly people of Yangon as well from US or another foreign invasion.

---

* Quotations from Maung Aung Myoe, 'The road to Naypyidaw,' Asia Research Institute Working Paper 79, Singapore: Asia Research Institute, 2006, 3–4, the key historical analysis of the event. The transcription into Latin script was first officially *Naypyitaw*, sometimes also *Nay pyi Taw*, but *Naypyidaw* has become the convention and corresponds better to the pronunciation.

Naypyidaw has apparently been built according to the same financial principle Hitler gave Speer for the new Reichskanzlei: 'Costs are immaterial'. The budget is not publicly known. Whatever else can be said about it, its construction in a matter of a few years was a remarkable feat of urban engineering, by a poor ex-colonial country at that.

A decade after its founding, the new Myanmar capital still makes a baffling impression on foreign visitors. Its megalomania is not in the buildings but in the size of the layout and its street system. Normal city streets are eight lanes wide and thoroughfares have twenty lanes, decisively overtaking the Grand Avenue of Germania – and they are all virtually empty of cars. Public employees are bussed to their offices from governmental residences distributed according to ministry, rank and marital status, but for the rest there is little public transport. The strict zoning does include hotels with restaurants, a modest Landmarks Garden, a more developed zoo and a number of golf courses, a favourite sport of the military.

The governmental buildings, usually in some kind of Southeast Asian modernism, distinguish themselves by their proximity and distance. The city hall, interestingly enough a replica of Yangon's, and the ministries are usually situated a hundred metres or so from the street and barred with an iron gate. The parliament is a big horizontal complex with Southeast Asian tiered roof towers, separated from its environment by a moat. There is no spectacular architecture, but original Asianism has been supplemented by an international-style convention centre, sports stadium and airport.

City iconography is religious, Buddhist above all. The emblem of the city is the Uppatasanti pagoda, a replica of the golden Shwedagon in Yangon, but thirty centimetres lower. There are also, as national icons, three gigantic golden bronzes of pre-colonial Burmese kings, the same as those standing outside the National Museum in Yangon – expanded in 1996 under the junta – but they are in a parade ground in the military sector and therefore beyond civilian contact. On a visit in 2010, I could only discern their silhouettes from afar, and they did not figure in the official Naypyidaw Directory of 2010.[36]

Before leaving our selected significant cases of capitals under modern military dictatorship and summing up their characteristic impact, a fifth case has to be put on the list, however briefly. The military junta ruling Argentina from 1976 to 1982 is mostly remembered for its torture and cruelty and for dumping its victims into the (sea-like) La Plata River. Ruling according to a neoliberal version of an ancient formula, it governed by death and circuses – that is, basking in the football World Cup of 1978, with its renovated stadiums and made-up city, an entertainment park and some green spaces. The junta entrusted the country to the different branches of the armed forces. Buenos Aires fell to the Air Force, and an energetic retired Air Force general, Osvaldo Cacciatore, was appointed mayor (*intendente*). His two main priorities were urban highways (he planned eight and managed to get two built) and cleansing the city of the poor and their 'villages of misery', in which he was 96 per cent successful.[37] Preparations were made for a monumental celebration of the retaking of the Malvinas/Falkland islands, which in the end was defeated, ending junta rule. Instead, the main monument of the bloodiest military dictatorship of South America is the big, sculptured Remembrance Park by the river, commemorating its cruelty and its victims.

Violence, Exclusion, Nationalism and Capitalist Development

Striking first is the extreme violence of the military takeover; it is incomparable to fascism, which in Germany and Italy actually mostly occurred peacefully and through constitutional channels. In Santiago the Presidential Palace was bombarded. The numbers of people killed exceeded those of fascism, outside the wars and the Holocaust. In about a year, the Indonesian regime killed something between 1 million and half a million people, which in Nazi Germany in the 1930s would have meant about 250–500,000 people. The killings of the Argentine junta, 30,000 people, would have meant 75,000 in Germany.

There is no post–World War II equivalent to the worst military violence, apart from the 1994 Rwandan genocide. The convulsions of the Chinese Cultural Revolution did include killings, but not on a scale comparable to up to 7 million Indonesian killings, or more than 1 million Argentine killings (adjusting for Chinese population size in 1973). First of all, military urbanism meant urban terror. Suharto called leaving killed bodies in the streets 'shock therapy'.[38]

Classical fascism was successful because, within its nationalist-imperialist programme, it took popular social concerns of employment, social security, leisure and entertainment seriously. The Italians set up a special organization for the latter, Dopo Lavoro ('after work'), which was emulated by the Nazis' Kraft durch Freude ('force by enjoyment'). Motoring, then a clearly middle-class interest, was pushed, with the Autobahn freeways. The Nazis' recognition of housing problems was spotty or limited, however, and fascist urbanism was generally geared to monumental representations of power. Authoritarian, top-down demolitions – in good Haussmannian tradition – were a city rule.

After World War II, military urbanism tended to be more exclusive, with cities from Santiago to Jakarta embracing US-inspired neoliberal capitalism. The Chilean regime did include an exceptionally large public housing programme on the outskirts of Santiago – as well as the expulsion (from 1979 to 1985) of 29,000 poor families, a total of 172,000 persons, from central Santiago to the eastern periphery.[39] The militarists of Buenos Aires and Jakarta were explicit, particularly in Buenos Aires, in their desire to expel the poor and the rustics from the central city. The housing secretary, later mayor, of Buenos Aires, del Cioppo, announced that only those people could live in Buenos Aires who were 'culturally prepared to live in it'. The informal slum population was drastically reduced, from 214,000 in 1976 to 12,600 in 1983.[40] According to the military governor of Jakarta, people lacking 'urban rationality' had no right to live in the city.[41] The modern military dictatorship shared the fear of the plebs (the *massa*, in Bahasa Indonesian) with nineteenth-century conservatism, something alien to people like Mussolini, Hitler and Goebbels, who were confident in their rabble-rousing skills.

Nationalism was common to fascism and modern militarism as well as to the nineteenth-century modern mainstream. There was little specific to military nationalism, but its invocations of religion, whether Christian, Muslim or Buddhist, distinguished it from fascism. Its national symbolism derived from traditional nationalism, avoiding new inventions like the fascio and the swastika. Given their geopolitical contexts, it is understandable that none of the post-war military dictatorships developed any imperialist nationalism. The ill-fated Argentine invasion of the Malvinas/Falklands was only a repetition of nineteenth- and early-twentieth-century irredentist nationalism. The nationalist Indonesian architecture of the 1980s and 1990s was not intrinsically militarist.

All of our five cases of military dictatorships – Franco's Spain, the Myanmar junta, Chilean Pinochetismo, the Indonesian 'New Order' and the Argentine junta, were crucial to capitalist development, of their countries as well as of their capitals. To Franquista Madrid, developmentalism came late, after World War II, and accelerated in the 1960s. In Myanmar, under military rule which is ending as I write, development was state-led and relied on bilateral state agreements with China and India. For late Franquismo as well as, from the beginning, the military regimes of Santiago, Buenos Aires and Jakarta, capitalist development and modernization were on the agenda. Urbanistically, this meant opening up the city to private developers and their current projects of highways, malls, offices and mixed-use towers. Modernist Brasília was saved as the national capital by the military dictatorship of Brazil – no doubt enjoying its then-secluded tranquillity from the masses of Rio – but a major part of its planning was undone by opening up to private lakeshore appropriations. In spite of all this, testifying to the complexity of Brazilian politics – even military politics – and culture, the junta invited the card-carrying Communist Niemeyer to design its headquarters in Brasília, which the comrade duly did. The modernizing impact of late Franquismo on Madrid is certainly still there, in the prolongation of the Paseo Castellana. In Myanmar, Naypyidaw remains a political and administrative capital, so the new economic times are mostly showing up in Yangon, the old capital and the remaining economic centre.

Jakarta, Santiago and Buenos Aires, probably in that order, had decisive capitalist developments under military rule, pushing them in a globalist direction of foreign investment, business services expansion, shopping malls, beginning sky-scraping, gating, credit consumption, private cars and congested motorways.* Their economic legacy was neoliberal capitalism, inspired by the Reagan-Bush regimes of the United States. None survived democratization unscathed, but its only outright repudiation – in Argentina of 2001, by a popular uprising followed by a populist presidency – is currently being revoked by the new President Mauricio Macri, a former *intendente* of Buenos Aires

---

* On Santiago, see also Miguel Laborde, *Santiago, región capital de Chile*, Santiago: Presidencia de la República, 2004; on Buenos Aires and Jakarta respectively, see Gutman and Cohen (eds), *Construir Bicentenarios Latinoamericanos en la Era de Globalización* and Kusno, *Behind the Postcolonial*. We shall return to the global moment below.

whose family was a major beneficiary of the military privatization of municipal services.[42] Jakarta, achieving a 'breakthrough of urbanism' under military rule, got a popular, reformist mayor, Jokowi, in 2012, who is currently president of the republic. Jokowi did change Jakarta in a more social direction. In 1990s Santiago, poverty decreased significantly, from 28.5 per cent in 1990 to 12.7 per cent in 2000, but overall income inequality rather increased to a Gini coefficient of 0.59.[43]

Democratic Reactions and Inheritances

In Rome, where some pieces of fascist iconography have been left in peace, there is to my knowledge no public commemoration or museum of the fascist dictatorship. Nor is there a museum of Franquismo in Madrid, although the current left-wing city government has announced a final cleansing of the remaining Franquista iconography. On the Suharto massacres there was total official silence until early 2016, when an officious seminar about them was held.* German Nazism, on the other hand, has inspired an impressive critical legacy of repudiation.

The contrast of Speer's Reichskanzlei and the chancellor's bungalow in Bonn together sum up the reaction. The latter is small, transparent with glass walls and accessible in a park, separated from a quiet street only by a very low hedge. The chancellor's office in Berlin of reunited Germany is taller and de facto much larger because of a large hidden back. In front is an iron gate. But with its glass front, light construction and easy public accessibility across a still-open field from the Reichstag, it is an eloquent manifestation against weight, closure and distance, and it deliberately hides its size. Furthermore, there is the roster of anti-Nazi memorials in Berlin, from the Topography of Terror museum to the memorials to the victims, Daniel Liebeskind's Jewish Museum, Peter Eisenmann's abstract memorial of the 'Murdered Jews of Europe' by the US embassy and the more anonymous ones to the murdered Roma and the persecuted homosexuals in corners of the Tiergarten. Nowhere else in the world is there as much monumental self-criticism as in Berlin.

---

* Joshua Oppenheimer's extraordinary documentary of the 1965–6 massacre, *The Act of Killing*, with the hired gangster-murderers themselves narrating and demonstrating their acts, has been prohibited from public showing but is widely watched via Internet streaming.

In Latin America, Buenos Aires and Santiago both publicly remember their bloody dictatorships and their victims. Brasília does not do so for its variant (less bloody, true). Buenos Aires has staged a very extensive commemoration of the victims of the military 'state terrorism' at a large number of sites across the city centre. A 2009 guidebook contains 203 different sites of remembrance. Most important is the Park of Memory, opened in 2007. A large landscaped monumental ensemble by the river, it pays respect to the 30,000 victims of the six years of military dictatorship.

In Santiago, the two main memorials are the Villa Grimaldi Park for Peace (of 1997), built at a former torture centre of Pinochet's security police, and the Museum of Memory and Human Rights, opened in 2010. The former focuses on the 4,500 victims of torture and murder in the Villa from 1974 to 1977. The latter combines remembrance of the dictatorship with a broader perspective on human rights, including a room devoted to the situation of the indigenous population in Chile.

8
The Coming and Going of Communism

Communism was one of the landmarks of the twentieth century, together with the two world wars from which it sprung. In the United States it was 'the American Century', but in most of the rest of the world, Communism summed up the aspirations, struggles, disappointments and, many would say, betrayals, disillusions and defeats of the popular classes and the radical intelligentsia. For better and for worse, Communism has an epochal significance to any modern history of power. What it means to urban history, and in particular to twentieth-century capital cities and their representations of power, is something we shall explore in this chapter.

The Bolshevik Revolution was launched in Petrograd, then the superior of the two official capital cities of Tsarist Russia. Moscow was the old capital, still the coronation site but not, since the early eighteenth century, the residence of the court and government. The revolutionary government moved to Moscow purely for military security reasons.

Tsarist Russia was not a nation-state but a patrimonial state of the Tsar, although since the Napoleonic invasion of 1812 the Tsarist regimes had used a number of nationalist rhetorical concepts – like the Fatherland War – and iconicity to back up their absolutism. Basically, Russia was part of the European path to modernity. Its pre-modern dynasty inter-married with the royal houses of Britain and Germany. Its working-class movement was of a Marxist, European type, and both the Bolshevik and the Menshevik wings of its Social Democratic Party were members of the Second International.

But since Peter I, knowledgeable ruling-class Russians had been acutely aware of the underdevelopment of their country vis-à-vis the main powers of Europe. Reactive modernization was part of the progressive Tsarist agenda of Peter I, of Alexander II, of the Stolypin government of the conservative Nicholas II – and of Lenin and Stalin. On the eve of World War I, Russia was still an underdeveloped part of Europe and had since 1870 been losing ground not only to Britain and Germany but also to Scandinavia, Hungary, Italy and Spain. Its GDP per capita was virtually on par with that of Bulgaria, but its human development index, taking literacy and infant mortality into account, was clearly lower, in comparison to Argentina, Chile and Japan, though not with respect to Brazil, Mexico and India.[1] The very (relatively European) underdevelopment of Russia meant a relative underdevelopment of popular nationalism, which the internationalist Bolsheviks used for their universalist socialist project as well as for their successful tactic of a defeatist peace.

The Russian road to modernity was a hybrid of a European development and reactive modernization from above. The February Revolution of 1917 did issue a brief Russian nation-state – throwing away the monarchy like the French had in 1792 – but committed to continuing a (for Russia) hopeless war in support of its Western allies. The October Revolution swept it away, significantly under the anti-nationalist (and anti-imperialist) banner of 'peace'. What followed was clearly a modern conception of state, but not a nation-state: a Union of Socialist Soviet Republics, intended as a prefiguration of a transnational revolution. When the latter did not happen, the Bolsheviks settled for 'building socialism in one country', meaning in one nation-state, multinational although increasingly Russian-dominated. Given the inherited underdevelopment, further deepened by civil war and foreign military interventions, this 'socialism' could only be built from above, by industrial classes of workers, engineers and managers. The 1917 revolutions in Russia were both outcomes of the European road to modernity and to the nation-state, but 'socialism in one [underdeveloped] country' was a socialist, and twentieth-century, equivalent to the Meiji Restoration in Japan, a variant of reactive modernization.

The reactive modernization of Qing China failed, from inner weakness through reactionary court intrigues and from blows by external predators, by Japan in particular. A national republic came out of the revolution of 1911, but one still semi-colonially governed by imperialist port-city 'concessions' and control of the customs, and internally in constant turmoil and armed conflict. In the 1930s China was invaded by Japan, opening a decade of external war during which the government had to retreat to Chongqing in the southeast.

On its route to modernity, China was a semi-failed country of reactive modernization, a semi-colony and a field of European-type class struggle, initially ploughed by Comintern cadres. The Communist Party was formed in 1920, inspired by the Russian Revolution, seen as an anti-imperialist beacon. It received a very substantial input of Comintern cadres and ideology in the 1920s, far from all of it very wise. But its legacy, through the Mao mutation, was the largest organized force of social change of the twentieth century. The Communist victory of 1949 was presented as a national victory, very different from the Bolshevik Revolution. But it also saw itself, and was seen from abroad, as a major extension of the Communist area.

While exploring the hypothesis further is outside the scope of this chapter, I do think it is more than accidental that the two main centres of Communism both emerged in countries with a particularly complex, hybrid pathway to modernity and the nation-state. The Communists came to the fore in the welter of brutal class exploitation and class struggle, but neither the Russians nor the Chinese confronted a constituted modern nation-state. Instead, both of them had to construct one, multinational and as a stage in a project of transforming national underdevelopment into the highest level of development imaginable: socialism and communism. The huge size of the countries made it possible for them to survive in a hostile world, but their imperial background left its traces on the new rulers of the state.

World Communism radiated from the two centres, first of all from the Soviet Union. After World War II, Eastern Europe had several strong indigenous Communist movements – in Albania, Bulgaria, Czechoslovakia, Greece, Yugoslavia – but even their strength and popularity derived largely from the aura of the successful Red Army resistance to Nazi Germany. Similarly, East Asian Communism, even when nationally strong, as in Vietnam, Malacca, Indonesia and the Philippines, owed much of its popular support to the Chinese example. The Koreans in particular, and the Vietnamese, survived to victory largely due to Soviet and Chinese material support.

Soviet and Chinese Communism became in the 1970s and 1980s role models for developing underdeveloped countries, especially in Africa, spawning fake Marxism-Leninism from Benin to Mozambique. It was no more than a veneer and an argument for help, although it has left street signs to this day – from Maputo, which still remembers Marx as well as Mao and Kim Il-sung, to Abuja in ecumenical Nigeria, which never claimed to aim for a dictatorship of the proletariat.

Cuba is a case apart. Its revolution was primarily nationalist and anti-imperialist. No proper Communist would launch the Fidelista revolution's slogan, *patria o muerte* (Fatherland or death).* It turned to Marxism-Leninism as a defiant response to the US-sponsored invasion of the Bay of Pigs in 1961. Being authentic, popular revolutionaries, the Cubans took their new-found Communism seriously – some leaders and cadres knowing it already. Havana belongs to an overview of Communist capitals, while, for example, Addis Ababa and Brazzaville may be left out.

Communism and the City

The Bolshevik revolution was urban and centred in Petrograd – as Saint Petersburg had been Russified during World War I – not only the political capital but the leading industrial city of the country. The Moscow Bolsheviks were advancing rapidly in the spate of elections in 1917, gaining a majority in the September district (*raion*) ones, but they followed their leaders in Petrograd, who ignited the revolution. After a week of armed struggle, the Bolsheviks held Moscow. Fearing for their lives in the ensuing, foreign-supported civil war, the Bolshevik leaders decided to transfer the capital to Moscow in March 1918, installing themselves in the Kremlin, which never had been their goal.

The October Revolution did not establish a multi-ethnic socialist nation-state but a universalist Union of Socialist Soviet Republics, which any Soviet republic could join or leave. The White secession of Finland was conceded directly, that of the Baltics as a recognition of Bolshevik defeat in complex wars, pitting White Baltic farmers supported by the British against working-class Bolsheviks and German baronial free corps. In the Caucasus and Central Asia, the Bolsheviks came to continue defending the old imperial borders against a variety of local nationalists.

---

* In its own way, the slogan does imply a non-consolidated nation-state, a fragile one under imperialist threat.

Revolutionary Moscow saw itself as the temporary capital of world revolution. Lenin and his comrades were acutely aware of Russian underdevelopment and were originally only hoping to hold the fort while triggering a world revolution, most likely to be centred in Germany. In 1919 the Communist International (Comintern), head-quartered in Moscow, was founded for that purpose.

Communism came to power with an ambitious, expanding and mutating iconographic programme. Inspired by Tommaso Campanella's utopia in *The City of the Sun*, Lenin outlined a programme of 'monumental propaganda' shortly after the October Revolution. It would consist of political inscriptions on walls and other places, and statues of various kinds. On 12 April 1918 the Bolshevik government issued a decree that 'monuments erected in honour of the tsars and their servants and of no historical or artistic interest . . . [would be] stored away [or] . . put to some utilitarian use'. Until May Day, 'inscriptions, emblems, street names, coats of arms' would be replaced with 'new ones reflecting the ideas and the mood of revolutionary working Russia'.[2]

The universalist conception of the revolution was put on full display for the 1918 anniversary in Moscow. Lenin's programme featured a rather broad international pantheon, much wider than the revolutionary Marxist tradition. It included ancient rebels such as Spartacus and Brutus; Enlightenment *philosophes* Voltaire and Rousseau; utopian socialists from Campanella to Owen and Fourier; a spectrum of French revolutionaries from Danton to Marat; Lord Byron; national democrats like Garibaldi; Russian anarchists Bakunin and Kropotkin; the Zionist Alexander Herzen; the contemporary French Socialist Jaurès (who died in 1914 in opposition to World War I); painters from Rublev to Cézanne; foreign writers such as Dante, Dickens and Shakespeare; and great Russian writers up to Dostoyevsky and Tolstoy.[*]

While 'monumental propaganda' was important Communist policy from early on, the Bolsheviks did not have, and Soviet Communist

---

[*] V. Bonnell, *Iconography of Power*, Berkeley: University of California Press, 1997, chapter 4; S. Michalski, *Public Monuments*, London: Reaktion Books, 1998, 109. Traces of the programme could still be found on memorial plaques on one side of the Kremlin when I visited in the late 1990s.

leaders never really developed, an elaborate conception of socialist urbanism. The revolution opened up an enthusiastic period of far-reaching urban theorizing and projecting and quite a bit of actual modernist building. Around 1930, Moscow and Russia constituted the most important international pole of actually existing modernist architecture. Le Corbusier was there on several visits, and many German star architects worked there: Ernst May, Hannes Meyer (dismissed as director from Bauhaus), Erich Mendelsohn and others. The fourth Congress of Modern Architecture (CIAM) was planned for Moscow in 1932 and 1933.

Remarkable buildings included the Izvestiya newspaper building by the Vesnin brothers (inspired by Walter Gropius's entry to the Chicago Tribune competition), the communal house for Finance Ministry employees by Moisei Ginzburg and Ignaty Milinis, and workers' clubs and local palaces of culture by Konstantin Melnikov and by the Vesnin brothers – in other words, constructions from significant public commissions. The Soviet period of the 1920s to early 1930s has a major place in the history of modernist architecture. The most influential architect in Moscow from the revolution to World War II was Alexei Shchusev, a non-party man, who designed the key monument of the period, the Lenin Mausoleum, but also the rather functionalist Ministry of Agriculture.[*]

The Soviet avant-garde was much less impressive in their garrulous conceptions of the city, on one hand flipping out into utopias of minutely regimented communal housing and, on the other hand, de-urbanizing and evacuating most of the Moscow population into 'green' garden villages.[†] The USSR's association with international architectural modernism was officially suspended in 1933, when the planned CIAM congress in Moscow was 'postponed'. Soviet modernists survived, but the 1937 All-Union Congress on Architecture asserted

---

[*] A beautiful photographic record of Soviet architectural modernism is provided by Richard Pare and Jean-Louis Cohen, The Lost Vanguard, New York: Monacelli Press, 2007. Cf. T. Colton, Moscow: Governing the Socialist Metropolis, Cambridge, MA: Belknap Press, 1995, 214–46.

[†] The sympathetic historian of Soviet architectural 'constructivism', Anatole Kopp, was palpably frustrated by his protagonists' loss of urban realism. Anatole Kopp, Town and Revolution: Soviet Architecture and City Planning, 1917–1935, London: Thames and Hudson, 1970.

Socialist Realism, a concept never properly defined except for being anti-modernist. Architectural discussion narrowed, though the 1937 congress had invited Frank Lloyd Wright as the most prominent of its international guests, who after some mild and vague criticisms of the 'left' and the 'right' wings of Soviet architecture cautiously expressed his hope that the USSR, 'liberated from private interests', would create a new architecture as an example to the world, including the United States.[3] This failure of the urbanistic avant-garde of the revolution at a time when debating channels were open and coeval with the emergence of Western European municipal socialism, was fatal to the development of a new socialist and Communist urbanism. In the wilderness of competing utopias, Stalinism could emerge as common sense and pragmatic historical realism.

The stake was the General Plan of Moscow, finally laid out in 1935, on the basis of top guidelines from 1932.* Stalin praised the plan drafters in 1934 for winning against 'those who would deny the very principle of a city and leave Moscow as a big village' and 'proponents of hyper-urban-ization along the lines of a capitalist city, with skyscrapers and extraordinary overcrowding'. In 1932 Lazar Kaganovich, then Stalin's Moscow builder, had declared on behalf of his boss that socialist urbanism should 'proceed first and foremost from the historically established forms of the existent city, rebuilding it in accord with the dictates of our epoch'.[4]

A cautious, pragmatic programme set the frame of Communist urbanism. Its main message was simple and modest: beware of radical utopias; respect history while not being confined to it. It has de facto been heeded throughout Communist history, except for Pyongyang, where the existent city had been totally destroyed by the American war. A pathetic illustration is Brezhnev's declaration to the 1971 Congress of the Communist Party of the Soviet Union (CPSU) that Moscow should be a 'model Communist city', without spelling out what that would mean. His loyal city lieutenant Viktor Grishin had no substance to add: 'A model Communist city is a city where people with

---

* Karl Schlögel, in his first great book on Moscow, in its original German edition called *Moskau lesen*, ('Reading Moscow'), 'reluctantantly' conceded that 'the General Plan probably struck a happy medium between conservation of the legacy of the past and changes that were essential' (*Moscow*, Cambridge: Cambridge University Press, 2008, 63).

a high level of culture and consciousness live, a city of model public order'.[5]

Some more, but not much, guidance was delivered by Soviet urban authorities to an East German study delegation in 1950, the systematized lessons of which were incorporated into GDR law in 1950 as sixteen *Grundsätze des Städtebaues* (principles of town planning). They begin by underlining the city's representative function: 'The city is in structure and architectural form [*Gestaltung*] an expression of the people's political life and national consciousness' (principle 1). The 'people's democracy' adaptation of Socialist Realism meant that architecture should have a 'democratic' content and a 'national' form (principles 1 and 14.) Much attention is given to the centre, 'the determining nucleus of the city' and the site of 'political demonstrations, processions [*Aufmärsche*] and popular festivities', as well as of 'the most monumental buildings' (principle 6). This may be seen as one variant of a political and civic opposite to the US notion of the city centre as the central business district (CBD). The 'face of the city' has its own basic principle (9), 'determined' by the 'squares, the main streets and their dominant buildings'. Principle 10 deals at relative length with housing, which should be concentrated in residential districts of multi-storied apartment buildings, with gardens, kindergartens, schools and 'provisions' [*Versorgungsanlagen*] for the 'daily needs of the population'. Traffic should not be allowed inside the residential complexes. There is a warning against 'excessive' urban growth, as well as a repudiation of efforts to turn the city into a garden. A city means 'urbane' [*städtisches*] living.[6]

The Communist contribution to urbanism and urban history has been much more modest than its role in twentieth-century power dynamics. However, it has in fact been more than the official banalities.*

* From the angle of architecture there are (at least) two major studies, both focusing on Eastern Europe. One is by the late Swedish architectural historian Anders Åman, whose *Architecture and Ideology in Eastern Europe During the Stalin Era*, first published in Swedish in 1987 and in English in 1992 (Cambridge, MA: MIT Press), was a trailblazer. The other is by the British architectural critic Owen Hatherley: *Landscapes of Communism* (New York: New Press, 2016). To my knowledge, there are hardly any towering works on the Communist city in a broader urbanistic sense, but there is a spate of retrospectives, some of which shed important light on the past. Of them, I have found the collective volumes edited by Gregory Andrusz, Michael Harloe, and Ivan Szelenyi (*Cities after Socialism: Urban and Regional Change and Conflict in Post-Socialist Societies*, London: Blackwell, 1995) and Ian Hamilton,

To urban history, in a wider sense than capital cities, communism also contributed modern industrial cities, beginning at Magnitogorsk in the Urals and continuing after World War II and Stalinism into Nowa Huta in Poland and Eisenhüttenstadt (formerly Stalinstadt) in East Germany, both of which today testify – in their architecture, their houses of culture, their greenery and their spatial layout – to a circumspect industrial modernism now silenced or muted by post-industrial capitalism.*

Four aspects of Communism in power

To get a grasp of the urban and, in particular, the capital-city meaning of Communism we have to look at the latter's identity, power base, power context and power structure and try to navigate through ideologically mined waters.

The identity of Communism was that of a working-class and poor peasant movement. It saw itself as the vanguard of the proletariat. The Bolshevik uprising in 1917 was undertaken by urban industrial workers, and all through their history, Communists everywhere paid close attention to the class composition of their parties and of the state institutions they governed. They always tried to ground their power in workplace

Kaliopa Dimitrovska Andrews, and Nataša Pichler-Milanovic, *Transformation of Cities in Central and Eastern Europe: Towards Globalization*, (New York: United Nations University Press, 2005) the most instructive. The past socialist city also appears clearly in the background of Sonia Hirt's 2012 Sofia-centred but generalizing book *Iron Curtains* (Oxford: Oxford University Press, 2012) on post-socialist Eastern Europe. Among the historical literature in Western European languages, one may signal Virág Molnár's East German and Hungarian-focused *Building the State* (New York: Routledge, 2013) and the penetrating Belgrade monograph by Brigitte Le Normand, *Designing Tito's Capital: Urban Planning, Modernism, and Socialism in Belgrade*, (Pittsburgh: University of Pittsburgh Press, 2014).

* Small Eisenhüttenstadt is now largely a city-cum-museum of post-Stalinist modern architecture designed as a working-class town, while Nowa Huta survives as a suburb of Krakow and the Lenin steelworks as a much reduced peripheral part of the transnational Indian corporation Acelor Mittal. Even before that, the Krakow diocese, home base of Pope John Paul II, had decisively defeated its secularist Communist challengers, the Catholic anti-Communist movement Solidarność, capturing the minds of most of the steelworkers (Kinga Pozniak, *Nowa Huta: Generations of Change in a Model Socialist Town*, Pittsburgh: University of Pittsburgh Press, 2014, 69). Today, this is, of course, well memorialized in a whole set of ecclesiastical buildings and monuments.

organizations and often, like in the GDR and in Czechoslovakia, formed armed workers' militias as class guards of their regimes.

However, before World War I, Lenin and the Bolsheviks/Communists were acutely aware of operating in a world of nationalities and nations, moulded in their opposition to the Tsarist Great Russian imperialism of a multinational empire. The power base of governing Communism was always a modern state with a central, but varying and problematic, relation to the nation. Lenin and Stalin gave much serious study to the 'national question' in a multinational empire. That nations were not resolvable into class was a basic Bolshevik tenet, in contrast to some other currents of radical Marxism. In turning the Russian multinational empire into a Union of Socialist Soviet Republics, they instituted national culture, development and self-determination as fundamental principles.

Under Stalin these fundamental principles were clearly subordinated to Russian imperial geopolitics, reasserting the imperial boundaries, including the Baltics and Bessarabia. But Stalin never forgot his Leninist lesson on the importance of nations. It was enshrined in the fundamental tenet of Socialist Realism: 'national in form, socialist in content'.[7] Communist Europe had been nationalized after World War I, Bulgaria and Romania in the last quarter of the nineteenth century. But they were hardly consolidated nation-states, nor properly European – i.e., internally driven – in their origin. Like Greece they owed their national statehood primarily to European geopolitics, to the external defeats of the Ottomans, Habsburgs, and Hohenzollerns. Borders, in particular those of Poland, Romania, Hungary and Bulgaria, and internal national relations – for example between Serbs and Croats or Czechs and Slovaks – were widely regarded as contingent and arbitrary, and often unjust.

The Eastern European Communists governing after World War II varied widely in their national rootedness and legitimacy, which were substantial, to put it cautiously, in Albania, Bulgaria, Czechoslovakia and Yugoslavia and significant but clearly minoritarian in East Germany, Hungary and, most pronouncedly minoritarian in Romania and Poland. Moscow instructed them all to pay utmost attention to the nation – while, of course, refraining from any nationalism critical of the Soviet Union. Even the weaker movements had some roots or achievements to point to: the German anti-fascist tradition, at a time when an important number of officials, judges, businessmen and professionals of the Third

Reich had been incorporated into West Germany; the Hungarians' break with pre-war conservative reaction as well as with Arrow Cross fascism; the Romanians successfully keeping contested Transylvania; the Polish western expansion to the Oder-Neisse line, always contested by the German right, arguably overshadowing its losses to the east, including Lwów (now Lviv).

The Chinese, Korean, Vietnamese and Cuban Communists all rose to power spearheading nationalist anti-imperialist revolutions. Ironically, the most nationalist turned chauvinist, the North Koreans, were the ones originally most dependent on foreign support: Soviet in the post-Japanese division of Korea between the United States and USSR, and Chinese military aid against the Americans in the Korean War.

The context of Communist power was economic underdevelopment in a world of hostile national and imperial geopolitics. Communist leaders were all very aware of this; Lenin very frankly and explicitly acknowledged it. The Communist powers were struggling against underdevelopment, with inferior resources in comparison with competing, hostile capitalist centres. Catching up, economically and militarily, was a constant preoccupation and constraint. It meant a very heavy mortgage on any social urbanist development. Industrial investment and armaments against much more resourceful hostile powers always weighed heavily on Communist social space, although to varying extents.

After class and nation, authoritarianism came to characterize Communism. It was not quite there from the beginning; Lenin could be outvoted in the party's Central Committee. The square in front of the Winter Palace of Petrograd was named for an important opponent of his Brest-Litovsk concessionary peace in 1918, Uritsky. But in some sense, authoritarianism was inherent in a 'scientific' conception of socialism as the guide of history, disqualifying all opposition; even within his own party, Lenin was known as the most intransigent against compromises and coalitions with others.

The terror dimension of ruling Communism, however, has to be seen as coming out of its origin in brutal and brutalizing war, in Eastern Europe as well as in Russia and Asia. The effects of comparatively minor attacks and threats from grouplets such as Al-Qaeda and the Islamic State on the powerful and secure Bush and Obama regimes in the US – from worldwide kidnapping and torture operations and a president signing off on weekly drone executions to two full-scale wars of invasion, explicitly launched for 'shock and awe' – provide us, the late-born, with some insight into the spiralling effects of political violence. Stalin added to that, and foisted on his henchmen an extraordinary paranoia and ice-cold indifference to human lives and suffering. It was decisive for the character of Communism that the international Communist movement, originally quite diverse, gelled around 1930 in a Stalinist mould: ruthlessly authoritarian and addicted to personality cults, something completely alien to Lenin but which Stalin, the former seminarian, may have learnt from the iconography of the Orthodox Church. After Stalin's death and under peaceful consolidation the movement did change and repent, but the human damage was, of course, beyond repair.

These four dimensions of Communism – its working-class identity, its idea of the importance of the nation, its rule of inherited underdevelopment and its authoritarian internal power structure – provide an explanatory framework for Communist urbanism. These dimensions had varying accentuations among the ruling parties and, above all, between different periods of rule.

The Moscow model

Pre-revolutionary Moscow, the coronation city of the Tsars, had a stronger conservative character than Saint Petersburg, as the cultural centre of Old Russia, of the Orthodox Church and of its increasingly economically successful Old Believers. Moscow's skyline was dominated by religious spires and cupolas around the Kremlin, after the move of the imperial court, which was mainly an ecclesiastical fortress. But by the early twentieth century it had also become a major industrial city, particularly in textiles, with 60 per cent of its population factory workers and artisans. It was also a site of vanguard artistic modernism, rivalled but not surpassed by Saint Petersberg. It was notorious as 'the worst-housed city of Europe', according to contemporary sociological studies.[8]

The Bolshevik government moved to Moscow in March 1918, acutely threatened in Petrograd by White and Western forces. Reluctantly, it settled in the Kremlin; there was no proper alternative available. The ecclesiastical space inside was cut down, but never completely eliminated. The Dormition,* Annunciation and Archangel Cathedrals remained throughout Communist rule.[9] Not much was done to the city in the first decade of Bolshevik power, a period which started with drastic urban decline in the wake of the Civil War. Moscow lost about 40 per cent of its population. Things started to change with Stalin's rise to power and the launch of a breakneck catching-up process through rapid industrialization, supported by the collectivization of agriculture. In Moscow, the characteristic reek of incense and sound of church bells were subjected to a full-scale attack. Churches, monasteries and convents were closed or dynamited en masse, including the landmark late-nineteenth-century votive Cathedral of Christ the Redeemer, a Tsarist monument to victory over Napoleon.

A General Plan for Moscow was prepared in the early 1930s and officially approved in 1935. It was meant to be the urbanist accompaniment to the grand plans of economic development and catch-up, making Moscow, as 'the capital of the world proletariat', a modern metropolis on a level with New York or Paris. But as the city's greatest historian Karl Schlögel has pointed out, it should also be seen as an 'emergency product', created while trying to cope with the enormous problems caused by a rural flight to the cities.[10] At the start of the first Five-Year Plan, Moscow had recovered its pre-revolutionary population: from 1930 to 1932 it increased by almost 50 percent, from 2 to 3 million.

The Plan, interrupted by the war, was never implemented in full, but this was not recognized before the death of Stalin. So it provided the blueprint for Eastern European Communism after the Red Army victories. What came out of the plan were three mega-projects: one exclusively representative – a huge Palace of Soviets topped by a 75-metre steel statue of Lenin – and two transport projects, the Moscow-Volga Canal as part of the city's and the nation's economic development, and a city Metro, given a lavishly expensive representative outfit.[11] The latter two materialized but the first was never built, and its ex-cathedral crater became an outdoor swimming pool in the late 1950s. It was restored as a cathedral after the fall of Communism.

---

* *Dormition*, literally 'falling asleep' (*uspenie* in Russian) refers to the death of the Virgin Mary. Sometimes the church is called the Asssumption Cathedral, referring to Mary's assumption into heaven. It is the oldest of the Kremlin churches and the coronation church of the Tsars.

Other features of the Plan included a large expansion of central public space, including doubling the size of the already extended Red Square; this was also not implemented. A major realization was the transformation of the old road to Tver and Saint Petersburg into a central artery of processions (to Red Square), luxurious apartment blocks and of night-life entertainment, 'low' and unofficial as well as high and sponsored. Tverskaya became Gorky Street and was widened from 20 to 60 metres, with corresponding housing demolitions.[12] Gorky was meant to be the principal of a number of wide boulevards criss-crossing the city; most were forgotten, but a large amount of green space materialized. Housing and consumer services were not neglected by the Plan, which included the construction of 15 million square metres of dwelling space in ten years, as well as schools, cinemas, hospitals and a new infrastructure of water, sewage and so on.[13] But these were clearly secondary to priorities of power representation and economic development. Moscow's dwelling space per capita exceeded its 1920 record of 9.5 square metres only after 1971. In 1940 it was at a trough of 4.1.[14]

Looking at this General Plan and the Moscow model, a latter-day observer may very well ask if there was anything socialist or working-class to it. Its socialist aspect was the comprehensive, *Gesamtkunstwerk* (Schlögel), all-city approach to town planning and the lack of need to take private property and private land rent into account, visible in the large open spaces in the centre. The class aspect was much more mediated. Negatively, it meant the absence of bank and other corporate offices of a CBD and of haute-bourgeois quarters. The Bolshevik leaders lived in very modest Kremlin apartments, subject to strict expense rules.[15] Star workers, Russian *Stachanovites*, could get plum housing, and the Moscow *mikrorayon* housing districts kept a vigilant record of their social composition in order to counteract housing segregation.[16] Class also meant the *komunalka,* communalizing the big bourgeois city apartments, reproduced under never-ending housing scarcity as multi-family apartments with common kitchens and bathrooms.

The officious message of the Moscow General Plan of 1935 was not so much that of a working-class socialist city as a that of a modern metropolis equivalent to New York, whose Rockefeller Center and Radio City Music Hall were lodestars to Boris Iofan, former assistant to the monstrous Roman Vittoriano monument and designer of the even more monstrous Palace of Soviets. The iconographic 1937 painting 'The New Moscow', by Yuri Pimenov, shows a young woman driving a cabriolet among other cars through a city, facing heavy new buildings.* (Only their heaviness tells us that this must be the USSR.)

The metropolitan drive was further underlined soon after the World War II victory by a city ring of seven high-rises, two ministries, two hotels, two apartment blocks and one university, in spacious settings, built in individual variants of the 'wedding-cake' style: heavy, pronouncedly vertical, symmetrical and closed (to outsiders) – ticking off the points of a grammar of authoritarian power – and richly ornamented with an eclectic mélange of motifs.[17] There were meant to be eight – one for each century of Moscow, celebrating 800 years – and were to make up the modern but non-Functionalist face of a historical capital rising again after an exhaustive, blood-letting war.

The Stalinist focus on representation was frontally attacked in December 1954 by Nikita Khrushchev, then secretary-general of the CPSU. He lambasted it from two angles: for its expensive waste, with the highest-quality materials and artisanal production, and for neglecting the huge housing needs of ordinary people. In November 1955 the Soviet government and the Party Central Committee issued a resolution titled 'On the removal of exaggerations in planning and building'. The turn was 180 degrees: 'Soviet architecture must be characterized by simplicity, austerity of form, and economy of layout'.[18] Mass housing was the new construction priority. Low-rise, pre-fabricated three- to five-storey apartment buildings sprouted all over the USSR, often popularly referred to as 'Khrushchev houses'. The CPSU was returning to its class roots.

However, for the international Communist imprint, the most important historical layer of Moscow was the Stalinist cityscape around 1950. What message of power did it convey? What were its main political landmarks? The messages, I think, were above all (if by no means exclusively) three: this power is national; it is based on popular mobilization; it is hedonistically developmentalist. The messages were cut in landmark stones.

'National' is, of course, first of all the Kremlin, the historical centre of Russia, purged of its pre-national Tsarist symbolism. As the metropolis of a big national power, Moscow was measuring itself with other world

* The picture is reproduced, for example, in Schlögel, *Terror und Traum*, 73.

metropolises, in particular New York, not by imitating them but by competing with them on its own terms. This was the message of the seven high-rises for the eighth centenary, some of which clearly drew inspiration from American skyscrapers of the 1920s and 1930s, with which the leading Moscow architects were familiar. One of the invitees for the Palace of Soviets competition in 1931 was William Lamb, the principal architect of the Empire State Building.* The whole architectural project of Socialist Realism was not so much about socialism as about finding a modern national style.

Whatever the actual importance of its repression, Communists saw their power as based on – though not necessarily as deriving from – popular mobilization. Red Square was inherited for free, although it required some work to suit modern mass demonstrations. The expressionist Lenin Mausoleum with its leaders' tribune provided a brilliant focal point. Parade grounds had to have their march routes – in contemporary air traffic lingo, feeder lines. Tverskaya Street, the beginning of the road from the Kremlin to Saint Petersburg, was a natural choice. In 1932 and 1933 it was renamed after the great writer Maxim Gorky into Gorky Street and became the iconic *magistrale* of Communist urbanism, doubling, in some plans trebling, its width, and the model for conceiving the street façades as the primary layout of street space. Particularly on procession days, street and façade banners, big posters and huge portraits of Lenin and the living leaders exhorted political direction.

The third aspect of Moscow and Socialist Realist power is not much worked out in the monographic literature. But there is a striking fit between, on one hand, the expensive, ornamental, luxurious Socialist Realist monumental buildings and, on the other hand, the explicit Stalinist anti-austerity turn in 1935 and 1936. Already, in 1931, Stalin had weighed against 'leftist' egalitarianism and for more wage differentiation. In November 1935, in a speech to elite Stachanovite workers, he proclaimed, 'Life has become more joyous'. After the traumatic, breakneck industrialization and famines from resistance to the collectivization of agriculture,

---

* Fabien Bellat, *Amérique–URSS: Architectures du défi*, Paris: Nicolas Chaudun, 2014, 82, 164ff. The connection is most visible in the case of the Ukraina and Leningradskaya hotels and in the New York hotels by the firm Schulze & Weaver, especially their Waldorf Astoria.

the time had come – for elite workers and loyal party functionaries – to enjoy life.* This was not capitalism à la Deng Xiaoping, but corresponded to the recent rise of a new developmentalist elite – all state-employed – coming out of the massive expansion of higher education in the Five-Year Plans. Through the terrorist 'purges', this stratum was rising fast in party and state. Stalinist doctrine told them they deserved their (unsecure) emoluments, elegant housing, caviar and champagne.

These people were clearly the main beneficiaries of the grand, expensive representative and by contemporary standards high-quality buildings: full-service apartment complexes, luxury hotels with their bars and restaurants, the luxury shops along Gorky Street and generous amenities for students as well as for faculty of the famous Lomonosov University.[19] Socialist Realist model streets and apartment blocks were expressions of the arrival of the new developmentalist elite: Stachanovite shock workers, engineers, managers, scientists and committed artists created by Stalinist modernization from above.

Hidden from the grand vistas of New Moscow, while further confirming the new hierarchical power structure, was the housing of the median worker. According to Colton, the Harvard political-science historian of Moscow, 'the median family in Stalin's Moscow' lived in one room of a *komunalka*.[20] In 1960, it seems that 60 per cent of Muscovites lived in communal flats.[21]

Eastern European Receptions and Mutations

From 1945 to 1950, Moscow was the Mecca of all the world's Communists, proud and enthusiastic about the Red Army's victories over fascism. Like it had during the first Five-Year Plan in the midst of the capitalist

---

* The Stalinist turn to a version of consumerism, which was not just propaganda but also included the end of rationing and the dispatch of delegations to study American department stores, is treated by David Hoffman in *Stalinist Values,* Ithaca, NY: Cornell University Press, 2003, 126ff. A connection between the mid-1930s explicit turn against egalitarianism and austerity, on one hand, and the expensive housing complex of 'New Moscow' is adumbrated by Monica Rüthers in her thorough and sharply observant 'Habilitation' thesis, *Moskau bauen*, 84–5, 95. The theme of Stalinist luxury has been excavated from among the many bizarre and obscene contradictions of the times by Jukka Gronow, *Caviar with Champagne,* Oxford: Oxford University Press, 2003.

Great Depression, the USSR had a broad left appeal far beyond the often small core of Communist cadres. How far is virtually impossible to gauge, and everywhere there were anti-Communists, some armed and continuing their wartime combat – alongside the German Nazis in the Baltics and the Ukraine – against them in Poland. My point here is obviously not to dive into post–World War II Eastern European history, but to situate the reception of the urbanistic signals from Moscow.

Eastern European architecture and urbanism had a strong current of left-wing modernism, participating in the pre-war modernist movement CIAM. This was particularly the case in East Germany, the home country of Bauhaus, as well as in Czechoslovakia, Poland and Serbia/Yugoslavia. Unsurprisingly, early Eastern European reconstruction often started in a modernist mode, though early on, national historical reconstruction was also given top priority, like rebuilding the Old City of Warsaw and resurrecting the historical Unter den Linden in East Berlin.

The freezing of the Cold War in 1948 and 1949, with the armed crushing of the pro-Communist anti-fascist movement in Greece, the (peaceful) Communist revolution in Czechoslovakia and the split-up of the Four Powers' lordship over Berlin dug a trench across the world, most deeply in Europe. Architecture and urbanism could not escape. The USSR, narrowly victorious after tremendous loss and devastation, saw itself as existentially threatened by the completely unscathed, nuclear-armed United States. Its message was no longer world revolution – which had been the hope of leftist modernism – but peace and national defence. 'We are against the Bauhaus because Functionalism is the height of imperialist cosmopolitanism', East German chief architect Kurt Liebknecht declared, adding that, characteristically, people like Gropius and van der Rohe had opted to stay in the United States.[22]

The new guideline – socialist in content, national in form – was asserted, in 1949–50 with typical Stalinist virulence, driven by Soviet pressure to conform; by some leaders of particular urbanistic concern, like the East German and the Polish party chiefs Walter Ulbricht and Bolesław Bierut; by the Hungarian head cultural *politruk*, Józef Révai; and, in day-to-day operational terms, by a handful of post-war returnee architects from the Soviet Union catapulted into urbanistic power: Liebknecht in the GDR, Edmund Geldzamt in Poland and Imre Perényi in Hungary.

However, it would be wrong to see Communist Eastern European capitals as simply imposed by Soviet transmissions. There were two other crucial elements: the Soviet infatuation of the local Communists and the post-war urban parameters.

The eighteenth of December 1948 was Stalin's seventieth birthday. All CP leaders of any significance were at the celebrations at the Bolshoi Theatre in Moscow. A number of monumental pledges were made: East Berlin offered the Stalinallee, the mayor of Budapest renamed his city's main street, Andrássy út, after Stalin; Prague, Budapest and Bucharest promised huge Stalin statues; cities from Bulgaria and Romania to East Germany were named after Stalin, and so was the coming Warsaw Palace of Culture and Science. The extra-Soviet origin of these proposals should be noticed, alongside the fact that they did not directly derive from the Moscow model. While it had some district monuments to the great leader, and some monstrous monumental proposals were floated after World War II, Moscow had neither a landmark Stalin statue nor a Stalinallee. Its main street was named after Maxim Gorky.

Intelligent Soviet Stalinists never forgot the national lessons of Lenin and Stalin. In December 1951, two Soviet commentators criticized the East German Stalinallee for following the Soviet example too closely.[23] In September 1953, the epitome of Soviet ideological orthodoxy, Mikhail Suslov, berated the Soviet editor of a Red Army publication in Poland, fighting for his publication's survival: 'And what about Poland's sovereignty? Poles themselves should be building socialism, and they should learn to write about our achievements and experience'.[24]

The new capitals of the western extension of Communism were all very different both from Moscow and from each other, although they did have some features in common. They were all – with some qualification for Budapest – capitals of nation-states coming out of inter-state wars either as beneficiaries of a victorious inter-state coalition (Bucharest, Sofia, Belgrade, Prague and Warsaw) or as the national capital of a defeated empire (post-Hohenzollern Berlin and, in part, Budapest). The borders of these states were precarious and contested. Their capitals, except for Berlin, had all changed their main ethnic character just before statehood and were all part of the multi-ethnic East-Central Strip of Europe, running between Prussia and Russia from the Gulf of Finland to the Black Sea.[25] However, there was no urbanistic or architectural commonality.

The central image of Warsaw was the Renaissance-era Old Royal City and the Baroque and Rococo mansions of the aristocracy. The hegemonic cultural tradition of the city was Catholic and military/aristocratic, with military strongmen ruling most of inter-war Poland. Prague had a grand medieval past; a mainstream tradition of Christian reformation and heresy, from the fifteenth-century Jan Hus onward; a vigorous Art Nouveau capitalism, with a corresponding labour movement; and an inter-war current of Republican modernism, including an avant-garde architectural cubism. Budapest emerged in the 1870s as the proud and increasingly opulent Magyar national capital of the Austria-Hungary empire of the Habsburgs. It lavishly displayed its national pride as well as its new wealth in a parliament modelled to surpass the Westminster model and challenge the dynastic castle up on the Buda Hills across the Danube, a Heroes' Square rivalling Vienna's Heldenplatz, and Europe's second underground. Belgrade, Bucharest and Sofia had once been Ottoman sites of power, something all three were trying to forget and overwhelm.

The capitals of Communist Eastern Europe were governed according to a very similar programme, but manifested in quite different ways for three reasons: firstly the cityscape in 1944–1945; secondly the national forms and traditions, the preservation and use of which the programme called for; and thirdly the rulers, who although all cast in the same mould were no clones.

Warsaw and Berlin were devastated by the war, Warsaw to such an extent that the much less ravaged textile city of Lodz functioned as the de facto capital of Communist Poland from 1945 to 1947. Lodz was the working-class and labour-movement centre of Poland, and there seem to have been at least some discussions about whether the capital should be relocated to this working-class base.* However, in spite of its ostentatiously aristocratic character, Warsaw was the capital of the Polish nation-state. So the Communist administration moved back to Warsaw, with the aim, in the words of its leader Bierut, of turning it 'through the development of industry . . . [into] the centre of production, the city of workers'.†

---

* I owe this insight to Agata Zysiak, an urban historian in Lodz, with whom I talked in September 2015.

† David Smith, 'The Socialist City', in Gregory Andrusz et al. (eds), *Cities after Socialism*,

Belgrade was badly damaged, Budapest and Sofia significantly so, Bucharest less; Prague was largely intact, if run down by the Nazi occupation. In Warsaw and Berlin new political centres had to be built, and in Belgrade and Sofia it was an obvious option, whereas in Prague and Budapest, old historical cities, it was a rather dubious one. Bucharest had got a new monumental centre from the inter-war right-wing governments, gloating over Romania's World War I gains. At the same time, the Communist urbanistic programme meant that, whether the political centre was new or old, national heritage had to be respected and, if need be, reconstructed. In Warsaw the first major city decision was to rebuild the Old Town, although the royal castle was restored only in the 1970s under a new leadership. In East Berlin a gradual reconstruction of the classical street of Berlin elegance, Unter den Linden, was one of the first building decisions.

According to the architectural canon of Socialist Realism, new monumental buildings had to have a 'national form'. This came to mean mostly neo-classicism in Berlin and Budapest, Renaissance in Warsaw and Prague and Byzantine elements in Sofia and Bucharest. Often, as in the Warsaw Palace of Culture, the national forms were mainly expressed in ornamental motifs recognizable only to architecture buffs.[26] Stalin's break with the Yugoslav Communists spared Belgrade the pastiches.[27]

The first major political building in Warsaw was for the party's Central Committee, a white classicist building unusually centrally located for such a building, at the crossing of Jerusalem Boulevard and Nowy Świat, but, in line with the Moscow model, it was not *the* landmark of the new political centre. That role fell to the enormous Palace of Culture complex, designed by the Soviet architect Lev Rudnev in Moscow style and built by Soviet workers, although with studied Polish historical motifs. In front of it was the political parade ground. The principal *magistrale was the* Marzsalkowska,* which ran on one side of it and at its palace end

---

Oxford, Blackwell, 1996, 85. Something similar happened in early Soviet Ukraine, where the capital was first located in the industrial centre Kharkov, but then moved to Kiev.

* The name refers to the mid-eighteenth-century Grand Marshal of the Crown, who headed an important city commission. The main streets of Warsaw tended to keep their historical names during Communism, although Saxon Square became Victory Square and Bank Square was rebaptized after Feliks Dzerzhinsky, the Polish first head of the Soviet security police, the Cheka.

included the principal residence and shopping area of new Warsaw, MDN. On a parallel street was a series of ministries. All this was several blocks south of the pre-war centre, and even further south of the Old Town.

In Prague, the preserved historical city was reused. The Communist presidents and governments stayed in the former Habsburg Castle, while party headquarters were lodged in a sombre former ministry by the Vltava River. The takeover of power in 1948 was announced by Klement Gottwald from the balcony of the Kinský Palace in Old Town Square; May Day and other political parades were held at the second inherited historical agora, Wenceslas Square.

In Czechoslovakia the Communists attached themselves to the national reformatory tradition of Jan Hus, who was burned at the stake as a heretic in Konstanz in 1415. The Bethlehem chapel where he preached was rebuilt in 1949.* The Gottwald mausoleum was a mutation of the one built before the war for President Tomáš Masaryk – who had the opportunity to reject it – far up from CP processions on Vítkov Hill, where a statue of the military commander of the Hussites, Jan Zilska sitting on his horse was installed there in 1951. A Stalin statue was raised on an opposite, higher hill, leading small bands of Soviets and Czechoslovaks in a forward march. The ensemble was put in place in 1955, less than a year before Khrushchev's anti-Stalinist turn. The Czechoslovak Communists dynamited it in 1961. Despite many attempts, no proper use has been found for the magnificent site and its solid platform.

The Budapest Castle, where the reactionary regent Admiral Miklós Horthy and after him, for a while, the fascist Arrow Cross Party leader Ferenc Szálasi had resided, was severely damaged in the final battle for the city. Restoration began in the early 1950s to turn it into a museum. The minion Sandor Palace nearby on the Buda Hills, the office of pre-war prime ministers – and now of post-Communist presidents – were left aside after the war. Communist power installed itself on the Pest side of the Danube, around the huge, Westminster-emulating parliament building, which also housed government offices, with ministries, and, very practically, party Central Committee and Politburo in a side street

---

* In Europe outside the Soviet Union, including the Sovietized Baltics (except Albania), churches were not closed, but reconstruction of damaged ones usually took a long time. The Lutheran East Berlin Domkirche was reconstructed only in the mid-1970s.

nearby. There were plans for creating a new political parade ground in pre-Communist Erzsébet Square and opening up a march route and a vista from the river, but like so many other plans of the time, they came to nothing.[28]

The provisional worked well enough. The most elegant avenue of the city, Andrassy út, named after a leading aristocratic statesman of the late nineteenth century, was appropriated for the procession calendar, for some years under Stalin's name (after 1956 under the impossible label of the People's Republic). The avenue led out to the major monumental ensemble of Hungarian nationalism, Heroes' Square. The Communists took out all the Habsburgs from the hemicycle of statues and replaced them with anti-Habsburg historical leaders, including Transylvanian princes, ending with the 1848 Hungarian hero Lajos Kossuth. Post–World War I *revanchiste* symbols and inscriptions were also deleted, but the square was kept free of Communism and Communists. Instead, in a very clever move of symbolic politics, the street which comes from the right where Andrassy ends, just before Heroes' Square, was widened, renamed and provided with a leaders' tribune. The renaming was full of national historical meaning. Before May 1945, it honoured István Werbőczy, a sixteenth-century noble statesman and lawmaker who suppressed a peasants' revolt. Under Communism the street was named after the leader of that revolt, György Dózsa. There was also a big statue of Werbőczy, which was destroyed in May 1945. It took six years for him to be succeeded by Stalin, who was not to be very long-lived there, hauled down in the anti-Communist uprising of 1956.*

Tito and the Yugoslav Communists were eager Stalinists but also proud of having liberated Belgrade on their own, without any direct help from the Red Army. The city had been occupied and was very severely damaged in both world wars. It was still to a large extent a Balkan city of one-storey traditional houses, still visible in the central city of the twenty-first century. The Communists made great plans. The

---

* Lenin was given a try after the suppression of the uprising, but times kept changing and he was later discreetly put away, first for 'repair'. On Heroes' Square, see further Andras Gerö, *Hungarian Society in the Making*, Budapest: Oxford University Press, 1995, chapter 11; on Dósza György út and more broadly Communist monuments in Budapest during the Stalinist period, Reuben Fowkes, 'The Role of Monumental Sculptures in the Construction of Socialist Space in Stalinist Hungary', in D. Crowley and S. Reid (eds), *Socialist Spaces*, Oxford: Oxford University Press, 2002, 65–84.

centre of the city, and of the capital of the country, was to move, into the marshlands across the Sava river, where a fully modern city should be built. Planning was inspired by the Athens Charter of CIAM, in which some Yugoslav architects had participated. But resources of the war-ravaged country to implement it were scarce, narrowing much further after Stalin's paranoiac break with Tito in 1948.

Plans for New Belgrade were both revised and postponed several times, but their modernist thrust was never broken by any Socialist Realist clampdown. In the course of the 1950s and 1960s, New Belgrade gradually emerged as a city of modern appearance, even if underdeveloped in quality and amenities, but it never became the new city and country centre. Instead it was redefined as one part of Belgrade, albeit an important one. It was not only a modernist residential area; it was also in a sense Yugoslavia's Ottawa or Canberra. It housed the federal government building and the ruling Party Central Committee, while most of the capital functions remained across the river, many of them, including other political institutions, along the Bulevar Revolucije.[29]

Bucharest and Sofia both had the early-twentieth-century Balkan village character with a central enclave of monumentality, but they were very different capitals of very different countries. Romania was a country of landowners exploiting a poor peasantry, with a small French-cultured urban upper class of merchants and real estate speculators* and a large, poor Jewish population, the target of virulent anti-Semitism. Bulgaria was peasant and had been broadly pro-Russian since Russia decisively helped it become indpendent from the Ottomans; it had a tiny, German-oriented political elite, which twice bet on Germany in the world wars. The Romanian CP was minuscule prior to the Red Army entrance, while the Communists were a major force in Bulgaria, although not a partisan army of Albanian or Yugoslav significance. With 973,000 inhabitants in 1940, Bucharest had more than double the population of Sofia, while the latter was the fastest-growing capital of the Balkans in the 1930s.[30]

Bucharest gained a centre of modernist boulevards in the inter-war period and a spate of monumental public buildings just before the war.[31] It was also provisioned with a major Victory Avenue and Victory Square,

* A good look into this 'Paris of the East' in its belle époque is provided by Paul Morand, *Bucarest*, Paris: Plon, 1935/1995.

celebrating victory against the Ottomans. While some ministerial buildings had been bombed during the war, most of Bucharest was still
standing in 1944 and 1945, with its modern monumental centre and its
dispersed village-like settlements, among which only half of the more
urbanized houses had electricity and running water.[32] The Romanian
Communists did not give priority to a new centre but to a landmark
building as a grand vista from the existing centre. This was the Casa
Scînteia, the newspaper and publishing house of the party, named after
Lenin's pre-revolutionary paper *Iskra* (both words meaning 'spark'). It
was a huge complex with an abundance of ornamental detail and a turret
on top, but nevertheless more linear and classicist than the Moscow
high-rises.[33] It was placed at the northern end of Victory Avenue, at the
far end of the city centre. Instead of a new centre, the Romanian
Communists from very early on gave much attention to the periphery,
its industries and its housing.[34]

Among Communists, the Bulgarians were the most infatuated with
the Soviet Union. The centre of Sofia had not been bombarded very
heavily, but it lacked the delimited splendour of Bucharest, and the
whole city lacked any continuous historical tradition. So the Bulgarians
asked their Soviet comrades for advice on creating a new political centre
towering over the royal one, which is still there. The original idea seems
to have been to focus on Moscow-type high-rises. But then party leader
Georgi Dimitrov died and all energy was concentrated on building his
mausoleum, in classicist white marble – built solidly despite the lack of
time before his funeral. When the anti-Communists wanted to demolish it in the years after 1989, it took them four attempts to blow it up,
which they finally accomplished in 1999.

After the mausoleum, a new central ensemble design was decided
upon, oriented to the party building: a triangle-shaped building with a
colonnaded façade and a turret with a red star on top. On both sides of
the rectangular square in front of it (the Largo) are two long, heavy
ministerial buildings with grandiose vestibules. In contrast to the East
Germans, the Bulgarians did realize core features of their new centre
design, but they too had to yield to urban resilience and to the compli-
cations of political art, even under authoritarian governments. The
planned statues of Lenin and Dimitrov were never built, and the royal
palace was never demolished to make room for the Council of
Ministers.[35] Even in Stalinist times, the main avenue of central Sofia was

that of the Tsar Liberator, i.e., Alexander II, who helped the Bulgarians to independence.*

Tirana was a small town of about 60,000 at the end of the war. Its centre had been laid out as a long boulevard – 'a boulevard without a city', as a French commentator wrote – for King Zog and had been extended during the Italian fascist occupation. The post-war Communist leader Enver Hoxha adhered to the programme of national reform and a representative political-administrative centre, but with the rider that 'buildings must be horizontal, not vertical'. The central square, projected before the war, was kept, with a horizontal Palace of Culture as its main building and an equestrian statue of Albania's medieval national hero Skanderbeg. (After he died, Hoxha was awarded an elevated statue in the square, but by 1990 the regime had not much time left.) New buildings of power were put up along the boulevard.[36]

Berlin was a very particular case. It was first divided into four sectors under occupation by the four big Allied powers, then, after the latter totally split during 1948, cut up into two cities, West and East. When Germany became two states in 1949, East Berlin became capital of the GDR, while West Berlin, surrounded by the GDR, had a special status under American protection in relation to the West German Federal Republic, governed from Bonn in the Rhineland. In the east as well as in the west a new capital had to be built. To Eastern European Communism, East Berlin had a special significance as a 'front-line' city in the Cold War.

East Berlin did include the old city centre, but Wilhelmstrasse had been bombed out, the badly damaged Reichstag was in West Berlin, the old imperial castle was a ruin and because of its centrality East Berlin was the most destroyed part of Berlin.

After clearing out all the rubble, the new city rulers set themselves three primary tasks. One was to begin restoring the most central parts of the city's national heritage, which meant Unter den Linden, Friedrichstrasse and the Museum Island. The second was to connect the centre with the working-class areas to the east in a representative

---

* He was also the emancipator of Russian serfs and was regarded as a friend of Finland. Apart from one in Sofia, his statue also stands in Helsinki, having survived the Red Finnish revolution, the White Finnish counterrevolution, and the Finnish 'Continuation War' with Hitler against the USSR.

manner and with new housing. The obvious choice was the existing eastward radial Frankfurter Allee, and construction started right after the proclamation of the new state in October 1949. On Stalin's birthday in December it was named Stalinallee. By default, it became *the* main construction of Stalinist Berlin, 'the first socialist street', although the original plan was to make the east-west line from Stalinallee and Alexanderplatz to Brandenburg Tor the 'central axis' of the city. This was because the third-priority task turned out to be much more complicated than expected; it was never fully realized and most parts that were realized came only a quarter of a century later. The third goal was the political centre of the city and the GDR.

The centre conception had two main components: a huge '*Demonstrationsplatz,* whereupon our people's will to fight and to build can find expression,' and a 'central building' at one end of the former. The square was the easy part. By dynamiting the ruins of the Wilhelmine imperial palace, the Palace Square was turned into a parade ground 60 per cent larger than Moscow's Red Square, and in May 1951 Marx-Engels-Platz claimed to have received a million people.

The 'central building' was intended as the *Stadtkrone* (City Crown), an idea the radical German architect Bruno Taut had raised in the early 1920s as a modern secular and republican successor to the age of cathedrals and Baroque palaces. Among the East German architects of the late 1940s and early 1950s there floated drafts of making a House of the People (*Volkshaus*) the central building, a house gathering not only political leaders and representatives but also ordinary people for culture and entertainment. Houses of the People were important institutions of the European labour movement. Unsurprisingly, this did not appeal to Walter Ulbricht and his leadership, who decided that the landmark building should be a high-rise government building like the recent Moscow high-rises, connected with a lower one for the (powerless) legislative branch. Like in Moscow and most of Eastern Europe save Sofia, the party Central Committee and its Politburo apex were to be

---

* Party leader Walter Ulbricht, quoted from B. Flierl, 'Der zentrale Ort in Berlin – Zur räumlichen Inszenierung sozialistischer Zentralität,' in G. Feist, E. Gilles and B. Vermiese (eds), *Kunstdokumentation 1945–1990,* Berlin: SBZ/DDR, 1996, 321. On East Berlin I am heavily indebted to the third part of the great historical work on art and architecture in East Germany, *Kunstdokumentation,* in which Flierl has a major contribution on the vicissitudes of the socialist political centre projects.

located somewhat off centre, and after 1959 were well housed in the former Reichsbank.

Exactly how and why this project, including a Marx-Engels monument on the square, was never even started escapes even an insider historian like Bruno Flierl.[37] Like the never-built Moscow Palace of Soviets, the only partly realized, quite mutated East Berlin political centre underlines that even the Stalinist city-builders were never all-powerful. Flierl points to internal discussions and disagreements among planners, artists and party functionaries about exact designs, locations and inter-monumental relations. But there must also have been some shifting political and economic parameters. The breakneck investment and construction programme of the regime ran into a serious, if not fatal, crisis in June 1953, when building workers on Stalinallee went on strike against yet another rise in work norms. Through inept handling by the authorities, who conceded too late, the strike escalated into insurrectionary demonstrations that were put down by Soviet tanks. Ulbricht narrowly survived in power, but the aftermath was clearly not the right moment for monumental self-representation. In the autumn of 1954 came Khrushchev's attack on Stalinist monumentalism, a clear signal not to be ignored. In 1961 the GDR had a new acute crisis, which led to the building of the Berlin Wall.

After another false start, in 1958, the twin problems of government housing and city symbolism gradually found solutions. The practical housing problems were solved first, in the mid-sixties. At the southern end of Marx-Engels-Platz, the Council of Ministers got a respectable but unremarkable horizontal building with a portico copied from a portal of the former imperial castle, from which in November 1918 Karl Liebknecht had proclaimed the Socialist Republic. Close by, to the west, the Ministry of Foreign Affairs got a standard, modern office rectangle.

The City Crown got a surprising form designed by Hermann Henselmann, the chief architect of the Stalinallee: a tall TV tower by Alexanderplatz, east of the original centre. The central building became in the end a modernist low-rise building with a façade of tinted glass on the eastern side of Marx-Engels-Platz: the Palace of the Republic, a popular place of entertainment and culture, where the never-hard-working GDR legislature was also lodged. The House of the People concept had finally triumphed. The Marx-Engels monument could not be fitted into their Platz and was instead, in 1986, like some, serene elderly couple, put up in a park east of the Palace of the Republic and surrounded by hologram plaques from the historical struggles of the labour movement, the Marx-Engels-Forum. Finally, Marx-Engels-Platz was in the 1970s abandoned even as a parade ground – replaced by the Karl-Marx-Allee (formerly Stalinallee). It became the main parking lot of central Berlin. The building efforts of the last decade of the GDR were concentrated on popular housing, on large ensembles of pre-fabricated apartment blocks for very low rent, under a political concept of 'unity of social and economic policy'.

East Asia

The Chinese nation-state was born out of the revolution in 1911. However, the republic could consolidate neither the nation nor the state, torn by almost constant civil wars big and small and hammered again and again by the Japanese army. But it did start modern China, and it did change Beijing from a site around the emperor to a national capital. Imperial Beijing was a set of walled cities, one inside and separated from the other, and these cities were inhabited by different populations. The centre was the Forbidden City, to which most people had no access. It was the ground of the imperial palace and court, surrounded by moats and a ten-metre-high red wall with four gates: one for the emperor only and each of the three others for specific categories. Outside that was the Imperial City, inhabited by the Manchu aristocracy and high court officials and also surrounded by walls with four gates, one solely for the emperor. Third was the Inner City, for the Manchu Bannermen (the military guard of the Manchu Dynasty), with greyish walls and nine gates. Finally, there was the Outside City, with colourless walls, where the Han Chinese lived.

The republic opened the partitions, turned the Forbidden City into a public museum and made Beijing one city for all its citizens, with a unified municipal administration. A large number of barriers, fences and gates and the wall of the Imperial City were taken down, and Chang'an Avenue was opened. However, because of the fragility of the new nation-state, Beijing could not develop into a national capital. In 1928 the central government moved to Nanjing, to the southern power base of the Guomindang Party. In 1935 North China, including

Beijing – or Beiping as it was called, Northern Peace instead of Northern Capital – was ceded to Japanese overlordship and soon to full occupation.[38]

In February 1949 the commanding Guomindang general surrendered Beiping to the Communist People's Liberation Army, and on 1 October, Mao proclaimed the People's Republic from Tiananmen Square, where imperial edicts and the triennial high examination results used to be handed down to the public. The new square was enlarged for the 1 October 1949 proclamation of the People's Republic, but this was not enough for the new politics of a huge country. In the course of the 1950s the square increased fourfold, from eleven to forty-four hectares, more than five times the size of Red Square.

In 1949, Soviet experts were invited to advise on city planning. There were three major issues at the top of the agenda. Most important was, where should the political centre of Beijing as the new capital be? The most distinguished Chinese architect at the time, Liang Sicheng, and others argued for a new centre to be built to the west of the historical one, while preserving old central Beijing as a museum city. With Soviet support, Mao decided to stay in the historical centre, in the Zhongnanhai park area of the old Imperial City, which had also provisionally housed the republic's presidential residence. Second, the Soviets were pushing for making Beijing an industrial, working-class city. Mao agreed in principle and big industrial suburbs sprang up, but the central Chinese government refrained from endorsing the industrial targets of the municipality.[39] Third, there was the issue of controlling city growth and capping the population, also insisted upon by the Soviets. It was accepted but continually revised upwards, and in the 1950s, Beijing had a de facto typical post-war Third World growth.[40] Urban growth control was institutionalized with a rural versus urban registration system, *hukou,* which divided the people of the People's Republic into two with very different social and educational rights and opportunities.

Monumentally, the two priority issues were Tiananmen Square and Chang'an Avenue. Tiananmen, the Gate of Heavenly Peace, was one of the southern gates of the old Imperial City. In front of it was a T-shaped area with a procession-way in the middle used only by the emperor, with a variety of imperial offices on the sides behind barriers and fences of different kinds. The national republic began opening the area as a public square which became the rallying ground for the nationalist and anti-Japanese demonstrations, including that of 4 May 1919 against the Versailles powers' delivery of the formerly German Tsingtao concession to Japan. The gate became a national tribune, where portraits of Sun Yat-sen (the father of the Republic) and later his successor Chiang Kai-shek hung. After 1949, Liang Sicheng persuaded Mao to make Tiananmen Square the centre of the new national emblem; Mao's portrait replaced that of Chiang Kai-shek. The public political-portrait culture must have come from the Soviet Union; the Republic and the Guomindang Party had important relations with the USSR in the early 1920s.

In imperial times, Chang'an Avenue had simply been two short wings of the T in front of the gate: the western associated with autumn, death, punishment and the military, and the eastern with spring, growth, business and celebration. The republic made it an avenue and the People's Republic made it *the* grand avenue of Beijing, tearing down the gates of West and East Chang'an and gradually filling it with monumental buildings. To some extent these still followed the ancient symbolism, so on East Chang'an rose the International Club, diplomatic apartments, the International Trade Centre and the Oriental Plaza mall. To the west were the headquarters of the Military Commission but also the national bank. The street was widened from fifteen metres in 1949 to between thirty-two and fifty metres.[41]

Chang'an means 'eternal peace' but was also the name of the capital of the imperial Han (202 BCE to 220 CE) and Tang (618 to 907 CE) Dynasties. The Ming Dynasty brought the name Beijing. Modern street (re-)naming had started with the Republic as part of the national unification of the city, displacing purely local, often 'vulgar' designations.[42] New political toponymy was relatively marginal to the Chinese Communists, although the central business street Wangfujing Street became People's Street for some time.[43]

Imperial statues were also absent from the Chinese tradition and were, on the whole, not imported in Mao's time. The only outdoor statue in the capital from the period, as I recall, commemorates a peasant uprising. However, there had to be a monument to the Heroes of the Revolution in Tiananmen Square, conceived in 1949. It is imperial in form and national-popular in content. The form is a traditional stele or pillar with calligraphic inscriptions: on the front side the writing of

Mao, on the back side that of Zhou En-lai. On the plinth of the stele are eight relief carvings of the main events of the revolution, as interpreted by the party after a thorough selection process, finally decided by the Central Committee.

The contrast to Lenin's 'monumental propaganda' in civil-war Moscow could hardly be starker. The former was international, ecumenical and individual, from Spartacus to Darwin and Kropotkin. The Chinese monument is exclusively national, focused on collective popular movements. It is also largely anti-imperialist and lacks any reference to twentieth-century working-class struggles. The front relief depicts the Crossing of the Yangtze River, referring to the beginning of the final victory of the Communists in 1949. The flashback history starts with 'Burning the Opium' (1840), followed by the start of the Taiping Rebellion in 1851; the Wuchang Uprising in 1911, which led to the Republic; the 4 May 1919 movement protesting the Versailles concession to Japan; the birth of modern student and intellectual radicalism in China; the anti-colonial march of 30 May 1925; the Nanchang Uprising of 1927; the birth of the People's Liberation Army; and, finally, the guerrilla war against Japan. Four of the eight events are anti-imperialist: one against the British-imposed imports of opium from India, two against Japan and one against both the Japanese and the British.* That May Day demonstrations disappeared from the Chinese calendar around 1970 should be understood against the background of this conception of the history of a Communist revolution.

In terms of architecture, the contribution of Chinese Communism was concentrated in the 'Ten Great Buildings' constructed for the tenth anniversary of the revolution in 1959. Two of them flanked Tiananmen Square: the Great Hall of the People, for major gatherings and for the state legislative body, and the Museum of Chinese History, divided by

---

* Wu Hung, *Remaking Beijing*, Chicago: University of Chicago Press, 2005, chapter 1. It is true that the 30 May 1925 movement did actually start as a working-class strike in Shanghai. But it was a rather special strike, as the strikers were paid by the Chinese Chamber of Commerce. The strike occurred in a Japanese textile mill, leading to clashes whereby one worker was killed. On 30 May, a big protest demonstration of workers and students was fired at by British police, killing another ten people. This then led to more than two months of further strikes, during which Chinese businessmen supported the strikers. See Elizabeth Perry, *Shanghai on Strike: The Politics of Chinese Labor*, Stanford, CA: Stanford University Press, 1993.

the Opium War into two sections. Most of the ten were built in some type of Soviet European classicism, without the Art Deco pastiche of the Moscow seven sisters high-rises and with Chinese roofing and other national motifs. Five were museums; three were guesthouses for foreign leaders, overseas Chinese and ethnic minorities of China; one was a train station; and then there was the Great Hall.[44]

Nothing grand was built for the ruling Communist Party, whose Central Committee and Politburo worked from within the walled-off compound of Zhongnanhai, the western part of the old Imperial City. Mao and the top Chinese leadership had been schooled by Comintern cadres and advised by Soviet town planners, but they were also very knowledgeable about and increasingly impressed by the great tradition of the Chinese empire. In that tradition there was a saying from the third century BCE: 'The Way of the Ruler lies in what cannot be seen, its function in what cannot be known'.[45]

The Maoist building cycle ended with the Chairman Mao Memorial Hall mausoleum on Tiananmen Square, with the two great buildings on the sides of the square. The mausoleum itself is flanked by two sculptured columns of revolutionary fighters. Inside, the Chairman makes two appearances: once as Lincoln, seated in an armchair, the other as Lenin, embalmed on *lit de parade*. It was inaugurated in 1977. In 1983 it was turned into a Pantheon when memorial chambers were opened to other defunct leaders, including Liu Shaoqi and later Deng Xiaping. From my experience, it is very often closed without explanation.[46]

Vietnam was a French colony, and Hanoi was the capital of all French Indochina. The Chinese city of Cholon was the largest city of colonial Vietnam, if put together with its smaller, Vietnamese-populated twin city, Saigon. As a colonial centre Hanoi was provided with a certain appropriate Beaux-Arts grandeur and, later, a dash of Third Republic avant-garde *urbanisme* directed by one of the latter's key figures, Ernest Hébrand. About half a millennium before, Hanoi had been a Vietnamese imperial capital and the colonial city had developed in the Citadel area, the core of the old Imperial City, clearly separated from the indigenous commercial city of 'thirty-six streets and corporations'.[47] During World War II the country and the city had been under Japanese occupation.

The making of a Vietnamese nation-state started in August 1945, in a power vacuum. Japan had surrendered, although its troops had not yet departed, and French troops had not yet returned. Collaborators with the Japanese tried to take power for themselves under the banner of anti-Communism, but lacked a popular force to back it up. The Communists rallied the people of the city, occupied strategic buildings and declared the task of forming a revolutionary government. No shots were fired.[48] The colonial collaborator and ceremonial emperor Bao Dai abdicated, and on 2 September Ho Chi Minh read the declaration of Vietnamese national independence from a small tribune in a square at the centre of the colonial city.

However, the Nazi occupation had not taught the French political and military elite that national independence had become a universal value. In the autumn of 1946 their colonial army and navy were back, in December launching the First Indochina War and soon reoccupying Hanoi, until they were finally defeated in 1954. But Vietnam was divided into two, North and South. The Americans soon succeeded the French as the 'protecting' power and vetoed the nationwide elections stipulated by the peace treaty. A new guerrilla war ensued, and in 1965 the United States launched an all-out war against North Vietnam. After ten years it too was defeated and had to depart, leaving a hecatomb of casualties and horrendous devastation, although Cold War diplomacy and tacit rules had largely spared Hanoi itself.

For obvious reasons, no great plans could be realized in Hanoi before 1975. A number of low-rise apartment buildings were constructed, many of them of the Soviet *kommunalka* type of two or multi-family apartments. The change that was realized was toponymical. The Japanese had begun changing the French colonial names of streets and places, allowing Vietnamese names instead. The Communists now embarked on large-scale political name change. Most significant was the new Ba Dinh Square in the ex-colonial centre, on which independence had been declared in 1945. The French had named it after a missionary bishop, Puginier; the Vietnamese called it after an uprising against the French in the 1880s.* Ba Dinh Square became the Red Square of Hanoi, and the Ba Dinh district the governmental district.

---

* Ba Dinh was a Vietnamese Dien-bien-phu, a fortress besieged, the heroic fall of which was the end of the uprising. In 1954 the Vietnamese storming of Dien-bien-phu was the final defeat of the French.

As in many ex-colonial capitals, the colonial governor-general's palace became presidential after 1954 – but with a difference. President Ho Chi Minh refused to reside in it and lived instead in the servants' quarters. Later, the government built him a replica of a house on stilts from his native village in the palatial garden.

Around the square are Ho's mausoleum, a sombre European temple-like building of square grey marble columns elevated on a concrete base – built against his explicit testamentary will – as well as the Central Committee and the National Assembly.[49] The mausoleum apart, they might perhaps be related to the architectural motto of the Vietnamese CP: 'modern, cultured, dignified and simple'.[50]

Communist Hanoi, until the turn to capitalism in the 1990s, was clearly more inspired by the Soviet Union than Beijing. It was also shaped by its colonial history, both in architectural survival and in anti-colonial rejection. A statue of Lenin was put on the spot where the French had raised one for the fallen of France. Although Ba Dinh square is a rather desolate place most of the time, Hanoi retains an intimate charm that is hard to find in Beijing or Pyongyang. In time for the city's millennium in 2010, a statue to Emperor Lý Thái Tổ, who made Hanoi his capital, was erected. Under the new capitalist dispensation, Hanoi risks being overshadowed by the economics of Saigon (currently officially Ho Chi Minh City), which was much larger and visibly more prosperous around 2000. But the government is trying hard, and not without success, to develop Hanoi also as an economic centre.[51]

Pyongyang is arguably the most modern of Third World cities: clean, well-ordered, full of (at least outwardly) well-kept high-rise housing reminiscent of Singapore (and, of course, of rival Seoul) and a number of creatively modernist buildings for sports and culture. It also houses perhaps one of the world's most spectacular hotels, Ryugyong, a 105-storey pyramid clad in blue-tinted glass. Construction started in 1989 and was suspended in 1992; by 2013 it was still only a shell. Construction (by the Egyptian company Orascom) allegedly recommenced, but in 2016 it was still empty. There are very probably backyards and dark holes I did not see, but North Korean poverty is mainly provincial and rural. Pyongyang has the character of a middle-class city – a middle class of public functionaries and employees.

The city's second major feature is less unexpected, given foreign media portraits: the quasi-religious cult of the ruling dynasty, expressed in innumerable statues, usually of superhuman size, murals and site naming. Its pervasiveness and its monumentality have no equivalent in the Stalin cult even at its peak. Dynastic ambitions and succession have always been alien to Communist conceptions of leadership, not only from Lenin but also from Stalin, Mao and all their successors. In this respect, Pyongyang is more similar to Buddhist and monarchical Bangkok than to Beijing, Hanoi or Moscow.

The Democratic People's Republic of Korea (DPRK) and its capital are indeed strange offshoots of Communism. The links were always tenuous. Kim Il-sung was an anti-Japanese guerrilla commander picked for leadership by the Soviets after the US–USSR partition of Korea in August 1945. There was a Communist underground in the Japanese colony of Korea, but it was never very significant, even less so north of the thirty-eighth parallel. Kim was not part of it; he had fought with the Chinese and later the Russians. The Korean Workers' Party was formed only in December 1945. Military nationalism was its main ideological drive, much more than Marxism-Leninism, which disappeared even officially in the 1990s. It was replaced by *Juche*: self-identity, self-reliance. Nevertheless, the (re-)construction of Pyongyang owes a great deal to the rulers' identification with Communism. In 1995 a large monument was erected to commemorate the fiftieth anniversary of the party's foundation, featuring three huge symbols of its class alliance: a working-class hammer, a peasant sickle and an intellectual pen.

The double signals of North Korean architecture come out of guidelines in *On Architecture* by Kim Jong-il: 'The architecture of our mould is an architecture centred on the masses of the people' that 'must be impregnated by the revolutionary view of the leader.'*

During the Japanese colonization Pyongyang had been relatively neglected in comparison with the capital, Seoul, so the first task in 1945 was to build a capital. There were five priorities: a government building, a building for the party paper, a university, a hospital and social housing.[52] During the Korean War (1950–53), Pyongyang, like Seoul,

---

* Here quoted from Philipp Meuser, *Architekturführer Pjöngyang*, Berlin, DOM, 2011, vol 2., 191 and 193. The translation should be read as approximate, first from Korean to German, then from German to English (by me).

changed hands more than once, and most of the city was obliterated. The Korean War is the background to the modernity of Pyongyang, which lacked the more recent royal traditions of Seoul.[*]

The central square of Pyongyang is Kim Il-sung Square, dominated by the People's Great Study Palace (a library and a cultural centre) in modern monumentalized Korean style. It is flanked by the Party Central and the Ministry of Foreign Trade, both more European neo-classicist. The square opens to the Taedong River, with the Juche Tower on its opposite bank. From the square, parallel to the river, runs the main parade street, Sungli (Victory). Underneath runs (since 1973) a subway, the public stations of which rival Moscow's in expensive décor. (Part of it is built as air-raid shelters and is not open to the public.)

The 1980s were a period of international opening and large-scale imports of international modernism, with a view to the World Youth Festival in 1989, a year after the Olympics south of the border, with similar upscaling efforts in Seoul. Since then the skyline of Pyongyang has been dominated by a few hotels, most of them operating. The typical landmark, though, is the huge statue of Kim Il-sung on Mansu Hill, with a palatial mural of the sacred Korean mountain Paktu behind him and a square flanked by two sculptural columns of marching fighters under red banners. The mausoleum of Kim I, and after 2012 of Kim II too, is another political landmark outside the city centre. It is actually a whole palace: first of the party, then the office of Kim I.[†] Size is a much-appreciated value in North Korean construction.

Cuba

Havana was the main port of the Spanish American empire, and in the mid-eighteenth century it was the third-largest city in the Americas, after the vice-regal cities of Mexico City and Lima.[53] At the time of the

---

[*] Pyongyang had been a dynastic capital for centuries before the Christian era, and also in the fifth century CE. In the second half of the nineteenth century it became the Korean centre of Christian missions.

[†] Leick, *Tombs of the Great Leaders*, 76ff. I am much indebted to the two-volume *Architekturführer Pjöngyang*, and not only for its informed texts and beautiful photos. Finding it in the great arts bookshop in Savigny-Platz in Berlin convinced me that Pyongyang was a city I had to visit.

revolution in 1959 it had about 1.3 million inhabitants. Its colonial centre, around the Plaza de Armas, was largely intact and its modern centre (El Prado) had a strong Spanish character, now with distinctive influxes of regional immigrants (Catalans, Galicians, etc.), including a House of the Arabs.

Further west, the US influence was expressed in neighbourhoods called Country Club, Biltmore and the like, and in US gangster hotels like Meyer Lansky's Riviera. The United States had stolen Cuba's independence in 1899 and occupied the island. After a short interlude at the end of the Spanish American War, a second occupation followed from 1906 to 1909, and until 1934 Cuba had to obey a set of US rules according to the so-called Platt Amendment. In the 1930s Havana became an important US entertainment centre. After World War II, ambitious plans were made for Havana, with the president of CIAM, Josep Lluís Sert, the main designer. It included building an artificial island just outside the Malecón, the axial seaside street and promenade of Havana, for casinos and luxury hotels.[54] This low-water mark of modernist architecture was not realized.*

The guerrilla revolutionaries who entered Havana, without resistance, in January 1959 had no articulated urbanistic visions. It so happened that they had a city waiting for them in the form of new, big Civic Square, surrounded by new governmental buildings – some finished, others almost – and even a ready-made national monument to the hero of Cuban independence, José Martí. The largest building, designed as a Palace of Justice in imposing classicism, became the building of the new government as Palace of the Revolution. The tallest was intended to be the City Hall, but now it became the Ministry of the Revolutionary Armed Forces. The architects' favourite was the office of the controller, a light, elegant office rectangle with rows of *brises-soleil* and a slightly concave concrete elevator block interrupting the façade. It became Ministry of the Interior, and the windowless elevator wall became from 1967 a canvas for pictures of the icon of the revolution, Che Guevara – first a huge photo portrait for the nightly vigil after his

---

* Sert returned to sympathizing with revolts against 'abuses of greed, speculation, and exploitation of resources by the few' in his preface to Le Corbusier, *The Athens Charter*, New York: Grossman, 1973, x.

death in 1967, then, from 1996, in a steel frame of the contours of his face in the same photo.

In contrast to all the other Communist rulers, Fidel Castro has never, to my knowledge, been iconized or monumentalized. Besides Che Guevara, one other Cuban revolutionary has his contours sculptured in lines of steel at the Plaza de Revolución: Camilo Cienfuegos, who died in an air crash in October 1959.

In April 1961, on the occasion of the failed US invasion and the proc-lamation of a socialist revolution, the square was renamed Plaza de la Revolución. No other regime and political leader has made as much and as intensive use of a rally square as Fidel Castro. The former presidential palace was turned into a Museum of the Revolution and the Congress Capitol became an event centre, as well as the site of the Ministry of Science and Technology. When the legislative was re-established, it began holding its short sessions in a new convention centre in western Havana.

The revolution owed nothing to the Soviet Union, but under mount-ing US pressure the Castro regime turned to the USSR for economic support and possibly military protection. This meant an increasing auto-Sovietization of ideology and politics, most marked in 1975, when a ruling Communist Party held its first congress there. In the inner city of Havana it is virtually impossible to find any traces of this, but in the southern outskirts a huge Lenin Park was laid out. Most of it is for popu-lar and children's amusement, but it does contain a big Lenin monument, by the late leading Soviet sculptor Lev Kerbel, and an ideologically committed Pioneers' House named after Che Guevara. In the 1980s the Soviet appeal started waning; after the Soviet collapse, capitalist Russia abandoned Cuba.

Against all odds, the Cuban Revolution survived its friendless 'special period' of the 1990s to recover at least in part in the new millennium. Foreign tourism was a lifeline to Cuban socialism in its direst moment – an unknown sector of a socialist economy, but an important one to pre-revolutionary Cuba. Havana turned to this chance with an extraordinary creativity. In 1993 the government entrusted the official historian of the city, Eusebio Leal, to set up an urban enterprise and make deals with foreign investors and whom-ever was willing to cooperate with a view to upgrading the dilapidated central city – a UNESCO World Heritage Site – primarily by renovating buildings for hotels and pensions, but also housing amelioration, for example putting parts of renovated buildings to commercial use. This process has significantly changed Old Havana for the better. The new city programme has also involved some monumental initiatives that would be quite original for almost any city in the world, but especially for a Communist-governed one. Communist Havana pays homage to Mother Teresa, to 'Diana de Gales [Princess of Wales]' (a small garden with an abstract flower sculpture probably financed, upon request, by the British embassy) and, since 2000, to John Lennon, who sits in bronze on a park bench in a thoughtful pose.*

The housing policies, urban infrastructure and services management of revolutionary Havana have not been on par with the regime's impressive achievements in education, health care and culture. One of the first acts of the revolution was to slash urban rents by half; they have been kept extremely low ever since, leaving no or very scarce resources for maintenance, and urban services were never given priority. In the 1960s the capital was largely neglected for support to the countryside and the provincial cities. When the bourgeoisie fled to Miami after the revolution, many of their mansions in western Havana were turned into schools and kindergartens. In others the servants stayed and invited their friends and family members. Some were taken over by functionaries of the new government. On and off, substantial efforts at housing construction have been made, including new estates in eastern Havana and often including promotion of cooperative self-building. The worst shantytowns were demolished after the revolution and their residents relocated to new housing. But housing quality was very uneven, at best, and public service institutions in the new estates were often delayed and/or deficient. Later, shantytowns were upgraded with water, electricity, schools and other services.

During the 'special period', flight from the poor countryside expanded the shantytowns again (although they are small by Latin American standards) and public transport broke down for lack of operating vehicles and fuel. Thereafter, the situation has improved, with Chinese buses and Venezuelan petrol. Under the heavy pressure of the 1990s, *talleres*

---

* In Spanish translation, a line from one his songs is added, no doubt intended as a subtle political message: 'You can say I'm a dreamer, but I'm not the only one'.

(workshops) for neighbourhood transformation were encouraged, which through local touristic projects and cooperation with foreign NGOs managed to get some resources for community development. On their limited scale they were apparently rather successful, and were selected as one 'best practice' at the 1998 UN Habitat Summit in Istanbul.[*]

Cuba is rich in culture and medical training but remains economically poor, and in spite of everything, Havana is still a nationally privileged city when compared, for example, with Santiago de Cuba.

The Social Mirror and the Power Topography of Communist Capitals

'Housing is the social mirror of a city', it has been said.[55] Communism had one clear achievement in this: providing cheap housing. Around 2000, households in the rich capitalist counties of the OECD paid on average between a quarter and a third of their income on housing and utilities (water, electricity, etc.) In Communist Europe in 1989, households paid 6 per cent of their income.[56] However, dwelling space was much smaller in Eastern than in Western Europe, while standing up rather well even to developed capitalist Asia. Only after the death of Stalin was mass construction of housing developed, to the point where the GDR finally overburdened itself by construction under the Honecker slogan of 'unity of economic and social policy'. The ensuing quality was uneven, as in parallel developments in Western Europe, but some was of high quality, for instance in East Berlin's Marzahn.[†]

---

[*] Scarpaci et al., *Havana*, 144; Jill Hamberg and Mario Coyula, 'Havana City Report', undated manuscript, 15. On urban planning and housing I have learnt most of what I know from Mario Coyula, the most brilliant – National Prize of Architecture 2001, National Habitat Award in 2004 – and the most outspoken of contemporary Cuban architects. He wrote the planning and housing chapters of the collective work *Havana: Two Faces of the Antillean Metropolis*. Sometime about 2005, when I met him personally, he gave me an undated but then recent manuscript. We also had a very informative, though short, conversation.

[†] My former student Martin Fuller is doing ethnographic research on Marzahn, and he has enlightened my mind on this.

Table 2. Floor space per person in Communist and capitalist countries, in square metres[57]

	1924	1940	1950	1961	1985	1992	2000
Moscow	6	4		6	11		
Bucharest			6				17
Prague							18
Sofia							15
W. Europe							36
Beijing						9	
Dhaka						4	
Hong Kong						7	
Jakarta						10	
New Delhi						9	
Seoul						13	
Tokyo						16	

Socio-spatial segregation is an important social mirror, but is very difficult to compare over a long period and between cities. However, most research indicates a decrease of segregation in Communist Europe.[58] Ownership of housing varied. Whereas in Beijing and Moscow, as well as no doubt in Pyongyang, all or almost all housing units were government-owned, in Czechoslovakia and Poland only 60 per cent were and in the GDR 40 per cent. In Hungary, Bulgaria and Cuba, private ownership dominated 70 to 85 per cent of the whole housing stock.[59]

The diversity of the cities and their change over time make the Cold War cliché of 'totalitarianism' look ridiculously passé. But what do these capitals tell us about Communist power? First of all, they underline the abiding importance and resilience of national city traditions, something which the Communist canon has always stressed. Moscow was a model, but it was replicated nowhere and was not intended to be. While the national was, so to speak, a common diversity, the project of working-class socialism was a 'common commonality'. It was expressed in several ways while never really corresponding to the dreams of socialists. Most surprising and blatant, perhaps, were the raised differences and barriers between the city and country, institutionalized in the Chinese *hukou* system.

The most immediately striking commonality of the Communist capitals was the absence of capitalism: of CBDs, banking districts, ostentatious corporation headquarters or corporate towers of speculative real estate, ostentatious display of private wealth in streets and public places and commerce catering to it. Nor were there any genteel quarters of aristocratic and bourgeois mansions. If the latter were still there, they were decaying and their proper inhabitants gone. The abolition of land rent made possible a central spaciousness of reconstructed cities, like parts of Moscow, Beijing, Berlin, Hanoi, Pyongyang and Warsaw, but not much visible in historical cities like Budapest, Prague and Havana, which got a new spacious centre just before the revolution that was never allowed to fill up.

Pre–World War II architectural modernism and its Charter of Athens paid no attention to city identity or the central identification function of a city. During and right after the war, the CIAM leaders Giedion, Le Corbusier and Sert came to see this as an error and a lack, arguing for a modern 'new monumentality' later realized in Le Corbusier's layout of Chandigarh in India.[60] (The Eastern European Communists had learnt the importance of a city centre from the pre-war Moscow programme, and went out to realize it in a civic-political rather than a business way.)

All capitals were concerned with industrializing the city and building up an industrial working class. An upper segment of the latter was given access to prime new housing. Culture, including entertainment, for the popular classes was everywhere given centrality in workers' clubs and Palaces of Culture, from the East German Palace of the Republic to the Korean Great Study Hall of the People. The Communist cities were workplace-centred, rather than street- and consumption-centred. You often got your housing through your workplace; you went to cultural, entertainment and political events with your workmates and very often you spent your holidays with them.

The working-class urban conception was naturally opposed to US-style middle-class suburbanization of sprawling one-family dormitory spaces. However, the 'urbane' living in the compact city that the GDR Principles of Town Planning defended is not exclusively working-class. On the contrary, it needs also a strong component of what Marxists would call 'petit-bourgeois': small shops, artisans, cafés, bars, restaurants. With some qualification for 1970s and 1980s Budapest, Communist rulers were largely tone-deaf to this aspect of urbanity.

Underdevelopment was the curse of governing Communists in their race against the leading powers of capitalism. Communist Europe did catch up substantially with the West, economically and in terms of human development, until about 1970, but relative scarcity was a constant problem.[61] There was always sharp tension between catching up investments and popular consumption. Housing provision suffered from this. Underdevelopment also meant that many efforts at mass housing came out with low quality buildings, whereas high-quality ones, like those along Gorky or Stalinallee, were available only to a minority. The excellent idea of *mikrorayon* housing with public-services planning, first developed by the American Clarence Perry in the 1920s, extensively applied in post–World War II Social Democratic planning and adopted in the Moscow programme, was often left partially or wholly unimplemented.

The repressive character of authoritarian Communism is hardly discernible from the townscape, as Karl Schlögel's captivating montage of Moscow at the height of the terror in 1937 shows.[62] You have to look into the buildings and their sealed flats of disappearances or deletions within city phonebooks and other urban records. But evidence of authoritarianism can be found. The monumental leadership cult is one example, although it should be approached with some caution, as most states and communities are prone to celebrate their leaders and their victories. The Stalin statues in Berlin, Budapest and Prague, as well as the Kim Il-sung and the Kim Jong-il statues in Pyongyang, did and do send signals of power adulation. The destruction of central Bucharest by Nicolae Ceauşescu – once the favourite not-quite-Communist of the US and British political elites – for his grotesque palace is perhaps the most telling manifestation. But throughout the Communist era, city planning, though always subject to internal debate and conflicts and occasionally put on big public display, as with the Moscow 1930s plan, did not allow any autonomous movement input. The late 1990s Havana Workshops were a novelty.

The authoritarian character of Communist urbanism may also be captured through its failures. The system was driven from the top in a political-ideological manner – of cavalry charges, as the Cuban president Osvaldo Dorticós once put it – with little time for preparation and maintenance. The constant underdevelopment of resources and the vicissitudes of political change, on bases far from solid, left even high-priority plans unfulfilled – like the central palace of Sofia – or delayed and mutated almost out of recognition, as in East Berlin.

Authoritarianism was brittle because Communism was changing. After Stalin, mass rather than elite housing became a priority, and Stalin himself was dynamited in Berlin and Prague. Socialist Realism gradually evaporated and joined the international dialogue of modernist architecture, from East Berlin to Pyongyang. But socialist urbanism ended before it could connect with kindred tendencies in postmodern (or neomodern?) urbanism, to create compact cities, public and non-motor transport, and cheap public housing (much in the foreground of the 2016 Architecture Biennale in Venice, if not in capitalist reality).

Post-Communism

'Towards globalization' was the subtitle of an important book on the post-Communist urban transformation in Europe, and the restoration of capitalism in former Communist states was indeed an important part of the ongoing global capitalist moment of urban history.[63] I shall therefore deal with it below. Here I shall touch upon a particular aspect. The Communist city had a particular, and for the regime very important, iconography, symbolic architecture and political toponymy. How did the victorious anti-Communists deal with that?

There were monumental removals, symbolic reuses of buildings, monumental substitutions, toponymic restitutions or other changes and new public narratives, religious and historical. Lenin was taken down everywhere outside Russia, Belarus, Kyrgyzstan and the eastern part of Ukraine. In post-Soviet Ukraine, the deeply divided political geography could be assessed by looking at the destruction or survival of Lenin. In Lviv and western Ukraine he was ousted in 1989, before the USSR; in central Ukraine west of the Dnipro, including Kyiv, he survived until the uprising of the winter of 2014. In the summer of 2014 the iconoclasm reached Kharkiv, Odessa, and the rest of the country west of the Donbass region. In Budapest, Lenin had been discreetly walked out even before the regime turn. In Sofia the mausoleum of Dimitrov was blown up after strenuous efforts. Enver Hoxha was blown out of Skanderbeg Square in

Tirana and Tito was removed from Belgrade and Ljubljana, while staying in Sarajevo and Zagreb. The numerous and often big Soviet war monuments, enormously important to the post-Soviet Russians as well as to the Soviets, who started planning them even before World War II had ended, have on the whole been left intact and are geopolitically respected, most clearly in Berlin.

Lots of lesser Communist monuments were removed or destroyed. The Hungarian anti-Communists exiled them to a special park well outside Budapest. The exiles included supporters of the Spanish Republic of the 1930s, sellers of the Communist newspaper and other similar representations of the Hungarian labour movement. In Berlin, Marx and Engels were left in peace, as was – against all West German intentions – the early 1930s Communist leader Ernst Thälmann, murdered as a Nazi prisoner, in a late heroic profile monument by Lev Kerbel.*

The most striking reuses of buildings still standing probably occurred in Warsaw and Berlin. In Warsaw, the Central Committee building has been recycled as the Warsaw Stock Exchange, with a Ferrari dealership as a sideshow. In Berlin, the East German Council of Ministers became the Treuhand (trustee), charged with selling out all collective enterprise. When everything had been privatized and Westernized, the building became a business school. In 1990 the GDR disappeared as a country, swallowed by West Germany, and the centre of East Berlin has since been subject to the most radical post-Communist change.

The final 'central building' of the GDR's Palace of the Republic, a popular venue of East Berlin urbanity as well as the site of the rare and insignificant sessions of the legislative People's Chamber, was destroyed,† as was the Foreign Ministry on the opposite site of the central square. After a prolonged business campaign, the West German powers in the national and city governments decided to rebuild the Wilhelmine

---

* Thälmann was a sectarian leader, never respected outsider party ranks, and in the GDR Kerbel's monument was regarded as out of date by many Communists in the 1980s. But when West German cleansing started, local residents of central East Berlin protested in various ways against his removal. And in the end, it seems, the West German powers simply lost their will to destruction. After all, the KPD leader is not in the central core of East Berlin.

† It was a good candidate, for two reasons. Symbolically, it destroyed the heart of GDR Berlin; argumentally, it was vulnerable because of its asbestos problem. A similar problem occurred with the EU Berlaymont headquarters in Brussels, but there no member state was complaining of the costs of sanitation.

imperial palace, the ruins of which had been blown up by the Communists in 1949 to open up a big political parade ground. The protracted debate about this proposal to turn Berlin back to the Wilhelmine Empire has changed direction considerably in a long process of decision-making. The palace will now be mainly a kind of Potemkin façade for what in Communist Europe would have been called a Palace of Culture, with a public walkway through it across Palace Square (Schlossplatz), aka Marx-Engels-Platz.

The two most intrusive buildings of Communist Europe have turned out to be too big to fall. The Warsaw Palace of Culture is still a much-used centre of culture, science and entertainment. It is now surrounded by a wreath of corporate towers which fail to overwhelm it. Ceauşescu's gargantuan palace is now used, at least in part, by the Romanian parliament.

The victory of capitalism is primarily manifested in capitalist build-ings – malls, corporate towers, luxury hotels – rather than in iconography, although Ronald Reagan (apparently after some gentle US prodding) is fêted in Budapest and Warsaw, for instance. Instead of victory, post-Communist iconography has focused on victimhood and victims of Communism. Some of these are graphically gripping. The most elab-orate, a monumental ensemble in Kyiv commemorating the *Holodomor* (famine), the great famine of 1932–3 and two other famines during the ruthless collectivization of agriculture, loses its symbolic focus – a thin, sad little girl holding a few sheaves of wheat in her hands – to an over-blown and overloaded thirty-metre column decorated with glass crosses and bronze storks rising from the ground. More captivating are simple installations that speak in a low, piercing voice, like 'Killed in the East' in Warsaw, a tipped railway wagon emptying a load of crosses (referring to Soviet deportations), and 'Victims of Communism' in Prague, in the centre but inconspicuous on a slight park slope, with a row of stylized humans gradually dissolving and disappearing in the distance.

Anti-Communist victimology also includes a set of museums of the victims of Communism or, less stridently, of life under Communism. In Moscow, this is a very modest, small but serious non-governmental institution. In Prague it is a commercial US enterprise, again rather small, more vulgar than serious. But Prague has also converted the former Gottwald mausoleum into a sober museum of Czechoslovak history. The Berlin DDR museum has a commercial odour and is lightweight. The thorough German historical museology is working slowly, but will certainly create something solid and serious.

The three Baltic capitals have three very different anti-Communist museums. The Tallinn one is coolly ethnographic, concentrating on everyday life in those days. The Riga one has taken over a building of symbolic significance, built in late Soviet times in memory of the Latvian Riflemen, Bolshevik shock troops during the civil war. It is professional, displaying a didactic history, with an abundance of written materials, quotations and statistics. The Vilnius one is the most ideological of all, along with the one in Budapest. Immediately after the fall of the USSR, some people occupied the former KGB building in Vilnius and turned it into a 'Genocide Museum'. However, here *genocide* does not refer to the Nazi destruction of the Jewish majority of Vilnius, originally not mentioned at all, but to 'the Soviet occupation', allegedly bent on the genocide of Lithuanians. Somewhat contradictorily, a large part of it is devoted to the several years of anti-Communist resistance by Nazi-armed partisans. This is a state institution. There is also a Jewish museum, which is private, marginally located and poor – although this seems to have changed in recent years.

Warsaw once had a projected ideological museum, SocLand, but it appears to have been discontinued. What the city has is a very professional and impressive museum of the 1944 Uprising and the conflict between the Polish underground and the Red Army, clearly influenced by the Holocaust Museum in Washington, D.C.

The Budapest 'House of Terror', curated by the far-right ideologue and businesswoman Maria Schmidt for her boss, Prime Minister Viktor Orbán, is less distortive than the Vilnius outfit, but it is by far the most strident of all such institutions. It is located in a building that once belonged to the Hungarian Nazi Arrow Cross movement and was expropriated after the war and used for a decade by the Communist security police. The aim of the museum is to assert that Communism in Hungary was a continuation of the Arrow Cross, Eichmann's helpers with the Holocaust in Hungary. Schmidt's project has a strong vindictive drive, with named photographs and, if available, addresses of living Communist targets. In the summer of 2015 the building was closed for renovation and the museum moved outdoors onto the pavement of Andrassy út with the theme 'GULAG is Soviet Power', dealing with Hungarian prisoners of war in the USSR. It included a long list of 'perpetrators', beginning with Stalin and ending with a curious selection of Western intellectuals such as John Kenneth Galbraith and Eric Hobsbawm, included for not denouncing that Hungarian soldiers of Hitler's war against the USSR were kept in Soviet labour camps for several years.

The alleged Nazi-Communist continuity is part of a larger narrative of revisionist history by the Orbán regime to exonerate the authoritarian anti-Semitic, Hitler-allied right-wing government which preceded the Arrow Cross in the last months of war. Another manifestation of this linkup with pre-war reaction is the new monument to István Bethlen outside the Presidential Palace. Bethlen was an astute conservative politician and prime minister for most of the inter-war period. His first major acts in office in 1921 were to deprive 30 per cent of adult Hungarians of their right to vote and to abolish the secret ballot.[64] The ruling party which calls itself the Young Democrats has a remarkable predilection for old anti-democrats (as long as they are right-wing).

In current Hungarian historical revisionism, right-wing Hungary was not an ally of Nazi Germany and Fascist Italy but an innocent victim of German occupation – the Germans intervened in 1944, when the Hungarian right began searching for ways out of a losing war. In 2014 a brazen monument was erected in the central core of Budapest 'in memory of the German Occupation', featuring a German eagle diving at Archangel Gabriel. However, this story has not been quietly accepted by all Hungarians, and even members of the regime seem to have got cold feet – the monument was never officially inaugurated. Instead, it has inspired the growth of an iconographic agora around it, where different, often radically opposing messages, denouncing the Orbán history are presented alongside memorabilia from the war and the Holocaust. A bit behind it is an informal platform used for small progressive demonstrations. The area has become a living monument, an ongoing symbolic politics of conflicting memories and opinions.

In the main square, Kossuth Square, there is also a recent underground museum built in a former ventilation chute and dedicated to the anti-Communist uprising of 1956, a kind of memorial crypt with sober, objective information, including some stating that it is still unknown who opened the fatal shootings and why.

When they came to power, the Communists renamed a large number of streets and squares as well as institutions. The anti-Communists did the same, most often reinstituting pre-Communist names. The West

Germans approached the toponymical issue with typical Teutonic systematization and appointed a high-level Commission, in which the prominent right-wing Social Democratic historian Heinrich August Winkler doubled as a formidable street fighter. The West German principle was that no mention should be made of anyone who had been connected with Communism after the October Revolution, which meant, for instance, that the classical socialist feminist Clara Zetkin of both the Second and the Third Internationals was persona non grata, as were all the murdered Communist underground fighters against Nazism. After the breakup of Yugoslavia, the Croatian government changed central Zagreb's Square of the Victims of Fascism into the Square of Great Croats. By the late 1990s this had become embarrassing, so the Victims of Fascism returned and the Great Croats were allocated a smaller place near the Stock Exchange Square.

Zagreb and Croatia exemplify the potentially explosive character of urban iconography. The breakup of Yugoslavia started with a nationalist Croat demand that the equestrian statue of Josip Jelačić should be returned to the central square of Zagreb, where it was before Communism.*

Post-Communist townscapes also changed with two new stories added to the city text – one religious, the other of pre-Communist history, represented as medieval or monarchical, and ironically enough, positively as authoritarian conservative.

Resacralizing political life has become a significant feature of the Orthodox post-Communist countries – with their historically close church-state relations – and in the most Catholic countries, Lithuania, Poland, Slovakia and Croatia.

The resurrection of the Cathedral of Christ the Saviour in Moscow is perhaps the most dramatic manifestation of this new tendency, followed in Kiev by the Uspenski Cathedral and the Mikhailovsky-Zlatoverkhy monastery. The first new monument in de-Communizing Vilnius was the restoration, in June 1989, of the Hill of Three Crosses, commemorating a legend of Franciscan martyrs, taken down in the Soviet period.

---

* Ban (Viceroy) Jelačić ruled in the mid-nineteenth century under the Habsburgs. In Croatia he is venerated for his abolition of serfdom and his uniting of Dalmatia with Croatia. The Communists took him out, presumably because of his important part in the Habsburgs' crushing of the Hungarian revolution of 1848.

Croatia has turned Archbishop Stepinac – condemned in 1946 to sixteen years' imprisonment for his collaboration with the fascist regime of 1941 to 1945 – into a national martyr, on parade in his sarcophagus in Zagreb Cathedral since 1993, beatified by John Paul II in 1998.

The most ambitious religious project is in Warsaw, decided in 1998 and still under construction in 2016: a Temple of Divine Providence 'votive church of the nation for the Constitution of 3 May [1791], the regained independence in 1989, for the twenty years of John Paul II's pontificate, and two thousand years of Christianity'.

Medievalism has been taken to bizarre lengths in Hungary, with an official (since 2000) republican cult of the 'Holy Crown of Hungary', an ancient crown of the Hungarian Kings, of uncertain age and origin. According to legend, it was the crown of Saint Stephen, the first king, crowned in the year 1000. The crown and other regalia were carried in procession from the national museum to Parliament and officers of the army swear allegiance to it.[65] More understandable to a modern mind is the new Lithuanian monument to the fourteenth-century Grand Duke Gediminas, the founder of Vilnius.

Moscow also exhibits a most ostentatious example of historical regression to pre-modern monarchical grandeur in the form of a naval monument on the Moscow river to Tsar Peter I. The heroic-military tradition of Polish nationalism was in a sense common to Polish Communism as well as anti-Communism. In Warsaw, the monument celebrating 'A Thousand Years of Polish Cavalry' was decided upon by the Communists, the design was selected during the reign of General Jaruzelski – the only military professional ever to rule a Communist country – and the column, topped by two charging cavalrymen, dedicated to Polish victories from 972 to Monte Cassino in 1944 and Schönfeld in Pomerania in 1945, was put up by the anti-Communists in 1994.

The illiberal, authoritarian conservatives who ruled virtually all of East-Central Europe outside Czechoslovakia prior to the Communists have been remarkably rehabilitated by the 'civil society' liberals of the 1980s. Post-Communist Warsaw has returned to its veneration of Poland's inter-war military strongman, Józef Piłsudski, standing by the central city square now bearing his name, and his successor Marshal Śmigly-Rydz. In Hungary, Admiral Horthy was given a state reburial in 1993, and I noted above the new veneration of his prime minister, who abolished (almost) universal suffrage. In Riga it was decided to pay homage in stone to the conservative Latvian dictator of the 1930s, Kārlis Ulmanis.

In Beijing and Hanoi, post-Communism does not mean anti-Communism but capitalist economics plus Communist Party government. In Beijing this has meant two things iconographically: first, above all a search for globally iconic architecture, of which Rem Kolhaas's CCTV building, Herzog & de Meuron's Bird's Nest Stadium and Paul Andreu's National Theatre are the most spectacular examples. In political iconography, the new orientation is a posthumous reunification of the party tradition. Mao's mausoleum now includes memorial chambers of post-1949 top leaders that Mao kicked out, and in one case had hunted to death. A big mural in the refurbished Historical Museum now includes the full leadership on the Tiananmen platform proclaiming the People's Republic. Nearby there is an outdoor group of sculptures depicting Mao in an amicable garden conversation with, among others, Liu Shaoqi and Deng Xiaoping.* The Vietnamese had no need for any such posthumous rehabilitation and few resources for global iconic aspirations, although Hanoi did, as noted above, remember the city's fifteenth-century royal founder. Instead, some of the colonial architecture was restored, with French help.

---

* There were also serious attempts at reviving Hitler's allies in Romania and Slovakia, Marshal Ion Antonescu and Father Jozef Tiso, respectively, but they were too associated with the Holocaust for the Western patrons and donors to accept them. On post-Communist Eastern European national memorials, see J. Stritecký, 'Das kollektive Gedächtnis oder die kollektive Selbstverdrängung? Zu den nationalen Identitätsmustern nach 1989', in A. Corbea-Hoisie, R. Jaworski and M. Sommer (eds), *Umbruch im östlichen Europa*, Vienna: Studien Verlag, 2004.

9

Global Moments in National Cities

The global moment is what we are living. There have been many globalizations before, but global is our time.[1] I am not going to approach it through the usual door of political economy and world capitalism. This is not rejection. I think the latter is not only valid but a valuable and important approach, although I have strong reasons to discard some conclusions from it,[2] to which we shall turn at the end of this book. It is another choice, one of political urbanism.

The current global moment of urban history has two principal components: one of style, the other of power. 'Style' is here meant as urban design style, which includes but is broader than architectural style. The latter is largely a cosmopolitan modernism, a mutation of the 'International Style' of the 1930s. Through the possibilities of computer-aided design, it has emancipated itself even from the modernist innovations of the European architectural repertoire. It operates through global architectural firms, usually based in the North Atlantic or East Asia, but no longer spreading any national models – as in the period of globalized nationalism – and competing on a planetary field. Global iconicity, not national representation, is the aim of the commissioner and the architect alike.[3] However, outside communities of Orthodox Christian believers, icons are rather rare – and have to be in order to function. The characteristic urban style in the current global moment is better grasped by three more general categories: *verticality* (skyscrapers), *novelty* (of business districts and shopping malls) and *exclusivity* (by gating and other means).

The power is that of transnational, post-industrial, financial, real estate and commercial capital and their upper-middle class clientele.

This power is not a priori to be seen as some impersonal external power; it may very well be local and national actors striving to globalize as an active verb, to board the global plane to wealth and power. The rationale of the global city is the creation, display and consumption of wealth. 'World City status is driven by wealth creation', the London Planning Advisory Committee emphasized in 1991.[4]

Corporate towers, shopping malls and, as protectors of privilege, gated communities and guards are emblematic of the global moment. But there are also other features following from the ambition to attract wealth-creating professionals and solvent tourists, like lavish cultural institutions, globalized entertainment and multicultural haute cuisine.

The style and the power both confront the national city head on. Below we shall see to what extent they have succeeded, where and why. But we shall start with the first modern globalization: the globalization of nationalism and, more specifically, the globalization of national capital cities.

Globalized Urban Nationalism

The late-nineteenth-century World Exhibitions, starting in 1851 with the 'Great Exhibition of the Works of Industry of All Nations' in London introduced a consciously international dimension to urban development. After the shorter-lived London Crystal Palace, the Eiffel Tower, for the 1889 Exhibition, was the modern world's first permanent globally iconic construction, generally abhorred by the national intelligentsia of the time. The World Exhibitions made global economic competition a world show. They also soon came to provide important stages of international scientific, intellectual and political networking. The First Workers' International came out of the British-Continental European labour contacts made at the 1862 London Fair;* the Second International was founded as a discreet sideshow to the Revolutionary Centennial Exhibition in Paris in 1889.

The notion of the 'world city' began to circulate in Europe just before World War I. In Germany, it was used to signal the rise of Berlin as a

---

* The International came into being in 1864 in the context of Franco-British labour support for Polish nationalism against Tsarist Russia.

Weltstadt, something more self-evident than Paris and London.* In the last third of the nineteenth century, a universal recognition of European 'civilization' and urban splendour began to develop. European colonialism had spread Iberian churches to Manila and Macau; Enlightenment Europe imported *chinoiseries* of royal park pavilions and aristocratic interior décor. But colonial cities were typically dual – colonial and native – the imports to Europe were no more than faddish add-ons and the huge uncolonized world – China, Japan, the Islamic heartlands and the African interior – remained unaffected.

Efforts at reactive modernization by threatened traditional realms, the pacification of Latin American nation-states after decades of turbulence and the nationalization of the Balkans together meant a globalized concept of 'a capital worthy of the nation'.

Khedive Ismail of Egypt wanted his country to become part of Europe, and ruined himself and his state in trying to emulate the Paris of the Second Empire. Japanese intellectuals coined the slogan 'Out of Asia', and the Meiji rulers of Japan invited architects from Europe and the United States, telling them not to pay any respects to Japanese tradition. The Japanese model was more London than Paris; the Mitsubishi conglomerate built a red-brick 'London Town'. When Korea emancipated itself from China in the 1890s – before falling prey to Japanese imperialism – Korean nationalists erected a simple replica of the Parisian Arc de Triomphe as an Independence Arch on the spot at the boundary of the capital where Korean governments used to greet their Chinese overlords. The curved central avenue of Bangkok, Ratchadamnoen (Royal Procession Road), connecting the old indigenous royal palace with a new Italianate one, is said to have been inspired by the Queen's Walk in Green Park.[5] In China, Shanghai became an international city along the Bund on the river, while European Beijing was largely confined to the Legation Quarter of imperial ambassadors. Istanbul began to Europeanize in the late nineteenth century; Germanic architecture designed by imported Austrian and

---

* In the English-only literature, the British urbanist Patrick Geddes is often credited as the baptist in 1915 of the 'world city', as in Peter Hall's *World Cities* (New York: McGraw-Hill, 1966, 1). But the German word *Weltstadt* was in use well before World War I (A. Lees, 'Berlin in der Vorstellungswelt der deutschen,' in G. Brunn and J. Reulecke (eds), *Berlin . . . Blicke auf die deutsche Metropole*, Essen: Reimar Hobbing, 1989, 46. As an example, see Leo Colze, *Berliner Warenhäuser*, Berlin: 1989 (1908), chapter 1.

German architects came to characterize the public look of post-sultanate Ankara. In 1929, the ill-fated modernizing king of Afghanistan, Amanullah, invited German architects to remake Kabul. Haussmann's transformation of Paris became the role model for Latin American capitals from Mexico to Buenos Aires via Santiago and Rio de Janeiro, as well as for Bucharest. While Paris offered impressive city design, London provided expert firms on urban engineering, sewage and water systems, gas works and public transport to locations as diverse as Hawaii, Odessa, Buenos Aires, Beirut, Bombay and Smyrna/Izmir.[6]

This was globalized nation-statism, aimed at providing the nation-state or the nationalist dynasty with a capital city 'worthy of the nation'. It was state-led and state-centred, driven by national powers seeing themselves as competing *qua* nations in a power and prestige system of nations. The urban competitions of World Exhibitions, with their emblematic landmarks were also state- and nation-centred. We have touched upon this kind of globalism above, when looking at the making of national capitals.

The current global moment has a very different dynamic, although, contrary to frequently peddled arguments, no capital city has cut its moorings to the nation-state nor been overwhelmed by any free-wheeling 'global city'.

Designing Global Cities: The Modernist Architect's Attempt

Before looking into the power dynamics of the current global moment, however, out of respect for our fundamental conception of cities as built environments of human settlements – and not just zip codes of power-holders, corporate or political – we shall look into the historical development of design and architecture of global cities. The current global moment does entail a particular style of urbanism dominated by corporate skyscrapers in 'International Style'. The trajectory of this style is a complex and ironic history of modernist architecture, the bare outlines of which are worth unravelling, far outside the specialized compartment of architectural historiography.

Architecturally, the global moment might be located at the New York Museum of Modern Art in 1932 and its exhibition of 'International Style' architecture. Well-promoted and highly influential, the

'International Style' was basically the European modernism of Bauhaus and Le Corbusier: non-ornamental, austerely streamlined, very different from the ebullient Art Deco high-rises of 1920s New York, which in the early Cold War were denounced as Stalinist 'sugar bakery'. American capitalists had first built skyscrapers; European modernist architects designed bolder and more stylish ones for the post-war future, in which they became the signum of global corporate power and ambitions.

This was a time when an international band of modernist architects tried to change the world. Their International, CIAM (Congrès International d'Architecture Moderne), was formed in 1928, largely out of a modernist protest against the academicism which, with the decisive support of the leading European politician at the time, the Frenchman Aristide Briand, had captured the competition for building the Geneva headquarters of the League of Nations. It was an international organization with an executive, national branches and a congress with delegates and individual members. Le Corbusier was its indefatigable spiritual leader, but the organization was mainly run by Sigfried Giedion, a Swiss architectural critic and historian who was its secretary-general from 1928 to 1957; Cornelis van Eesteren, a chief planner from Amsterdam who was its president from 1931 to 1947; Walter Gropius (vice-president), the founding director of Bauhaus, had been since the Nazi takeover in exile – first in Britain, then at Harvard; and, in its later years, Josep Lluís Sert, an exiled Catalan planner at Harvard, who was president from 1947 to 1957.

It was an extraordinarily intellectual movement, producing not only ideas but urban designs – often unheeded, like Le Corbusier's unsolicited plans for Algiers and Bogotá – for housing, traffic and spatial city layout. Compared to vanguardist movements in literature, painting and music, CIAM was long-lived, dissolving itself only after more than thirty years, in 1959. It attracted and involved most modernist architects and planners of the world – except for US-born Americans.[*]

While no more than an 'attempt' at world change, CIAM was more than a radical talk shop. In 1941 it boasted, without exaggerating, *inter alia*:

---

[*] The story of CIAM is narrated by Eric Mumford in *The CIAM Discourse on Urbanism*, Cambridge, Mass.: MIT Press, 2002; and is given a brief summary in Giedion's *Space, Time, Architecture*, Cambridge, MA: Harvard University Press, 1982, 696–706.

> The plans for Amsterdam are in the hands of the president of this group; Stockholm is developing its eminently social structures on the CIAM doctrine; Brazil and Argentina invite CIAM personalities to conduct lectures in urbanism and to lay foundations for major plans; Finland has entrusted the Finnish delegate of the CIAM as the director of its reconstruction . . . Harvard University . . . has conferred its chair of architecture and urbanism upon another vice-president of the CIAM [Gropius].[7]

After World War II, its ideas directly produced Chandigarh in India and Brasília in Brazil and, somewhat less so, Islamabad in Pakistan and Abuja in Nigeria (see the National Foundations section of this book). The team which, under the leadership of the Rockefellers' house architect Wallace Harrison, designed the UN headquarters in New York included Le Corbusier and four other CIAM members, including Oscar Niemeyer, who seems to have made a crucial design input out of an idea by Le Corbusier.

It spanned a wide political spectrum, from Italian Fascism (Giuseppe Terragni) to Communism (André Lursat, Hannes Mayer, Hans Schmidt and Helena and Szymon Syrkus, among others), including reformist Scandinavian Social Democrats. Le Corbusier himself was publicly politically ambiguous, but his intimate personal circle belonged to the French far right.[8] He competed for the Palace of Soviets in Moscow and, in 1941, he approached the Vichy regime and published the fundamental CIAM document, the Charter of Athens, in 'the hour of National Revolution' (while its 1957 edition situated the first edition 'in the depth of the occupation').[9] Leaving the labyrinths of Le Corbusier's personality aside, the ecumenism of CIAM can be rendered intelligible out of its positioning in architectural and political history.

Architecturally, CIAM was a fighting avant-garde, not without some successes – above all in Weimar Germany, the Netherlands, the early Soviet Union and Scandinavia, after the Stockholm Exhibition in 1930 – regrouping after its defeat in Geneva in 1927 and hotly contested everywhere. Nazi power dispersed CIAM architects across the planet, from Moscow to Cambridge, Massachusetts; from Ankara and Dar es Salaam to Shanghai. Bourgeois academicism and historicism were its main urbanistic enemies.

From its first congress, CIAM's main architectural focus was on housing; the whole theme of its second congress was on low-cost housing, for

'minimal existence'. Politically, the 1920s was when working-class housing emerged on the mainstream agenda in Europe, either as 'an insurance
against Bolshevism and Revolution', as it was put in Lloyd George's
government,[10] or as part of building a working-class city, as it was envisaged in Amsterdam and Vienna (see the chapter on Popular Moments).

Though initiated just before, CIAM emerged in the Great Depression
of the early 1930s. Right-wing liberalism, the one major non-tradition-
alist current absent from CIAM, was at its nadir. Planning was widely
regarded as necessary to transcend the self-destructive chaos of capitalist markets. Soviet planning attracted even right-wing Social Democrats,
like the Webbs. The USSR had harboured vanguard modernist arts and
architecture in the 1920s and was still in flux. Italian fascism included
explicit modernist currents, not least 'rationalist' architecture, and was
still, before the gas invasion of Ethiopia, respectable in large sectors of
Europe. The advent of Nazism and the war in Spain were yet to draw the
frontlines between fascism and antifascism.

The Stalinist abandonment of modernism for Socialist Realism was
about to occur. In 1932, Giedion sent two telegrams to Stalin protesting
the outcome of the Palace of Soviets competition (which Le Corbusier
and other modernists lost) as 'an insult to the spirit of the Russian
Revolution and to the realization of the Five-Year Plan'.[11] The telegrams
may not have reached Stalin, to the luck of Ernst May and other Western
architects then working in the USSR.[12] CIAM's fourth congress, planned
for Moscow in 1933, was 'postponed' by the Soviet authorities and
replaced by an epic cruise from Marseille to Athens and back, with a
celebratory week in Athens under the auspices of the Greek government. The break was not total, though. At CIAM7 in Bergamo in 1949,
the Communist Warsaw architect and CIAM veteran Helena Syrkus
made a spirited defence of Socialist Realism. And something of the original ecumene was still remembered. In his opening speech the Italian
host Piero Bottoni commemorated both the fascist Terragni – dead in
combat against the USSR – and Gian Luigi Banfi, a Jewish Italian resistance fighter killed in a Nazi camp.[13]

However, for all its circumspection and diplomacy, the main thrust of
CIAM was towards some kind of socialist urbanism. Giedion was a
socialist. His telegrams to Stalin were written 'in the spirit of the Russian
Revolution', but in the autumn of 1933 he understood that the red flag
had to be kept under wraps. In a letter to Le Corbusier, provoked by the

Czechoslovak leftist Karel Teige, he laid out two alternative public stands of the CIAM: 'Technicians or politicians?' He answered:

> 1. Technicians: the only possibility to have an international influence at the moment. But when the true social development becomes really effective we will be turned out instantly, without a doubt. 2. Politicians: impossible for us to have an influence with anyone important at the moment. Only means to have influence is a socialist situation.[14]

The most famous document of CIAM, the Charter of Athens, of 1933, is an explicit blueprint for a social urbanism, even in Le Corbusier's Vichy redaction of the terse *constatations* of CIAM4, within an overall framework of 'machine age' modernism. Of the 'four functions' of the city, dwelling or housing (before leisure, work and communication/traffic) is prime. The first working congress, CIAM2, was devoted to low-income housing. Changing the class structure of housing was a high-priority task:

> No one has the right to transgress rules that ought to be inviolable by allowing only the favoured few to benefit from the conditions required for a healthy and well-ordered life. (Point 15)

> Henceforth, residential districts must occupy the best locations within urban space. (Point 23)

> The selection of residential zones must be dictated by considerations of public health. (Point 24)

> At one time open spaces had no other reason for existence than the pleasure and amusement of a privileged few. The social point of view which today gives new meaning to the use of these spaces, has not yet emerged. (Point 30)

> Even when open spaces are of an adequate size . . . being remote from working-class districts . . . they will actually be forbidden ground for the masses. (Point 31)

> The places of work . . . are no longer rationally located within the urban complex.

Dwellings and places of work should be close to each other, in parallel bands separated by a 'verdant zone'. (Points 46 and 47)

The pedestrian must be able to follow other paths than the automobile network. (Point 62)

By no means can any narrow cult of the past bring about a disregard for the rules of social justice. (Point 67)

The practice of using styles of the past on aesthetic pretexts for new structures erected in historic areas has harmful consequences. (Point 70)

The pre-eminence of private interests, motivated by self-interest and by the lure of profit, is at the root of this deplorable state of affairs where the majority of cities do not at all fulfil their purpose which is to satisfy the . . . needs of their population. (Points 72 and 71)

Urbanism is a three-dimensional . . . science. Introducing the element of height will solve the problems of modern traffic and leisure by utilizing the open spaces thus created. (Point 82)

It is a matter of the most urgent necessity that every city draw up its programme and enact the laws that will enable it to be carried out. The soul of the city will be brought to life by the clarity of the plan. (Point 86)

The first of the functions that should engage the urbanist's attention is that of housing – and good housing. (Point 89)

To pass from theory to action still requires a combination of the following factors: a political power such as one might wish – clear-sighted, with earnest conviction and determined to achieve those improved living conditions . . . an enlightened population that will understand, desire, and demand what the specialists have envisaged for it; an economic situation that will make it possible. (Point 91)

Architecture presides over the destinies of the city . . . Architecture is the key to everything. (Point 92)

For years, at every point . . . attempts at urban improvement have been dashed against the petrified law of private property . . . The ground should be open to mobilization whenever it is a matter of the general interest. (Point 94)

Private interest will be subordinated to the collective interest. (Point 95)

The 'points' refer to the ninety-five theses of the Charter of Athens, of 1933, as published by Le Corbusier.[15]

CIAM was not primarily a movement of modernist architecture. It was a movement of modernist social urban design. It was a movement demanding cities for people, 'in the machine age' – but not cities by the people, which obviously facilitated the movement's public political ambiguity and actual technocratic ecumenism.

That this urbanism explicitly aiming at subordinating private interests and private property, with its priorities turned to the living and working conditions of workers and low-income people, had little attraction to architects raised and socialized in the United States should be no surprise. CIAM's polar opposite is the most powerful American city designer of the 1920 and 1930s, Robert Moses in New York. He has gone down in posthumous notoriety for his various tricks to make public parks and beaches inaccessible to poor people in general and African Americans in particular, including making bridges across his parkways too low for buses to pass under.[16] Nevertheless, there is a connection between modernist architecture and the current global capitalist moment. It runs through the International Style.

Modernism, Skyscrapers and Mutations of the International Style

'Skyscrapers are the ultimate architecture of capitalism', the American architectural historian Carol Willis has written.[17] They have certainly become landmarks of global capitalism. The victory of the global capitalist direction in 1980s London characteristically spawned a spurt of corporate towers in Canary Wharf, transforming also the rest of the former Docklands and under Boris Johnson's right-wing mayoralty becoming the signum of the whole city, even allowing the Qatari-owned 'Shard' to overshadow the national icon of Saint Paul's Cathedral. In Panama City, the national capital huddles in the old colonial centre, where civic militancy is still (in November 2015) struggling to hold corporate 'developers' at bay, completely overwhelmed by recent towers for money laundering and other banking, luxury hotels, corporate offices and upscale malls.

Architectural modernism was not synonymous with skyscrapers. On the contrary, there was originally not only a gap but even a modernist antagonism against the latter. In the famous and epoch-making 'Modern Architecture International Exhibition' at the New York Museum of Modern Art in 1932, when and where the concept of 'International Style' was minted, there were only two skyscrapers on show. Most of the existing ones were dismissed with contempt by the authors of the style-making accompanying book, Henry-Russell Hitchcock and Philip Johnson.[18] The curator, Alfred Barr, noted with satisfaction in his preface an American influence from the International Style in the 'passage . . . from accentuation of verticality to that of horizontality in numerous recent metropolitan buildings'.[19]

Skyscrapers are an invention of American engineering and real estate capital, first in the 1880s and 1890s, in Chicago above all, then followed with gusto in New York. There were some technical preconditions: industrial steel production, pioneered in England, and elevators, dating from the Second French Empire. But also crucial were the socioeconomic conditions in the Chicago historical and topographic context. Chicago was a booming industrial metropolis which had to be rebuilt after a devastating fire in 1871, in a small business district between Lake Michigan to the east and the Chicago River to the north and west, bordered on the south by railway yards and established industries.[20] In those circumstances the wisdom of the contemporary *Architecture Record* was, 'An office building's prime purpose and only object is to earn the greatest possible return for its owners, which means that it must present the maximum of rentable space possible on the lot' – which obviously meant building tall.[21] Cass Gilbert, the architect who built the Woolworth Building in New York, from 1913 to 1930 the world's tallest, defined a skyscraper as 'a machine that makes the land pay'.[22] European architects, particularly but not only in France and Germany, became fascinated with skyscrapers in the 1920s. In Paris, tall tower designs were pushed by Auguste Perret and Le Corbusier, whose Plan Voisin of 1925 (for the car manufacturer Voisin) of a new business district in central Paris with 200-metre-high buildings was the most daring. In Germany, Mies van der Rohe also began skyscraper designs in the 1920s. One of the most prolific Germans in the genre was Ludwig Hilberseimer, whose Welfare City model of high-rises eerily presages the huge housing complexes built all over Europe in the 1960s and 1970s and was included in an exhibition catalogue in Stuttgart in 1927.[23] Nothing of this was built, though.

The four stars of MoMA's International Style were Le Corbusier, Walter Gropius, the Dutchman J. J. P. Oud (who lived until 1960 but who did not build much after the 1920s) and Mies van der Rohe. The illustrations in Hitchcock and Johnson's catalogue show overwhelmingly low-rise buildings with a marked horizontality. Barr and the authors showed their respect for the early skyscraper architect Louis Sullivan but not for his followers, both because of their accentuation of a tower-type verticality and because of their infatuation with historicist, in Gilbert's case neo-Gothic or Art Deco, ornamentation. Simply put, Barr, Hitchcock and Johnson found the typical American skyscraper a manifestation of bad taste. While the Exhibition and its catalogue did pay some attention to the social concerns of the European avant-garde with popular housing, Hitchcock and Johnson's influential book concentrated on style and aesthetics.[24]

What then happened was that the aesthetic of the International Style was adopted by wealthy, ambitious corporate skyscraper builders and their architects, while the CIAM programme of social urbanism was dying out. By the MoMA Exhibition, one of the most prominent American business architects, Raymond Hood, had already moved in the International Style direction; Rockefeller's upcoming house architect Wallace Harrison was an early convert whose impact is visible in the monumental Rockefeller Center of the late thirties.

Avant-garde international architecture and American capital first came together in the United Nations Secretariat Building (154 metres), built from 1947 to 1952 on land donated by Rockefeller, under the day-to-day direction of Wallace Harrison but basically designed by Le Corbusier and Oscar Niemeyer. Lewis Mumford found it appalling:

A type of building that to distant peoples is a stock emblem of the things they fear and hate – our slick mechanization, our awful power, our patronizing attitude toward lesser breeds who have not acquired the American way of life.[25]

Mies van der Rohe became the iconic skyscraper builder after World War II, with his Lake Shore Drive Apartments in Chicago and his Seagram Building in New York. Early on, corporate building generated a big firm (still) producing business buildings in high International Style, the Chicago-based multinational Skidmore, Owings & Merrill (SOM) with its early 1950s landmarks, Lever House and Chase Manhattan Bank in New York.[26]

The ending of European avant-garde architecture and of radicals like Gropius and van der Rohe as stylists for American capital is a significant part of a wider process of European self-destruction (through fascism) boosting an American mid-century.

Mies van der Rohe was once a member of the revolutionary German November (1918) Group of committed artists. His first striking construction was an expressive tomb monument to the murdered revolutionaries Rosa Luxemburg and Karl Liebknecht. In English exile before his influential chair at the Harvard Graduate School of Design, Gropius had surrendered. In 1934 he wrote to the CIAM General Secretary: 'I have resolved . . . as far as possible, not to start with social housing for workers, but to make a breach into the class of the wealthy'.[27]

There is another trajectory of modernist architecture, also with a full share of ironic twists. As we noted above, egalitarian, low-income housing was a central part of the original CIAM project. Not much of it was built before World War II, but there remains the Dutch tradition from Oud of neat, brightly coloured rows of working-class and popular city housing. Hans Scharoun's 'city landscapes' of low-rise apartment buildings in landscapes of grass and trees, such as the Siemensstadt in Berlin (of 1930), still characterize many of the urban inner peripheries of Scandinavian towns and cities, including my own local town of Kalmar. This aspect of modernism, too, had its belated and ironic victory after World War II. First and most authentic was its contribution to Scandinavian welfare-state building (see the chapter on Popular Moments).

Much more important, however, were the big mass housing projects which started in the mid-1950s in both Eastern and Western Europe, in the peripheries of or, as in Paris, around the capitals and other large cities. The projects had no specifically architectural aims and focused on providing low-cost modern housing to meet soaring popular demand as fast as possible. But it may well be argued, as Javier Monclús and Carmen Díez Medina have most recently, that it was inspired by (parts of) CIAM and its Charter of Athens.[28] The stone cities of the West and often greener cities of the East both succumbed to urbanization in the form of concrete slabs and tower blocks. In the East this was an egalitarian victory led by Nikita Khrushchev over hierarchical Stalinist Realism, in the West a translation of pre–World War II social ambitions and traditions.

However, it was a Pyrrhic victory, particularly the further west you got from Moscow. Charles Jencks famously claimed that 'modern architecture died in Saint Louis, Missouri, on July 15, 1972', when the Pruitt-Igoe housing block by Minoru Yamasaki (the architect of New York's World Trade Center) was dynamited.[29] Thirty years later Jencks himself presented a wider view, with some self-irony, but hardly more convincing.[30] Popular high-rise housing was not an intrinsic part of the great housing concerns of the European modernist avant-garde and was absent from all its actual pre–World War II manifestations: Oud's buildings in Hoek van Holland and Rotterdam, Mies van der Rohe's Weissenhof in Stuttgart, Scharoun's Siemensstadt in Berlin, Ernst May's large-scale housing programme in late 1920s Frankfurt.

The background to the demolition of the Pruitt-Igoe and to the collapse of London's Ronan Point is not modernist architecture but Anglo-Saxon housing ideals and social realities. In both the United States and the United Kingdom, the single-family home was the ideal, even in its caricatured form of the morose rows of wall-to-wall British working-class houses, backing onto a communal alley, with an outhouse in the backyard. Under urban housing pressure, this was, of course, a slow response, and apartment building was tried. The Pruitt complex of eleven-storey apartment buildings was built in the mid-1950s for a White middle class, but under budget constraints, cheaply and shoddily designed. Initially it did function as intended, but then the middle class moved out, the elevators stopped functioning and social as well as material rot set in. The causal sequence of the spiral of housing and social decline need not concern us here. In most other cases of Anglo-Saxon 'modernist' architecture for the poor, the main problem was not the architectural style but the concentration of poor people, addicts and dysfunctional families in shoddily built and poorly maintained public housing estates, magnifying self-destructive tendencies. To use these tragic experiences for purposes of polemics about architectural style seems obscene.

Mass fabrication of large-scale, moderately high, five- to twenty-storey popular housing became from the 1960s a major feature of the peripheries of big European cities, in the West as well as in the East. They did not have the inbuilt social stigma of the Anglo-Saxon public projects for the poor – and remained socially mixed in Eastern Europe – but were usually cursorily planned and hastily built, with promises of services unfulfilled or delayed and, in western Europe, increasingly housing the precarious and immigrants. Obviously not optimal neighbourhoods, these projects and their inhabitants became extremely vulnerable to fast-changing and hard-hitting mass media opinion, particularly in Berlin and Paris. Several of them, for instance those of the Swedish 'million programme', have lately been subject to rehabilitation, with varying success. Cheap modernism for people held to be cheap became a cheap target for expensive architectural critics. But the story of mass modernist housing does not end in Europe.

Somewhat later, higher buildings, twenty storeys and up, became popular middle class housing in East Asia, not only in crowded cities like Hong Kong and Singapore but also in a nation-state metropolis with acute housing shortages from rural emigration, like Seoul. High-rise living got its middle-class attraction in Seoul, after some failures, from its new 'Western' amenities: central heating, bathrooms and flush toilets, practical kitchens, American-style living rooms and European-type neighbourhood services such as kindergartens, schools, playgrounds and shops. The 1988 Olympic Athletes' Village provided a fashionable

---

* Florian Urban, in his contemporary history of mass housing, gives a number of arresting examples: how the Märkisches Viertel in northern West Berlin from 1966 to 1968 changed from a positive model to a nightmare (Urban, *Tower and Slab*, 62ff); how Gropiusstadt, planned by Gropius himself, in southern West Berlin, came to be seen, in a bestseller of reportage, as the breeding ground of the desolate and addicted in 'Children of the Zoo Station' (Urban, *Tower and Slab*, 72). Similar denunciations befell several of the *grands ensembles* in the *banlieue* of Paris (Urban, *Tower and Slab*, 49ff).

model.[31] From East Asia, the free-standing high-rise condominium has spread both east and west. Among the world's twenty-five tallest completed buildings (by early 2016), five are residential: two in the United States and three in the United Arab Emirates. The tallest building in Western Europe, the London Shard, is at least partly residential.[32]

One lesson of all this is that architecture cannot trump sociology. Rather, architecture is sociology turned into built form. Another is the irony of architectural modernism. Its most radical constructivism ended up providing the preferred form of corporate capitalist power. Its political ambition of social change was discredited as a breeding ground for social outcasts. A third lesson is that architecture is a constitutive part of the global moment of cities.

Context and Contingency: The Battle for London

Although we can discern both a capitalist developmental dynamic and preparatory historical antecedents, the arrival of the current global moment in urban history was neither a natural evolution nor a foregone conclusion. It was decided in the contingency of battles. London was the crucial arena, Tokyo was the failed prophet; the turn of New York tipped the balance.

In the 1980s, Japan seemed to be on its way to becoming the world's number one, economically.* Euphoric expectations unleashed great urban plans, ultimately aiming at making Tokyo Bay a kind of urban pond and positioning Tokyo as a global city. Tokyo's master architect Kenzō Tange was drawing up big and bold projects for Tokyo Bay, unparalleled in any other city. Tokyo in the 1980s was riding on a property boom and the nationalist prime minister Yasuhiro Nakasone and Governor Shunichi Suzuki were invoking it as a 'world city', 'which will lead the world'.[33] In the end not much, though something, came out of this, as Japan was plunging into stagnation by the early 1990s, with Tokyo diving deepest.

In the 1970s, New York was in dire straits, directly facing the necessity of declaring bankruptcy. After 1977 it managed to get out of its

---

* This was also a scholarly American view at the time (Ezra Vogel, *Japan as Number One*, New York: Harper, 1979).

financial trap and started to grow again, economically as well as demographically, fuelled by finance and real estate. This turnaround was the first major victory of post-industrial, financially driven capitalism, capable also of sustaining a vibrant metropolitan culture. It set the agenda of the coming world-city wanna-bes. Its political context was decided nationally, by the Reagan presidency, rather than by any major city battle.

Why London? After all, London was an Old World city, until the aftermath of World War II ruling the planet's largest empire, where the sun never set and wages never rose (Alice Amsden). Even after the end of most of the empire, London remained the global centre of financial transactions. However, London was not just its financial square mile, 'the City' with a capital C. It was also, and above all, the capital of a complex national society and state, the world's first and most industrialized country run by an oligarchy deeply steeped in monarchical and aristocratic mores and manners, presiding from their rural country houses over a bustling modern capital largely laid out and owned by noble landowners.

Capitalist industrialism culminated around 1970, as measured in the proportion of industrial employment in the rich core countries. As Marx had predicted, the peak of industrial capitalism was also the peak of the working-class movement, in terms of political party membership and voter turnout and of trade union organization. There was no socialist revolution, but there were Labour governments and large and successful strikes. The problem was that time was running out for Labour. Economic history was about to tip, towards de-industrialization in the centres of capitalism, seriously weakening the industrial core of the working class. Conditions for capitalist revenge were building up. Margaret Thatcher promised to be the Death Angel of trade unionism and Labourism. She was very much helped by the divisions of industrial strife and, decisively, by the British electoral system, which gave her absolute power with the support of never more than a third of the electorate.

London had never been a strong industrial working-class city, like Berlin or the centres of the British North,[34] and its political preferences had changed back and forth. It did have a hefty contingent of blue-collar employment, which in the 1970s and 1980s was shrinking fast, generating structural unemployment. Part of this economic change was the closing of the East London docks due to the new container shipping. In

1967 the East India Docks were shut, then in 1982 the Royals, the last of the working docks, closed.[35] More unemployment ensued.

London in the 1980s was a city of mounting social problems. But it was also a maturation of the 'Swinging London' of the 1960s: multi-cultural, multi-ethnic, multi-sexual, with its New Left, now spread out from its initial Soho centre and hardened in countless campaigns. In 1981 Labour gained a majority in the Greater London Council (GLC), the replacement (in 1965) for the smaller but more powerful London County Council, and a New Left coalition under the dynamic leadership of Ken Livingstone took over. The GLC had few powers and resources but tried heroically to make up for that with ideas, symbolic projects and civic engagement.

The lines were clearly drawn. On the right was the central government, with minority support but almost unlimited constitutional powers, hell-bent on crushing any labour or popular opposition to its neoliberal project, which also included getting rid of the oligarchic 'old boys', regarded as indolent and inefficient. On the left was a city government with few powers, dependent on alignments with the (thirty-three) boroughs of London but riding on a crest of radicalism (soon to decline) and bristling with ideas and initiatives.

At stake was the orientation of the capital city. 'Speculative building has no place in a socialist London', the GLC declared in 1983.[36] The decisive battlefield was found in the Docklands of East London, historically poor, now dilapidated and full of unemployment. Clearly this was a part of the city where something had to be done. What?

Left concerns were local and popular, concentrated on employment, social services, housing and democracy – in the sense of popular participation in planning. The best example is perhaps the People's Plan for the Royal Docks: trying to keep some of the docks, developing fruit and timber depots, supporting cargo handling and boosting public housing as well as the care and education of children.[37]

Right concerns focused on nation-blind rather than globalist economic development, offices, and business connections such as a city airport and Docklands Light Railroad. A tax-exempt 'Enterprise Zone' was set up in 1982. Democracy was a problem, so the Tory government recycled an old instrument of British urban policy in the empire as well as in the UK's 'New Towns', the 'development corporation' of appointees accountable only to the central government. The London Docklands

Development Corporation was put up in 1981. The Thatcher government were firm believers in what may be called the dictatorship of capital. The objections of the Docklands' local authorities could be dismissed, as they were 'all run by communists'.*

For all their campaigns and the logistic and propagandistic support of the GLC, the not-very-united ordinary people of East London stood no chance against the might of unbridled political power and international capital. In 1985, the Thatcher government announced the end of elected London government and the globalist star piece of Docklands development, Canary Wharf, was launched by an American-Swiss bank consortium. By 1987 it was virtually bankrupt and bought up by three of the Reichmann brothers from Canada under the label of their real estate development company Olympia and York. The latter laid out a new business centre in the east, with a plan by SOM and an iconic landmark tower by the Argentinian-American architect César Pelli, who had designed the Petronas Towers in Kuala Lumpur and the World Financial Center in New York for the Reichmanns. Olympia and York soon also faltered financially and in 2004 Canary Wharf was in the control of Morgan Stanley, who then sold it to a 'Songbird' consortium headed by one of the Reichmann brothers and a Saudi prince.[38] Later, China Investment Corporation became a major shareholder of Songbird, which then in early 2015 was bought by the Qatari Investment Authority together with the Toronto-based Brookfield Properties.

Canary Wharf is an exemplary part of a global city: laid out by foreign capital, designed by foreign developers, built with foreign techniques and materials as a forest of high-rises and involving a foreign replica as a landmark, designed by a foreign architect. The cleaners came from the Global South and post-Communist Eastern Europe and were denied the right to assemble (in 2004) because the whole area was private property.[39] Nevertheless, after a quarter of a century, it seems to have been included in the city as well as in the national patrimony.[40] It signals the successful arrival of the global moment. In 1989, the long post-war demographic decline of London reversed into population growth.

---

* Michael Heseltine in his memoirs, quoted in Sue Brownill and Glen O'Hara, 'From planning to opportunism? Re-examining the creation of the London Docklands Development Corporation', *Planning Perspectives* 30:4 (2015): 550. Heseltine was a 'wet' or moderate of the regime who later came to lead the coup against Thatcher.

Canary Wharf was the urbanist fulcrum of the new globalist transformation of London. But there were also other crucial decisions and
plans in the 1980s. Economically, the most important was the de-regu-
lation of the City in 1986, opening up the London Stock Exchange to the
financial sharks of all the seven seas, who devoured the quaint gentlemen of one-nation, pre-neoliberal Tories. Politically, the abolition of
elected London government spawned a government consultancy with
world-city visions.

The London Planning Advisory Committee (LPAC) was established
by the same act which abolished elected government. In 1988 it presented
an innocuous 'Four-fold Vision' for London:

- Civilized city offering a high quality of environment for all
  Londoners
- World centre of international trade and business
- City of opportunities for all
- City of stable and secure residential neighbourhoods,
  capable of sustaining community development

The real question, however, was 'London's future as a world city'. The
firm Coopers Lybrand & Deloitte was hired by the LPAC in 1990 to
answer: 'What is London's future competitiveness as a world city and
how can this position be sustained and enhanced by the right urban
policy framework?'[41] The consultants' main report, 'London: World
City', was published by HMSO in 1991, the same year as Sassen's
book.

In 1999 LPAC put out strategic planning advice on high buildings
and strategic views in London. After noting that 'high buildings have
been promoted as essential to London's success as Europe's pre-eminent
world city',[42] the Committee stated bluntly,

Research has failed to reveal significant evidence to suggest either a
need or desire for a radical change in London's skyline through the
addition of high buildings in order to secure, sustain or enhance
London's importance as a World City . . . London's character is already
well defined. It does not need new high buildings to define itself as a
World City.[43]

When he returned to power in 2000, Ken Livingstone acknowledged the new times. The London Plan of 2004 embraced economic globalism, although a bit less ostentatiously than its first draft: 'The London Plan cannot realistically reverse these strong deep-rooted factors, nor does the Mayor wish it to do so.' Now, the global moment is not totalitarian, any more than actually occurring Communist urbanism. Livingstone II's London had a significant social, public and, above all, environmental agenda, including affordable day care and (some) housing and public space – transforming Trafalgar Square from a traffic circus, occasionally interrupted by concerned and courageous citizens demonstrating, into a public pedestrainized area for citizens and visitors – as well as introducing congestion charges on cars in the city and promoting public transport.

The successful bid for the 2012 Olympics, crucially supported by Livingstone's old foe Tony Blair, was aimed at funding, in a globalist way, the social development of East London.[44] But a capitalist world city project of course demands its pound of flesh. In the 2000s business interests had privileged access to the mayor, and the corporate towers started sprouting.[45]

After a brief hiccup from the 2007 financial crash, it was soon more business than usual – including new ownership of the Shard project – with the crisis shunted off as austerity for the plebs. Under Boris Johnson's mayoralty, London skyscrapers proliferated like never before. By mid-March 2014 the London press was informed that 236 new twenty-plus-storey buildings were being built or planned. Most of them are (at least partly) residential: the new gentrifying classes of London are following the East Asian middle classes upwards.

Johnson scrapped Livingstone's public spaces plan, first of all the one for remaking Parliament Square, and has downplayed, if not quite abandoned, concrete proposals of affordability building. 'Affordability' quotas in new housing developments have been reduced and have come to mean 80 per cent of the market price – with a separate 'poor door'

---

* Gordon, *Planning Twentieth Century Capital Cities*, 9–10; Massey, *World City*, 86. Doreen Massey was herself, as a radical urbanist, associated with the first Livingstone administration. Her book also expresses a resigned mood, across its perceptive and penetrating analyses.

entrance – which is far beyond the financial capacity of the popular classes. Social housing construction ended with Thatcherism. Instead, London is competing with Los Angeles in housing the largest expat homes in the world, up to 90,000 square feet (about 8,400 square metres). The value of the London real estate market is about the same as that of the GDP of Brazil.*

The Tory mayor's two primary objectives were clearly globalist:

> London must retain and build upon its world city status as one of the three business centres of global reach. It must be somewhere people and business want to locate . . . London must also be among the best cities in the world to live, whatever your age and background.[46]

(As long as you don't have to rely on a median Atlantic income, presumably.) It should be noted that Johnson hedged his Mayor's Vision by excluding any reference to housing in his city 'for everyone'.[47]

But official Tory London is not Panama City. Johnson's 2011 version of the London Plan stipulated that applications for tall and large buildings should include 'an urban design analysis' demonstrating that the project will meet a list of nine conditions.[48] As an old world city, London is globalizing with some style. This may be seen in the election of a new mayor in May 2016, a Labour politician of Pakistani origin, Sadiq Khan, who decisively beat a Tory candidate running a campaign of innuendos against allegedly relevant Islamist extremism and anti-Semitism.

Nor is this city, the world's largest financial gambling den, a stateless global city without national moorings. Not only are its financial and real estate markets dependent on national British state protection – including against EU infringement, however minimal – and

---

* Serious journalism provides valuable insight into the London property market. Here I am indebted to *Financial Times* architecture critic Edwin Heathcote ('The gentrification and petrification of London's heart', *Financial Times*, 17 June 2015) and many others: the *Daily Telegraph* columnist Reni Eddo-Lodge; *New York Times*, 28 October 2014; Stefanie Bolzen et al., 'Metropolis Merciless', *Welt am Sonntag*, 22 March 2015; Ruth Bloomfield, *Financial Times*, 13 and 14 December 2014; Peter Haldeman, *New York Times*, 9 December 2014.

their terms of trade set by national legislation. The basic infrastructure of London, planned and existing, depends on national permits and national co-finance: the Underground, the Crossrail, Heathrow Airport, the Thames Gateway, etc. And as the mass turnout at the Queen's jubilees demonstrates, London's national moorings are not just economic shackles. They are chosen and deeply felt. On the other hand, beneath the current architectural glitz, fed by a seemingly never-drying-out pool of 'developers', an explosive social brew is brewing of mega-rich Arab oil sheikhs, Russian oligarchs and expat magnates from all continents, with their huge, lavish and most of the time empty mansions; of mass poverty immigrated from Bangladesh, Eastern Europe and the Global South in general; and with the native popular classes increasingly expelled or marginalized from London proper. In the language of the times, this is hardly a sustainable development.*

The Battle for London was a crucial event as it pitched not only national popular interests against those of global capital, but also, somewhat less prominently, two projects of a global city against each other, a city of global multiculturalism against a city of global capital. In both respects, global capital was the winner.

A similar, though politically less dramatic, battle was fought out in Tokyo. In the 1970s, Tokyo had something of a popular moment under Governor Ryokichi Minobe, elected in 1971 under the banner of 'Open Squares and Blue Skies', promoting civic participation in urban planning (i.e., 'open squares'). The government focused on low-income housing, schools and parks – in contrast to the preceding Olympic expressways and flyovers – and argued for a 'civil minimum' for a decent standard of living. The turn to a 'world city' came in the mid-1980s, in the second term of Governor Suzuki, first elected in 1979, with his 1986 Second Long-term Comprehensive Plan for Tokyo Metropolis. Then, in 1990 and 1992, the Japanese bubble burst and the world-city dreams took a hard hit, decisive with

---

* Actual London development runs opposite to Boris Johnson's sixth programmatic objective in his 'London Plan' (32): 'A city where it is easy, safe, and convenient for everyone to access jobs, opportunities, facilities'. To what extent Sadiq Khan will be able to change the direction remains to be seen. It should be kept in mind that the power resources of the mayor of London are very much limited in comparison with those of the governor of Tokyo.

respect to the grandeur of the Tokyo Bay landfilling project, less so ideologically and with respect to private corporate development. The 1995 election buried the world city ambitions for a while, but only until the 1999 election, won by the conservative Shintaro Ishihara. He staked his ambition on making Tokyo a 'dominant world city'. It should be noted, though, that Ishihara was no Anglo-Saxon neoliberal but a Japanese nationalist, unafraid to take on corporate power in a perception of national city interest. Against the national government and the business lobby, but with impeccable right-wing credentials he managed to push through a metropolitan tax on bank profits, something the progressive governor of the 1970s had failed to get passed.[49]

Saskia Sassen was right in pointing to a global city surge through diverse histories, cultures and politics,[50] but her uncritical followers have failed to pay attention to the enduring, yet very different, constructions and therefore experiences and functioning of global cities.

The Urban Moment of Global Capitalism

The current global moment is the hour of global capital. To nation-state capitals this is a particular challenge. Are they losing their national character or are they being marginalized by cities more receptive to the new constellations of power?

First, we have to take stock of the different geopolitical meanings of 'globalization'. In East Asia, South and North, 'globalize' is an active verb, referring to a chosen policy option, not some external force to which one has to adapt, as in most Euro-American globalization discourse.[51] This choice to globalize is nowhere more explicit, emphatic and enthusiastic than in China. In the second half of the 1990s it became almost a craze in political China to build 'global cities' in order to modernize and integrate China into the world. Forty-three Chinese cities announced global city plans![52] As part of its plan to become a 'modern international city' (an English translation preferred by the Beijing mayoralty), Beijing, after central government approval, decided to build a 'CBD' (Central Business District) in the eastern centre of the city. Two international competitions for its design were held. The official master plan captures well the spirit of the current global moment: 'The core area of the CBD is designed to concentrate a large number of skyscrapers . . . The design is to create a perfect urban image with outstanding symbolic buildings and to form a focal point in the mass of high-rise towers.'[53] The Chaoyang CBD opened for business in 2004. Since then the city has built a second business district, west of Tiananmen: Financial Street.

Under the slogan 'New Beijing, Great Olympics', the globalization project was pushed forward, with massive housing demolitions as well as large-scale metro extensions and iconic architecture. In the competitive selection process, national motifs were sifted out. The well-known result was indeed stunning, although Rem Koolhaas's television building was partly ravaged by fire, Paul Andreu's National Theatre for the Performing Arts has had leaking problems with its underwater entrance passage and Herzog & de Meuron's Bird's Nest Stadium stands mostly empty. The two latter icons are the two city buildings on Beijing's official website.

A globalist project was bluntly set out by the Seoul Metropolitan Government in 2006:

> In a future society, urban competitiveness determines national competitiveness . . . The influence of nations will dwindle drastically, while some 10 megapoles will dictate world policy . . . In the past, nations formulated ways to make cities properly function . . . But now, it's time for cities to set specific visions for themselves.[54]

The city think tank had already specified the meaning of urban competitiveness:

> These efforts in the recent years [to ensure sustainability of the city's growth and development] can be summarized as competition among cities to become an international centre – a node in the network of corporations, work forces, resources and finance. A fierce competition is taking place to become the centre of economy, politics, culture, as well as transportation and telecommunications by attracting the headquarters of multinational corporations and

high-level service functions, high-quality workforce and international events.*

However, it should be noted that this strategy of becoming an 'international centre', 'attracting multinational corporations' and vying for
'international events' (conventions of all kinds, big international sports
games) is deployed by the national capital of a fiercely nationalistic,
ex-colonial country. As Korea's then-president put it in January 1995,
'Globalization is the quickest way to build the Republic into a first-rate
nation in the coming century.'[55] In 2011, Seoul elected a more socially
concerned mayor, Park Won-soon (re-elected in 2014), who has
scrapped some of the globalist prestige projects.

The global capitalist moment in urban history means a major shift in
city power and a dramatic change in the cityscape. The most important
shift of power, however, is not from the national to the global. It is the
shift from the people, the citizenry, to capital, national and global. The
prime aim of a global city is not the satisfaction of its inhabitants, that of
a global capital city not to represent its nation and its citizens, but to
attract foreign capital and consumer spending, to benefit (some sectors
of) national capital and to compete with other cities for the title of Miss
Capitalist Universe.

Now, urban globalism should not be taken as a category but as a
variable, of which a given city can have more or less. It does not
usually rule alone. In democratic cities, mayors and city governments
have to get elected by the local population. National governments
keep a watch on national interests; most have to face uncertain elections, too.

Approaching the urban imprint of global capitalism, we may use two
sets of variables, one referring to the degree of a city's insertion into or
connectivity with global capitalism, the other referring to a city's openness or its systemic subservience to global business. 'Systemic' is used

---

* Seoul Development Institute, *Can Seoul Become a World City?* 2003, 11. The text is an
  introduction to a detailed study, undertaken together with the analytical arm of the
  Japanese finance corporation Nomura Securities, with a view to giving policy answers
  to the title question. Around that time, Seoul boosters and consultants were also
  toying with the 'Beseto' idea, a networked urban mega-centre of Beijing, Seoul, and
  Tokyo. It got little traction in Beijing and Tokyo, as I found out interviewing planners
  there.

here to distinguish a market system from patterns of cronyism and of collusive kleptocracy. In order to make large-scale comparisons possible, for the first variable, I shall here make use of a partial index out of the urban economic network analyses developed by Peter Taylor and his collaborators, from an ambitious Chinese-led project on global urban competitiveness of which two major reports have emerged so far.[56] They call it 'global connectivity', and it basically places cities into a hiearchy based on the location of the world's most important multinational corporations, according to *Forbes*.[57]

As the designers of the composite urban competitiveness index are enlightened academics and not hard-nosed businesspeople or business ideologues, it includes a number of items not directly related to capitalist profitability. So for our purposes here of looking at capitalist power, we have to look elsewhere.* The best I have found has been developed by true believers in unbridled capitalism, the US Heritage Foundation and the *Wall Street Journal*: the 'index of economic freedom'.[58]

I shall here use two of their ten-part indices. One we may call capitalist openness: it is an average of the authors' trade, investment and financial freedoms. The other I shall call freedom from taxation, although the original title is 'fiscal freedom'. It reaches its maximum of 'freedom' where there are no taxes at all.† It should be noted that both these two indices refer to whole states, not just to the capital city, but that is the way contemporary global capitalism is organized, although individual cities may offer special tax breaks and services.

First we shall look into the extent to which nation-state capitals are enmeshed in the tentacles of global capitalism by looking at how they score on two sets of variables: global capitalist connectivity and global capital power.

---

* The first Competitiveness Report had a partial index called 'Market System', which might have been usable in spite of the fact that one of its three items was irrelevant: the ratio of local to national revenue. It was dropped without explanation in the second report.

† There was another good candidate, 'Labor Freedom', the true capitalist credentials of which, as business freedom against labour, are demonstrated by its claims to find more labour freedom in Saudi Arabia and in the United Arab Emirates than in Germany or Sweden. But it is a composite of several items and not exactly the reverse of worker freedom. 'Labor freedom' is found to be even higher in the United States – where trade unions, although harassed, are not illegal – than among the almost totally rights-less immigrants labouring in the Arabian peninsula.

Table 3. Capitals under global capitalism: the twenty-five most entangled cities

Cities	Global Corporate Connectivity	Global Capital Power	
		Capitalist Oppeness	Freedom from Taxes
Singapore	0.976	0.85	0.91
London	0.966	0.86	0.65
Tokyo	0.957	0.71	0.69
Beijing	0.849	0.44	0.70
Paris	0.847	0.77	0.48
Moscow	0.745	0.43	0.82
Seoul	0.728	0.75	0.74
Madrid	0.725	0.81	0.58
Bangkok	0.710	0.63	0.81
Buenos Aires	0.660	0.42	0.66
Mexico City	0.633	0.70	0.75
Warsaw	0.624	0.78	0.76
Kuala Lumpur	0.581	0.67	0.85
Budapest	0.576	0.78	0.79
Brussels	0.572	0.78	0.44
Jakarta	0.568	0.60	0.83
Dublin	0.570	0.83	0.74
Prague	0.527	0.83	0.83
Vienna	0.525	0.83	0.51
Santiago de Chile	0.525	0.81	0.75
Athens	0.505	0.61	0.64
Delhi	0.498	0.49	0.77
Cairo	0.468	0.55	0.86
Stockholm	0.464	0.84	0.44
Manila	0.457	0.65	0.79
Berlin	0.415	0.83	0.62
Washington, D.C.	0.403	0.76	0.66

Notes: All indices have a maximum of 1. 'Connectivity' refers to the city's place in the location of office hierarchies by leading multinational corporations. 'Capitalist openness' refers to the absence of barriers to trade, private investment and financial moves. 'Freedom from taxes' involves both maximum tax rates and total taxation as share of GDP.[59]

European national capitals are still at the centre of global capitalist networks, making up twelve of the twenty-five capital cities. By comparison, there are only nine Asian capitals, three Latin American, one North African/Arab and not a single capital of sub-Saharan Africa. Nairobi is the highest scorer of the latter with 0.2. (Among sub-Saharan African non-capitals, Johannesburg got 0.442 and Lagos 0.211.) The specialized political capitals are not deeply entangled in world capitalism. Washington is the most so – 0.403 on the index – followed by Ottawa with a score of 0.284, and Wellington with 0.247, well ahead of Ankara, Brasília, Canberra, Islamabad, Pretoria and the Hague. Abuja and Astana are not even listed. Washington is the fourth most globally corporate-connected city in the United States, after New York, Los Angeles and Houston.

Capitalist penetration of post-Communist capitals is impressive: in Europe four of them more so than Berlin and Rome, six more than Lisbon. But the reliability of the index is not always transparent: Hanoi (0.314), for instance, appears in the index to be more broadly entangled in global capitalism than Seattle or Detroit.*

Capital's freedom to move is very pronounced in Europe. Of the capitals with the nine highest values (greater than 0.80) six are European; London scores highest of all. Surprising, perhaps, is the large freedom given to capital in welfare-state cities like Stockholm, Vienna and Berlin, more than in Washington. Capitalists also find more barriers in Tokyo, Paris and Brussels. Putting the two capital power indices together, Singapore, for all its strong state capitalism, appears as the ideal capitalist city, followed by Prague, Budapest, Dublin, Santiago de Chile and Warsaw. London is below the top on the combined power indicators because of its taxes, although it offers more freedom from taxation than all Western European cities except Dublin.

In the current global moment, urban representations of power take three main style expressions: *verticality, novelty* and *exclusivity.* The verticality of skyscrapers has become a signal of global aspirations, of longing for world power or at least for world prestige. Today's skyscrapers correspond to the grand wide avenues of the global nationalism of the late nineteenth century. This is not a verticality of housing, although

---

* How the index-makers deal with the globalism of Starbucks and General Motors I don't know.

a growing minority of skyscrapers are residential, but of luxury, wealth and power. Skyscrapers are enormously expensive to build; their builders tell the world that they have the capital to erect them. In growth cities with high land prices, these buildings, with a huge floor area per square metre of land, are also extra profitable – when their space can be sold or let out, which is far from always the case.

Contrary to contemporary hype, world cities are not necessarily important incubators of innovation – neither the electronic nor the biomedical revolution arose in cities – but they are hubs of novelty to which the new and its wealth gravitate and are put on display. In terms of cityscapes, novelty is, above all, new business and shopping districts. Here we shall deal with novelty in connection with verticality. But we shall also pay attention to the construction of new, non-national, globalist city landmarks and their relative significance to new national iconography.

Exclusivity is a third distinctive feature of the global urban moment. Not in the sense of city closure, as these cities have a huge demand for a low-wage 'service class', as well as for new, ambitious talent: 'exclusivity' here means slicing the city into exclusive segments. Gating is the most cutting instrument, but unregulated market pricing in growing cities is also very effective.

On 25 April 2003, the real estate group Mori Building hosted the Roppongi Hills Opening Exhibition in the Mori Tower in Tokyo. Its theme was 'the global city', and it presented models of a number of international cityscapes to 'demonstrate the direction taken by global cities that have developed under the motto "Vertical Growth: Towards the Sky"'. The exhibition was part of a programmatic ambition expressed by the president and CEO of the firm, Minoru Mori: 'We must transform Tokyo's horizontally dense city into a vertical urban area'.[60]

Bearing in mind our earlier findings that skyscrapers rose to maximize profits in urban construction and as capitalist claims to public power and prestige, the history of tall buildings gives us a picture of a remarkable global shift in such claims. In 1940, all of the hundred tallest buildings of the world were in North America (read: the United States). By the mid-1950s some additions had been erected, seven in Moscow – topped by the 240-metre Lomonosov University and the 206-metre Hotel Ukraine[61] – as well as the Soviet-built 231-metre Culture and Science Palace of Warsaw and the insurance corporation

Torre Latinoamericana in Mexico City (182 metres). There were also single 140-plus-metre towers in São Paulo and Buenos Aires. On the eve of the surge of the current wave of globalization by 1980 and 1990 respectively, the North American share (overwhelmingly, if no longer exclusively, in the United States) had gone down to 81 and 80 per cent. Then the skies changed, to 50 per cent in 2000, to 30 in 2010 and down to 17 by 2015.[62]

Table 4. Skyscraper geography and the relative decline of US urban capitalism: location of the world's 100 tallest buildings, 1940–2015

Year	Location	No. of 100 tallest skyscrapers
1940	USA	100
1990	North America	80
2000	North America	50
2020	USA	13 (incl. no. 6)
	East Asia	61 (incl. no. 2)
	(of which Mainland China)	44 (incl. no. 2)
	Arab Peninsula & Gulf	21 (incl. no. 1)
	Eastern Europe	5 (all Russian; incl. no. 14)
	Western Europe	0
	Latin America	0
	South Asia	0
	Africa	0

Note: Communications towers uncounted.[63]

The skyscraper race is becoming increasingly Asian; additions from Southeast and South Asia are to be expected.[64] American supremacy is clearly under strong attack and, since 1998, American capital has left the race for the world's tallest building. In 1998 the Malaysian state-capitalist Petronas Towers overtook the Sears/Willis Tower of Chicago at the top of the world, to be dethroned by the Taipei financial centre Taipei 101 in 2004, in turn overtaken in 2010 by the Burj Khalifa in Dubai, which in its turn is planned to be overtaken by the Saudi Kingdom/ Jeddah Tower (under construction).

However, while skyscrapers are indicators of *urban* capitalist power and ambitions – and, at one time, of Stalinist aims of emulating them – they are not very reliable as pointers to capital power per se. Some of the world's most powerful corporations, like Apple, Microsoft and Walmart, have their headquarters in rustic (though well connected) locations and characterized by a pronounced horizontality.

Now let us see how urban globalism has affected national capital cities.

Table 5. Skyscrapers in national capitals, in 2015

City	No. Tall Buildings[65]	No. Buildings 200m or Higher
Tokyo	207	23
Jakarta	201	23
Singapore	155	27
Seoul	141	14
Moscow	119	14
London	95	5
Metro Manila[a]	92	18
Mexico City	91	3
Bangkok	88	9
Beijing	87	8
Panama City	78	21
Kuala Lumpur	68	16
Paris Banlieue[b]	43	1
Ankara	42	0
The Hague	42	0
Paris Ville	39	1
Buenos Aires	36	0
Berlin	33	0
Brussels	24	0
Warsaw	23	2
Tehran	23	0
Cairo	22	0
Vienna	21	2
Bratislava	21	0
Athens	20	0
Madrid	19	4
Santiago de Chile	19	1

Hanoi	18	4
Caracas	17	2
Lima	15	0
Kiev	14	0
Santo Domingo	14	0
Baku	13	1
Astana	13	0
Nairobi	13	0
Oslo	13	0
Beirut	12	0
Pretoria	12	0
Bogotá	11	0
Bucharest	11	0
Riga	11	0

Notes: a. The Metro Manila agglomeration does not have the clear French demarcation of city and suburb, so cities of Makati, Mandaluyong and Taguig are here merged with data for Manila, b. Paris *banlieue* here refers to the western suburbs of Courbevoie and Puteaux, which together include the Paris buisness district La Défense.

In this book we are concerned only with capital cities of nation-states, but before looking more closely at them, we should relate them to other cities of the world. The Tall List is actually headed by six non-capital, very capitalist cities: New York, the outstanding leader with 1,226 registered buildings, Hong Kong with 582, then Chicago, Toronto, Shanghai and Dubai, which has the highest number of buildings more than 200 metres tall – sixty-four, against Hong Kong's sixty-three and New York's fifty-eight. At 300 metres up, Dubai towers over all others, with eighteen buildings – including the very highest, at 828 metres – as compared to New York's seven.

Until 2000 the tallest buildings in the world were overwhelmingly office towers, from the early American ones on – usually not exclusive corporate headquarters but partly or mainly for corporate rent. In this century there has been a drastic increase in mixed-use skyscrapers, mixing offices, apartments, hotels, shopping and entertainment. By 2012 only forty-nine of the hundred tallest buildings were solely offices and eighteen were (mainly) residential.[66]

National Capitals under Global Capital

Among the national capitals the preponderance of East Asia is to be expected, but it is more broadly based than is often implied in the conventional world-city discussion. Jakarta has fifteen skyscrapers more than 210 metres high; fourteen were built during the oil and commodities boom of 2005 to 2015. Bangkok and Manila, however nationally different, both have a strong globalist record of soliciting and receiving foreign investment. Kuala Lumpur is also trying to posit itself as a global player but is more driven by national state capitalism, as expressed in the city's iconic landmark, the twin towers of Petronas, the state oil company. The absence of Delhi is noteworthy; and ahead of India's skyscraper centre, Mumbai, are five Chinese cities. Delhi has proclaimed 'world-class city' ambitions, but so far the Congress Party tradition has kept globalist capital aspirations within bounds. On the other hand, post-Communist Hanoi, like Moscow and Beijing, has embraced the global game of sky-scraping. But Beijing, as the political centre of a strongly governed country, has opted to follow rather than to lead the Chinese race of globalist capitalist urbanism and is parked on the sixth national rung, with the hierarchy led by Shanghai.

Sky-scraping should not be reduced to capitalist calculations of floor-space ratios. It has also an important status-competitive component, incarnated in the persona and practices of Donald Trump, the builder and owner of a number of 'Trump Towers'. The Trump World Tower, towering over the UN Secretariat in New York, for instance, was built (in 1980) as 'the world's tallest residential building' and was only recently overtaken by competitors. It illustrates how height has become a status symbol, important enough to be manipulated. Its official height exceeds the measurement of the expert of the Council on Tall Buildings and the number of floors was increased by skipping some numbers. Trump's ninetieth floor is actually the seventy-second floor.[67]

Skyscraper building has become a significant indicator of the state of contemporary capitalism. It indicates a capitalist boom and often, as with the Empire State Building and the Moscow Federation Tower, the boom's approaching end. Above all, it tells us something about the character of capitalism in a given place. On the whole, I think it holds from experience, current as well as historical, that the more skyscrapers a city has the more brash and brazen its capitalism.

'The cities of Europe have remained silent as the world's cities compete on a new stage – the sky – to become the tallest in the world', wrote a Japanese architect in the Global City catalogue mentioned above. It is true that the race has become one mainly between East Asians and Arabs, with the Americas well behind, and that Western Europe is largely staying away.

In Western Europe, after the victorious battle for it, globalist capital has its undisputed centre in London, for which Arab oil sheikhs and Russian oligarchs vote with their feet. In France, Paris and its suburbia or *banlieue* are two very different social entities, but even if an insolent Scandinavian should try to merge them, London maintains its advantage. In the city of Paris, high-rise construction was stopped by the Conservative president Valéry Giscard d'Estaing after the 209-metre Tour de Montparnasse, inaugurated in 1973. On 30 June 2015 the Socialist mayor Anne Hidalgo finally succeeded in pushing through a divided city council the 180-metre Triangle Tower, an office building designed by Herzog & de Meuron, in the Exhibition Park by Porte de Versailles in southwestern Paris. The mayor sold the project, financed by a French-Dutch commercial property investor, as 'a work of art', adding to the grand Parisian collection.

Absence from the top high-rise club does not indicate an absolute absence of high-rise buildings, only fewer. But Europe has quite a number of no-shows, particularly if we remember the still respectable wealth of Europe. The listing highlights a significant European resilience to the sirens of high-rise globalism. The main absentee is Rome, still mainly a national political capital and the world centre of Catholicism, while Milan and Turin participate.*

---

* The face of crude Roman capitalism is generally hidden, infested as it is with corruption and 'mafia capital'. Corruption thrived under the rightwing mayor Gianni Alemanno, in office 2008–2013, and blew up as a scandal under his left-of-centre successor, Ignazio Marino, a man of probity who unfortunately lacked both public office experience and a political base. Marino was forced to resign under public pressure from the prime minister. In June 2016 a young lawyer from the populist Five Star Movement, Virginia Raggi, was elected the new mayor, who after little more than two months had a new Roman crisis blow up in her face, with administrative conflicts and ghosts from the corrupt Alemanno administration popping up. Urban services have been at the centre of the recurrent difficulties, in particuar the municipal bus company and the city's deficient garbage collection.

Out of the four Nordic welfare-state capitals, only oil-rich Oslo is in the game. All four have strong public town-planning traditions, opinions and legal instruments as well as predominantly rural and peasant historical traditions. High-rises and any kind of ostentation have always been subject to vigilant scrutiny with respect to fitting into context. This did not prevent all of them from generating and commissioning innovative architecture in the mid-twentieth century (Alvar Aalto in Helsinki, Gunnar Asplund and Sven Markelius in Stockholm, Arne Jacobsen in Copenhagen) or contemporary modernism (Snöhetta in Oslo; Henning Larsen, Schmidt Hammer Lassen and BIG in Copenhagen). Local rejection in Helsinki of a costly deal with Guggenheim is characteristic of a critical ambience for globalist hype, although the politicians of Stockholm are aggressively trying to brand their city as the 'capital of Scandinavia'.

Ireland has posited itself very successfully as a trampoline for American capital to European markets, but the city of Dublin has played its hand more cautiously than the Irish banks and has not publicly joined the race for the skies. For all its influx of illicit gains, Switzerland is still basically a country of old-money capitalism, discreet and restrained, like the famous business street of Zürich, Bahnhofstrasse. Neither the capital, Berne, nor any of the three other main business centres of Switzerland (Basel, Geneva, Zürich) figures on the lift queue to the sky. The exclusion of Lisbon at the same time as the inclusion of Athens indicates some interesting differences between semi-peripheral Southern European capitalisms. Athenian high-rises seem to have primarily been products of the brash military junta period (1967 to 1974), without significant input during the build-up to the 2004 Olympics. Lisbon, more conservative – and briefly, after the 1974 revolution, anti-capitalist – hilly and peripheral has not faced any strong corporate office demand; its 1998 World Expo promoted a horizontal architecture in line with the latter's oceanic theme.*

The statistical ranking of Athens above Madrid is an artefact, depending on the cut-off points chosen. While Athens had one more registered

* I am here indebted to my Greek friend and colleague Sokratis Koniordos and ditto my Portuguese friend José Luis Cardoso. A single, relatively modest high-rise built for the Lisbon event of 1998 failed to get enough office tenants.

high-rise than Madrid, the latter had thirteen more buildings taller than 100 metres. Actually, Madrid was among European pioneers of high-rise building, with the vanguard, 'organicist' White Towers of the 1960s. It is a 71-metre tower of eight cylindrical forms with semi-circular balconies, now looking a bit run down from the outside but still impressively original.*

A massive verticality of skyscrapers is usually connected with urban novelty, in the form of new CBDs. The Parisian was the first in Europe. Having rejected one proposal in 1951, the city council launched a new business district in 1956 to be developed by a public body, EPAD. That was the beginning of La Défense, west of the city proper. EPAD intended it as an *ensemble monumental,* which it has become over the decades, under mounting business pressure for tall buildings, standing out all the more since President Giscard d'Estaing and public opinion stopped further skyscrapers.[68] The business towers of La Défense had become a public issue when they were found to disturb the view along the Champs Élysées and the Arc de Triomphe. Only the intervention of President Pompidou saved the business ambitions, but this led to a project of a 'Tête de la Défense', some kind of architectural portal. The competition was won by an unknown Danish architect, Johan Otto von Spreckelsen, with a simple but genial design, a white 'open cube' of two thin 'office slabs with a lid on',[69] which came to correspond beautifully to the Arc de Triomphe and became known as the Grande Arche de la Défense. It was arguably the world's most successful connection of a new business district to a historical city.

The arch of La Défense got incorporated into President Francois Mitterrand's 'grand projects' for Paris, mainly aimed at updating Paris's nineteenth-century standing as the capital of world (read: Western) culture. This endeavour, also part of the contemporary global moment, was largely successful, but in terms of global iconicity it did not match two buildings erected under his predecessors: the Roissy Airport by Paul Andreu – not the most traveller-convenient airport, especially after all traffic expansion, but still the world's most original – and Beaubourg or Centre Pompidou, by Renzo Piano and Richard Rogers, which was selected after spirited jury work by Philip Johnson and became a global

---

* It was designed by the Spanish architect Francisco Javier Sáenz de Oiza for a private real-estate firm, Huarte, and houses apartments, offices and a rooftop swimming pool.

model of postmodernism. Mitterrand himself did choose a remarkable global monument the daring, non-national yet elegant and unobtrusive glass pyramid by I. M. Pei in the courtyard of the historical Louvre, as a canopy to the museum entrance.

Next was the new business centre of Madrid. It had been planned in the last decade of the Franco dictatorship and indeed implemented an idea in the 1940 master plan for Madrid. It is called AZCA, where A stands for the mixed corporate association of the development of the Zona Comercial de la Avenida del Generalísimo. The latter is the north-south artery of Madrid, known among democrats earlier, then and after, as Paseo de la Castellana. AZCA was a northern prolongation of the Paseo, opened (in 1996) by two inward reclining towers (by Philip Johnson and John Burgee), the Gate of Europe, and featuring a set of ambitious business towers with the Torre Picasso, a white striped rectangular tower by Minoru Yamasaki (who also designed the Twin Towers of New York). In 2007, ill-timed just before the crash, this prolongation was further prolonged by a Four Towers district, of which Norman Foster and César Pelli were the most famous authors. In spite of its deviant high-rise defiance, AZCA and the Four Towers fit remarkably well into the Madrid cityscape, neither a rival centre nor an ostentatious enclave but an extension of the city.

For all its globalism, the district remains nationally embedded. On your way up to it (from the old centre) you pass one of the world's rare, perhaps unique, monuments to a Constitution, the 1978 one of post-Franco democracy. Then, just before entering the Gate of Europe – built by the Kuwait Investment Office – you stand by a monument 'of Spain' to the extreme right politician José Calvo Sotelo, who was, after ordering another assassination, killed in the tensions leading up to the military uprising of 1936 and the Civil War. In 2016 Sotelo was taken down by the newly elected left-wing city government.

Since the end of World War I, Vienna has been a big city without a big country. After World War II and the peace treaty of 1955, the national and city governments in tandem have strived to remake Vienna an international metropolis and a UN meeting-place. In this vein the Vienna International Centre opened in 1979 as the start of a UN city on a Danube island. Since the late 1990s this has expanded into a business and entertainment area, Donau City, with a cluster of skyscrapers driven by a consortium of Austrian banks.

Remarkably, all post-war changes occurred in Vienna under the same label of Social Democratic government which had been in power since 1920. Whereas in 1930 a Social Democratic magazine had proudly proclaimed that 'the Red Million City is the hope and the advancement of the working people of all capitalist countries in the world',[70] in 2004 the city presents itself beside an office-tower picture as 'a top location for business'. Donau City was promoted in 1994 as an example of 'large projects [which] should bring international investors to Vienna'. In 2004, the city withdrew from public housing.[71]

In contrast to the three above, built mainly by national private or public capital, though for an increasingly globalized clientele, London's new business centre at Canary Wharf was global from the start, as we noted above, even if crucially backed up by a conservative national government.

We shall also look at two European capitals in which the contemporary global moment is secondary to national political concerns. Neither the Hague nor Berlin is very much entangled in global capitalism. Yet both have recently transformed themselves in very ambitious and interesting ways.

The rather high high-rise rank of the Hague is noteworthy, given its limited size and relative domesticity. It is part of a significant Dutch high-rise urbanism, even more evident in Rotterdam and Amsterdam and largely absent or only belatedly embryonic in Scandinavia. The Hague is remarkable on its own, for two reasons. First, in terms of general city remaking, it is arguably the most successful inner-city transformation of any major historical city, at least in Europe and perhaps in the world. It was undertaken in the two decades from around 1990 to 2010 as a vigorous city and state response to an Anglo-Saxon-type inner-city decline and middle-class suburbanization. Around the Central Station a high-rise modernist area has been constructed, which is connected to the lower, more historical rest of the city centre by an exquisite postmodernist quarter, the Resident, of medium height and in variable shapes. The high-rise Wine Harbour Quarter by the station was laid out by the American architect Richard Meier and the Resident by the Luxembourgian Rob Krier. The city's striving for global iconic status is most tellingly exemplified by a forty-two-story twin set of residential towers called The Iron, by a local architect.[71]

Second, most of the city's new high-rises and other modern buildings are not corporate towers but public buildings. While the new city hall is a rather unremarkable functionalist complex, the national government has provided itself with a group of skyscrapers, occasionally shared with business renters. The Ministries of Justice and the Interior occupy the tallest (and least interesting) and the Ministries of Education and Welfare are installed in the most striking, designed by the New York firm Kohn Pedersen Fox. The Ministry of Foreign Affairs got its new home in 1984, a large but unostentatious curved medium-height structure with the look of middle-class condominiums.*

A rather specialized political and administrative centre, the Hague has never been a stronghold of radical politics – but its city and national governments, the latter under a centrist Labour-led coalition in the 1990s, have shown that even in a country wide open to global capital, cities have different options.

Berlin is the lonely heart of Europe, centrally located geographically but no traffic hub, the political pump of EU economic circulation but itself a capital of relative poverty and as such attractive to young artists and writers for its (still) cheap rents. Rather than a global moment, Berlin is living a *new national moment*, of German reunification with the Western absorption of East Germany. Berlin's world-city discussion was in the 1910s and 1920s and it has not yet returned.†

The city has some high-rises, but in the class of over 100 metres, Berlin ranks only as number nine among European capitals, after Moscow, London, Paris, Warsaw, Brussels, Madrid, Kiev and Vienna. Strict height regulations have been imposed in the reconstruction of the new, unified central city and many proposals for skyscrapers, concrete ones by architects, generally by developers, have been rejected. The city's official 1992 'Principles of Town Planning' did acknowledge, 'in view of the demand pressure for office space with an image-conscious construction stamp [*baulicher Ausprägung*] after the model of leading world cities as high-rise cities', the need to pay

---

* See the lavish picture album by van Oppen 2012. I have also been lucky in being able to consult the Amsterdam geography professor Herman van der Wusten and my Dutch friend Don Kalb.

† The leading political weekly of Germany, *Der Spiegel*, did try half-heartedly in its 6 September 1999 issue, announcing its cover story as 'Aufbruch zur Weltstadt' (Decamping for the World City), but the story itself does not elaborate the idea.

attention to the 'height profile' of the city. However, that had to be approached in a differentiated manner. In the city centre 25 metres should be the maximum height; while high-rises were conceivable outside, they would have to respect the view of the 'typical Berlin [building] dominants'.[72] As it turned out, the demand for office space in Berlin was soon satisfied. Instead of aspiring to become a global business city, the Berlin city planners concentrated on making different versions of a middle-class city.[73] Incessant pressure by some architects and developers has recently led to a loosening of height restrictions in and around Alexanderplatz, a hub of former East Berlin. The outcome so far is not impressive.

A very active and broad public and political opinion has given priority to respecting the history of the city's pre-war and pre-Nazi patrimony. This was on its way to take a bizarre expression in the decision to rebuild the imperial palace of the Wilhelmine Reich. In the end a seemingly good compromise was found: the façade of the palace will be rebuilt, but the building will be part of an ensemble of cultural institutions, the Humboldt Forum, in a quite new design (by Franco Stella) of the Palace Square, turning it into a big cultural courtyard.

The two largest building projects of reunified Berlin included no CBD. One was building a new government centre; the other was the Potsdamer Platz area, a pre-war social and traffic centre in the eastern part, which had been devastated by the war and then turned into a wasteland by the city division. The government edifices were designed according to principles of democratic architecture developed in Western Germany after Nazism, though they shed the pronounced small-scale modesty of the Bonn Republic and were more adjusted to a great Germany: light construction, glass transparency and public accessibility. The Chancellor's Office, with a narrow glass façade hiding its huge back bulge; the Reichstag, with a new glass cupola which citizens (and other visitors) can walk up to look down at the MPs; and the open grass space between the Reichstag and the Chancellor's Office, on which kids can play football, are the best realizations of the idea. The West German political elite was the decisive force in shaping the new architecture of German power. Key words were 'confidence, modesty, dignity' (Chancellor Kohl on the new Chancellor's Office) and 'an unmistakeable yet unobtrusive building' (President Herzog on the new Presidential Palace).[74]

The Potsdamer Platz project was guided by the city government and intended to reintegrate the eastern and western divisions of the core of the city. It was left to four different private developers, within a public set of guidelines (and legal height regulations), although a few relatively modest high-rises were allowed. The two largest lots were given to Daimler-Benz and Sony, which launched two rather different neighbourhoods of offices, shopping and entertainment, one designed (successfully, in my opinion) by Renzo Piano as a (post)-modern version of a European city tradition, the other, by the German-American Helmut Jahn, more inspired by US commercial centres. A third part, the Beisheim Centre, is built as an updated *quartier bourgeois* of serene residences, discreet professional offices and two expensive, moderately sized hotels.

Berlin's second national moment had, of course, an iconographic dimension. For its first twenty-five years (at least) it has not been focused on national unity, not to speak of national glory or victory over Communism. Instead, in a strikingly original way, it has concentrated on national remorse and national shame. There came the Jewish Museum by Daniel Liebeskind; the prime central site 'Memorial of the Murdered Jews of Europe' by Peter Eisenmann, a field of concrete slabs very close to Brandenburger Tor; followed by a less central memorial to the murdered and persecuted Roma and Sinti in a corner of the Tiergarten; followed by a much smaller commemoration of the Nazi persecution of homosexuals. And there is the final development of the Topography of Terror project into a systematic informational museum of Nazi repression and genocide. National Berlin is a unique manifestation of national expiation and repentance.

The implosion of Communism meant a restoration of capitalism, first of all of global capitalism, in search of new markets and profitable investment, sending experts on selling public property, firing employees and cutting social benefits. No restoration of pre-Communist national capitalism was possible, but under the new global dispensation, new national variants of free-for-all capitalism could develop.

The Russian was the most brutal of all. According to the great British epidemiologist Sir Michael Marmot, the restoration of capitalism led to 4 million extra deaths from 1989 to 1999 in the former USSR.[75] At one pole, enormous private fortunes were made by grabbing formerly public assets of oil, gas and minerals; at the other pole, mass unemployment and mass impoverishment were created. This was the time when the Mayor of Moscow announced (in 1999) that in the next fifteen years sixty forty-storey high-rises would be built. (Conveniently, the mayor's wife, Yelena Baturina, owned what had become one of the city's largest construction and real-estate companies.)

The Moscow designed by Yuri Luzhkov, mayor from 1992 to 2010 (then fired by President Medvedev for fraud), was a city of Russian imperial capitalism. While aiming to make Moscow a financial centre of global capitalism, the design reconnected with the Orthodox Church, now an ostentatious part of Russian official life, rebuilding the Christ the Saviour Cathedral – once dynamited by Stalin for the never-built Palace of Soviets – and with Tsarist traditions, commissioning a huge statue of Tsar Peter I standing on a ship of concrete by the Moscow River. Tsarist emulation is also on full display in the current televised Kremlin interior décor and protocol. The enormous residential 'Triumph Palace' in northern Moscow evokes another Russian tradition, a capitalist variant of Stalinist Realism in its affinity with the seven high-rises of the 1940s.

However, the rehabilitation of Tsarism and the resurrection of the state-church marriage and of national Russian traditions are, of course, only one side of capitalist Moscow. The other is modernist, or post-modernist.[76] The Moscow City began in the early 1990s as a project of the mayor, with the leading Moscow building firm as constructor. Building was suspended in 2010 for economic reasons and looks too big for the current economic situation and prospects of Russia. But several tall buildings have been completed, including Europe's highest to date: the OKO Tower, built by the US firm SOM for the Russian real-estate developer Capital Group. The City has already four completed buildings higher than 300 metres. But the one intended to become Europe's tallest, the eastern (Vostok) of the two Federation Towers, for another Moscow real-estate firm, has been scheduled for 2016.

Moscow City in particular and the new European business districts generally, except Canary Wharf, are more manifestations of global aspirations of national capital than of national ambitions of global capital. The developers are local firms; architecture and engineering are in Moscow both domestic and international, but without recourse to iconic celebrities. The buildings try to develop specific forms, but their main competitive asset is their height.[77] The core buildings are corporate investments in mixed-use buildings of offices, luxury apartments and high-end entertainment, not branded corporate headquarters. The toponymy of the Moscow City high-rises are notably national: the Federation Tower, Eurasia Tower, the twin Capital City Towers (referring to the two official capitals, Moscow and Saint Petersburg).

Post-Communist Warsaw hosts an iconic Stalinist skyscraper, the Palace of Culture and Science, designed by Lev Rudnev, who also laid out the Moscow State University, the two highest skyscrapers of the world outside the United States in the 1950s. There was naturally strong anti-Communist pressure to demolish it, though this would be neither easy nor cheap, and it fulfilled a number of cultural functions. In the end, the city government opted for embedding and overshadowing it in a grove of capitalist skyscrapers. The economic means, and perhaps the final political drive, seem to have been lacking for that, although Warsaw has become an important financial centre of the region. There are now a set of high-rises around the Culture Palace, hotels and corporate offices, obviously more contemporary but hardly more striking and none beating the palace in height. The latter still functions as a major cultural centre of the city and seems to be rather widely accepted as a historical landmark. As a city icon it still has no rival.

From the Eastern European skyscraper list, three absences, Belgrade, Budapest and Prague and one contrasting presence, of Bratislava, call for a comment, however brief. Belgrade has built three buildings taller than 100 metres since 1980 and has not been able to globalize very well, as Serbia lost the wars of the Yugoslav Succession due to US interventions. It has built no new skyscraper until now. Prague and Bratislava both had two skyscrapers taller than 100 metres before 1989 and both cities have got into high capitalist growth, fuelled by foreign investment. In the 2000s the rise of Bratislava, without the great history of Prague and Budapest, has been remarkable, into the sixth most prosperous region of the EU, measured in purchasing power parities, ahead of Prague and of Stockholm. Bratislava completed three towers taller than 100 metres in the 2000s and recently Penta Investments – with offices in Jersey, UK, as well as in Prague and Bratislava – has contracted Zaha Hadid for a mixed-use complex in a new city centre. It is scheduled for 2019, but has already been scaled down (and perhaps may wind down after the death of Hadid). Budapest has kept stringent height regulations of 55 metres and high-rise proposals have been rejected,* in tune with the contemporary conservative nationalist government. The tallest building is the Parliament (of 1903), at 96 metres. Like high Stalinism, globalizing post-Communism has its national variety, and European city tradition still weighs upon the fervently capitalist capitals of Eastern Europe.

Settler capitalism has a specific brash – or simply nouveau-riche – character from making huge profits in a new country. As we have seen above, skyscrapers originated in the Americas, spreading from New York and Chicago to Montreal and Toronto and trickling down to Mexico City, São Paulo and Buenos Aires before getting any foothold in Eurasia (outside the USSR) or Africa. However, settler politics in the British Empire and after generated new, specialized political capitals not run by capital.

In Washington, D.C., the US Congress has so far kept stringent height rules, probably the one major American city where political power is still keeping business developers at bay. But in contrast to the other specialized political capitals, Washington is also, as we saw in table 3 above, significantly enmeshed in global corporate networks. As the seat of the World Bank and the IMF, Washington is furthermore the most important 'command post' of global economic governance.

Notable in Latin America is the absence of skyscrapers in the modernist capital, Brasília, underlining my previous argument that architectural modernism was not intrinsically wedded to skyscrapers. Brasília has become a large city, but it is the national capital of a big, nationally self-centred country. Like Berlin, it has a good national life in the world, but without globalist yearnings. Opposite to the absence of Brasília is the presence of Panama City, in which eighteen skyscrapers above 200 metres have been completed since 2010. The high-rises of US and expatriate finance and leisure capital overwhelm the peninsula of the national centre.

Mexico is *the* city of Latin American verticality, among cities of the southern hemisphere, not only the capitals. While the first Latin American high-rises of 100 metres or more were built in the 1920s and 1930s in Buenos Aires and São Paulo, the Torre Latinoamericana, of the insurance company by that name, was for a long time after the

---

* Judit Bodnar and her graduate student Judit Vere have been helpful guides to Budapest.

mid-1950s Latin America's tallest building, built well enough to survive the 1985 earthquake basically unscathed. Since the neoliberal turn of 1988 and the 1994 North American Free Trade Agreement, the global push in Mexico City has materialized in two areas: a new business district, Santa Fe, and the vertical transformation of one of the main avenues of the city, Paseo de la Reforma, which 'represents everything that this city and this country has desired to be in modern times', the official tourist guide has written.[78] It is not much of a promotional exaggeration. As noted earlier, the Paseo was made a parade ground of national and liberal iconography in the last third of the nineteenth century. Major statues of Columbus and of the last Aztec emperor Cuauhtémoc were raised in the middle of the avenue; on low pedestals along the sidewalks were minor ones of the pantheon of Mexican liberal nationalism. For the centenary of the revolt against Spain, the Angel of History, turned into an Angel of Independence, was hoisted on to a high column further down the street. The column was later proclaimed the Altar of the Fatherland. Adjacent to the Paseo is also a 1952 monument to economic nationalism, the *Fuente de Petróleos* (Fountain of Oil), commemorating the nationalization of the oil industry in 1938. From 1984 to 2003, the tallest building in Mexico was the Executive Tower of the state oil company, Pemex.

Today, the grand avenue might be called Paseo del Nacionalismo al Globalismo. Walk southwest along the tree-lined boulevard, preferably on a Sunday without car traffic, from the Glorieta Simón Bolívar and you can watch how the national iconography is increasingly overwhelmed first by international hotels and then by corporate skyscrapers.* Particularly the Zona Rosa – once a bohemian quarter allegedly named after Edith Piaf's *La Vie en Rose* – has become a battlefield of corporate competition, not for a world but a regional or at least national championship of height. From 2003 to 2010 the Torre Mayor was the Latin American champion and until 2016 the national. It was developed by Paul Reichmann, the key Reichmann brother behind Olympia and York of Canary Wharf notoriety. In February 2016 the Spanish bank BBVA opened its Bancomer Tower nearby, which – after adding five metres to its original plan – overtook Reichmann's tower, but probably only for

* See also the great boulevard monograph by Carlos Martínez Assad, *La Patria en el Paseo de la Reforma*, Mexico City: Fondo de Cultura Económica, 2005.

months rather than years. Well under way and planned for opening is Torre Reforma, still ten or eleven metres higher.

As in Europe outside London, we find in Mexico an imbrication of national and global forces and interests, under the auspices of the former. The global Torre Mayor developed in tandem with the then-chief of government in the Mexico Federal District, the left-of-centre Andrés Manuel López Obrador (AMLO), whose government also included a popular moment, as we have seen. In a joint press conference with AMLO, Reichmann claimed that his tower was a physical representation of the economic force of Mexico.[79] The Mexican developers of the upcoming Torre Reforma are explicitly flaunting the 'Mexican construction' of their steel skyscraper, in contrast to the 'big glazed volumes' of 'so-called "international architecture"'. In truth, the most convincing argument was probably: 'The enterprises forming part of it will enjoy the prestige and the reputation which a building like this transfers'.*

The new business district in Western Mexico City, Santa Fe, which was projected in the 1970s, started in the 1980s and took off in the 1990s, remains well behind the southwestern end of Paseo de la Reforma in corporate significance, but it is clearly a purpose-built business city. It is built for private cars; a public pedestrian is suspect. It does have several architecturally interesting buildings, more stylish than tall, but when your writer was taking a picture of one he was immediately assaulted by a small platoon of private guards who demanded the film, 'private copyright'. The separate business and residential buildings are closed in on themselves. However, for all its exclusive, private image, Santa Fe was launched by a public consortium of the national and the city governments and its first building was a progressive Jesuit university.

The tallest building of Latin America today is the 300-metre tall Gran Torre of Santiago de Chile, completed in 2014. It was built by an old Chilean construction firm and designed by César Pelli, with local collaborators. Santiago has also created a special Ciudad Empresarial (Entrepreneurial City), more visitor-friendly than Santa Fe but without any striking architecture. Only 30 per cent of its enterprises are multinational.

---

* The architect is local, although with some Latin American productions outside Mexico: Benjamin Romano.

Bogotá's reach for the skies is more international. Spanish capital is financing its coming height champion, the hotel plus mixed-use BD Bacatá, at 260 metres. Its current one, Colpatria, is actually, despite its name, a part of the Canadian Scotiabank. Next in rank is, tellingly, Centro de Comercio Internacional (World Trade Centre), the latter completed in 1979. Lima is a historical city without high-rise modernism, but it has had strong economic growth in the last two decades which has yielded a couple of transnational towers, of rather limited height (at most 120 metres). Noteworthy is that from 1976 to 2001, the tallest building of Peru was the Civic Centre in Lima (102 metres).

Rich, brash Buenos Aires was among the pioneers of high-rise construction outside the United States in the 1920 and 1930s, but its post–World War II development has been less spectacular, except for its crash in 2001. Buenos Aires is not competing at 200 metres and above. The major urbanistic project in recent times has been a waterfront project, in part inspired by Barcelona's successful Olympic development, Puerto Madero. The area does include business towers, but the main focus is on leisure and residence, including high-rise condominiums. Like Santa Fe but probably more so, Puerto Madero is developed and run by a joint national and city government body, with a rotating presidency. Over the years, the district seems to have become more national and less multinational.

The Latin American settlers have always strived to become and be recognized as members of the First World, of their motherlands or, increasingly, of their big brother in the north and of First World 'global cities'. Though the latter is a very fuzzy set, few would argue that any Latin American city has fully arrived yet.* In organizing their efforts, some big Latin American capitals (Mexico City and Buenos Aires), appear more similar to European ones in the significance of public actors, national as well as local, than to US cities (outside Washington). But in their (varying) vertical ambitions and in their tolerance or even promotion of inequality, segregation and a deeply fractured quality of living, they are all quite similar to their big brother.

The colonial experience brought Africa and Asia together as subject to the same empires, with their oppression, racism and modernization. The struggle for national independence and the tasks of turning an

* The main contender would be São Paulo.

imperial colony into a nation-state were basically similar. Peripheral status in the world economy was a commonality of ex-colonial countries, but their capacity for confronting it was vastly different, for historical reasons too difficult and complicated to be explained here. In the current global moment there is a major divide of the ex-colonial zone, between sub-Saharan Africa on one hand, and Asia and North Africa on the other.

In addtion national experiences separated colonies from countries surviving by reactive modernization. Under current capitalist globalization this group separation has become less significant, while individual national developments still leave their imprint, for example on Addis Ababa, Bangkok, Tehran and Tokyo, as well as on the ex-colonial capitals.

As we saw above in table 3, Cairo is more entangled in global capitalism than Stockholm and Manila more than Rome, but only Nairobi, of capitals south of Sahara, is better corporately connected than Minsk. Even so, it is well below Wellington, at the end of the world.

Nairobi is the capital of free-wheeling Kenyan capitalism, a UN meeting-ground and the seat of the UN Habitat. In 2008 it announced its ambition of becoming a 'world-class African metropolis' by 2030. With Pretoria, it is the only sub-Saharan capital on the skyscraper centre list of the 200 cities with highest number of tall buildings. While still harbouring a couple of the world's largest slums, Nairobi did upgrade itself in the first decade of the current century, including comfortable inner-city buses, functioning public telephones and clean public toilets, as well as shopping malls deliberately built to discourage visitors coming on foot from the street and mainly catering to White expatriates. Independent Nairobi has always had a flamboyant character, which included high-rise buildings. But while a Kuwaiti Hazina Tower may be built and trump everything, so far the high-rises have been national: the insurance-company UPA Tower of 2015, the local *Daily Times* building of 1997, the governmental Kenyatta International Conference Centre of 1974 and the Social Security House of 1973. All are above 100 metres and below 200.

Once, about fifteen years ago, I flew into Abidjan, the capital of Côte d'Ivoire, from Mali. Coming from a vast, dusty and friendly village with occasional public buildings built decades earlier by the Soviets,

Yugoslavs and Chinese, the Abidjan central plateau in its lagoon looked like an African Manhattan. Driving around central Abidjan was like driving in a proper city and, for a Scandinavian, even a high-rise one. The 1980s cocoa boom put an end to Abidjan's ambitions, returning the centrality of Francophone West Africa to Dakar. Abidjan does have four buildings higher than 100 metres, two of them public but all built by 1984. In terms of global capitalist connectivity Abidjan has become negligible, albeit currently recovering; it is well below Accra and Maputo, for instance in verticality above 100 metres. Maputo is more a national than a global assertion, as its two leading skyscrapers are the state central bank and another national bank. Although there are global aspirations, driven by the early twenty-first century boom, in Lagos as well as in Nairobi and global inspirations all over, the full moment of global capitalism is only beginning to change sub-Saharan African cities. Change is visible, though, even in once-sleepy Dar es Salaam, where the national Bank of Tanzania has inspired a recent skyscraper development.[80]

Cairo, unlike all sub-Saharan capitals, is quite well connected in the world of multinational corporations, presumably as a metropolitan gateway to a substantial and solvent Arab market. However, Cairo is not in the global race of the Arab peninsula. Its tallest building, at the Arabically modest height of 143 metres, dates from 1994 and is the Foreign Ministry building. Among its twenty tallest buildings, only two are private offices, three are public offices, three are international hotels and the rest are part of a south city residential complex.

As we are here concerned with nation-states and their capitals, I leave out the high-towering dynastic ambitions of the monarchies of the Arab peninsula, while noting, as above, that they are leading the pack for the skies.

There is also a clear-cut divide inside Asia between the two most populous regions of the South and of the East, more with respect to verticality than to corporate connectivity. Of Asia's twenty tallest buildings, four are in the Arab peninsula and all the rest in East Asia, of which ten are in mainland China. The absence of Delhi is quite remarkable. Disregarding a radio mast, its tallest building is the minaret Qutb Minar, completed in 1368. Delhi has, so far, been built more for the state than for capital.

In Mumbai, on the other hand, there has recently been a capitalist and high-rise boom. Since 2009, nineteen buildings of 173 metres and more have been completed, topped by a residential 'Palais royale' [sic] at 320 metres, not yet completed and legally contested. The new business city Gurgaon outside Delhi will get a tower of 178 metres in 2016. Asian capitals between the Arab peninsula and Thailand are short on, but not without, skyscrapers, which underlines the singularity of Delhi, after independence no longer a specialized political capital but a big metropolis. Tehran has a 2007 International Tower of 162 metres; Islamabad – which remains a specialized political centre – recently got a 200-metre hotel and a telephone company tower above 100 metres; Dhaka has, since 2006, added four office and bank towers to its central bank building.

The new capital of Myanmar, Naypyidaw, has no skyscrapers but instead three gigantic statues of medieval kings. The power style of the buildings in this spread-out, often empty-looking city is assured by horizontal distance. Most public buildings, even the city hall, are fenced off and built at a considerable distance from the road. The old capital, Yangon, is a somewhat dilapidated nineteenth–twentieth century city, where Hilton opened a high-rise hotel in 2014.

The East Asia of skyscrapers starts in Bangkok with a quintet of residences and hotels above 200 metres with varying ownership, the tallest Thai-owned. At the same time, the non-colonial history of Bangkok remains on lavish display through its royalist (non-architectural) iconography. Vietnam is following China along the capitalist road with gusto. It has designated a special international business district in Hanoi whose highest buildings are South Korean, including the Landmark Tower, about twenty metres higher than the London Shard.

High-rise construction has been frenetic in the region, fuelled by commodities and the (now ended) oil boom: from 2006 to 2016, Jakarta completed nineteen buildings above 210 metres, Kuala Lumpur eighteen above 200 and Metro Manila twenty between 2009 and 2014. Few are headquarters or regional offices of private banks and corporations. Many have mixed uses: offices, residences, hotels and/or shopping. As in Bangkok, the thrust in Manila and Jakarta seems to come from real-estate speculators, domestic and international, openly disregarding planning regulations. Private capitalist development in Jakarta also includes whole suburban cities built and governed by private developers.*

Kuala Lumpur stands out for its state capitalism. To the two Petronas Towers, a third Petronas Tower has been added and a new state-directed building is under construction, Warisan Merdeka (Heritage of Independence), planned for 644 metres. The Kuala Lumpur high-rises clearly have architectural ambitions, including contributions by Pelli and Foster, but the architecture centre of South-east Asia remains Kuala Lumpur's nearest rival, Singapore, the master builder of state capitalism. Its latest coup is the Marina Bay Sands complex, opened in 2010, the most spectacular feature of which is a triad of skyscrapers topped and connected by a 'skypark'. The government laid down a detailed set of specific development demands, for which a bid by the US casino mogul Sheldon Adelson and a design by the Israeli architect Moshe Safdie was accepted.

In Northeast Asia the power pattern is also varied, although nowhere is foreign capital the dominant actor. At one end is Pyongyang, where the quasi-dynastic state holds all the reins. No corporate buildings, but a score of high-rises taller than 100 metres, three of them hotels and the rest apartment buildings. The residential high-rises, together with some well-made sports complexes, convey an air of modernity to the city. In Seoul and Tokyo, the forest of skyscrapers does manifest the wealth and the power of national private capital, but within effective planning in Seoul and in Tokyo alongside a uniquely resourceful metropolitan government.

The South Korean upper class tends to live in villas in the mountains, but by, say, Mexican class criteria they are not ostentatious. Guards can be spotted around some of them, but the streets are not closed off. Asking for a gated community, I was taken to a concierged high-rise in a posh district of Gangnam (a new business and residential part of the

---

* On Jakarta 'super-blocks' overtaking planning permits by factors of two and three, see H. Cairns and E. Friedrich, 'Big floods, hard infrastructure and "weak" plans: Megacity vulnerability and the case for diversified instruments for city-making,' pp. 146–65 in Saskia Sassen, Fulong Wu, et al., *Cities in Transition: Power, Environment, Society,* Rotterdam: NAi010, 2015: 152. Private property rights trump any common good planning. A friend of mine showed me in January 2014 how her garden had lost its access to the sun because of a wall her neighbour had built. There was no public authority to complain to.

city south of the Han River, developed since the mid-1970s) with a little playground in front, which was accessible to an obviously alien-looking visitor like me. Novelty in globalizing Seoul is, first of all, a move south across the Han River. Gangnam, South Bank, has become a 'style' of mass culture, as well as the new centre of business. Invoking early 1970s South Korean forays into international construction, the main business street of Gangnam was originally Teheran-ro. In its nation, Seoul is a very dominant city, like Bangkok, Jakarta, Kuala Lumpur, Manila and, increasingly, Tokyo, but it is a testimony to national planning that out of the twenty current tallest buildings of South Korea, only seven are in Seoul, including the highest by far, the Korean Lotte World Tower (556 metres), designed by Kohn Pedersen Fox.

As noted above, Beijing seems to have given up in the intense Chinese race for the skies. Currently, not a single one of China's twenty tallest buildings is in Beijing. However, Beijing is definitely in the running in global iconic architecture. From the Olympics there are Norman Foster's new airport and Herzog & de Meuron's Bird's Nest stadium, Paul Andreu's National Theatre by the Tiananmen and Rem Koolhaas's TV headquarters. Worth noting about Beijing's architectural development are two more things. More than other capitals, it makes use of international star architects (although not exclusively), from grand corporate collectives like the American SOM and KPF or the Japanese Nikken Sekkei to the individually iconized firms of Norman Foster, Zaha Hadid and John Portman. This is, of course, a product of resources and ambition. Second, Chinese media also have a predilection for the skies in building. Three of the twenty tallest Beijing buildings are for television and a fourth is for the *People's Daily* newspaper. Beijing manifests a more political globalism than capitalist Shanghai

Tokyo is the high-rise capital city of the world. Jakarta has as many buildings above 200 metres, but Tokyo leads the 100-metre league 177 to 109 and the 150-metre list 117 to 60. Sky-scraping did not come early to Tokyo, for long a vast, low-rise city. The first tall building, an unremarkable functionalist slab of thirty-six floors in the government quarter of Kasumigaseki, was erected in 1968.

From the rich urbanism of Tokyo, the non-Western originality of which I first discovered in 1977, adding crucially to my infatuation with global studies, I would here highlight two contradictory features. One is the power of private property, which you notice from the often strange heterogeneity of central city streets: odd, incongruous buildings catching your eye from all sides. The opposite of this is the harmonious state-imposed homogeneity of the *grand boulevards de Paris*, for instance the Avenue de l'Opéra. As a political urbanist in Tokyo you will never forget the prime minister's bungalow: elevated on a low hill, but overshadowed by a non-descript high-rise of an unremarkable insurance company. The positive side of this private power is the large-scale, publicly accessible urban developments by Japanese capital, mimicking the Rockefeller Center of New York. Like their New York model, they are well planned, culturally oriented and public, but much more green, for example, than the Roppongi Hills of 2003 by the Mori group, the Mid-Town Centre of 2007 by Mitsui and the Tokyo Skytree City of 2012.

The second feature of Tokyo to be underlined is the resourcefulness of its metropolitan government. As we just saw, it is not something arising from legal planning power but from tax-based income. Whereas the 2010 budgets of London, Paris and New York totalled around 1 per cent of their countries' national budgets, Tokyo's was 13 per cent of Japan's.[81] In the 1980s the governor of Tokyo decided to build a new metropolitan headquarters, although the previous one had been completed in 1959, creating a new vertical centre of the city in Shinjuku around the new grand government complex, on land which the city happened to own. It was built by Japan's first-rank star architect Kenzō Tange, who also had built the previous city hall, now torn down, with typical Japanese lack of interest in construction permanence. The third-tallest building in this now very competitive race is still the city hall of 1991, for sixteen years the peak of built Japan.[82]

Exclusivity and Urban Privatization

The global moment of urban connectivity is at the same time a moment of important urban social disconnection. The most blatant and brutal manifestation of the latter is gating: the construction of walled and fenced-off privileged enclaves, so-called 'gated communities', although they may not be very much of a community. In the international urban literature, the notion got traction in the 1990s.*

---

* By far the best empirical overview as well as a literature compass is the volume *Private Cities*, edited by Goerg Glasze, Chris Webster and Klaus Frantz, New York: Routledge,

The link between globalism and gating exclusivity has to be sorted out with some care, however. It is not self-evident that the same process which has brought multi-cultural music, fashion and cuisine to world cities should generate social exclusion. And intra-urban gating is an ancient phenomenon (extensively deployed in imperial Beijing, as noted above) and characteristic of classical Islamic cities. The top *nomenklatura* of the Communist regimes had their fenced-off and well guarded residences, such as the Mayakovsky Ring in East Berlin Pankow and the surveilled *dachas* outside Moscow. Furthermore, the term and modern practices of 'gated communities' emerged in that most provincial society, the United States, primarily in southern California in the late 1950s and early 1960s, after an initial launch in the 1930s.[83] Nobody knows how many there are in almost any city, let alone in the whole world, and there is no clear consensus of how to fence off the concept. Two British scholars claim to have identified 'around 1,000' gated communities in England, for instance.[84] But this seems to mean (necessarily) no more than a housing estate, to which entrance is by key or punch card only, a definition which de facto amounts to a trivialization of the phenomenon.

When I talk of gating here, I am primarily referring to secluded private cities or private urban areas to which the public has no access rights and in which modern urban services have been privatized, at a minimum through policing, but often also in cleaning, garbage collection and utilities and sometimes kindergarten, schools and leisure facilities.

This kind of gating is mainly a late-twentieth-century phenomenon, reversing a more than century-old expansion of public urban services. It has two quite different but contingently related causes. The first is a reassertion of upper-middle-class privilege in a maturing pioneer-settler society: southern California, Arizona and other parts of the US Sunbelt.[85] Operating under weak US municipal legislation, urbanized enclosure is developed to keep up house values, avoid or minimize taxes and keep out people of low income and dark skin colour. These exclusivist 'homeowners' associations' were behind the notorious

---

2006. There is also a thinner volume edited by Samer Bagaeen and Ola Uduku, *Gated Communities*, New York: Routledge, 2010, and Thierry Paquot's *Ghettos des riches*, Paris: Perrin, 2009.

Proposition 13 of 1970s California, which crippled state taxation for a generation.

California and the US Sunbelt are provincial, but there is a connection to later global developments, safe-keeping upper-middle-class privilege and opting out of any commonality with the national plebs. The first link between US provincialism and the global moment was probably the Alphaville complex of gated areas in a suburb of São Paulo, dating from the 1970s. São Paulo had become the South American hub of industrial world capitalism; money was flooding in, adding to the stark historical inequality of Brazil. The extended Castelo Branco highway connected the new suburb with the CBD. There might have been another historical link running via Manila, until World War II a US colony. My first personal experience of privatized gated cities was in Manila in the 1990s, taking notice of the closed-off streets and their guards.

Anyway, the global breakthrough came in the 1990s. In Mexico City, for instance, gated neighbourhoods with 50,000 housing units were built from 1990 to 2012.[86] In Buenos Aires 29 per cent of all private investment between 1990 and 1998 went into gated communities.[87] Lots of former 'country clubs' have been converted into enclosed permanent upper-middle-class residences and a special private city has been built, the Nordelta. In Santiago, Chile, the enclosure wave got into gear in the first decade of this century[88] – like in Argentina after redemocratization, though with a sort of lag. In Malaysia and Kuala Lumpur the process took off after the financial crisis of 1997 and the state's withdrawal from housing,[89] while in Indonesia, Chinese developers started the process in the last years of the Suharto dictatorship.[90]

The 1990s were also when post-Communist global capitalism descended on Eastern Europe and China, spawning a rapid upper- and upper-middle-class urban exclusivism.[91] The impact on Tokyo and Seoul and on Western Europe (with some qualification for Madrid and Lisbon[92]) seems to have been marginal, at most.

The necessary infrastructure of fast motorways connecting central business districts and gated enclosures had started in Buenos Aires in the late 1970s, when the city was under the rule of General Osvaldo Cacciatore, and developed later in Santiago, post-Communist Moscow, Mexico City and Kuala Lumpur. In Budapest the new bourgeois developed another exclusive habitat of walled-off, guarded 'residential parks' inside the inner city. Between 2002 and 2007, 14,000 such dwellings were built.[93]

Exclusivist urban gating has become part of the current global moment of urban history in several ways and for several inter-connected reasons. Their globalism is first of all manifested in their pricing in US dollars and in their toponymy, which is usually extra-national. Among the new desert satellites, rigidly planned class-specific cities of Cairo to which the Stock Exchange has moved, you have gated areas called Golf City, Dreamland, Beverly Hills.[94] Around Beijing you can find not-very-welcoming areas called Chateau Glory, Palm Springs, Purple Jade Villas and Upper East Side.[95] While most global names are American, some are English ('Oxford', for example) or Mediterranean (including 'Venice'), one Russian closed development is advertised as 'Benelux', with the Luxembourg division for the richest.[96]

There are four main global mechanisms behind contemporary urban gated comunities. Most direct are the housing demands of multinational corporations, which then spill off into local business demands. Around 2000 in Beijing, 70 per cent of 'foreign housing' was bought by local businesspeople.[97] Second and most importantly, there is the global First World prestige and status vividly transmitted by globalized media and aspired to by world-city upper-middle-class inhabitants.[98] The other side of this coin is an abdication of the public authorities' responsibility to provide good urban services, quite explicit in cases like Jakarta and Kuala Lumpur. In the Third World, only an exclusive private development is presumed to provide First World urban services. Third, there is promotion by global development players, quite important in Africa and in Cairo (from Dubai and the Gulf).[99] Finally, underlying them all is a global upper-middle-class contempt and fear, in that order, of the popular classes. The global moment came not only after the most dramatic popular moments but, more generally, after major secular advances of the popular classes and their erosion or implosion: the welfare state in Western Europe, Communism in Eastern Europe, the New Deal in the United States, democratization in Latin America and in the world of reactive modernization, anti-colonial popular mobilizations in the ex-colonial zone, the end of apartheid in South Africa. Fear of crime is part of this, but to a greater extent these communities exemplify the fear of the poor exhibited by the rich.

Common to the provincial American and the global is upper-middle-class revulsion, contempt and fear of ordinary people; the contingent causal link between the two is a global diffusion of upper-middle-class admiration for the US upper-middle class, its consumption and its 'lifestyle'.

Verticality-cum-novelty and exclusivity do sum up the specificity of the global moment of urban history, while not eclipsing the national foundations or obliterating all memories of preceding popular moments. Urban social exclusion remains quite varied among nations.

In Western Europe, Patrick Le Galès and his collaborators found the upper-middle-class managers of Madrid and Paris well rooted in their cities and connected to their non-gated neighbourhoods.[100] In the first decade of this century there was a dramatic increase in social segregation in Madrid, Tallinn, and Stockholm, with the first two becoming the most segregated European capital regions and Stockholm reaching fourth place after London. Least segregated was Oslo out of a ranking of twelve cities and regions. Residential dissimilarity is related to but not very tightly correlated with economic inequality.[101] This is something also seen in Latin America. Buenos Aires is not one of the worst offenders in the fierce regional competition for the title of most-income-unequal city, but its highly educated stratum is the most exclusively segregating (with a dissimilarity index of 0.414, compared to, for instance, Brasilia's 0.258).[102]

Urban exclusivity and segregation are aspects of inequality – existential inequality, kindred to racism and sexism. Urban gating runs against an uneven but worldwide trend in the last few decades of trying to erode racism, patriarchy and sexual discrimination. But it accompanies a global tendency of mounting intra-national economic inequality.

There does not seem to be enough reliable data to make a metric table of urban economic inequality in the world. Even the UN Habitat databases include some incredible anomalies and self-contradictory data.* However, a broad world pattern is discernible, showing an interesting and rarely noticed picture.

---

* For instance, according to its latest income distribution table and the latest available *State of the World's Cities* (for 2012–13), Beijing should be the least unequal and most equitable city of the world; according to the same publication, Bucharest should have the third most equitable distribution of income, services and gender positions in the world, something which is clearly contradicted by another Habitat report, *The State of European Cities in Transition 2013*, 175.

Table 6. World patterns of urban economic inequality: capital cities

Least unequal[102]	Medium inequality[103]	High inequality[104]	Extreme inequality[105]
• European cities except Moscow, probably headed by Copenhagen and Oslo • Seoul and Tokyo	• Moscow • Most Asian capitals, incl. Beijing, Delhi and Jakarta • Some African cities: Brazzaville, Dakar, Dar es Salaam, Harare, Tunis • A few Latin American exceptions: Caracas, Lima, Montevideo	• Most African capitals, incl. Abidjan, Addis Ababa and Nairobi • All remaining Latin American capitals, except Brasília	• Washington, D.C. (0.61) • Brasília (0.67) • Tshwane (Pretoria) (0.72)

No correlations can be calculated at this point, but it is noteworthy that the least economically unequal capitals are also the ones in which gating exclusivity is least developed. The capitals of rapidly rising Asia are not emulating Latin American inequality, historically inherited from Iberian colonialism and slavery and replenished by recurrent military regimes. The trio of extreme inequality, Washington DC, Brasília and Tshwane C Pretoria, are not often seen together and their presence at the peak of inequality points to another noteworthy phenomenon. That is, current globalization is not *the* driver of urban economic inequality. None of the three is a top 'global city' in the economic sense. Furthermore, they tend to be at least as unequal as their respective nation's first global city,

---

* UN Habitat, 'Income distribution table, excl. Western Europe, North America and highly developed countries in Asia and Oceania', New York: United Nations, 2014, http://unhabitat.org; CEPAL, *State of Latin American Cities 2012*, fig. 2.6; *The State of Asian and Pacific Cities 2015*, table 2.16; *The State of African Cities 2014*, tables 5.8–5.9; *State of the World's Cities 2008/2009*, 65, 79, extrapolated from 1999 to 2012 assuming the inequality of Beijing has increased about as much it has in all China, according to *Inequality UN Habitat in Focus* 22, 2013. For Western Europe and Seoul, *State of the World's Cities 2012/2013*, table 1, equity index, after checks of national income statistics for Seoul. See H. Koo, 'Inequality in South Korea', *East Asia Forum*, 2014, eastasiaforum.org, for possible anomalies.

although the official records have to be read with a margin of error in mind. Washington appears statistically somewhat more unequal than New York City,[107] Tshwane slightly less unequal than Johannesburg, and Brasília more unequal than São Paulo.[108]

Image Capitalism and the Imagined
Tribe of Capitalist Globalism

I noted above a historical global moment in the globalization of nationalism and of what a national capital should look like to be 'worthy of the nation'. This global moment was concentrated in the last quarter of the nineteenth and the first decade of the twentieth century and was much inspired by the Paris of the Second Empire and Baron Haussmann. It focused on general street widening – a central task of 'modernization' in Cairo, Tokyo and Seoul, for instance – on laying out grand avenues and hubs of circulation and erecting dignified public buildings for culture – operas, theatres, etc. – as well as for politics. Paris was indeed the capital of the nineteenth century. The current global moment has no equivalent model city. The nearest is probably Singapore, the predominant role model of rising Asia.

In the new global style, the verticality of corporate skyscrapers and of their skylines to the tourist gaze has replaced the horizontality of the wide avenues and broad sidewalks of the flâneur; private malls have overtaken the public spaces of squares, cafés and teahouses; nervous fences, walls and barbed wire have followed upon the serene, open mansion neighbourhoods of the self-confident upper classes. Global nationalism was, of course, driven by local nationalists. More surprising, perhaps, is our finding that the current global capitalist moment and its proclaimed and aspiring 'global' or 'world' cities are driven mainly by national and local actors, by national developers and bankers and by local city politicians, usually with active national government support. Looking at skyscraper launches and new business district plans, we see this pattern all over the world: in Paris and Madrid; in Moscow, Beijing and Hanoi; in Mexico, Santiago and Buenos Aires; in Dar es Salaam and Nairobi; in Kuala Lumpur and Jakarta; in Tokyo and Seoul. The only clear exception was London, where the Canary Wharf project has all the time been driven by global capital and capitalists, albeit with decisive national government support initially.

East Asian politicians and intellectuals were more honest or lucid than their North Atlantic counterparts in explicitly conceptualizing 'globalization' as an option rather than as an external force you had either to adapt to (liberal interpretation) or resist (left-wing reading).

But why have so many national and local actors chosen the globalist option? Here I think a comparison of nationalism and globalism is fruitful. Benedict Anderson argued persuasively, in a brilliant work, that nationalism fed on imagining the nation as a community of people who had never met, and that the emergence of the nation as an 'imagined community' was crucially dependent on 'print capitalism'[109] – that is, on the commerce of books and newspapers, which made possible a leap of the imagination out of the local circle of people known to each other.

In a similar vein, current urban globalism is not so much a rule of cities by foreign or transnational capital as a striving by local upper and upper-middle classes and their urban managers and real estate developers to become part of an imagined community of global urbanity. Or, perhaps more exact, of an *imagined tribe*, hierarchical and competitive, of capitalist globality, a tribe of 'wealth creation', display and consumption. This imagined global tribe is dependent on global image capitalism*: that is, on a commerce of images through satellite television, global marketing, property websites, tourism imagery, stock photography, Facebook, Instagram, movies and magazines like *Cosmopolitan*, *Vogue* and others. This is an image capitalism of a rich world 'lifestyle' of boundless consumption, urban vertical glamour, iconic culture, residences similar to the upper (middle) classes of the rich world secluded from the local populace, of luxury brands and 'world-class' leisure, at the least with golf and swimming pool.

---

* A perceptive analysis of the image production of the capitalist skyscraper is provided by Monika Grubbauer's essay 'The high-rise office tower as a global "type"', in Michael Guggenheim and Ola Söderström (eds), *Re-Shaping Cities*, New York: Routledge, 2010.

10
Envoi: Global Capital, the Future of National Capitals and of Their People

The future of capital cities will depend, first of all, upon the future of nation-states.

In time, this future will turn out to be bright, contrary to global city consultancies. At the time of writing, this was underlined by the British referendum on leaving the EU, where the Conservative government was risking tearing its party asunder on a referendum pitting two conceptions of the British nation-state against each other. That the outgoing mayor of London, Boris Johnson, challenged his own party government in campaigning for 'Brexit' adds a nice embarrassing twist to the argument of global cities as unmoored from their original nation-states; so does the fact that his successor, Sadiq Khan, was actively campaigning for Britain to stay in the EU.

The rise of immigration and border control as central political issues in most of Europe is not only redrawing national political maps to the right, it also hammers home that nations and nation-states still matter to majorities of people. New nation-states are emerging, unlucky South Sudan being the most recent (in 2010). The demand for them is still growing: Catalonia and Scotland in Europe, Kurdistan and perennial Palestine in West Asia are the most visible. The international as well as national uproar against Russia's reincorporation of Crimea (a Russian-speaking, largely pro-Russian, historically Russian peninsula which, following an internal 1950s Soviet redivision, became part of Ukraine) reaffirms the classical ideology of state nationalism:* The soil of the national territory is sacred, however recently and contingently acquired. The new Cold War between the United States and its NATO clientele, on one hand and Russia, on the other; the increasing national assertiveness of China and the reactions to it: all point more to a world of nation-state geopolitics than to a stateless world economy of capital flows and business services.

Recent 'globalization' has not drained capitalist nation-states of resources and capacity, even if it has challenged their complacency. Between 2000 and 2014, total public expenditure in the six largest economies of the rich OECD area increased from an average of 41.8 per cent of GDP to 46.2.[1] Public social expenditure has risen substantially in Asia as well as in Latin America. Neither the nation-state nor the welfare state is shrinking, although the demand for the latter from populations of increasing age and with growing numbers of poor children are mounting even faster.

Capitals and Other National Cities

National capital cities are in general very well placed in urban hierarchies and networks, international as well as national and they are well connected in the global corporate networks.

Table 7. The best corporately connected cities of the world in 2013: index values[2]

The Top Ten		Other Cities >0.60	
New York	1.000	Madrid	0.725
Singapore	0.976	Shanghai	0.717
London	0.966	Buenos Aires	0.660
Hong Kong	0.959	Sydney	0.634
Tokyo	0.957	Mexico City	0.633
Beijing	0.849		
Paris	0.847		
Moscow	0.745		
Seoul	0.728		
São Paulo	0.726		

---

* So does, of course, Putin's decision to no longer recognize the post-Soviet borders of Ukraine, although 'enlightened' Western opinion could attribute that to some peculiar Russian nationalist atavism or imperial nostalgia.

Seven of the top ten are national capitals; only New York, Hong Kong and São Paulo are not. Among the fifteen with more than 60 per cent of possible index value, ten are capitals of nation-states.

Not all capitals are dominant cities of their nations, but most of them are, many of them very heavily so, such as Addis Ababa, Athens, Bangkok, Budapest, Buenos Aires, Cairo, Dakar, Dhaka, Jakarta, Manila, Lima, Paris, Santiago, Seoul, Tehran and Vienna, for example. Since São Paulo overtook Rio some eighty years ago, no second city has overtaken the capital since then in demographic or economic weight. Instead, the predominance of many capital cities has been reinforced: of London over the cities of the industrial north, of Tokyo over Osaka and of virtually all the post-Communist capitals of Eastern Europe over second cities, including Moscow in relation to Saint Petersburg. Some originally specialized political capitals have grown into multifunctional metropolises, such as Ankara, Brasília, Delhi and Washington. Abuja and Astana are well under way. New constructions of a national capital have rapidly become the dominant city of their country, such as Gaborone in Botswana, Nouakchott in Mauritania, and Kigali in Rwanda. The future of specialized capitals built after independence is less certain and more dependent on the vicissitudes of national politics, but some of them, like Dodoma in Tanzania and Lilongwe in Malawi, have already shown a resilience transcending the lifespans of their original sponsors.

Polycentric and bifocal national city systems certainly exist, most importantly in Western Europe – Germany, Italy, the Netherlands, Spain and Switzerland – but also in Cameroon, China, Colombia, India, Libya and Vietnam, among others. In the examples just mentioned, the capital makes up one important node of the system, but Canberra and Ottawa do not and Tshwane, Washington and Wellington not quite.

Summing up, while capital cities show a fascinating variety, the great majority of them have a major, absolutely non-negligible social, economic and cultural importance in their countries alongside their defining function as the seat of national power. Furthermore, this broad importance is not in decline. On the contrary, more often than not, it is increasing. In terms of political economy, within any foreseeable future, the world is not going to be run from supposedly supra-national global cities like New York, Shanghai, Hong Kong or Dubai but from national capitals: Washington and Beijing, first of all, but also Berlin, Delhi, London, Moscow, Paris and Tokyo, and in a longer perspective perhaps also Brasília, Jakarta, Mexico, Seoul and other national capitals. Brussels is likely to remain a place of important decisions, not as a supra-national city but as a site of international deal-making and cooperation.

National Symbolism in the Global Era

Are nations and national symbolism losing their meaning in more heterogeneous, multicultural societies? Will national monuments become as invisible as in Robert Musil's *Kakanien*? It might very well happen. I remember driving around with Brazilian friends in Rio twenty years ago, looking at monumental statues, and I was the only one who knew anything about the figures. However, general amnesia is not for the foreseeable future. Berlin is still developing its new national moment, with its semi-resurrected imperial castle and its Humboldt Forum and its plans for a major anti-Communist commemoration. All post-Communist Europe has invested heavily in nationalist and nation-religious iconography as we saw above; Skopje, Macedonia, has indulged in a monumental spree, from Alexander the Great onwards.

Madrid is cleansing the city of the remnants of Francoism. In Washington a very belated African-American museum opened in September 2016. Buenos Aires, Lima and Santiago are monumentally remembering their recent dictatorships and repression. South Africa's Freedom Park is the crown of national iconography worldwide in the twenty-first century.

In a number of cities around the world, political urban iconography is still hotly controversial, which is the surest sign of its vitality and meaningfulness. Above, we took note of ongoing iconographic controversies in Budapest, Madrid and Kyiv. Others may be added: about the Arab Spring in Cairo's Tahrir Square, Macedonian history in Skopje or whether Ottawa should monumentalize victims of Communism. The *statuemanie* of the Third French Republic is probably ebbing after its revivals by European Communism and post-Communism. But the interest in public symbolic and museum representations and narratives of national and world history as well as the present clearly remains, and I see no signs of its disappearance any time soon.

The Capital of the Early Twenty-First Century

This century is young and will in due course, without doubt, deliver its full capacity of surprises and unexpected turns. But at least for its first fifteen years, the best place to see the opportunities and the intertwining of national and global urbanism and the political economy of the early twenty-first century on display and in interaction has been Astana, the new capital of Kazakhstan.*

Astana ('capital city' in Kazakh) was laid out as a national project of the least nationalist of the former Soviet republics. Like the rest of Soviet Central Asia, the country's cities were predominantly Russian in language and culture. The capital of the Republic, Almaty (Russian Alma-Ata, once internationally famous for its fast skating rink) was dramatically off-centre in this country the size of Western Europe, now with 17 million inhabitants, in the extreme south, close to the Chinese border. A move of the capital was announced in 1994, motivated by ethno-political as well as geopolitical interests. The ethno-political subtext was to create a Kazakh capital in the centre of the country, in the largely Russian-speaking regions.

The capital project was driven by one of the great (and authoritarian) political entrepreneurs of small countries of the late twentieth and early twenty-first centuries, along with Lee Kuan Yew of Singapore, Mahathir Mohamad of Malaysia and Paul Kagame of Rwanda, Nursultan Nazarbayev, the last leader of Soviet Kazakhstan. It was made financially possible by the oil and mineral boom, now ending and casting its shadows over Astana.

On the northern steppe, the nineteenth-century Russian garrison town of Akmolinsk – later the outback Soviet Tselinograd, which Khrushchev once dreamt of as the centre of a solution to the perennial problems of Soviet agriculture – on the river Ishin (in Kazakh, Esil), a stunning new capital has been constructed in about fifteen years, starting in 1998. The 'metabolist' Japanese architect Kisho Kurokawa won the international competition for a master plan, which has not played much of a master role, and it was deliberately intended as a platform for organic growth – in that sense somewhat similar to Doxiadis's conception of Islamabad – not as a city blueprint, like Costa's Plan Piloto for Brasília.†

---

* In 2019 the city was renamed Nur-Sultan after the departing President.
† More important and effective was Kurokawa's emphasis on urban metabolism in prioritizing water and sewage infrastructure and a forest belt around the city to placate the harsh climate.

The government district is laid out in a grand west-east axis with a clear association to the Washington Mall. It starts with the headquarters of the main state oil and gas company, an almost circular building in classical Soviet style, with an archway to the east. A green mall then leads you to the central national symbol, the Bayterek, a sleek 105-metre-tall construction representing a tree with a golden egg (the sun) on top, taken from an old legend. Then the mall continues, flanked on both sides by long rows of ministerial buildings ending in two golden towers, marking the entrance to the next square, with parliament and court buildings on one side, the presidential administration and a concert hall on the other and, at the end of the axis, Ak Orda (the White Camp), the Presidential Palace, under its blue dome looking like a double-sized Washington White House.

This is monumental nationalism, obviously inspired by both of the superpowers of the Cold War, thought to be long gone. There is much more post-Communist nationalism. The concentration camps in Kazakhstan and the cruel collectivization famine of the 1930s are remembered. There is a big monumental ensemble to national defenders, with one side referring to World War II and the defence of the USSR against Nazi Germany and the other to Kazakh nomadic warriors against the (Tsarist) Russians. National independence is celebrated by two big monuments: one from 2008, a tall column topped by an eagle, with President Nazarbayev standing at its base, the other from 2011, in the form of a triumphal arch. In good Stalinist tradition, several institutions and buildings are named after the president. Lenin was stowed away in the early 1990s, replaced by the Kazakh poet Abay; Marx and Soviet leaders have disappeared from the streets. Curiously enough, the 1980s Communist leader Dinmukhamed Kunayev, whom Mikhail Gorbachev fired for corruption and unwisely replaced with an ethnic Russian (before turning to Nazarbayev), has survived in a major street.

However, this nationalism is only one part of the Astana story. From the beginning the city has simultaneously been conceived as a globalist project, including its own 'Special Economic Zone' of corporate tax breaks. Part of the urban nationalism has actually been sub-contracted. The first big mosque, on the government mall (Nur Astana), was a gift from Qatar. The Chamber of Deputies was built by a Turkish firm – Astana is part of the Turkish States Convention for

Architecture and Urban Planning – and the Senate building was a gift from Saudi Arabia.

The little river has been dammed up and widened to Thames-Seine proportions, with a riverside promenade. After the first round of national buildings, which left me quite unimpressed on my first visit in 2005, Nazarbayev's Astana has embarked on globalist imagery and iconicity, including seductive image-capitalism offers of 'country club villas', an 'English quarter' and 'Europolis'. Noman Foster has been recruited for two big projects. One is a Palace of Peace and Reconciliation, a pyramid full of number symbolism which looks much better from afar than close by and inside, as a meeting-ground for an inter-religious ecumene, one of Nazarbayev's grand international projects.* Another, Khan Shatyr, is a standard globalist shopping and entertainment centre, with an indoor pool and a beach of sand from the Maldives inside, spectacular 150-metre-high marquee or transparent tent, closing the governmental axis to the west (across the river from the Presidential Palace). Currently the big building projects are a new commercial centre, Abu Dhabi Plaza, made with Gulf money, and the 2017 World Expo, designed by the Chicago firm of Adrian Smith and Gordon Gill.

Astana has come to house a very high number of spectacular post-modernist buildings, most of them for culture or sports. Some of the best have been designed by a local architect, Shokhan Makyabetov, the chief city architect from 2005 to 2007.†

What Astana shows in its abundant splendour is, first of all, the possible intertwining of the national and the global. They remain distinct but are not necessarily incompatible. Above we noted the wisdom of the Asian conception of globalizing as an active verb. To globalize in Asia has been a national choice of political and business leaders. The rulers and the architects of Astana have been much more sophisticated than

---

* Post-Soviet Kazakhstan is about 70 per cent Muslim and 25 percent Christian (mainly Orthodox). Other religious are tiny, but a prominent synagogue is included in the new cityscape.

† My picture of Astana derives first of all from two visits, in 2005 and 2011, which (thanks to the kind collegial help of my two interepreters, Tapani Kaakuriniemi and Larisa Titarenko) included a number of interviews. The literature is not large but includes an excellent architectural guide edited by Philipp Meuser (*Astana: Architectural Guide*, Berlin: DOM, 2015).

the skyscraper developers of Mexico or Jakarta – precisely for that reason, they demonstrate more convincingly how globalist economics and nationalist political symbolism can coexist.

The Nazarbayev regime is now entering stormy waters. The long commodities boom has ended and people are obviously quite angry at the new long-term lease of national lands to foreigners, protesting in the spring of 2016. A typical post-Communist turn to religion has not prevented the emergence of militant Islamism. Whether the World Expo of 2017 will make Astana into a 'global city' looks increasingly uncertain. However, Astana has become part of world urbanism. True, Almaty remains the economic and cultural capital of Kazakhstan, but Astana has grown into a social fact. According to the 2014 census it had 835,000 inhabitants, up from about 250,000 in the 1980s and two-thirds are Kazakhs instead of one-sixth. This city is not likely to disappear with regime change. It will remain an architectural monument.

Globalism and the Future of the People

The future of globalism, of skyscrapers as well as of global corporations, looks pretty sure and well laid out: continuing and, most probably, increasing in influence and impact. The main difficult question is the future of the people. Will the people *have* a future in the world of ruthless global capitalism? Almost a lifetime of political commitment, observation and analysis has taught me not to expect anything inclusive and egalitarian from unbridled capitalism, and that rebellions are impossible to predict – but that they do occur, again and again.

In fact, I think there are two reasons for moderate optimism about the prospects of future popular moments.

One is the recent return of popular urban revolutions. The international costs of national repression have increased and are likely to stay high. Such revolutions or regime changes by popular street protests will remain unlikely in the consolidated electoral democracies, but there they might mutate into movement-parties successfully playing the electoral game. Recent southern European embryonic examples show that such a scenario is not beyond the pale of political realism. Outside countries with intact constitutional and electoral legitimacy, repetitions of recent successful popular uprisings will happen again and might very well spread in sub-Saharan Africa, where armed violence has so far decided most contested political outcomes.

The other is the possibility of urban reformism. It was pioneered by European 'municipal socialism', but in recent times the main thrust of radical, socially transformative urban reformism has come from the Global South, with long-term inputs in Montevideo and Mexico City and recent breakthroughs in Delhi and Jakarta. It is a very vulnerable project, dependent on the national economy, often under pressure from a hostile national government and facing a volatile metropolitan electorate, now that the historically stable European working-class base is largely gone. But it should not be forgotten 'that its major achievements in the South are of this century'. A tri-continental multiplication of the projects of AMLO, Jokowi and Kejriwal is certainly not impossible.

After Ken Livingstone's first mayoralty, Euro-American urban politics has been much more cautious; Euro-American city governments are usually boxed in by superior state governments, more so in the United States than in Europe. The left in Madrid was ousted in 2019 after only one term, but an ecological-social democratic coalition now into its third decade has had an impact in Paris, if more environmental than social. The possibility of wider social change is not to be ruled out. Ordinary people are not going away. They will continue to disturb the visions of global image capitalism. Their chances of social transformation are better in cities than elsewhere – and for urban social change, capital cities of power turned into cities of transformation are likely to be decisive.

Endnotes

Introduction

1 Göran Therborn, 'Monumental Europe: The National Years: On the Iconography of European Capital Cities', *Housing, Theory and Society* 19:1 (2002), 26–47.

2 Patrick Le Galès and Göran Therborn, 'Cities', in Stefan Immerfall and Göran Therborn (eds), *Handbook of European Societies: Social Transformations in the 21st Century*, New York: Springer, 2010, 59–89.

1. Cities, Power and Modernity

1 Lewis Mumford, *The Culture of Cities*, New York: Harcourt Brace, 1938, 3.

2 Lewis Mumford, *The City in History*, New York: Harvest, 1961/1989, 571.

3 Gary Cohen and Franz Szabo, *Embodiments of Power*, New York: Berghahn Books, 2008.

4 Leonardo Benevolo, *Die Geschichte der Stadt*, Frankfurt: Verlag Zweitausendeins, 1983 (orig. ed. *Storia della cittá*, Rome: Laterza, 1975), chapter 13.

5 Peter Hall, *Cities in Civilization*, London: Pantheon, 1998.

6 Charles Tilly, *Coercion, Capital, and European States, AD 990–1992*, Oxford: Oxford University Press, 1992 (1975).

7 Ibid., 190, 185.

8 Peter Hall, 'Six Types of Capital City', in J. Taylor, J. Lengellé, and C. Andrew, *Capital Cities/Les Capitales*, Ottawa: Carleton University Press, 1993; Peter Hall, 'Seven Types of Capital City', in David Gordon (ed.),

Planning Twentieth Century Capital Cities, London: Routledge, 2006. Most of the other chapters of Taylor et al. and Gordon are very interesting and useful.

9 Michel Foucault, *Les mots et les choses*, Paris: Editions Gallimard, 1966, 7.

10 Saskia Sassen, *The Global City*, 1st ed., Princeton, NJ: Princeton University Press, l991; P.J.Taylor *World City Networks*, London, Routledge, 2004.

11 Lawrence Vale, *Architecture, Power and National Identity*, 2nd ed., New York: Routledge, 2008.

12 Wolfgang Sonne, *Representing the State*, New York: Prestel, 2003.

13 Vadim Rossmann, *Capital Cities: Varieties and Patterns of Development and Relocation*, New York: Routledge, 2016.

14 Deyan Sudjic, *The Edifice Complex*, New York: Penguin, 2006.

15 Rowan Moore, *Why We Build*, New York: Harper Design, 2014.

16 Owen Hatherley, *Landscapes of Communism*, New York: New Press, 2016.

17 Ingeborg Flagge and W.J. Stock, *Architektur und Demokratie*, Stuttgart: Hatje,1992; Deyan Sudjic, *Architecture and Democracy*, New York: Te Neues, 2001.

18 Henri Lefebvre, *The Production of Space*, Oxford: Oxford University Press, 1991 (1974).

19 Spiro Kostof, *The City Shaped*, London: Thames and Hudson, 199, 209.

20 Mike Davis, *Planet of Slums*, New York: Verso, 2006, 95.

21 Simon Bekker and Göran Therborn (eds), *Capital Cities in Africa: Power and Powerlessness*, Cape Town: Human Sciences Research Council, 2012.

22 Thomas Thiis-Evensen, 'Arkitekturens maktgrammatik', in C. Kullberg Christophersen (ed.), *Maktens korridorer*, Oslo, Norsk Form, 1998.

23 Göran Therborn, 'Modern Monumentality: European Experiences', in James Osborne (ed.), *Approaching Monumentality in Archaeology*, Albany: SUNY Press, 337f.

24 *El País*, 23 November 2014, 18.

25 See, e.g., K. Marton, 'Hungary's Authoritarian Descent', *New York Times*, 4 November 2014, 6.

26 Ben Weinreb and Christopher Hibbert (eds.), *The London Encyclopedia*, London: Papermac, 1993, 444ff, 864, 986f.

27 Jacques Hillairet, *Dictionnaire historique des rues de Paris*, Paris: Editions de Minuit, l963, 38.

28 Madeleine Yue Dong, *Republican Beijing*, Berkeley: University of California Press, 2003, 71ff.

29 On Teragini see further Aristotle Kallis, *The Third Rome, 1922–1943*, Basingstoke: Palgrave Macmillan, 2014, 57–8, 64ff.

30 Liah Greenfield, *Nationalism: Five Roads to Modernity*, Cambridge, MA: Harvard University Press, 1992, though she was mostly interested in national identity.

31 Quoted in Patrick Dillon, *The Last Revolution: 1688 and the Creation of the Modern World*, London: Pimlico, 2006, 212, 217.

32 Anthony Giddens, *The Consequences of Modernity*, Stanford, CA: Stanford University Press, 1990, 1.

33 Göran Therborn, 'The Right to Vote and the Four Routes to/through Modernity', in Rolf Torstendahl (ed.), *State Theory and State History*, London: SAGE, 1992, 62–92.

34 Eugene Weber, *Peasants into Frenchmen*, Stanford: Stanford University Press, 1976.

35 N. Chanda, *Bound Together*, New Haven: Yale University Press 2007, 165.

36 Leopoldo Zea, *El pensamiento latinoameriocano*, Mexico City: Pormaca, 1965, vol. 1, 65ff, 103ff; cf. Antonio Annino and François-Xavier Guerra, *Inventando la nación. Iberoamérica. Siglo XIX*, Mexico City: Fondo de Cultura Económica, 2003.

37 A. Simpson and B.A. Oyètádé, 'Nigeria: Ethno-Linguistic Competition in the Giant of Africa', in Andrew Simpson (ed.), *Language and National Identity in Africa*, Oxford: OUP, 2008, 172

38 Tariq Rahman, *Language and Politics in Pakistan*, Oxford: Oxford University Press, 1997, ch. 6.

39 D.Z. Poe, *Kwame Nkrumah's Contribution to Pan-Africanism: An Afro-Centric Analysis*, London: Routledge, 2003, 94.

2. National Foundations: Europe

1 Margaret Whitney, *Wren*. London: Thames & Hudson, 1971, 45.

2 Mark Girouard, *Cities and People*, New Haven and London: Yale University Press, 1985, 120ff.

3 A. Ságvari, 'Studien der europåischen Hauptstadtentwicklung und die Rolle der Hauptstädte als Nationalrepräsentanten', in T. Schieder and G. Brunn (eds), *Hauptstädte in europäischen* Nationalstädten, Munich: Oldembourg, 1983.

4 Jacques Le Goff, 'Le phénomène urbaine dans le corps politique francais',

in Georges Duby (ed.), *Histoire de la France urbaine*, vol. 2, Paris: Seuil, 1980, 322.

5 On Versailles and its relationships with Paris, see Jean-Francois Solnon, *Historie de Versailles:* Paris: Perrin, 2003; Joël Cornette (ed.), Versailles, Paris: Pluriel, 2012.

6 M. Riddle, 'Winchester: The Rise of an Early Capital', in B. Ford (ed.), *The Cambridge Cultural History of Britain*, Cambridge: Cambridge University Press, 265, 434.

7 L. Barea, *Vienna: Legend and Reality*, London: Pimlico, 1993, 39.

8 G, Brunn, 'Die deutsche Einigungsbewegung und der Aufstieg Berlins zur deutschen Hauptstadt', in Schieder and Brunn (eds), *Hauptstädte in europäischen*.

9 S. Juliá, 'Madrid – Capital del Estado (1833–1993)', in S. Juliá et al., *Madrid. Historia de una Capital*, Madrid: Fundación Caja de Madrid, 1995, chapter 2.

10 S. Rokkan, 'Cities, states, and nations: A dimensional model for the study of contrasts in development,' in S.N. Eisenstadt and S. Rokkan (eds), *Building States and Nations*, vol. I, London: 1973.

11 Perry Anderson, *Lineages of the Absolutist State*, New York: Routledge, 1974.

12 Gilbert Gardes, *Le monument public français*, Paris: Presses Universitaires de France, 1994, 14, 24ff, 90ff.

13 Nikolaus Pevsner, *London I: The City of London*, Pevsner Architectural Guides, New Haven, CT: Yale University Press, 1957, 73.

14 M. Settele, *Denkmal. Wiener Stadtgeschichten.* Vienna: 1995, 68–9.

15 Richard Cleary, *The Place Royale and Urban Design in the Ancien Régime*, Cambridge: Cambridge University Press, 1999.

16 This argument is elaborated in my *The World*, Cambridge: Cambridge University Press, 2011, 54ff.

17 Wang Hui, *China from Empire to Nation-State*, trans. Michael Gibbs Hill, Cambridge, MA: Harvard University Press, 2014, chapter 2.

18 C. Amalvi, 'Le 14-e Juillet,' in Pierre Nora (ed.), *Les lieux de mémoire, Vol. I, La République*, Paris: Gallimard, 1984, 424.

19 Hillairet, *Dictionnaire historique*, 38.

20 David Harvey, *Paris: Capital of Modernity*, New York: Routledge, 2003.

21 Claudine de Vaulchier, 'La recherche d'un palais pour l'Assemblée Nationale,' in *Les Architectes de la Liberté*, Paris: Ecole Nationale Supérieure des Beaux-Arts, 1989.

22 Jean Favier, *Paris: Deux mille ans d'histoire*, Paris: Hachette, 1997, 301ff.

23 Two excellent contributions to the latter question are Linda Colley, *Britons: Forging the Nation, 1707–1837*, New Haven, CT: Yale University Press, 2005, and Krishan Kumar, *The Making of English National Identity*, Cambridge: Cambridge University Press, 2003.

24 Quoted in Dillon, *Last Revolution*, 239, 128.

25 Jean Hood, *Trafalgar Square: A Visual History of London's Landmark Through Time*, London: Batsford, 2005, 35.

26 Howard Nenner, *The Right to Be King: The Succession to the Crown of England, 1603–1714*, Chapel Hill: University of North Carolina Press, 1995, 248.

27 Norman Davies, *The Isles*, London: Macmillan, 1999, 629.

28 Colley, *Britons*, 216.

29 Pevsner, *London I*, 87–101.

30 Göran Therborn, 'Monumental Europe: The national years: On the iconography of European capital cities', *Housing, Theory and Society* 19(1), 2002: 26–47.

31 V. Gjuzelev, 'Die Hauptstadt-Entwicklung in Bulgarien', in Harald Heppner (ed.), *Hauptstädte zwischen Save, Bosporus und Dnjepr*, 145–70, Vienna: Bohlau, 1999, 159ff.

32 Eleni Bastéa, *The Creation of Modern Athens*, 18ff.

33 Gjuzelev, 'Die Hauptstadt-Entwicklung in Bulgarien', 163.

34 Tommy Book, *Belgrad*, Belgrade: Växjö, 1987, 130.

35 Herbert Wilhelmy, *Hochbulgarien II: Sofia*, Buchdruckerei Schmidt & Klaunig Kiel, 1936, 119.

36 Ioana Iosa, *Bucarest: L'emblème d'une nation*, Rennes: Presses Universitaires de Rennes, 2011, 35.

37 See Göran Therborn, *European Modernity and Beyond: The Trajectory of European Societies, 1945–2000*, London: SAGE, 1995, 43ff.

38 Z. Hojda and J. Pokorný, 'Denkmalkonflikten zwischen Tschechen und Deutschbömen', H. Haas and H. Stekl (eds), *Burgerliche Selbstdarstellung*, Vienna: Böhlau, 1995, 214ff.

39 R. Toman, *Wien: Kunst und Architektur*, Köln: Köneman, 1999, 164.

40 Carl Schorske, *Fin-de-siècle Vienna*, New York: Vintage, 1980, 29ff.

41 G. Kapnert, *Ringstrassedenkmäler*, Wiesbaden, 1973, 29ff.

42 See further Therborn, 'Monumental Europe'.

43 *La Civiltá Cattolica*, 28 December 1871, here quoted from A. Riccardi, 'La

Vita Religiosa', in Vittorio Vidotto (ed.), *Roma Capitale*, 'Bari': Laterza, 2002, 273.

44 L. Berggren and L. Sjöstedt, 'Legitimering och förändringspropaganda – monumentpolitik i Rom 1870–95', in *Kulturarvet i antikvarisk teori och praktik*, 45–71, Stockholm: 1993.

45 Dejanirah Couto, Histoire de Lisbonne, Paris: Fayard, 2000, 236–7; cf., on Madrid, Fidel Revilla González and Rosalía Ramos, *Historia de Madrid*, Madrid: La Librería, 2005, 151ff.

46 Andrea Ciampani, 'Municipio capitolino e governo nazionale da Pio IX a Umberto I', in Vittorio Vidotto (ed), *Roma Capitale*, 43ff.

47 Rokkan, 'Cities, states, and nations'.

48 Baron Haussmann, *Memoires*, Paris: Seuil, 2000 [1890–1893], 575, 705, 735.

49 Favier, *Paris*, 87.

50 Gunter Peters, *Kleine Berliner Baugeschichte: Von der Stadtgrundung bis zur Bundeshauptstadt*, Berlin: Stapp, 1995, 84.

51 M. Cacciato, 'Lo sviluppo urbano e il disegno della città', in Vidotto (ed.), *Roma Contemporanea*, 128, 147.

52 Thomas Hall, *Planung europäischer Hauptstädte*, Stockholm: Kunglign Vitterhots Historie och Antikuitets Akademien, 1986.

53 Haussmann, *Memoires*, 257

54 Ibid., 791.

55 Roy Porter, *London: A Social History*, Cambridge, MA: Harvard University Press, 1996, 321.

56 J. Hargrove, 'Les statues de Paris', in Pierre Nora (ed.), *Les lieux de mémoire, Vol. II, La Nation*, Paris: Gallimard, 1986.

57 S. Leprun, 'Exposition colonial internationale 1931', in B. de Andia (ed.), *Les Expositions universelles à Paris de 1855 à 1937*, Paris: 1989, 167–71.

58 H.V.D. Wusten, S. De Vos, and R. Deurloo, '"Les Pays-Bas Tropicaux": L'imaginaire colonial dans la toponymie néerlandaise', *Géographie et Cultures* 60 (2006): 97–98.

3. National Foundations: Settler Seccessions

1 Joseph Passonneau, *Washington Through Two Centuries*, New York: Monacelli Press, 2004, 16ff.

2 Idem., chs 2–3.

3 Jeffrey Meyer, 'The eagle and the dragon: Comparing the designs of Washington and Beijing', *Washington History* 8(2), 1996: 13.

4 Lucie-Patrizia Arndt, *'Imperial City' versus 'Federal Town'*, Münster: Lit Verlag, 1998.

5 C.M. Harris, 'Washington's "federal city," Jefferson's "federal town"', *Washington History* 12(1), 2000: 49–53.

6 Passonneau, *Washington*, 42.

7 Charles Dickens, *American Notes for General Circulation*, New York: Penguin, 2000 (1842), 129–30.

8 David Berman, *Local Government and the States*, Armonk, NY: M.E. Sharpe, 2003.

9 Frederick Douglass, *A Lecture on Our National Capital*, Washington, D.C.: Smithsonian Institution Press, 1978 (1875), 21.

10 Passonneau, *Washington*, 39.

11 Carl Abbott, *Political Terrain: Washington, D.C., from Tidewater Town to Global Metropolis*, Chapel Hill: University of North Carolina Press, 1999, 50.

12 Constance McLaughlin Green, *Washington: Village and Capital*, Princeton, NJ: Princeton University Press, 1962, 399; E. Caretto, 'Italian Imprints', in Luca Molinari and Andrea Canepari (eds), *The Italian Legacy in Washington D.C.: Architecture, Design, Art, and Culture*, New York: Skira Rizzoli, 2007, 173.

13 McLaughlin Green, *Washington*, 221ff.

14 Christopher Thomas, *The Lincoln Memorial and American Life*, Princeton, NJ: Princeton University Press, 2002, 143.

15 Savage, *Monument Wars*, 292, 353n.

16 R. Bellamy, 'The architecture of government', in Jeff Keshen and Nicole St -Onge (eds), *Construire une capital – Ottawa: Making a Capital*, Ottawa: University of Ottawa Press, 2001, 435; cf. John Taylor, *Ottawa: An Illustrated History*, Toronto: Lorimer, 1986.

17 National Capital Planning Commission, *Capital in the Making – Bâtir une capitale*, Ottawa: Government of Canada, 1998, 12.

18 Ibid., 102.

19 Roger Pegrum, *The Bush Capital: How Australia Chose Canberra as Its Federal City*, Sydney: Hale & Iremonger, 1983.

20 Sonne, *Representing the State*, chapter 4.

21 Pegrum, *Bush Capital*, 184; Crowley and Reid, *Socialist Spaces*.

22 David Headon, *The Symbolic Role of the National Capital*, Canberra: National Capital Authority and the Commonwealth of Australia, 2003.

23 City of Pretoria, *Official Guide*, Pretoria: n.d., but probably from the mid-1950s, 90, 222.

24 Z. Nuttall, 'Royal ordinances concerning the layout of new towns', *Hispanic American Historical Review* 4(4), 1921: 743–53; cf. Porfirio Sanz Camañes, *Las ciudades en la América hispana: siglos XV al XVIII*, Madrid: Silex, 2004.

25 Alexander von Humboldt, *Ensayo político sobre el Reino de Nueva España*, Mexico City: Porrúa, 1966 [1822], 64, 79.

26 Patrice Elizabeth Olsen, *Artifacts of Revolution: Architecture, Society, and Politics in Mexico City, 1920–1940*, Lanham, MD: Rowman & Littlefield, 2008, chapter 6.

27 Raúl Porras Barrenechea and Edgardo Rivera Martínez (eds), *Antología de Lima*, Lima: Fundación M. J. Bustamante de la Fuente, 2002, 11.

28 Ibid., 11ff, 412; Ortemberg, *Rituels du pouvoir*.

29 Gabriel Ramón, 'The Script of Urban Surgery: Lima, 1850–1940', in Arturo Almadoz (ed.), *Planning Latin American Cities, 1850–1950*, London: Routledge, 2002; and Anonymous, *Lima, Paseos de la Ciudad y su Historia*, Lima: Guías Expreso, 1998.

30 Herbert Wilhelmy, *Südamerika im Spiegel seiner Städte*, Hamburg: De Gruyter, 1952, 238; M. Rapoport and Maria Seoane, *Buenos Aires: Historia de una ciudad*, Buenos Aires: Planeta, 2007, 48.

31 Rapoport and Seoane, *Buenos Aires*, 167ff.

32 L. González, S. Condoleo, and M. Zangrandi, 'Buenos Aires festeja el Centenario. Periferias, conflictos y esplendedores de una ciudad en construcción', in Francisco Xavier González (ed.), *Aquellos años franceses*, Santiago: Taurus, 2012, 261ff.

33 Rapoport and Seoane, *Buenos Aires*, 182ff.

34 Horacio Salas, *El Centenario: La Argentina en su hora más gloriosa*, Buenos Aires: Planeta, 1960, 160ff.

35 Rodrigo Gutierrez Viñuales, *Monumento conmemorativo y espacio público en Iberoamérica*, Madrid: Catedra, 2004, 710.

36 Ramon Gutiérrez, 'Buenos Aires, A Great European City', in Almadoz (ed.), *Planning Latin American Cities*, 68ff.

37 Alfonso Ernesto Ortiz Gaitán, *Bogotá, El Dorado: Arquitectura, historia e historias*, Bogotá: Universidad de Gran Colombia, 2005, 72.

38 Twentieth-century population figures from Alan Gilbert and Julio Dávila, 'Bogotá: Progress Within a Hostile Environment', in David Myers and Henry Dietz (eds), *Capital City Politics in Latin America*, Boulder, CO: Lynne Rienner, 2002, 30, 127.

39 Santiago Montes Veira, *Bogotá: La metrópoli de los Andes*, Bogotá: I.M. Editores, 2008, 38, 66.

40 Herbert Wilhelmy, *Südamerika im Spiegel seiner Städte*, Hamburg: De Gruyter, 1952, 203.

41 Ramon Gutiérrez, *Arquitectura y urbanismo en Iberoamérica*, Madrid: Catedra, 2002, 289.

42 Gutiérrez Viñuales, *Monumento conmemorativo*, 618.

43 B. Vicuña Mackenna in 1870, quoted in Gustavo Munizaga Vigil, 'Les grandes étapes du dévéloppement urbain de Santiago', in *Santiago Poniente: développement urbain et patrimoine*, Santiago: Ministry of Culture and Communication, 2000, 34.

44 Carlos Lessa, *O Rio de todos os Brasis*, Rio de Janeiro: Editora Record, 2005, 71, 82.

45 Jaime Benchimol, *Pereira Passos: Um Haussmann Tropical*, Cidade do Rio de Janeiro, 1992, 36ff.

46 Ibid.; Berenice Seara, *Guia de roteiros do Rio antigo*, Rio de Janeiro: Globo, 2004.

47 Giovanna Rosso Del Brenna, *O Rio de Janeiro de Pereira Passos*, Rio de Janeiro: Routledge, 1985, 19.

48 The inauguration programme is reprinted by Laurent Vidal, *De Nova Lisboa à Brasília*, Brasília: UNB, 2002, 280–1.

49 James Holston, *The Modernist City: An Anthropological Critique of Brasilia*, Chicago: University of Chicago Press, 1989, 70.

50 Juscelino Kubitschek, *Por Que Construí Brasília*, Brasília: Senado Federal, Conselho Editorial, 2000 (1975), 31ff.

51 On modernist Brazilian architecture, see Elisabetta Andreoli and Adrian Forty, *Brazil's Modern Architecture*, New York: Phaidon, 2004, chapter 3; on MoMa and Brazil, see Zilah Quezado Dekker, *Brazil Built. The Architecture of the Modern Movement in Brazil*, London: Taylor & Francis, 2001.

52 Kubitschek, *Por Que*, 7ff.

53 Vidal, *De Nova Lisboa à Brasília*, 238; Holston, *Modernist City*, 76ff.

54 Gustavo Lins Ribeiro, *O Capital Da Esperança: A Experiência Dos Trabalhadores Na Construção De Brasília*, Brasília: UNB, 2008, chapters 2 and 4.

55 Lúcio Costa interviewed in Vidal, *De Nova Lisboa à Brasília*, 241; cf. Holston, *Modernist City*, chapter 6.

56 Lins Ribeiro, *O Capital Da Esperança*, 240.

57 UN Human Settlement Programme, *State of Latin American and Caribbean Cities 2012*, Nairobi: United Nations, fig. 2.6.

4. National Foundations: Nationalizing Colonialism

1 Jurgen Osterhammel, *Colonialism: A Theoretical Overview*, Kingston, Jamaica: Markus Wiener, 1997, 51.

2 Narkayani Gupta, 'Concern, Indifference, Controversy: Reflections on Fifty Years of "Conservation" in Delhi', in Véronique Dupont, Emma Tarlo and Denis Vidal (eds), *Delhi: Urban Space and Human Destinies*, New Delhi: Manohar, 2000, 167ff.

3 Krishna Menon, 'The Contemporary Architecture of Delhi: The Role of the State as Middleman', in Dupont et al., *Delhi*, 147.

4 See Jon Lang, Madhavi Desai and Miki Desai, *Architecture and Independence*, Oxford: Oxford University Press, 1997, and Khanna and Parhawk, *Modern Architecture*.

5 Sten Ake Nilsson, *The New Capitals of India, Pakistan, and Bangladesh*, Lund: Studentlitteratur, 1973, 134.

6 Lang et al., *Architecture and Independence*, 201ff.

7 Khanna and Parhawk, *Modern Architecture*, 33.

8 Denis Vidal, Emma Tarlo and Veronique Dupont, 'The alchemy of an unloved city', in Dupont, et al., *Delhi*, 20; B. Mishra, R.-B. Singh, and A. Malik, 'Delhi: housing and quality of life', in R.P. Mishra and K. Mishra (eds), *Million Cities of India*, Vol. I, New Delhi: Sustainable Development Foundation, 1997, 204ff.

9 Ranjana Sengupta, *Delhi Metropolitan*, New York: Penguin, 2007, chapter 5.

10 Vidal et al., 'Alchemy of an Unloved City', 16.

11 Mishra et al., 'Delhi', 199; cf. P. Cadène, 'Delhi's place in India's urban structure', in Dupont, et al., *Delhi*.

12 Constantinos Doxiadis, 'Islamabad: The creation of a new capital', *Town Planning Review* 36:1 (1965): 17.

13 M. Hanif Raza, *Islamabad and Environs*, Islamabad: Colorpix, 2003, 71–81.

14 Kwaja, *Memoirs*, 944ff.

15 Ibid., 122.

16 Susan Abeyasekere, *Jakarta: A History*, Oxford: Oxford University Press, 1987, 154.

17 Jo Santoso, *The Fifth Layer of Jakarta*, Jakarta: Tarumanagara University, 2009.

18 See Lai Chee Kien, *Building Merdeka, Independence Architecture in Kuala Lumpur, 1957–1966*, Kuala Lumpur: Petronas, 2007, chapter 10.

19 Cf. the lavish hagiographic publication on the Petronas Towers edited by Gurdip Singh, *Sculpting the Sky: Petronas Twin Towers*, Kuala Lumpur: Petronas, 1998.

20 See Kwang-Joong Kim (ed.), *Seoul, 20th Century: Growth and Change of the Last 100 Years*, Seoul: Seoul Development Institute, 2003, chapters 2 and 3.

21 Soon-won Park, 'Colonial industrial growth and the emergence of the Korean working class', in Gi-Wook Shin and Michael Robinson (eds), *Colonial Modernity in Korea*, Cambridge, MA: Harvard University Asia Center, 1999, 47.

22 Ki-Suk Lee, 'Seoul's Urban Growth in the Twentieth Century: From the Pre-modern City to a Global Metropolis', in Kwang-Joong Kim (ed.), *Seoul, Twentieth Century*, 32, 47.

23 Ki-baik Lee, *A New History of Korea*, Cambridge, MA: Harvard University Asia Center, 1984, 349, 351.

24 Schmid, *Korea Between Empires*, 172.

25 Andrei Lankov and Sarah L. Kang, *The Dawn of Modern Korea*, Seoul: EunHaeng NaMu, 2007, 216.

26 Sei-Kwan Sohn, 'Changes in the residential features of Seoul in the 20th century', in Kim (ed.), Seoul, *20th Century*, 240–1.

27 City History Compilation Committee of Seoul, *The Launch of Seoul as the Capital of the Republic of Korea (1945–1961)*, Seoul: CHCCS, 2004, 124–5.

28 Kyo-Mok Lee, 'Seoul's urban growth in the 20th century: From pre-modern city to global metropolis', in Kim (ed.), *Seoul, 20th Century*, 130.

29 Sohn, 'Changes in the residential features'.

30 Quoted in James Jankowski, 'Egypt and Early Arab Nationalism, 1908-1922', in Rashid Khalidi, Lisa Anderson, Muhammad Muslih and Reeva S. Simon (eds), *The Origins of Arab Nationalism*, New York: Columbia University Press, 1991, 263.

31 Raafat, *Cairo: The Glory Years*, Cairo: AUC Press, 2003, 71ff, 283ff.

32 Yoram Meital, 'Central Cairo: Street naming and the struggle over historical representation', *Middle Eastern Studies* 43:6 (2007): 857.

33 Al Jazeera, 2 January 2011.

34 Sarah Sabry, 'Informal housing: An Introduction', in Marc Angélil et al. (eds), *Housing in Cairo*, Berlin: Ruby Press, 2015, 243.

35 Zeynep Çelik, 'Post-Colonial Intersections', *Third Text* 13:49, 63–72.

36 See, e.g., Richard Hull, *African Cities and Towns before the European Conquest*, New York: W. W. Norton, 1976.

37 Charles-Robert Ageron and Marc Michel (eds.), *L'Afrique noire francaise : L'heure des indépendances*, Paris: Biblis, 2010 (1992).

38 Cf. Michael Crowder, *Senegal: A Study in French Assimilation Policy*, Oxford: Oxford University Press, 1962, 4ff.

39 K. Twum-Baah, 'Population Growth of Mega-Accra – Emerging Issues', in Ralph Mills-Tettey and Korantema Adi-Dako (eds), *Visions of the City: Accra in the 21st Century*, Accra: Woeli, 2002, 33.

40 The so-called Devonshire White Paper, quoted in Janet Hess, 'Imagining architecture: The structure of nationalism in Accra, Ghana', *Africa Today* 47:2, 2000: 39.

41 See ibid.; Janet Hess, 'Spectacular nation: Nkrumahist art and iconography in the Ghanaian independence era', *African Arts* (Spring 2006): 16–21; and Ato Quayson, *Oxford Street, Accra*, Durham, NC: Duke University Press, 2014, chapter 2.

42 A. Bremer, 'Conflict moderation and participation – prospects and barriers for urban renewal in Ga Mashie', in Mills-Tettey and Adi-Dako (eds), *Visions of the City*; Quayson, *Oxford Street*, chapters 1 and 2.

43 Blackpast.org.

44 Adebawi, 'Abuja'.

45 Marie Huchzermeyer, *Cities with Slums*, Claremont, South Africa: Juta Academic, 2011, 101.

46 See further Adebawi, 'Abuja', 91ff; Nnamdi Elleh, *Abuja: The Single Most Ambitious Urban Design Project of the 20th Century*, Berlin: Weimar Bauhaus University Press, 2001; Huchzermeyer, *Cities with Slums*, 95ff.

47 See Jerome Chenal, *The West African City*, New York: Routledge, 2014; cf. A. Dioup, 'Dakar', in Bekker and Therborn, *Power and Powerlessness*.

48 See Thomas M. Shaw, *Irony and Illusion in the Architecture of Imperial Dakar*, Lewiston, NY: Edwin Mellen Press, 2006.

49 A. Dubresson, 'Abidjan: From the public making of a modern city to urban management of a metropolis, in Carole Rakodi (ed.), *The Urban Challenge in Africa*, Tokyo: United Nations University Press, 1997, 285.

50 R. Kobia, 'European Union Commission Policy in the RDC', *Review of African Political Economy* 93/94 (2002): 431–43.

51 Filip De Boeck, 'La ville de Kinshasa, une architecture du verbe,' *Esprit* 330 (2006).

52 Fumunzanza Muketa, *Kinshasa d'un quartier à l'autre*, Paris: l'Harmattan, 2008, 61.

53 Marco d'Eramo, *The Pig and the Skyscraper – Chicago: A History of Our Future*, London: Verso, 2002, 44.

54 A. O'Connor, *The African City*, Cambridge: Cambridge University Press, 2007, 45.

55 Paul Bairoch, *Cities and Economic Development*, Chicago: University of Chicago Press, 1988, 430.

56 L. Nzuzi, 'Kinshasa: Mégacité au Coeur de l'Afrique', in A.-M. Frérot, *Les grandes villes d'Afrique*, Paris: Ellipses, 1999, 130.

57 Anja Kervanto Nevanlinna, 'Interpreting Nairobi', Helsinki: Finnish Literature Society, 1996, chapter12; cf. S. Owuor and T. Mbatia, 'Nairobi', in Bekker and Therborn, *Power and Powerlessness*.

58 Davis, *Planet of Slums*, 92ff, 142ff.

59 Shadi Rabharan and Manuel Herz, *Nairobi, Kenya. Migration Shaping the City*, Maastricht: Lars Muller Verlag, 2014, 26ff; on favelas, see Licia Valladares, *La favela d'un siècle à l'autre*, Paris: Maison des Sciences de l'Homme, 2006, 20ff.

60 Cf. Caroline Wanjiku Kihato, 'Kibera: Nairobi's Other City', *Cityscapes* 3 (2013), 39–41.

61 Bernard Calas, *Kampala: La ville et la violence*, Paris: Karthala, 1998, 69.

62 Philippe Gervais-Lambony, *De Lomé à Harare: Le fait citadin*, Paris: IFRA, 1994, 385.

63 UN Habitat, *State of the World's Cities 2012/2013*, London: Routledge, 2013, table 2.

64 UN Human Settlement Programme, *State of the World's Cities 2008/2009*, Nairobi: United Nations, 2009, 111ff.

5. National Foundation: Reactive Modernization

1 Quoted in Takii Kazuhiro, *The Meiji Constitution: The Japanese Experience of the West and the Shaping of the Modern State*, Tokyo: International House of Japan, 2007, 150.

2 Quoted in William Coaldrake, *Architecture and Authority in Japan*, New York: Routledge, 1996, 208.

3 Edward Seidensticker, *Low City, High City: Tokyo from Edo to the Earthquake*, San Francisco: Knopf, 1985, 26; Takashi Fujitani, *Splendid Monarchy: Power and Pageantry in Modern Japan*, Berkeley: University of California Press, 1998, chapter 2; Nicolas Fiévé and Paul Waley (eds), *Japanese Capitals in Historical Perspective*, New York: Routledge, 2003.

4 Seidensticker, *Low City, High City*, 68, 98.

5 Fujitani, *Splendid Monarchy*, chapter 2; T.A. Bisson, 'The constitution and the retention of the emperor', in Jon Livingston, Joe Moore and Felicia Oldfather (eds), *Postwar Japan: 1945 to the Present*, New York: Pantheon, 1974, 24–8.

6 Coaldrake, *Architecture and Authority*, chapter 3.

7 Quoted in Koompong Noobanjong, 'Rajadamnoen Avenue: Thailand's transformative path towards modern polity', in Nihal Perera and Wing-Shing Tang (eds), *Transforming Asian Cities*, London: Routledge, 2013, 39; see also Douglas Webster and Chuthatip Maneepong, 'Bangkok: Global actor in a misaligned governance framework', *City* 13:1 (2009), 80–6.

8 See Çelik, *The Remaking of Istanbul*, Seattle, Unversity of Washington Press, 1986.

9 Toni Cross and Gary Leiser, *A Brief History of Ankara*, Vacaville: Indian Ford Press, 2000, 135ff.

10 S. Türkoglu Önge, 'Spatial Representations of Power: Making the Urban Space of Ankara in the Early Republican Period', in J. Osmund and A. Cimdina (eds), *Power and Culture: Identity, Ideology, Representation*, Pisa: Plus, 2007, 89n.

11 Sibel Bozdogan, *Modernism and Nation Building: Turkish Architectural Culture in the Early Republic*, Seattle: University of Washington Press, 2001.

12 J.D. Gurne, 'The transformation of Tehran in the later nineteenth century', in C. Adle and B. Hourcade (eds), *Téhéran Capitale Bicentenaire*, Leuven: Peeters, 1992, 38.

13 See, e.g., Ervand Abrahamian, *Iran between Two Revolutions*, Princeton, NJ: Princeton University Press, 1982, 73ff, 81ff.

14 On Pahlavi urban planning, see M. Habibi, 'Reza Chah et le développement de Téhéran (1925-1941)', in Adle and Hourcade (eds), *Téhéran Capitale Bicentenaire*; on its architecture, see Marefat, 'Protagonists,' 100.

15 B. Hourcade, 'Urbanisme et crise urbaine sous Mohammed-Reza Pahlavi', in Adle and Hourcade (eds), *Téhéran Capitale Bicentenaire*, 214ff.

16 Marc Angélil and Dirk Hebel, *Cities of Change: Addis Ababa*, Basel: Birkhäuser, 2010, 207, 62ff, and 112, respectively.

17 José Luis Romero, *Latinoamérica: las ciudades y las ideas*, Buenos Aires: Siglo XXI Editores Argentina, 2001 (1976), 198ff.

6. People Rising

1 W. Vogel, *Bismarck's Arbeiterversicherung*, Braunschweig: Dr. Müller, 1951, 152ff and passim.

2 R. Roberts, 'Teoria, prassi e politica del socialismo municipale in Inghilterra, 1880–1914,' in Maurizio Degl'Innocenti (ed.), *Le sinistre e il governo locale in Europa*, Pisa: Nistri-Lischi, 1984, 146–66.

3 Tim Willis, 'Contributing to a real socialist community: Municipal socialism and health care in Sheffield (1918–1930),' in Uwe Kühl (ed.), *Der Munizipalsozialismus in Europa*, Munich: Oldenbourg, 2001, 101–15.

4 H. Searing, 'With red flags flying: Housing in Amsterdam, 1915–1923,' in Henry Millon and Linda Nochlin (eds.), *Art and Architecture in the Service of Politics*, Cambridge, MA: MIT Press, 1978, 230.

5 Most importantly by Otto Neurath, 'Städtebau und Proletariat,' *Der Kampf*, June 1924, 236–42.

6 The decisive urbanistic study is Eve Blau, *The Architecture of Red Vienna, 1919–1934*, Cambridge, MA: MIT Press, 1999, quoted on page 46. Also valuable is Helmut Weihsmann, *Das rote Wien*, Vienna: Promedia Verlagsges, 2002.

7 R. Stremmel, 'Berlin–Aspekte und Funktionen der Metropolenwahrnehmung auf Seiten der politischen "Linken" (1890–1933),' in G. Brunn and J. Reulecke (eds), *Metropolis Berlin*, Berlin: Bouvier, 1992, 93ff.

8 For two overviews, see Degl'Innocenti (ed.), *Le Sinistre e il Governo locale in Europa*, and Kühl (ed.), *Munizipalsozialismus*.

9 P. Hedebol, 'Jens Jensen,' in Poul Nørlund, Erick Struckman and Erick og Thomsen (eds), *Köbenhavn 1888-1945*, Copenhagen: Biblioteksstämplar.

10 Blau, *Architecture of Red Vienna*, 228.

11 E. Bellanger, 'Les maires et leurs logements sociaux,' *CAIRN Info* 3 (2008): 95–107.

12 Anne Haila, *Urban Land Rent: Singapore as a Property State*, New York: Wiley-Blackwell, 2015, tables 5.1. and 5.3.

13 See Florian Urban, *Tower and Slab: Histories of Global Mass Housing*, New York: Routledge, 2013.

14 Swenarton, Avermaete, and van den Heuvel (eds), *Architecture and the Welfare State*.

15 Kumiko Fujita, 'Conclusion: Residential segregation and urban theory,' in

Thomas Maloutas and Kumiko Fujita (eds), *Residential Segregation in Comparative Perspective*, New York: Routledge, 2012, table 13.1.

16 E. Klein, *Denkwürdiges Wien*, Vienna: Falters, 2004, 40.

17 Vasconcelos, *Raza Cósmica*.

18 Marie-Danielle Demélas, *La invención política*, Lima: IFEA-IEP, 2003, 389.

19 Gutiérrez Viñales, *Monumento commemorativo*, 482–83.

20 G. Schönwälder, 'Metropolitan Lima: A New Way of Making Politics,' in Daniel Chávez and Benjamin Goldfrank (eds), *The Left in the City*, London: Latin America Bureau, 2004.

21 Danilo Martucelli, at the University of Paris–Diderot, first alerted me to the cultural change of Lima. My friend Narda Zola Hernández confirmed I was on the right track and connected me with Pedro Pablo Ccopa, whose very perceptive essay 'Música popular, migrantes y el nuevo espiritú de la ciudad' (in *Colégio de sociólogos del Peru, Los nuevos rostros de Lima* (2009): 113–40), provided the context and the documentation. The lyrics are quoted from him. Their interpretation is my responsiblity.

22 Anahi Ballent, *Las huellas de la política. Vivienda, ciudad, peronismo en Buenos Aires, 1943–1955*, Quilmes, Universidad Nacional de Quilmes, 2005.

23 The horror story is vividly told in a paper by Alejandro Grimson, 'Racionalidad, etnicidad y clase en los orígenes del peronismo', Desigualdades.net, Working Paper 93, 2011; Rapoport and Seoane, *Buenos Aires*, 729.

24 Göran Therborn, 'Moments of equality: Today's Latin America in a global historical context,' in Barbara Fritz and Lena Lavinas (eds.), *A Moment of Equality for Latin America?*, New York: Routledge, 2015, 13–28.

25 Economic Commission for Latin America and the Caribbean (CEPAL), *Social Panorama of Latin America 2014*, New York: United Nations, 2015, table I.A.3.

26 Benjamin Goldfrank and Andrew Schrank, 'Municipal neoliberalism and municipal socialism: Urban political economy in Latin America,' *International Journal of Urban and Regional Research* 33:2 (2009): 443–62.

27 Daniel Chávez, 'Montevideo: From Popular Participation to Good Governance', in Chávez and Goldfrank (eds), *Left in the City*.

28 CEPAL, *Social Panorama of Latin America* 2014, table IIA.2.

29 Asa Cristina Laurell, 'Health Reform in Mexico City, 2000-2006,' *Social Medicine* 3:2 (2008): 149; Asa Cristina Laurell and A.I. Cisnertos Lujan,

'Construcción de un proyecto contra-hegemónico de salud: El caso del Distrito Federal, México', in C. Teitelboim Henrion and A.C. Laurell (eds), *Por el derecho universal a la salud*, Buenos Aires: CLACSO, 2015, 53–54.

30 See Justin McGuirk, *Radical Cities*, London: Verso, 2014, chapter 6.

31 Misagh Parsa, *Social Origins of the Iranian Revolution*, New Brunswick, NJ: Rutgers University Press, 1989, 78.

32 See Valladares, *La favela d'un siècle à l'autre*.

33 See Castells, *City and the Grassroots*, chapters 18–19.

34 Alan Gilbert (ed.), *The Mega-City in Latin America*, New York: United Nations, 1996.

35 See further Owuor and Mbatia, 'Nairobi', 129ff.

36 Davis, *Planet of Slums*, 102.

37 Jean-Louis van Gelder, Maria Cristina Cravino, and Fernando Ostuni, 'Housing Informality in Buenos Aires: Past, Present and Future?', *Urban Studies* 2015: 7.

38 See P. Lundin, 'Mediators of modernity: Planning experts and the making of the 'car-friendly city in Europe', in Mikael Hård and Thomas Misa (eds.), *Urban Machinery: Inside Modern European Cities*, Cambridge, MA: MIT Press, 2008, 257–79.

39 Jane Jacobs, *The Death and Life of Great American Cities*, New York: Vintage, 1961.

40 Schrag, 'Federal fight'. Having checked it against several other sources, I would say the Wikipedia entry on Three Sisters Bridge is a good entry to the topic.

41 Norma Evenson, *Paris: A Century of Change, 1878–1978*, New Haven, CT: Yale University Press, 1979, 285.

42 Klemek, *Transatlantic Collapse of Urban Renewal*, 139.

43 See further, Squatting Europe Kollective (ed.), *Squatting in Europe*, London: Minor Compositions, 2013; Hans Pruijt, 'The Logic of Urban Squatting', *International Journal of Urban and Regional Research* 37:1, 2013, 19–45.

44 This story is well told in great detail by Anders Gullberg, *City – drömmen om ett nytt hjärta* [City – The Dream of a New Heart], Stockholm: Stockholmia Förlag, 1998, 2 vols. The second volume is my main source.

45 L. Stanek, 'Who Needs "Needs"? French Post-War Architecture and Its Critics', in Swenarton, Avermaete, and van den Heuvel (eds), *Architecture and the Welfare State*.

46 S. Malhotra and M. Comeau, 'Moscow', in Francesa Miazzo and Tris Kee (eds.), *We Own the City*, Hong Kong: Valiz/Trancity, 2014, 110–51.

47 F. Engels, 'Einleitung zu Karl Marx' and 'Klassenkämpfe in Frankreich 1848 bis 1880', 1895, *Marx-Engels-Werke*, vol. 22, Berlin: Dietz, 1970, 513, 520–2.

48 See George Katsiaficas, *Asia's Unknown Uprisings*, vol. 2, Oakland, CA: PM Press, 2013, chapter 2.

49 See, for example, Lincoln Mitchell, *The Color Revolutions*, Philadelphia: University of Pennsylvania Press, 2012, chapter 4, and Sakwa, *Frontline Ukraine*, 52ff, 86.

50 E. Porio, 'Shifting spaces of power in metro Manila,' *City* 13:1 (2009): 115.

7. Apotheosis of Power

1   Vittorio Vidotto, 'La capitale del Fascismo', in Vidotto (ed.), *Roma Capitale*, 390–91.

2   Ibid., 385.

3   The pre-Fascist "Nationalist" paper Idea Nazionale 1.11.1922, quoted in Vidotto 'La Capitale', 385.

4   Italo Insolera, *Roma moderna: Un secolo di storia urbanistica 1870–1970*, Rome: Piccolo biblioteca Einaudi, 1993, 143.

5   Italo Insolera, *Roma moderna: Da Napoleone I al XXI secolo*, Rome: Piccolo biblioteca Einaudi, 2011, 128.

6   Vidotto, *Roma contemporanea*, Barí: Laterza, 184.

7   Insolera, *Roma moderna: 1870–1970*, 136ff.

8   Vidotto, *Roma contemporanea*, 257.

9   *Corriere della Sera*, 18 April 2015, 13.

10 Antonio Cederna, *Mussolini Urbanista*, Rome: Laterza, 2006 (1979), chapter 7; Insolera, *Roma moderna: Da Napoleone I*, chapter 13.

11 Ingeborg Flagge and W.J. Stock, *Architektur und Demokratie*, Berlin: Hatje, 1992.

12 See Perry Anderson, *The New Old World*, London: Verso, 2009, 333ff.

13 Hitler, March 1942, quoted in Laurenz Demps, *Berlin-Wilhelmstrasse: Eine Topographie preussisch-deutscher Macht*, Berlin: Ch. Links, 1996, 231.

14 Peters, *Kleine Berliner Baugeschichte*, 175f.

15 Gitta Sereny, *Albert Speer: His Battle with Truth*, London: Picador, 1996, 225.

16 Engeli and Ribbe, 'Berlin in der NS-Zeit (1933–45)', in Wolfgang Ribbe (ed.), *Geschichte in Daten – Berlin*, Vol. II, Munich: Fourier Verlag, 1988, 952ff.

17 Alexandra Ritchie, *Faust's Metropolis: A History of Berlin*, New York: Carroll & Graf, 1998, 461.

18 Speer, *Inside the Third Reich*, 197.

19 Demps, *Berlin-Wilhelmstrasse*, 225ff; Speer, *Inside the Third Reich*, 157ff.

20 Speer, 159, On Thiis-Evensen see ch. 1, quote 22.

21 Speer, 118ff.

22 Ibid., chapters 10–12.

23 Shown by Peters, *Kleine Berliner Baugeschichte*, 171.

24 Speer, *Inside the Third Reich*, 158.

25 Vidotto, 'La Capitale', 397; Speer 1995, 115, 159.

26 Speer, 197.

27 Cederna, *Mussolini Urbanista*, chapter 4; Insolera, *Roma moderna: Da Napoleone I*, 434ff and chapter 14.

28 Ritchie, *Faust's Metropolis*, 428

29 See Ramos and Revilla, *Historia de Madrid*, 223 and chapter VIII; Juliá et al., *Madrid*, 434 and chapter 10.

30 Dan Hancox, 'Race, God and Family', London Review of Books 37:3 (2 July 2015), 16; *El País*, 6 July 2015.

31 Quoted in *The Clinic*, Santiago de Chile, 28 October 2004, 7.

32 Cf. Nas, 'Jakarta', p. 117, above.

33 Hans-Dieter Evers, 'Urban symbolism and urbanism in Indonesia', in Peter Nas (ed.), *Cities Full of Symbols*, Leiden: Leiden University Press, 2011.

34 Kusno, *Behind the Postcolonial*, 72.

35 See ibid., 85ff, and Kusno, *Appearances of Memory*, 216ff.

36 See Donald M. Seekins, '"Runaway chickens" and Myanmar identity', *City* 13:1(2009), 63–70; Naypyitaw Development Committee, *Naypyitaw Directory 2010*, Naypyitaw, 2010; Matt Kennard and Claire Provost, 'Burma's bizarre capital: A super-sized slice of post-apocalypse suburbia', *Guardian*, 19 March 2015, theguardian.com.

37 See Rapoport and Seoane, *Buenos Aires*, 2007, chapter VII.

38 Kusno, *Appearances of Memory*, 57; Margarita Gutman, 'Hidden and exposed faces of power in Buenos Aires', *International Journal of Urban Sciences* 19:1 (2015): 20–8.

39 R. Hidalgo Dattwyler, 'La vivienda social en Santiago de Chile en la

segunda mitad del siglo XX: Actores relevantes y tendencias especiales', in Carlos de Mattos, María Elena Ducci, Alfredo Rodríguez and Gloria Yáñez Warner (eds), *Santiago en la Globalización*, Santiago: SUR, 2003, 228.

40 Mario Rapoport and María Seoane, *Buenos Aires: Historia de una ciudad*, vol. 2, Buenos Aires: Planeta, 2007, 483.

41 Abidin Kusno, *Behind the Postcolonial*, London: Routledge, 2000, 108.

42 Rapoport and Seoane, *Buenos Aires*, 424.

43 Ramiro Segura, 'Conexiones, entrelazamientos y configuraciones socio-espaciales en la (re) producción de desigualdades en ciudades latinoamericanas (1975–2010)', desiguALdades working paper 65, 2014, Table 1, desigualdades.net.

8. The Coming and Going of Communism

1 N. Crofts, 'Globalization and growth in the twentieth century', Washington, D.C.: International Monetary Fund, 2000, table 1.1.

2 V. Tolstoy, I. Bibikova and C. Cooke, *Street Art of the Revolution*, London: Thames and Hudson, 1990, document no. 1.

3 Karl Schlögel, *Terror und Traum: Moskau 1937*, München: Fischer Taschenbuch, 2008, 316–7.

4 Colton, *Moscow*, 277,174.

5 Ibid., 391–2.

6 Peters, *Kleine Berliner Baugeschichte*, 320.

7 See Åman, *Architecture and Ideology*, chapter VII.

8 Blair Ruble, *Second Metropolis: Pragmatic Pluralism in Gilded Age Chicago, Silver Age Moscow, and Meiji Osaka*, Cambridge: Cambridge University Press, 2001, chapters 3 and 9.

9 Catherine Merridale, *Red Fortress: History and Illusion in the Kremlin*, New York: Picador, 2013, 312.

10 Schlögel, *Terror und Traum*, 80.

11 Being unable to read many Russian primary sources, I am heavily indebted to Schlögel, *Terror und Traum*; Monica Rüthers, *Moskau bauen*, Vienna: Boehlau Verlag, 2007; Colton, *Moscow;* and Greg Castillo, 'Cities of the Stalinist Empire', in Nezar AlSayyad (ed.), *Forms of Dominance*, Aldershot, UK: Avebury, 1992.

12 See Rüthers, *Moskau bauen*, 75–150.

13 Schlögel, *Terror und Traum*, 70.

14 Colton, *Moscow*, 798.

15 Merridale, *Red Fortress*, 318.

16 Colton, *Moscow*, 417.

17 Ibid.

18 Åman, *Architecture and Ideology*, 218–9.

19 On the latter, Schlögel, *Moscow*, 30–1.

20 Colton, *Moscow*, 342.

21 Rüthers, *Moskau bauen*, 49.

22 Åman, *Architecture and Ideology*, 163; Molnár, *Building the State*, 41.

23 Åman, *Architecture and Ideology*, 61.

24 Patryk Babiracki, *Soviet Soft Power in Poland*, Chapel Hill: University of North Carolina Press, 2015, 196.

25 Therborn, *European Modernity and Beyond*, 43ff.

26 Åman, *Architecture and Ideology*, 115ff.

27 Le Normand, *Designing Tito's Capital*, 37ff.

28 Dr. Judit Bodnar, in conversation in September 2015.

29 See Le Normand, *Designing Tito's Capital* and the historical geography of the city by Book, *Belgrad*.

30 Joachim Vossen, *Bukarest – Die Entwicklung des Stadtraums*, Berlin: Reimer, 2004, 157; Hirt, *Iron Curtains*, 82.

31 Luminita Machedon and Ernie Scoffham, *Romanian Modernism*, Cambridge, MA: MIT Press, 1999.

32 Vossen, *Bukarest*, 232.

33 Åman, *Architecture and Ideology*, 135ff.

34 Vossen, *Bukarest*, 224ff.

35 Åman, *Architecture and Ideology*, 141ff.

36 See further Dorina Pojani, 'Urban design, ideology and power: Use of the central square in Tirana during a century of political transformations', *Planning Perspectives* 30:1 (2014), 67–94. The Hoxha quotation is from page 76.

37 Ibid., 327 ff.

38 See Madeleine Yue Dong, *Republican Beijing*, Berkeley: University of California Press, 2003.

39 Victor F. S. Sit, *Beijing: The Nature and Planning of a Chinese Capital City*, London: Belhaven, 1995, 95.

40 Ibid., 181.

41 Shuishan Yu, *Chang'an Avenue and the Modernization of Chinese Architecture*, Seattle: University of Washington Press, 2012, 17ff.

42 Yue Dong, *Republican Beijing*, 72ff.

43 Xuefei Ren, *Building Globalization: Transnational Architecture Production in Urban China*, Chicago: University of Chicago Press, 2011, 66.

44 Hung, *Remaking Beijing*, 108ff.

45 Han Feizi, quoted in ibid., 58.

46 Hung, *Remaking Beijing*, 126ff; Gwendolyn Leick, *Tombs of the Great Leaders*, London: Reaktion Books, 2013, 61ff.

47 Pierre Clément and Nathalie Lancret, *Hanoï, Le cycle de métamorphoses*, Paris: Editions Recherches, 2001; William Logan, *Hanoi: Biography of a City*, Seattle: University of Washington Press, 2000, chapter 3.

48 David Marr, *Vietnam 1945: The Quest for Power*, Berkeley: University of California Press, 1995.

49 Leick, *Tombs of the Great Leaders*, 54.

50 Logan, *Hanoi*, 200.

51 Ibid., 91ff.

52 Ahn Chang-mo, 'Koreanische Baukultur. Stadt-und Architekturgeschichte in Pjöngjang,' in Philipp Meuser (ed.), *Architekturführer Pjöngjang*, vol 2, Berlin: DOM, 2011, 115.

53 John H. Elliott, *Empires of the Atlantic World*, New Haven, CT: Yale University Press, 2006, 262.

54 Joseph Scarpaci, Roberto Segre and Mario Coyula, *Havana: Two Faces of the Antillean Metropolis*, Chapel Hill: University of North Carolina Press, 2002, 83ff.

55 Scarpaci et al., *Havana*, 196.

56 Robert Buckley and Sasha Tsenkova, 'Urban Housing Markets in Transition: New Instruments to Assist the Poor', in Sasha Tsenkova and Zorica Nedovic-Budic (eds), *The Urban Mosaic of Post-Socialist Europe*, Heidelberg and New York: Physica, 2006, 180.

57 Liviu Chelcea, 'The "Housing Question" and the State-Socialist Answer: City, Class and State Remaking in 1950s Bucharest', *International Journal of Urban and Regional Research*, 36:2, 2012: 291; Kiril Stanilov, 'Housing Trends in Central and Eastern European Cities during and after the Period of Transition', in Kiril Stanilov (ed), *The Post-Socialist City*, Frankfurt and New York, Springer. 2007: 176; Yue-man Yeung, 'Housing the Masses in Asia: Two Decades after Habitat I', in Yue-Man Yeung (ed), *Urban Development in Asia*, Hong Kong: Chinese University of Hong Kong, 1998: 148.

58 Hirt, *Iron Curtains*, 87.

59 Yue-man Yeung, *Housing the Masses*, 148; Olga Medvedkov and Yuri Medvedkov, 'Moscow in Transition', in Ian Hamilton et al. (eds), *Transformation of Cities in Central and Eastern Europe: Towards Globalization*, Tokyo: United Nations University Press, 2005, 438; Hartmut Häussermann, 'From the Socialist to the Capitalist City: Experiences from Germany', in Gregory Andruz, Michael Harloe, and Ivan Szelenyi (eds), *Cites after Socialism*, Oxford: Blackwell, 1996, 228; Stanilov, *Housing Trends*, 177.

60 Eric Mumford, *The CIAM Discourse on Urbanism, 1928–1960*, Cambridge, MA: MIT Press, 2002, 150ff.

61 Therborn, *European Modernity and Beyond*, chapters 7–8.

62 Schlögel, *Terror und Traum*.

63 Hamilton, Andrews, and Pichler-Milanovic, *Transformation of Cities*.

64 Bryan Cartledge, *Mihály Karolyi and István Bethlen: Hungary*, London: Haus, 2009, 121.

65 Paul Nemes, 'Crown Power', *Central Europe Review*, vol. 2, no. 1, 2000

9. Global Moments in National Cities

1 Therborn, *The World*, 35ff.

2 G. Therborn, 'End of a Paradigm: The Current Crisis and the Idea of Stateless Cities', *Environment and Planning*, A, 43, 272–285; K. Fujita (ed.), *Cities and Crisis*, London: Sage, 2016.

3 Cf. Leslie Sklair, 'Iconic architecture and urban, national, global identities', in Diane Davis and Nora Libertun de Duren (eds), *Cities and Sovereignty*, Bloomington: Indiana University Press, 2011, 179–95.

4 London Planning Advisory Committee (LPAC), 'London: World City: Report of Studies', mimeographed, London: LPAC, 1991, 5.

5 Nattika Navapan, 'Absolute Monarchy and the Development of Bangkok's Urban Spaces', *Planning Perspectives*, 29:1, 2013: 7.

6 Girouard, *Cities*, 341

7 Le Corbusier, *The Athens Charter*, New York: Grossman Publishers, 1973, 37.

8 Francois Chaslin, *Un Corbusier*, Paris: SEUIL, 2014.

9 Le Corbusier, *Athens Charter*, 108 and xiii, respectively.

10 Peter Hall, *Cities of Tomorrow*, Chichester: Wiley Blackwell, 2014, 73.

11 Eric Dluhosch and Rostislav Svacha, *Karel Teige: L'Enfant Terrible of the Czech Modernist Avant-Garde*, Cambridge, MA: MIT Press, 1999, 243.

12 Mumford, *CIAM Discourse*, 73.

13 Ibid., 186–7, 193.

14 Ibid., 87.

15 Le Corbusier, *Athens Charter*, 43–105.

16 Robert Caro, *The Power Broker: Robert Moses and the Fall of New York*, New York: Vintage, 1975, 318–9.

17 Carol Willis, *Form Follows Finance: Skyscrapers and Skylines in New York and Chicago*, Princeton, NJ: Princeton Architectural Press, 1995, 181.

18 Henry-Russell Hitchcock and Philip Johnson, *The International Style: Architecture since 1922*, New York: Norton, 2001(1933), 33.

19 Ibid., 25.

20 On the Chicago context, see George Douglas, *Skyscrapers: A Social History of the Very Tall Building in America*, New York: McFarland, 1996, chapters 1–2; D'Eramo, *Pig and the Skyscraper*.

21 Quoted in Willis, *Form Follows Finance*, 19.

22 Ibid.,19; see also David Nye, 'The sublime and the skyline', in Roberta Moudry (ed.), *The American Skyscraper*, Cambridge: Cambridge University Press, 2005, 255–69.

23 Jean-Louis Cohen, *Scenes of the World to Come*, New York: Flammarion, 1995, chapter 5.

24 C. Massu, 'Préface à l'édition francaise', in Hitchcock and Johnson, *International Style*, 6–7.

25 Quoted in L. Vale, 'Designing global harmony: Lewis Mumford and the United Nations headquarters', pp. 256-82 in Thomas Hughes and Agatha Hughes (eds), *Lewis Mumford: Public Intellectual*, Oxford: Oxford University Press, 1990, 270.

26 Douglas, *Skyscrapers*, chapter 14; Hasan-Uddin Kahn, *International Style: Architektur der Moderne von 1925 bis 1965*, Köln: Taschen, 1998, 117ff.

27 Dluhosch and Svacha, *Karel Teige*, 240.

28 Javier Monclús and Carmen Díez Medina, 'Modernist housing estates in European cities of the Western and Eastern Blocs', *Planning Perspectives* 31:4 (2016).

29 Charles Jencks, *The Language of Post-Modern Architecture*, New York: Rizzoli, 1977.

30 Charles Jencks, *Critical Modernism*, London: Academy Press, 2007,18ff.

31 Sohn, 'Changes in the residential features of Seoul', especially section VII.

32 Council on Tall Buildings and Urban Habitat, *Skyscraper Center*, 2016, skyscrapercenter.com.

33 Tokyo Metropolitan Government, '2nd long-term plan 1987', quoted in A. Saito and A. Thornley, 'Shifts in Tokyo's World City Status and the Urban Planning Response', *Urban Studies*, 2003: 672.

34 Gareth Stedman Jones, *Outcast London*, London: Verso, 1971.

35 Sue Brownill, *Developing London's Docklands: Another Great Planning Disaster?* Thousand Oaks, CA: SAGE, 1990, 19.

36 Ibid., 124.

37 Ibid., 129–30.

38 Colin Lizieri, *Towers of Capital: Office Markets & International Financial Services*, New York: Wiley, 2009, 254.

39 Doreen Massey, *World City*, London: Polity, 2010, 139.

40 Cf. Richard Williams, *The Anxious City: English Urbanism in the Late Twentieth Century*, New York: Routledge, 2009, 163, 176ff.

41 LPAC, 'London: World City', Preface.

42 Ibid., Point 1.4.

43 Ibid., Points 1.7 and 1.9.

44 John Allen and Allan Cochrane, 'The urban unbound: London's politics and the 2012 Olympic Games', *International Journal of Urban and Regional Research* 38:5 (2014): 1616.

45 Gordon, *Planning Twentieth Century Capital Cities*, 11; Thornley et al., 'The Greater London Authority: Interest representation and the strategic agenda', Discussion Paper 8, London: London School of Economics, 2001.

46 Greater London Authority (GLA), 'The London Plan', 2011, Preface.

47 Ibid., 32.

48 Ibid., 217–8.

49 Toshio Kamo, 'Reinventing Tokyo: Renewing city image, built environment and governance system toward the 21st century', paper presented at Hong Kong Real Estate Developers Association Conference on Re-inventing Global Cities, November 2000, Faculty of Law, Osaka City University 2000; Asato Saito and Andy Thornley, 'Shifts in Tokyo's world city status and the urban planning response', *Urban Studies* 40:4(2003), 665–85; Shun-ichi J. Watanabe, 'Tokyo: Forged by market forces and not the power of planning', in Gordon (ed.), *Planning Twentieth-Century Capital Cities*, 101–14.

50 Saskia Sassen, *The Global City*, Princeton, NJ: Princeton University Press, 1991, 4.

51 For references, see Göran Therborn, 'Europe and Asia: In the global political economy and in the world as a cultural system,' in Göran Therborn and Habibul Khondker (eds), *Asia and Europe in Globalization*, Leiden: Brill, 2006, 292ff.

52 Ren Xuefei, *Building Globalization*, 12.

53 Quoted in ibid., 70.

54 Seoul Metropolitan Government, *Seoul, A Clean and Attractive Global City*, Seoul, 2006, 6.

55 Quoted from Gil-sung Park, Yong Suk Jang, and Hang-Young Lee, 'The interplay between globalness and localness: Korea's globalization revisited,' Seoul: Korea University, 2007, 8.

56 Pengfei Ni and Peter Karl Kresl, *The Global Urban Competitiveness Report 2010*, Cheltenham, MA: Edward Elgar, 2010; Pengfei Ni, Peter Karl Kresl, and Wei Liu (eds), *The Global Urban Competitiveness Report 2013*, Cheltenham, MA: Edward Elgar, 2013.

57 Ibid., 2013, 10.

58 Heritage Foundation, 'The 2016 Index of Economic Freedom', Washington D.C.: Heritage Foundation, 2015, www.heritage.org/index.

59 Ni et al., *Global Competitiveness Report 2013*, 10 (definition) and chapter 16 (data on connectivity); Heritage Foundation, '2016 Index'.

60 Roppongi Hills Opening Exhibition Catalogue, *The Global City*, Tokyo, 2003, 5, 97.

61 A. Latour, *MOCKBA 1890–2000*, Moscow, 1997 (Originally published in Italian as *Mosca 1890–2000*, 1992), 296ff.

62 Antony Wood, 'Introduction: Tall trends and drivers: An overview,' in David Parker and Antony Wood (eds.), The *Tall Buildings Reference Book*, New York: Routledge, 2013, 6.

63 Council on Tall Buildings and Urban Habitat, 'Buildings', Skyscraper Center, 2020, skyscrapercenter.com.

64 *China Daily*, 19–25 September 2014, 5.

65 Council on Tall Buildings and Urban Habitat, 'Criteria', www.ctbuh.org/HighRiseInfo/TallestDatabase/Criteria. The Skyscraper Center does not give any clear minimal criteria: 'It is not just about the height, but about the context in which it exists.' It then goes on to say that 'a building of perhaps 14 or more stories – or more than 50 meters (165 feet) – could perhaps be used as a threshold for considering it a "tall building"'. Emporis uses 35 metres and twelve floors as a bottom line. The list is cut off after the first 196 cities, ranked by their total number of tall buildings.

66 Wood, 'Introduction', 6

67 Jon Ronson, 'Breaking into the 800 club', *New York Times* 4–5 June 2016, 2.

68 Anthony Sutcliffe, *Paris: An Architectural History*, New Haven, CT: Yale University Press, 1993, 174; Simon Texier, *Paris Contemporain*, Paris: Parigramme, 2005, 166ff.

69 Sutcliffe, *Paris*, 192

70 Blau, *Architecture of Red Vienna*, fig. 1.2, 4.

71 M. Grubbauer, 'Architecture, economic imaginaries and urban politics: The office tower as socially classifying device', *International Journal of Urban and Regional Research* 381 (2014), 336–59, fig. 2.

72 Quoted in Bruno Flierl, *Berlin baut um – Wessen Stadt wird die Stadt?* Berlin: Verl. für Bauwesen, 1998, 137.

73 Cf. S. Hain, 'Berlin's urban development discourse', in Matthias Bernt, Britta Grell and Andrej Holm (eds.), *The Berlin Reader*, 53-65, Bielefeld: Transcript-Verlag, 2013.

74 Quoted in Michael Wise, *Capital Dilemma: Germany's Search for a New Architecture of Democracy*, Princeton: Princeton Architectural Press, 1998, 72, 85.

75 Michael Marmot, *The Status Syndrome: How Social Standing Affects Our Health and Longevity*, New York: Owl Books, 2004, 196.

76 B. Schulz, 'Moskau 2002', in W. Eichwede and R. Kayser (eds.), *Berlin-Moskau*, Berlin, 2003, 27–34.

77 Cf. Peter Knoch, *Architekturführer Moskau*, Berlin: DOM, 2011.

78 Gobierno del Distrito Federal, *Gran Guía turística de la Ciudad de México*, Mexico City: 2003, 106.

79 C. Parnreiter, 'Formación de la ciudad global, economía immobiliaria y transnacionalización de espacios urbanos. El caso de Ciudad de México', *Eure* 37 (2011): 15.

80 *Citizen* (Dar es Salaam), 8 August 2014.

81 For sources, see Göran Therborn, 'Global Cities', World Power, and the G20 Capital Cities', in K. Fujita (ed.), *Cities and Crisis*, London, Sage, 2013, Table 2.1.

82 See Coaldrake, *Architecture and Authority in Japan*, 266ff.

83 Mike Davis, *City of Quartz*, London: Verso, 1990, chapters 3–4; Klaus Frantz, 'Private Gated Neighbourhoods: A Progressive Trend in US Urban Development', in Georg Glasze, Chris Webster and Klaus Frantz (eds), *Private Cities*, London: Routledge, 2006.

84 Rowland Atkinson and John Flint, 'Fortress UK? Gated communities, the spatial revolt of the elites and time-space trajectories of segregation,' *Housing Studies* 19:6 (2004): 875–92.

85 Davis, *City of Quartz*; R. Le Goix, 'Gated Communities as Predators on Public Resources,' in Glasze et al., *Private Cities*, 76–91.

86 Michael Janoschka and Axel Borsdorf, '*Condominos fechados* and *barrios privados*: The rise of private residential neighbourhoods in Latin America,' in Glasze et al., *Private Cities*, 102.

87 P. Cicciolella, 'Globalización y dualización en la Región Metropolitana de Buenos Aires. Grandes inversiones y restructuración territorial en los años noventa,' *Eure* 25:76 (1999): table 1.

88 Axel Borsdorf, R. Hidalgo and R. Sánchez, 'A new model of urban development in Latin America: The gated communities and fenced cities in the metropolitan areas of Santiago de Chile and Valparaíso,' *Cities* 24:5 (2007), 365–78.

89 P.A. Tedong et al., 'Governing enclosure: The role of governance in producing gated communities and guarded neighbourhoods in Malaysia,' *International Journal of Urban and Regional Research* 38 (2014): 112–28.

90 Harald Leisch, 'Gated communities in Indonesia,' *Cities* 19:5 (2002): 341–50.

91 Wu Fulong and K. Webber, 'The rise of "foreign gated communities" in Beijing: Between economic globalization and local institutions,' *Cities* 21:3 (2005), 203–13; Sebastian Lenz, 'More Gates, Less Community? Guarded Housing in Russia,' in Glasze et. al., *Private Cities*; G. Giroir, 'The Purple Jade Villas (Beijing): A golden ghetto in red China,' in Glasze et al., *Private Cities*; Mikhail Blinnikov, Andrey Shanin, Nikolay Sobolev and Lyudmila Volkova, 'Gated communities of the Moscow green belt: Newly segregated landscapes and the suburban Russian environment,' *GeoJournal* 66 (2006): 65–81; P. Stoyanov and K. Frantz, 'Gated Communities in Bulgaria: Interpreting a new trend in post-Communist urban development,' *GeoJournal* 66 (2006): 57-63; Z. Cséfalvay, 'Gated Communities for security or prestige? A public choice approach and the case of Budapest,' *International Journal of Urban and Regional Research* 35:4 (2011): 735–52; S. Hirt and M. Petrovic, 'The Belgrade wall: The proliferation of gated housing in the Serbian capital after socialism,' *International Journal of Urban and Regional Research* 35:4 (2011): 753–77.

92 K. Verhaeren and R. Reposo, 'The rise of gated residential neighbourhoods in Portugal and Spain: Lisbon and Madrid,' in Glasze et al., *Private Cities*.

93 Cséfalvay, 'Gated Communities for security or prestige?' 741.

94 Field notes, 2007. Thanks to professor Samir Riad and his wife, M. Iskander, who took us around.

95 B. Ferrari, 'The noble, the traditional, and the cosmopolite: Globalization and changes of urban landscapes in Beijing,' *Pacific News* 30 (2008): 18–21.

96 Blinnikov et al., 'Gated communities of the Moscow green belt', 77.

97 Wu and Webber, 'Rise of "foreign gated communities" in Beijing', 212.

98 Verhaeren and Reposo, 'Rise of gated residential neighbourhoods'; Cséfalvay, 'Gated Communities for security or prestige?'; Tedong et al., 'Governing enclosure'.

99 Marianne Morange, Fabrice Folio, Elisabeth Peyroux and Jeanne Vivet, 'The spread of a transnational model: "Gated communities" in three Southern African cities (Cape Town, Maputo, and Windhoek)', *International Journal of Urban and Regional Research* 36:5 (2012): 890–914; Verhaeren and Reposo, 'Rise of gated residential neighbourhoods'.

100 Alberta Andreotti, Patrick Le Galès, and Francisco Javier Moreno-Fuentes, *Globalised Minds, Roots in the City*, New York: Wiley, 2015.

101 Szymon Marcinczak et al., 'Inequality and Rising Levels of Segregation', in Titt Tammaru et al. (eds), *Socio-economic Segregation in European Capital Cities*, London: Routledge, 2016, 369.

102 CEPAL, *Social Panorama of Latin America 2014*, table V.A2.3a.

103 Guideline: Gini index for income<0.40.

104 0.40>Income Gini<0.50

105 0.50>Income Gini<0.60.

106 Income Gini>0.60.

107 Natalie Holmes and Alan Berube, 'City and metropolitan inequality on the rise, driven by declining incomes,' Washington, D.C.: Brookings Institution, 14 January 2016, brookings.edu.

108 UN Habitat, *State of the World's Cities 2008/2009* and *State of African Cities 2014*.

109 Benedict Anderson, *Imagined Communities*, London: Verso, 1983.

10. Envoi: Global Capital

1 OECD iLibrary, 'General government expenditure statistics'. The economies are France, Germany, Italy, Japan, UK and United States.

2 Ni et al., *Global Competitiveness Report 2013*, chapter 16.

Index